D1456823

"I'M NOT AFRAID TO DIE ANYMORE. I'VE SEEN WHAT LIES BEYOND, AND IT IS FAR MORE BEAUTIFUL THAN ANYTHING IN THIS LIFE."

— ELVIS

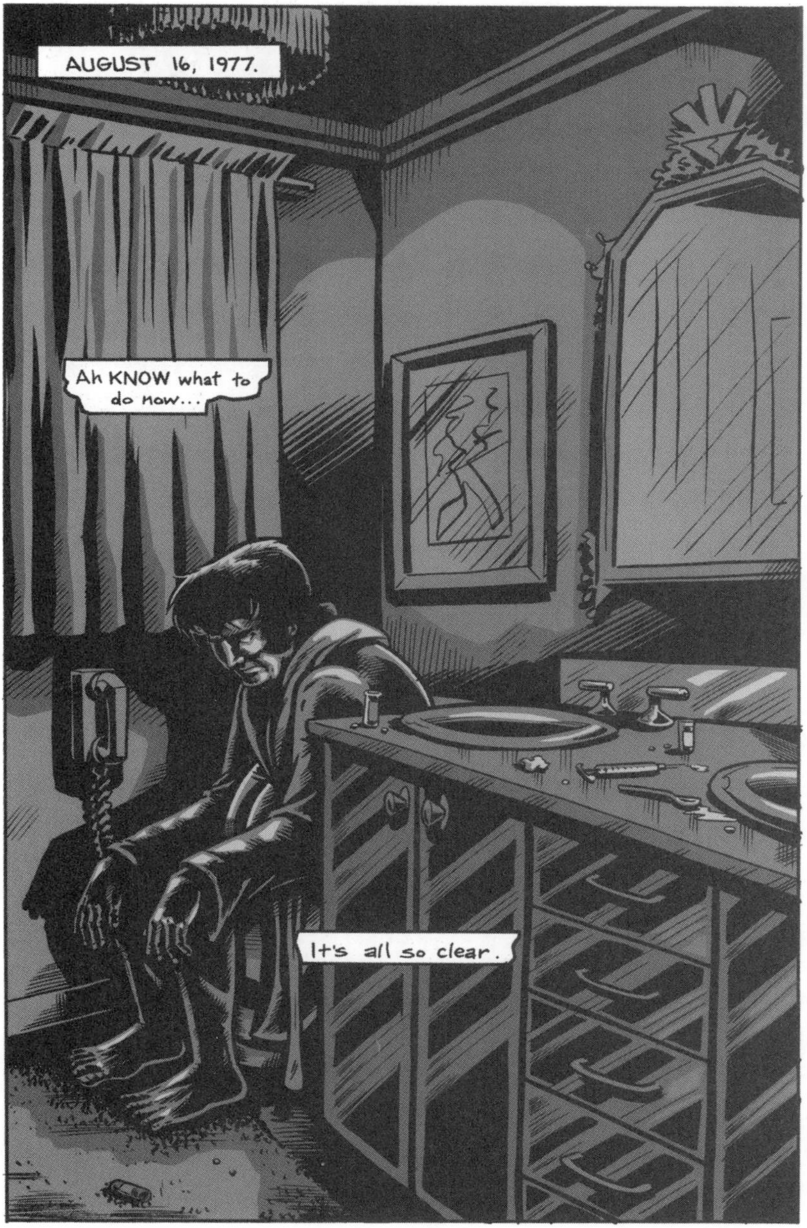
AUGUST 16, 1977.
Ah KNOW what to do now...
It's all so clear.

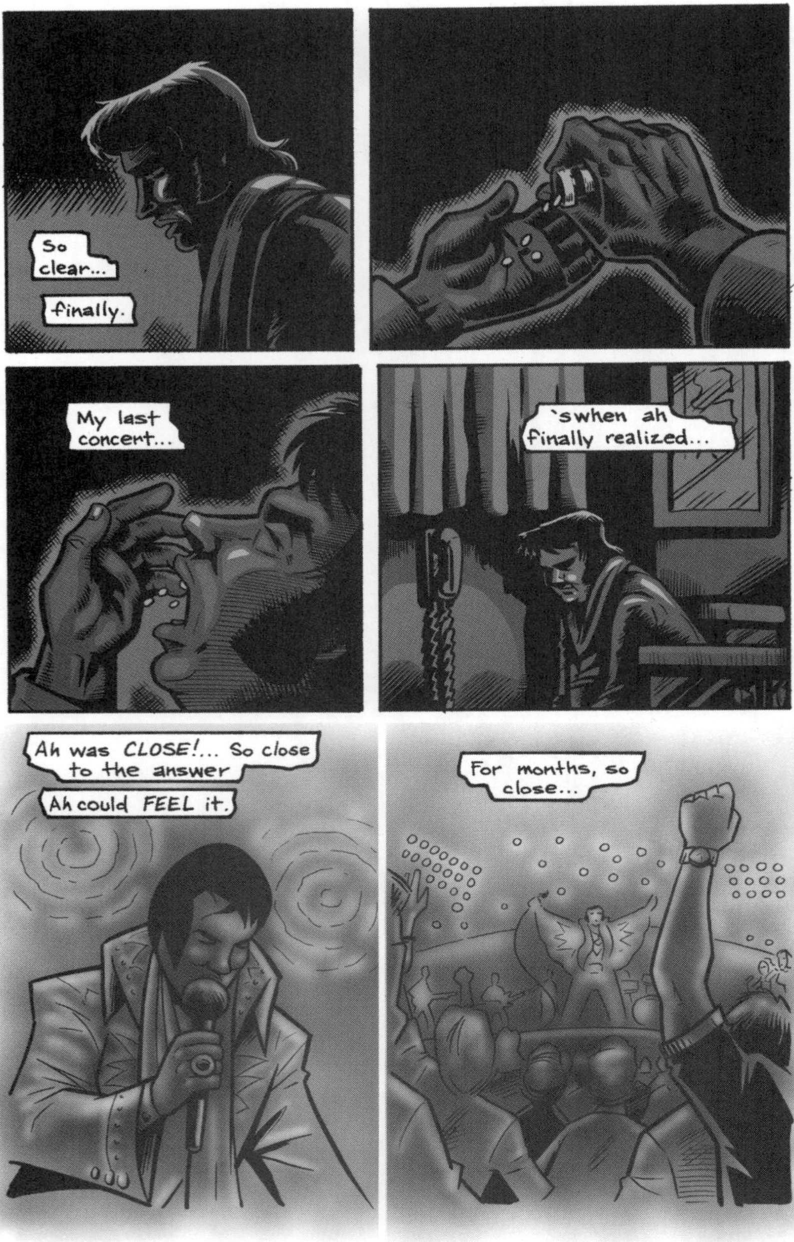
So clear...
finally.
My last concert...
`swhen ah finally realized...
Ah was CLOSE!... So close to the answer
Ah could FEEL it.
For months, so close...

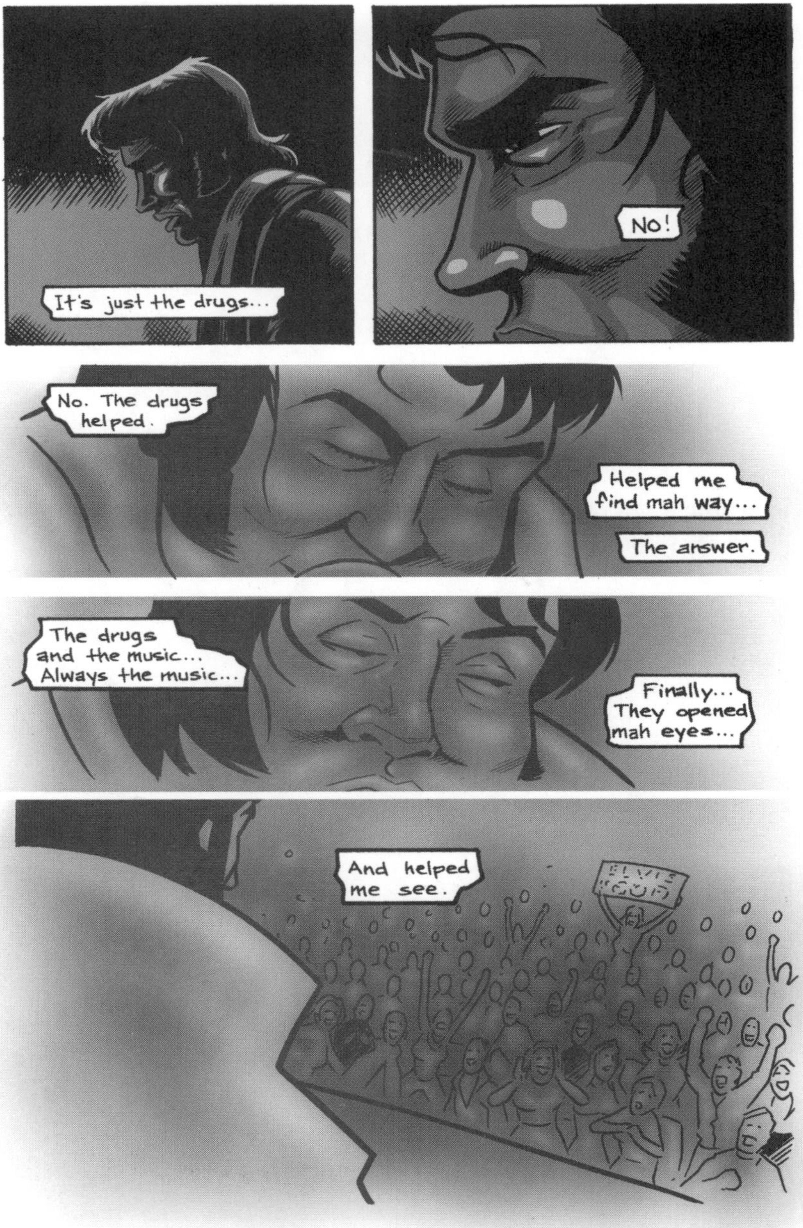
It's just the drugs...
No!
No. The drugs helped.
Helped me find mah way...
The answer.
The drugs and the music... Always the music...
Finally... They opened mah eyes...
And helped me see.

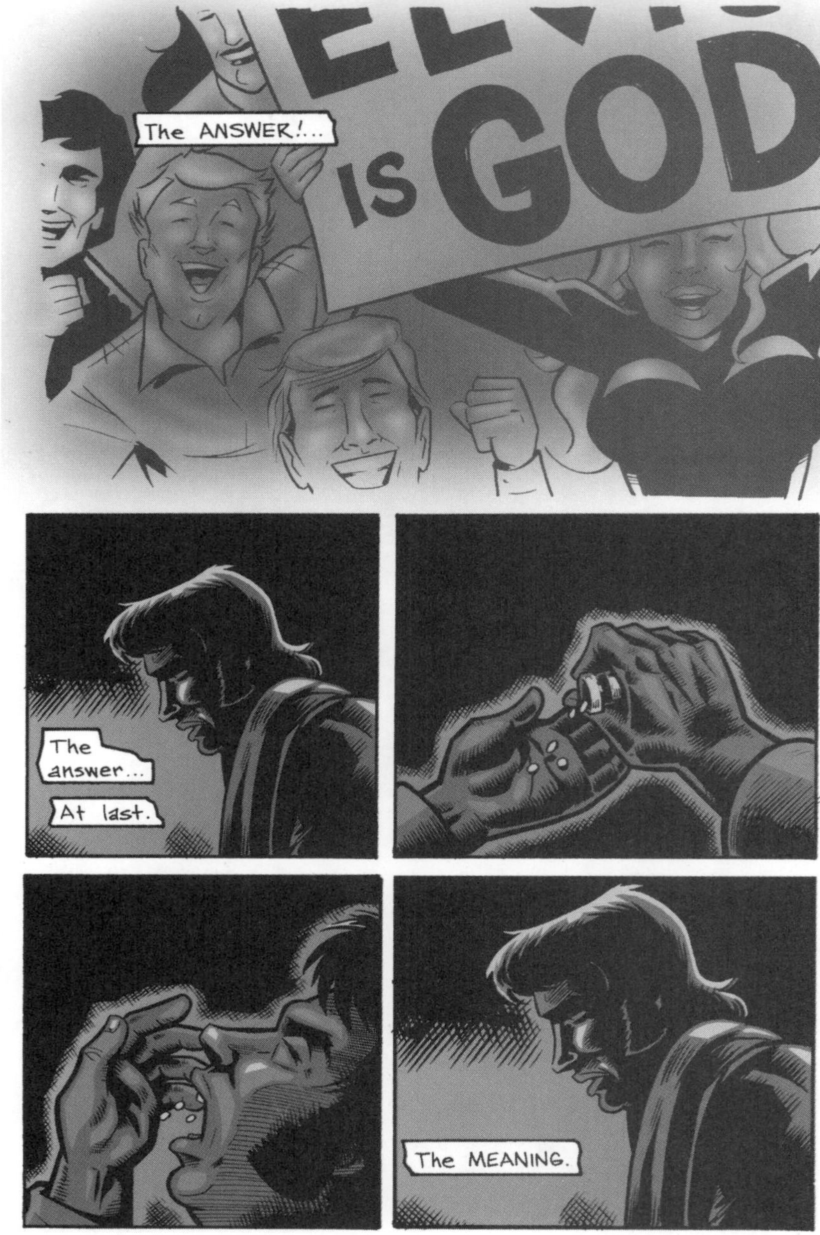
IS GOD
The ANSWER!...
The answer...
At last.
The MEANING.

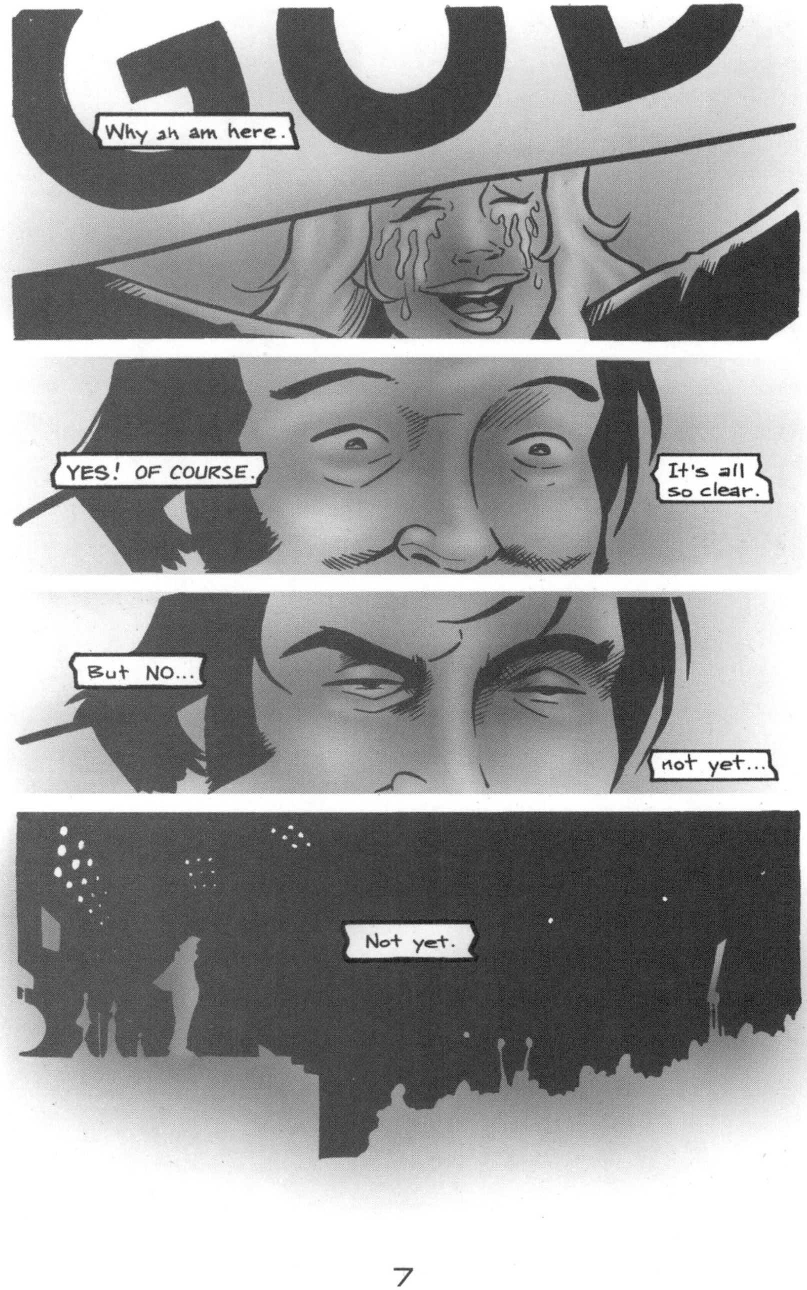
Why ah am here.
YES! OF COURSE.
It's all so clear.
But NO...
not yet...
Not yet.

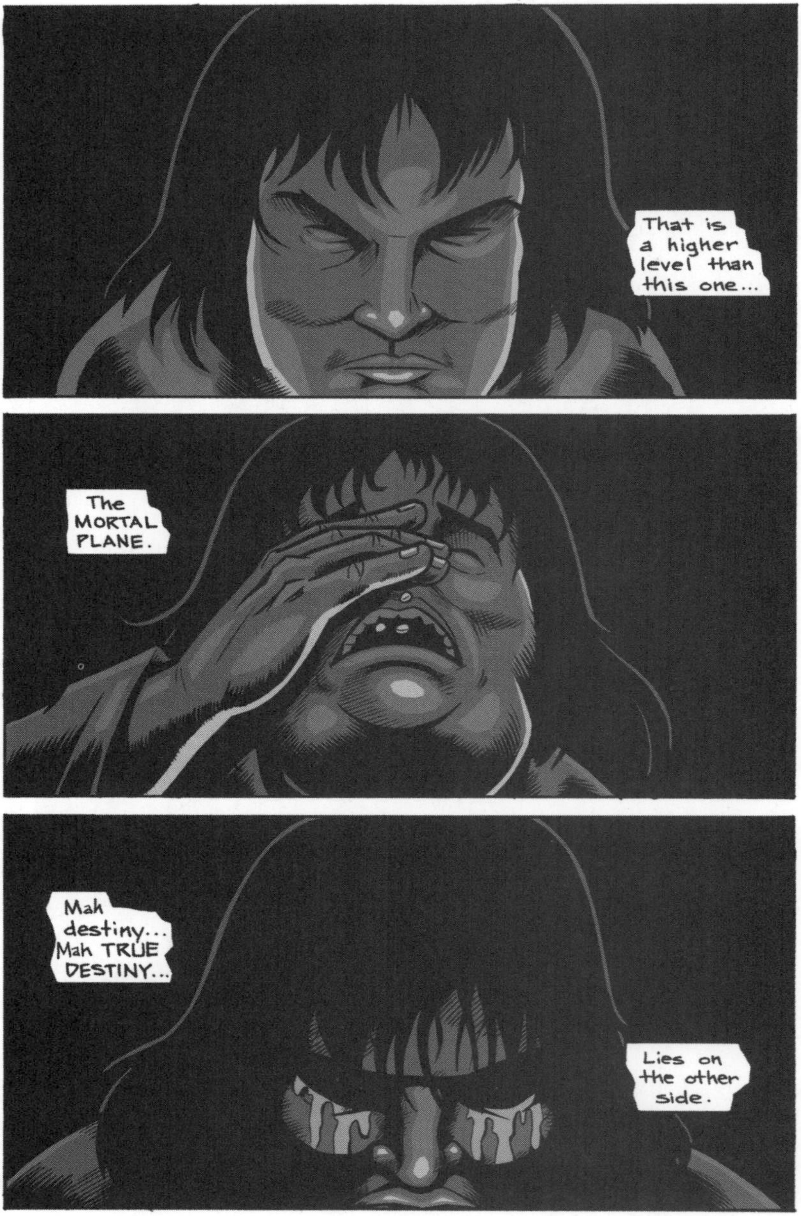
That is a higher level than this one...
The MORTAL PLANE.
Mah destiny... Mah TRUE DESTINY...
Lies on the other side.

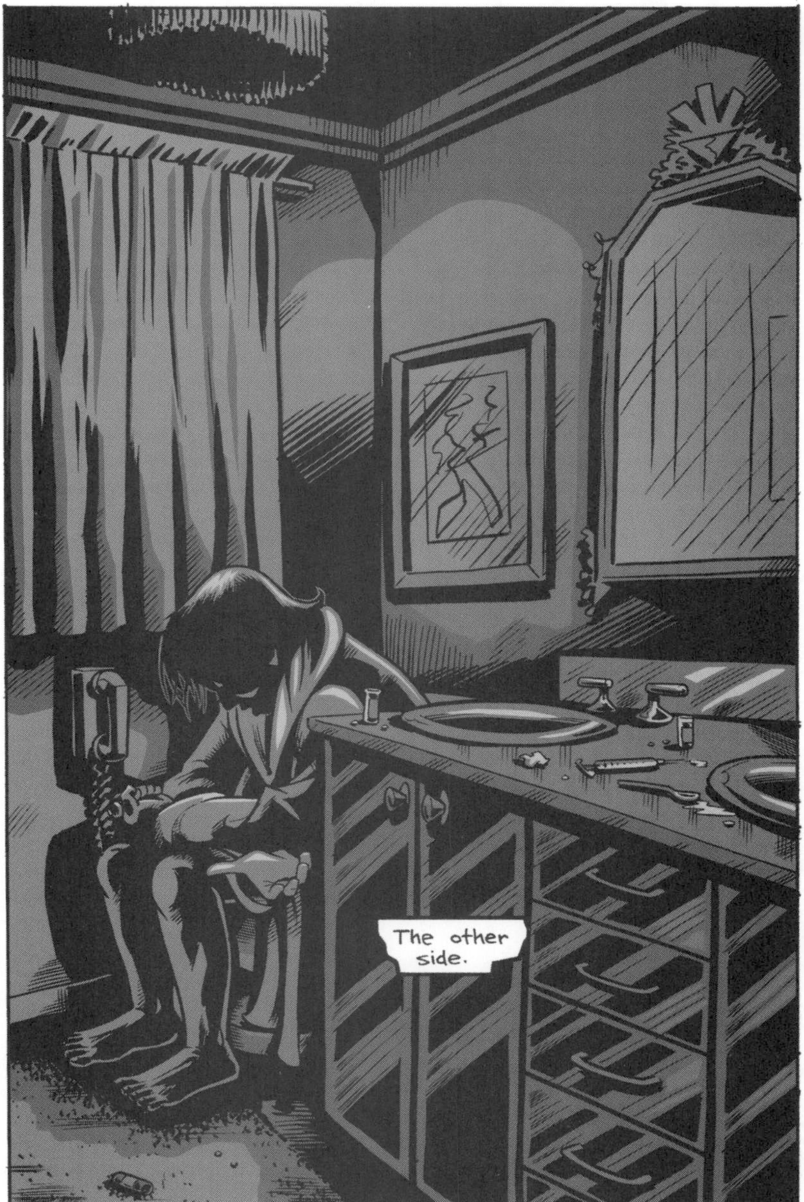
The other side.

THE

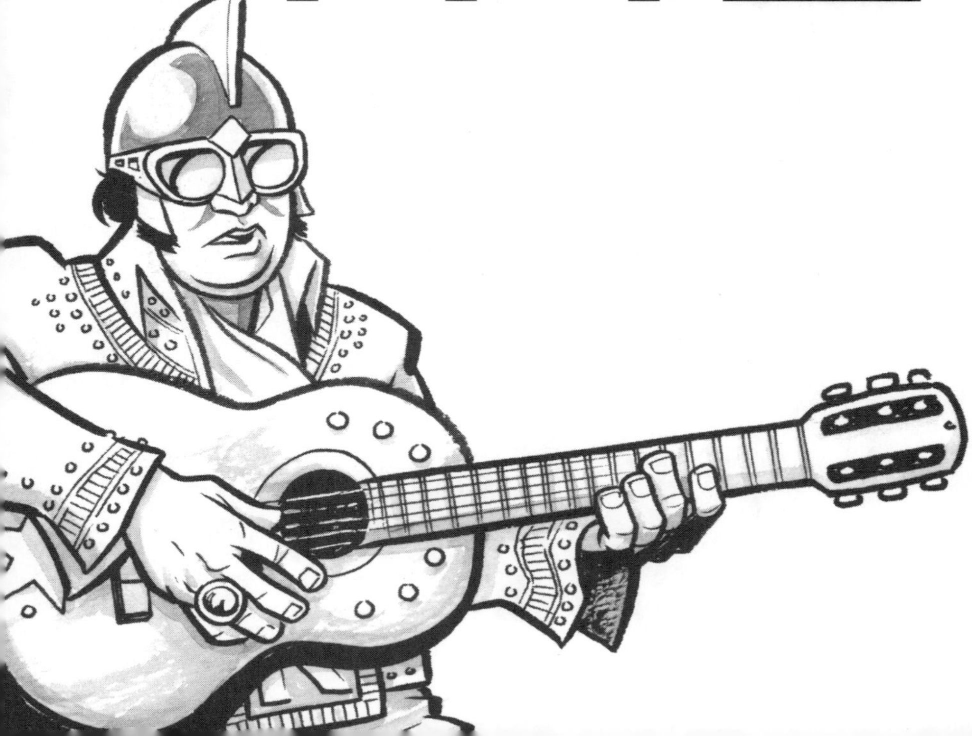

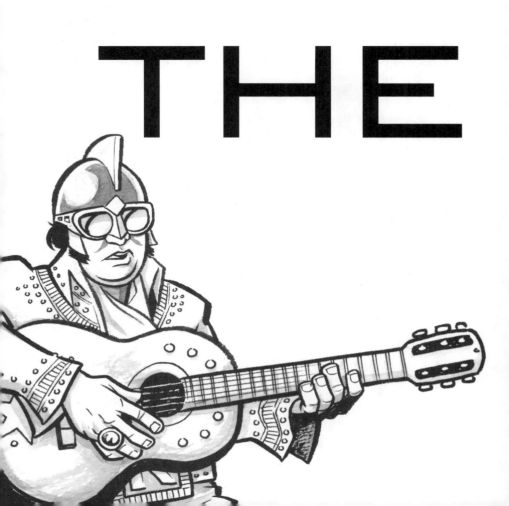

KING

BY RICH KOSLOWSKI

•WITH COLOR TONES BY ADAM WALLENTA•
•COVER ASSISTS BY DOG ON A BONE STUDIOS•
•BACK COVER ILLUSTRATION BY ZACH HOWARD•
•EDITED BY CHRIS STAROS AND ROBERT VENDITTI•
•PRODUCTION AND BOOK DESIGN BY BRETT WARNOCK•

ISBN 1-891830-65-1
1. Music / Music History
2. Graphic Novels
3. Elvis

The King © 2005 Rich Koslowski. Published by Top Shelf Productions, PO Box 1282, Marietta, GA 30061-1282, USA. Publishers: Brett Warnock and Chris Staros. Top Shelf Productions® and the Top Shelf logo are registered trademarks of Top Shelf Productions, Inc. Visit our online store at www.topshelfcomix.com. First Printing, July, 2005. Printed in Canada.

"A LOT OF THESE GUYS AREN'T REPORTERS, THEY'RE MARKSMEN."

—ELVIS

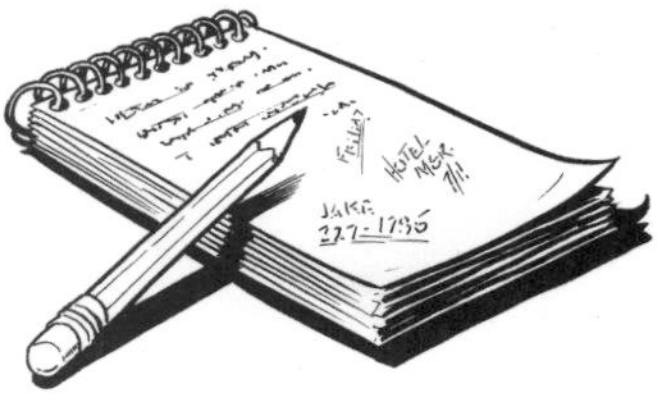
FRIDAY?
HOTEL MGR.
JAKE

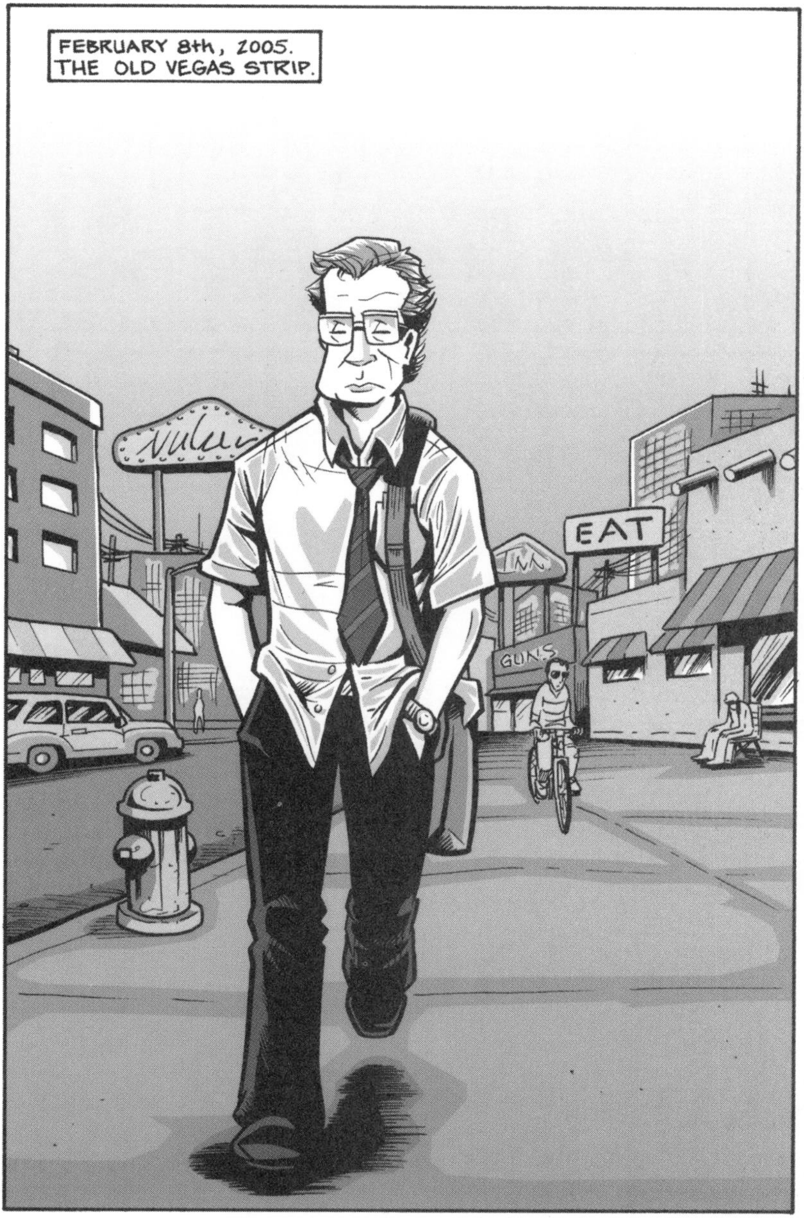
FEBRUARY 8th, 2005.
THE OLD VEGAS STRIP.
EAT
GUNS

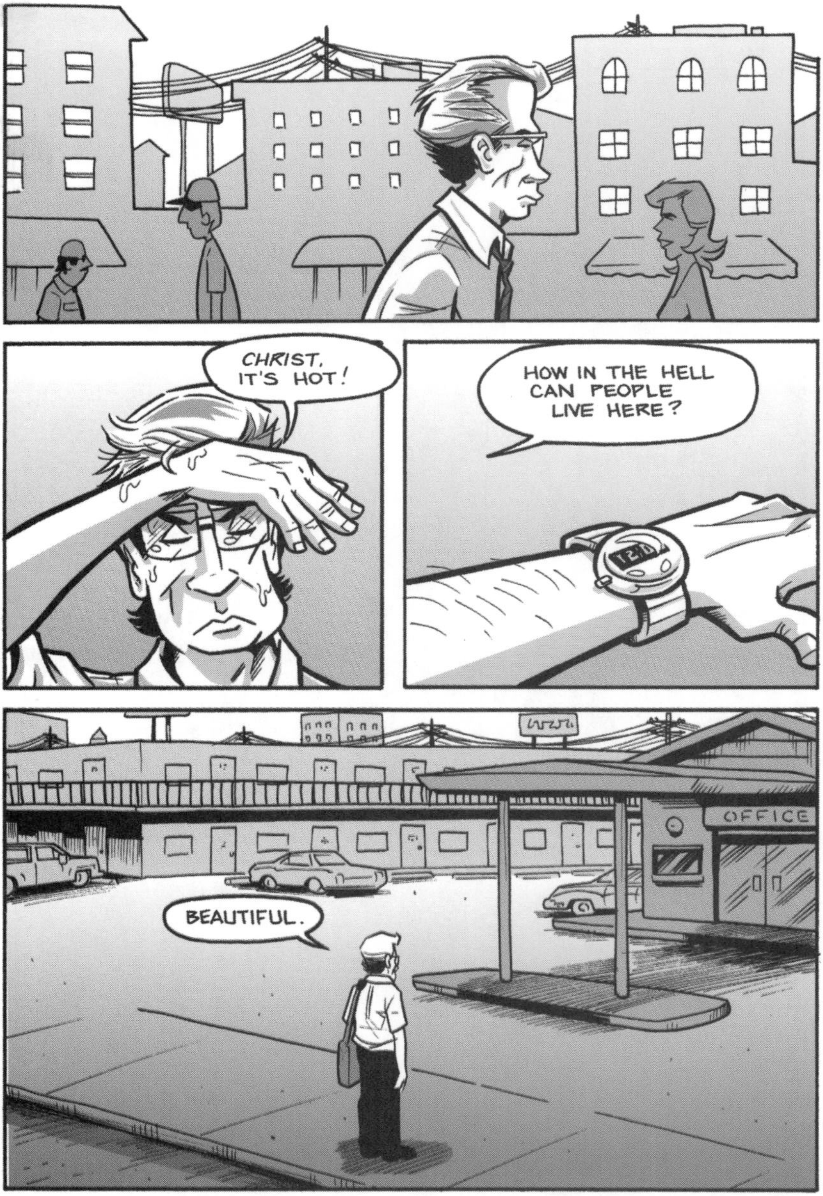
CHRIST, IT'S HOT!
HOW IN THE HELL CAN PEOPLE LIVE HERE?
OFFICE
BEAUTIFUL.

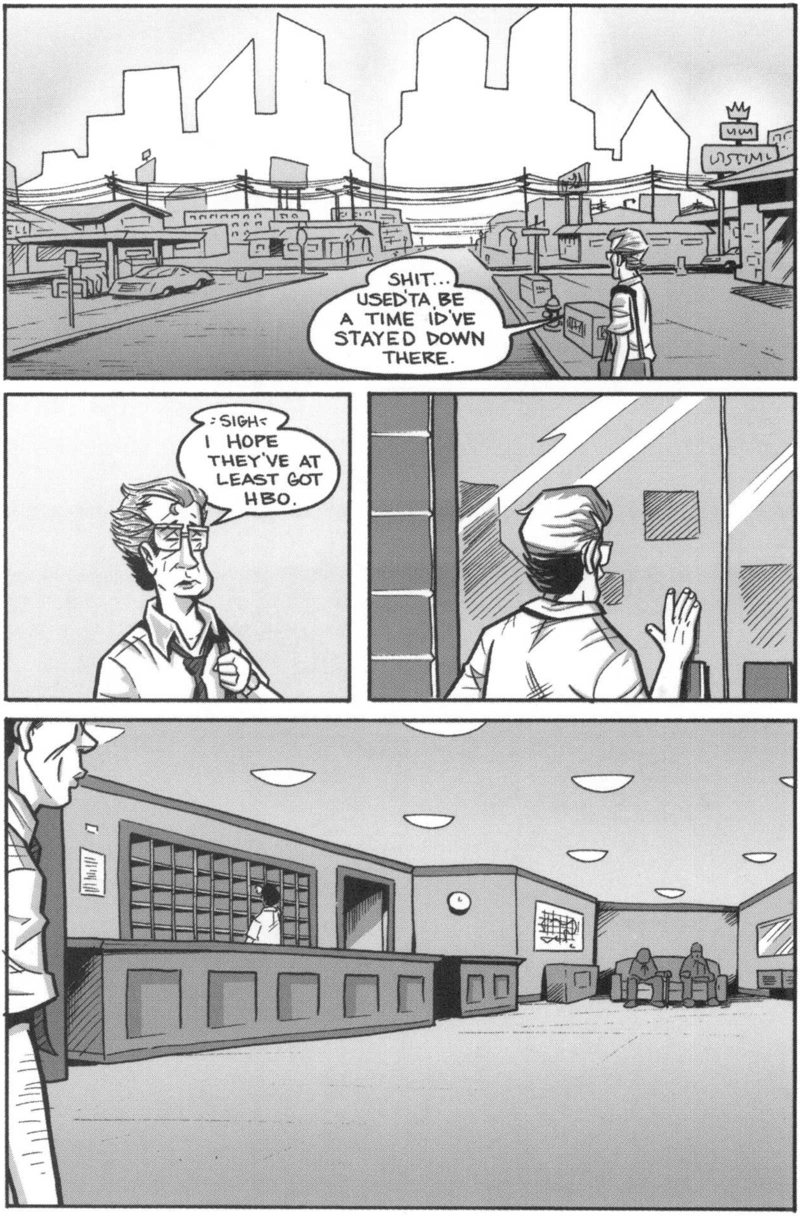
SHIT... USED'TA BE A TIME ID'VE STAYED DOWN THERE.
=SIGH= I HOPE THEY'VE AT LEAST GOT HBO.

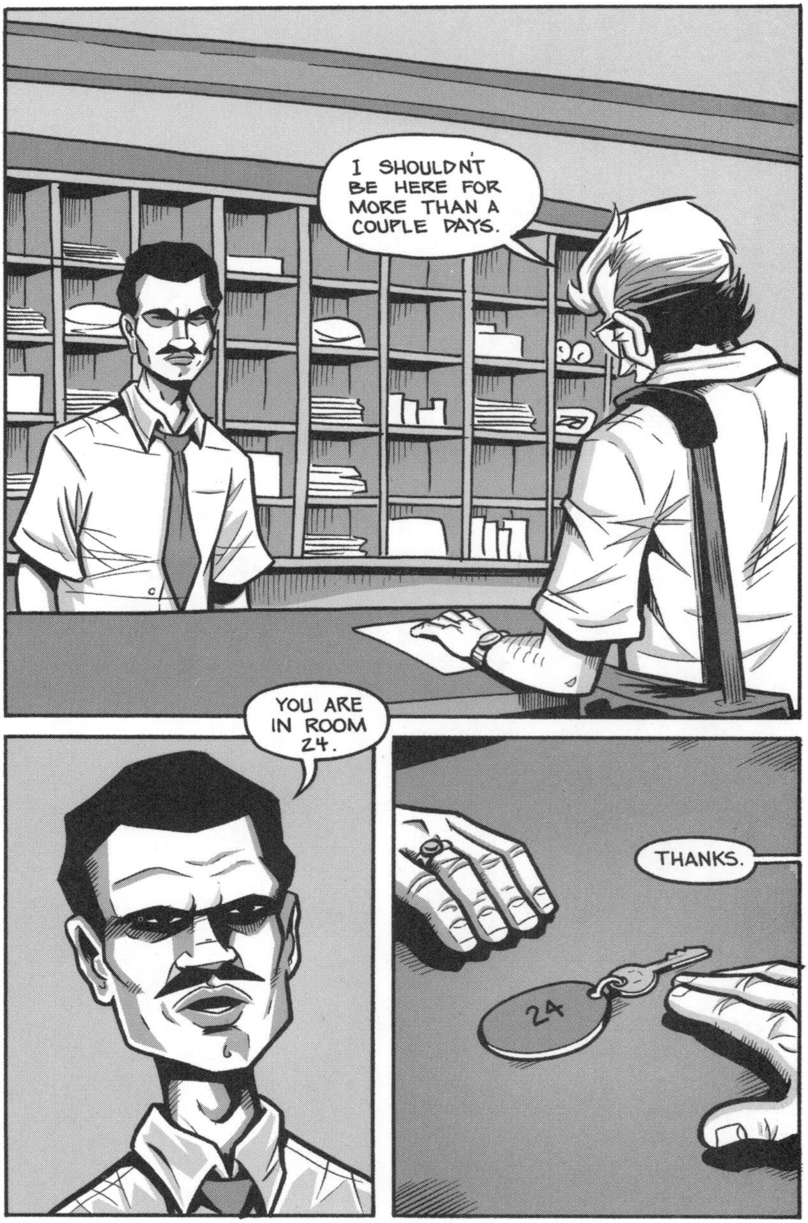
I SHOULDN'T BE HERE FOR MORE THAN A COUPLE DAYS.
YOU ARE IN ROOM 24.
THANKS.
24

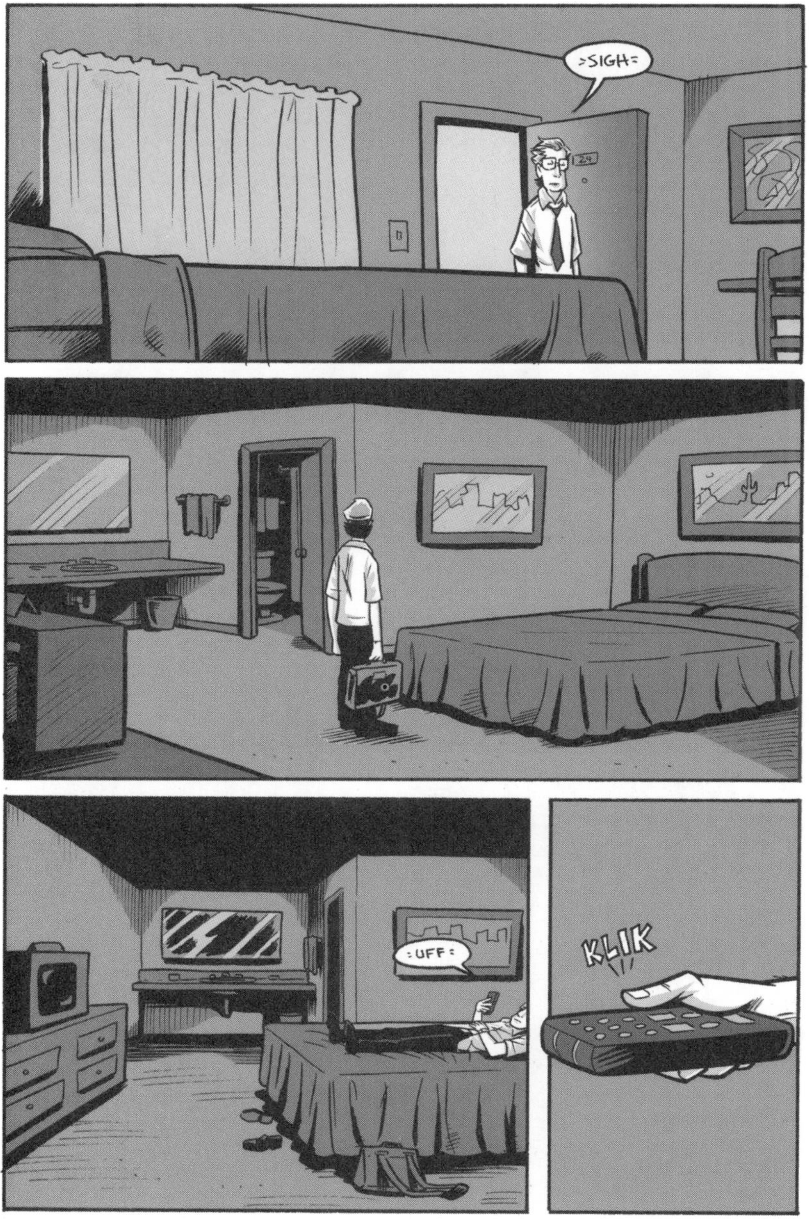

=SIGH=
24
=UFF=
KLIK

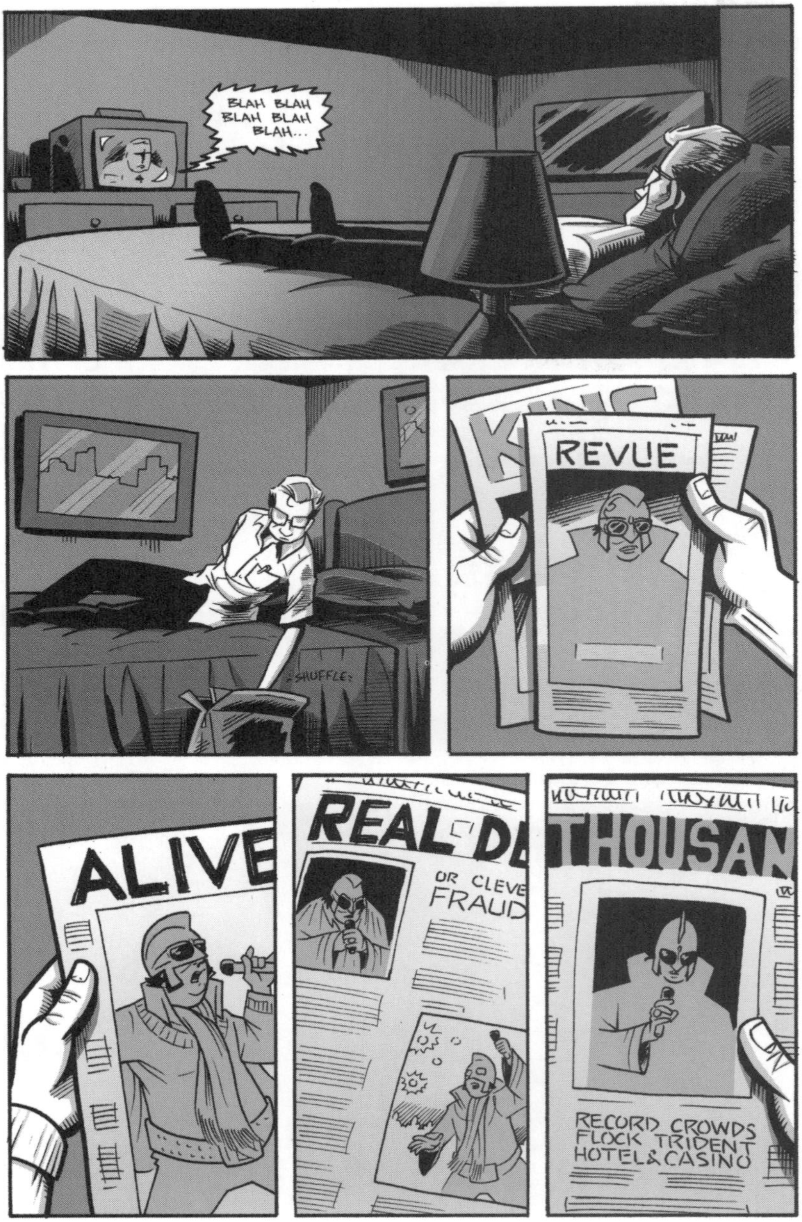
BLAH BLAH BLAH BLAH BLAH...
SHUFFLE
REVUE
ALIVE
REAL DE
OR CLEVE
FRAUD
THOUSAN
RECORD CROWDS FLOCK TRIDENT HOTEL&CASINO

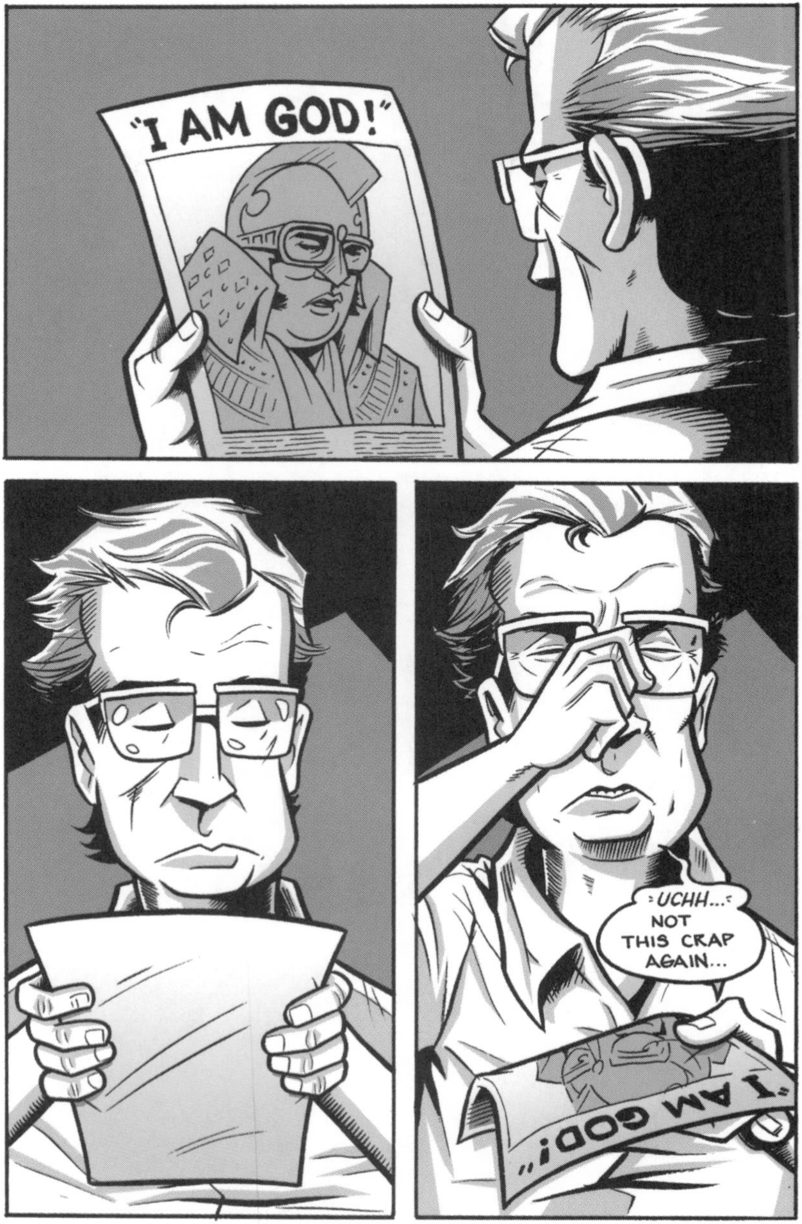
"I AM GOD!"
UCHH... NOT THIS CRAP AGAIN...
"I AM GOD!"

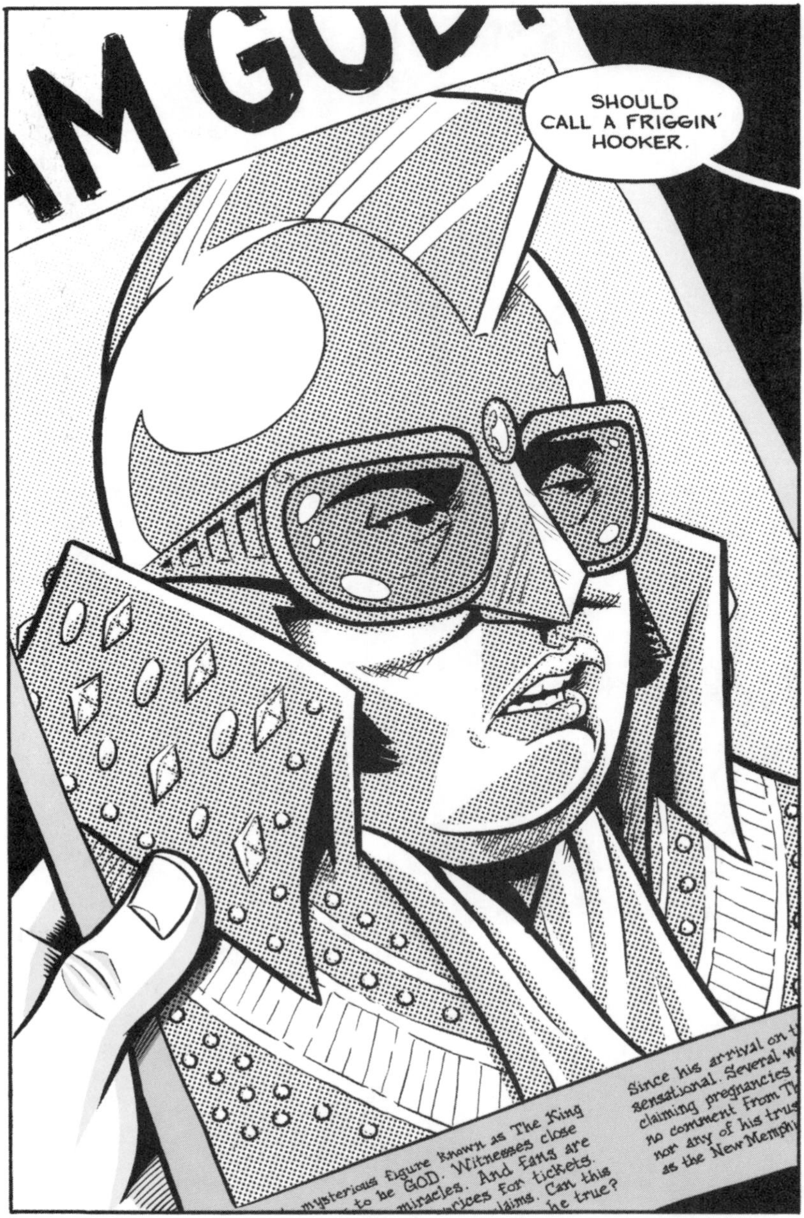
AM GOD
SHOULD CALL A FRIGGIN' HOOKER.
mysterious figure known as The King
to be GOD. Witnesses close
miracles. And fans are
for tickets.
Can this
true?
Since his arrival on
sensational. Several
claiming pregnancies
no comment from
nor any of his
as the New

"THE AUDIENCE IS THE OTHER HALF
OF ME."

—ELVIS

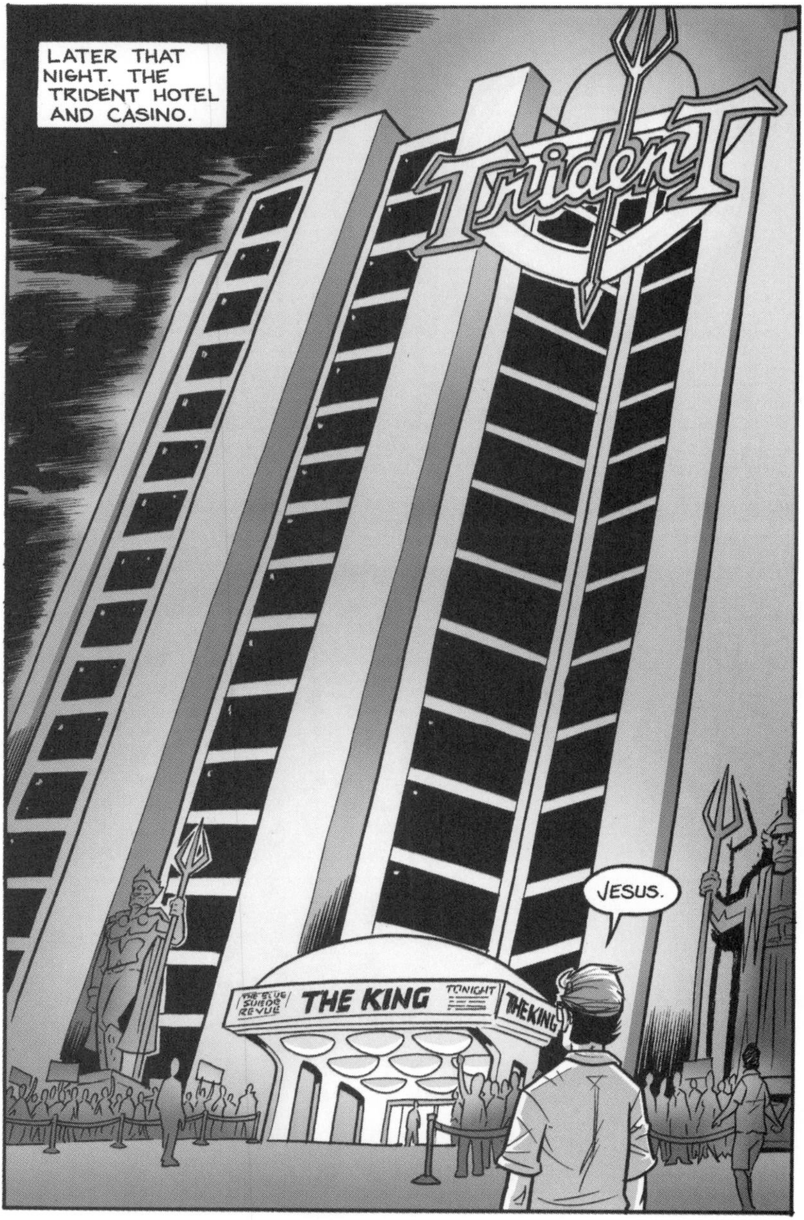
LATER THAT NIGHT. THE TRIDENT HOTEL AND CASINO.
TRIDENT
THE BLUE SUEDE REVUE
THE KING
TONIGHT
THE KING
JESUS.

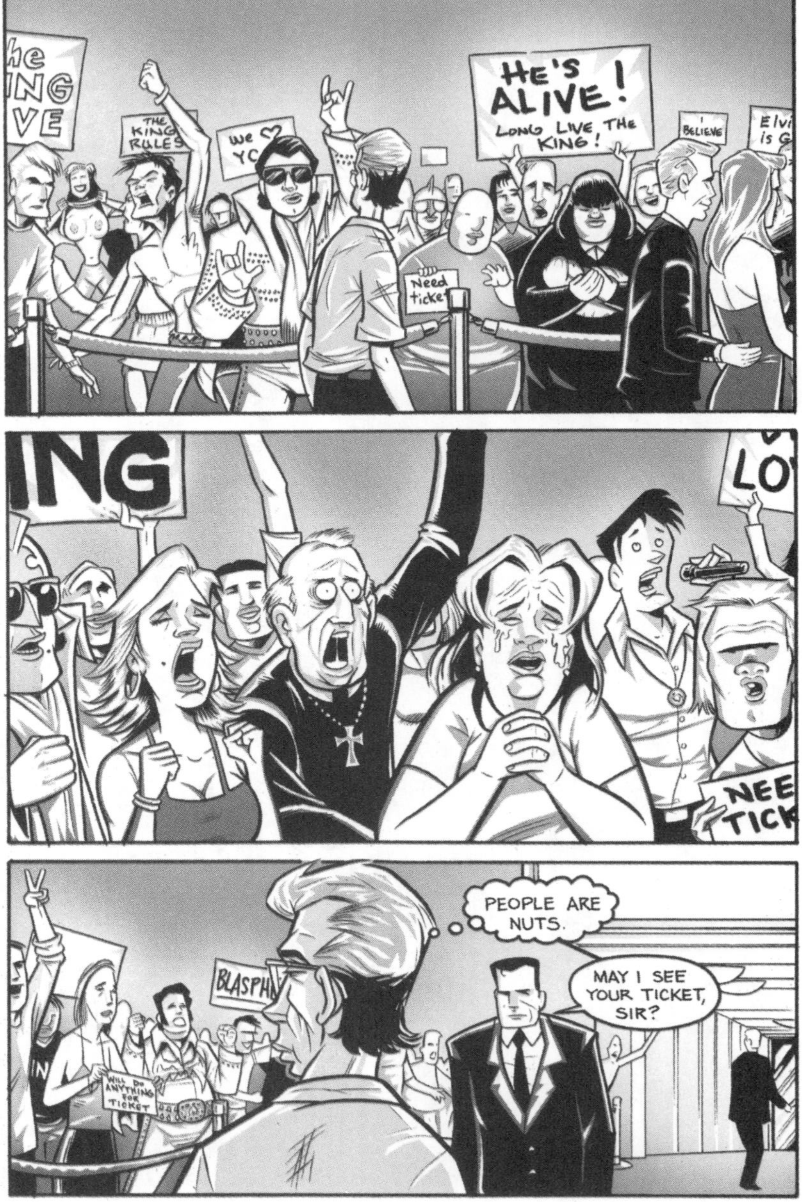
THE KING RULES
HE'S ALIVE! LONG LIVE THE KING!
I BELIEVE
WILL DO ANYTHING FOR TICKET
PEOPLE ARE NUTS.
MAY I SEE YOUR TICKET, SIR?

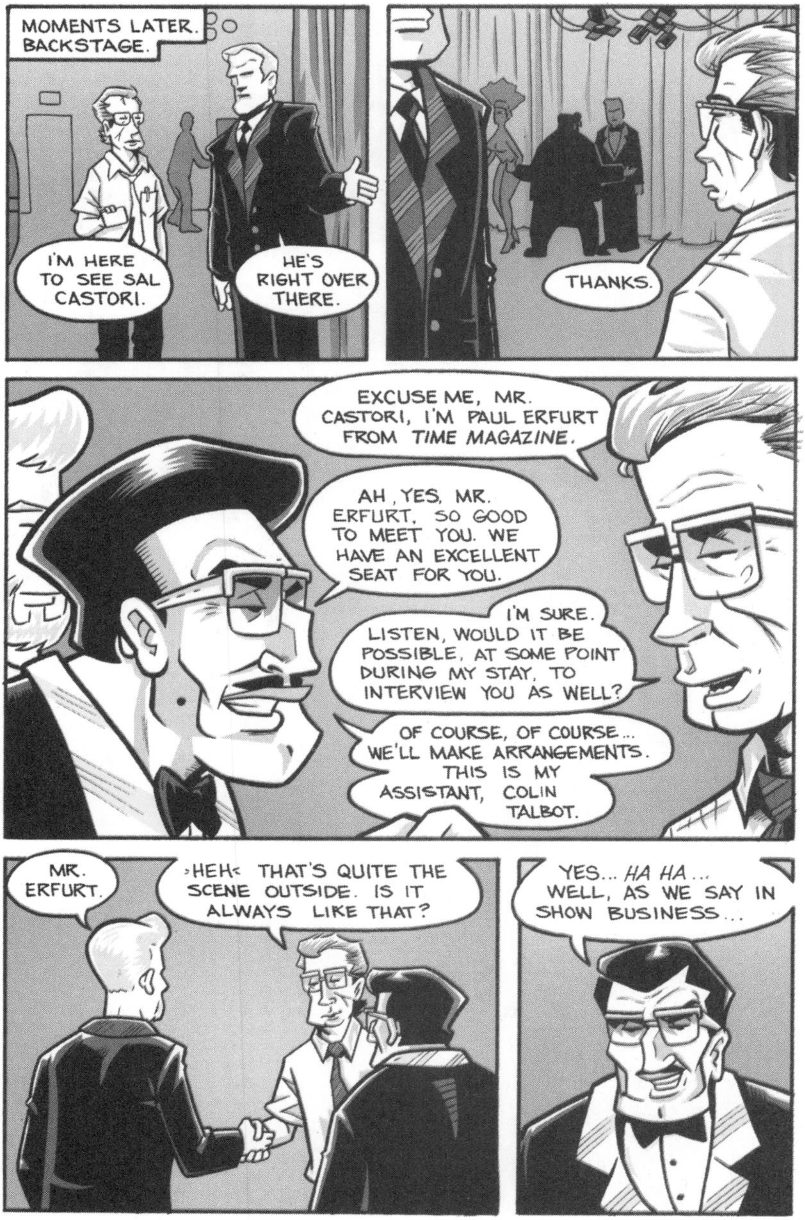
MOMENTS LATER. BACKSTAGE.
I'M HERE TO SEE SAL CASTORI.
HE'S RIGHT OVER THERE.
THANKS.
EXCUSE ME, MR. CASTORI, I'M PAUL ERFURT FROM *TIME MAGAZINE*.
AH, YES, MR. ERFURT. SO GOOD TO MEET YOU. WE HAVE AN EXCELLENT SEAT FOR YOU.
I'M SURE. LISTEN, WOULD IT BE POSSIBLE, AT SOME POINT DURING MY STAY, TO INTERVIEW YOU AS WELL?
OF COURSE, OF COURSE... WE'LL MAKE ARRANGEMENTS. THIS IS MY ASSISTANT, COLIN TALBOT.
MR. ERFURT.
>HEH< THAT'S QUITE THE SCENE OUTSIDE. IS IT ALWAYS LIKE THAT?
YES... *HA HA*... WELL, AS WE SAY IN SHOW BUSINESS...

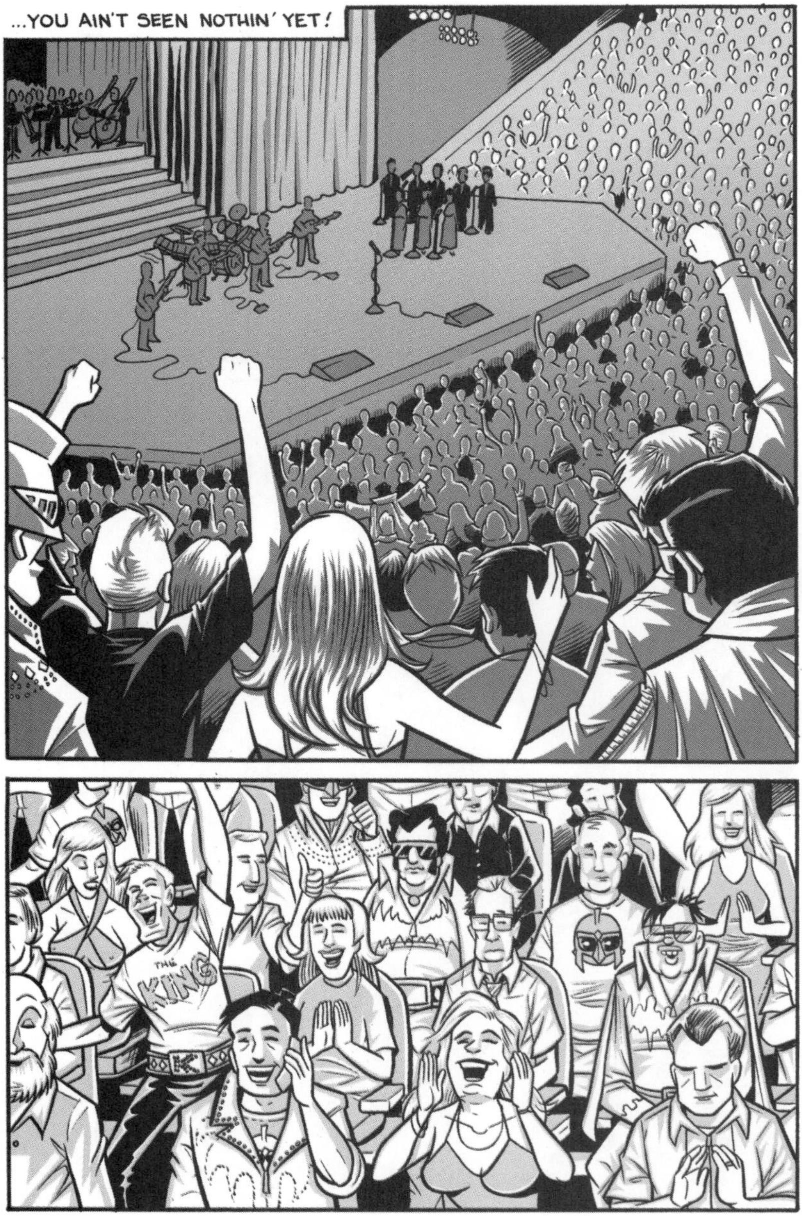
...YOU AIN'T SEEN NOTHIN' YET!
THE KING

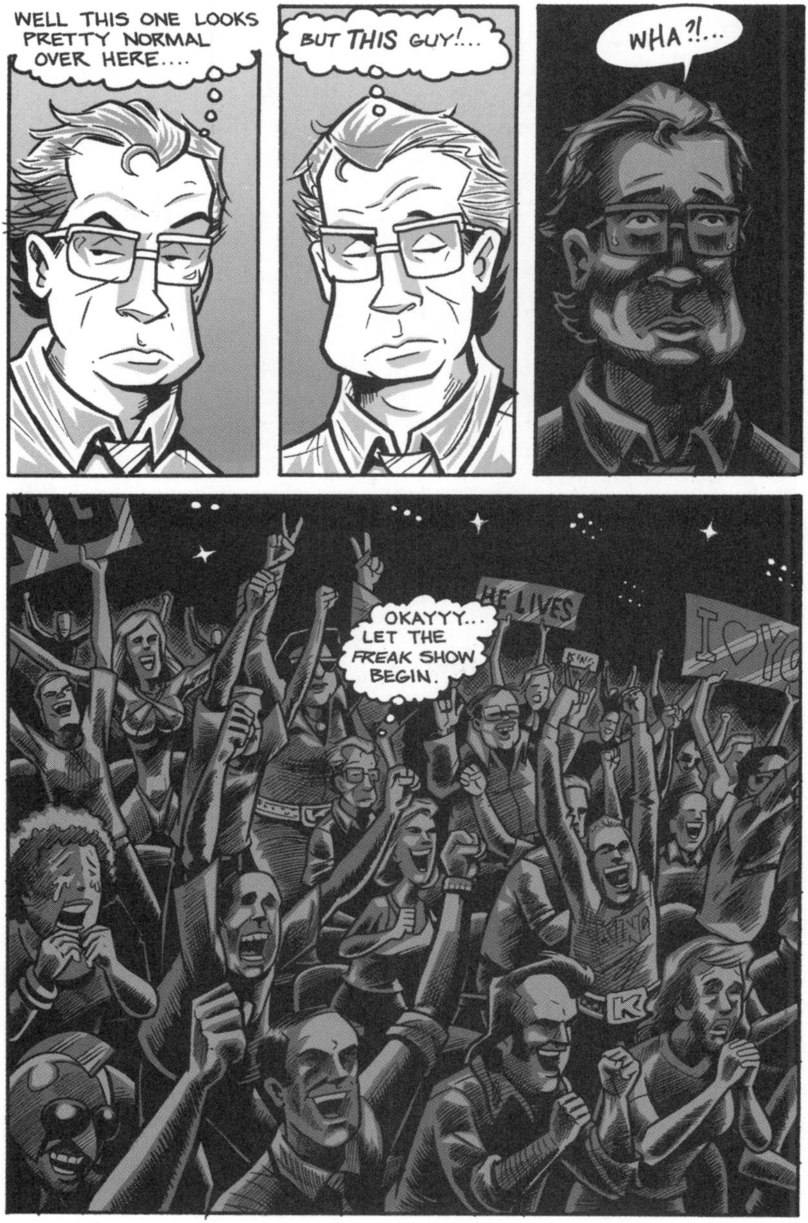
WELL THIS ONE LOOKS PRETTY NORMAL OVER HERE....
BUT THIS GUY!...
WHA?!...
HE LIVES
OKAYYY... LET THE FREAK SHOW BEGIN.

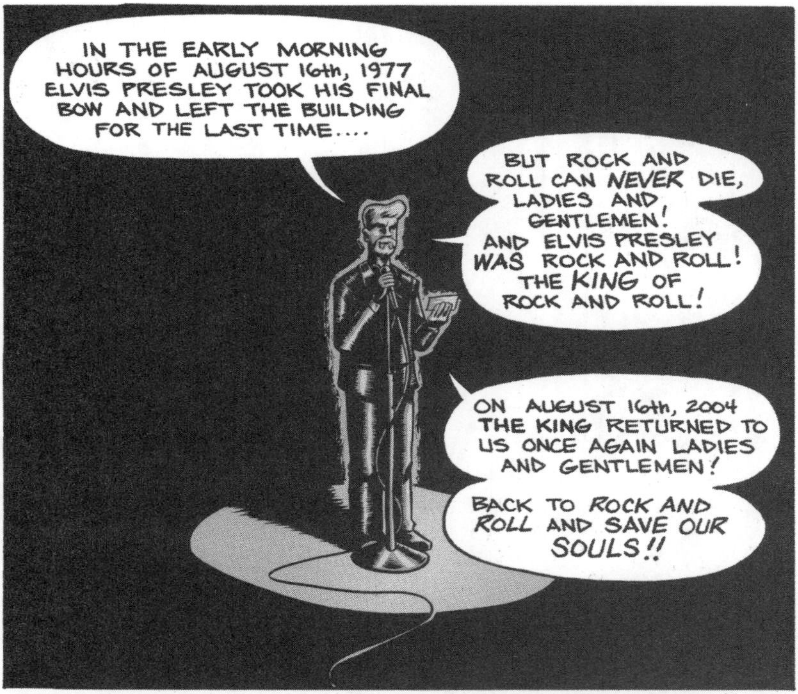
IN THE EARLY MORNING HOURS OF AUGUST 16th, 1977 ELVIS PRESLEY TOOK HIS FINAL BOW AND LEFT THE BUILDING FOR THE LAST TIME....
BUT ROCK AND ROLL CAN *NEVER* DIE, LADIES AND GENTLEMEN! AND ELVIS PRESLEY *WAS* ROCK AND ROLL! THE *KING* OF ROCK AND ROLL!
ON AUGUST 16th, 2004 THE KING RETURNED TO US ONCE AGAIN LADIES AND GENTLEMEN!
BACK TO *ROCK AND ROLL* AND SAVE OUR *SOULS*!!

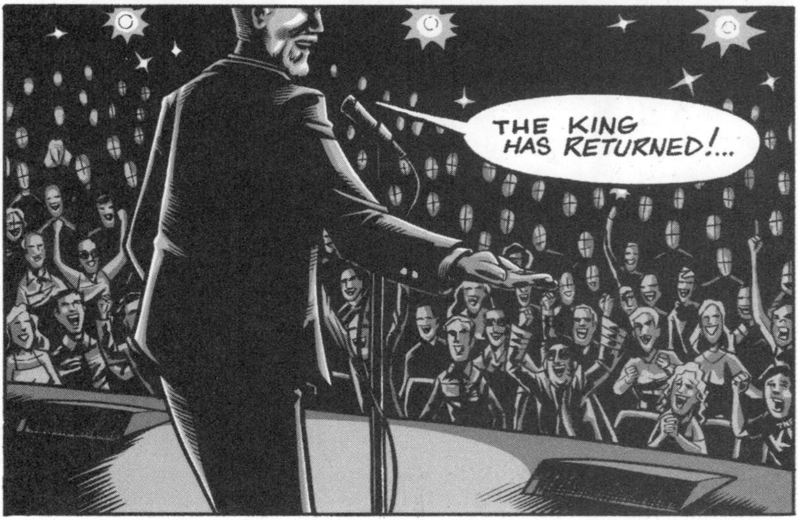
THE KING HAS *RETURNED*!...

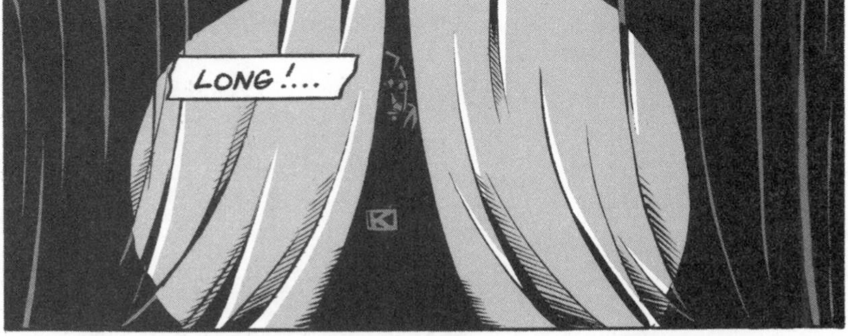
LONG !...
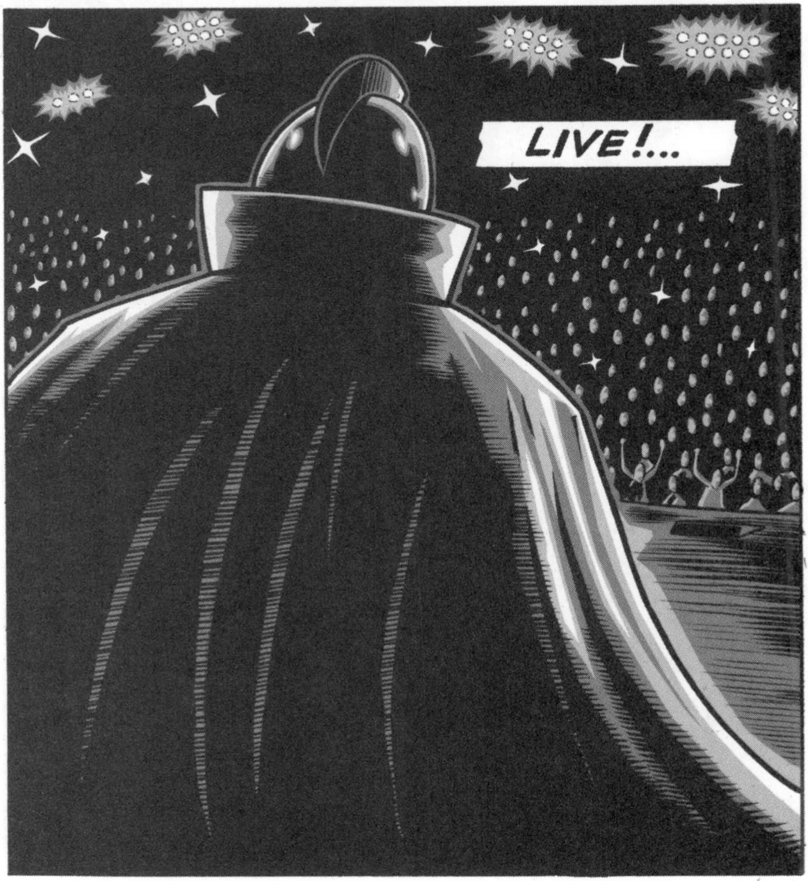
LIVE !...

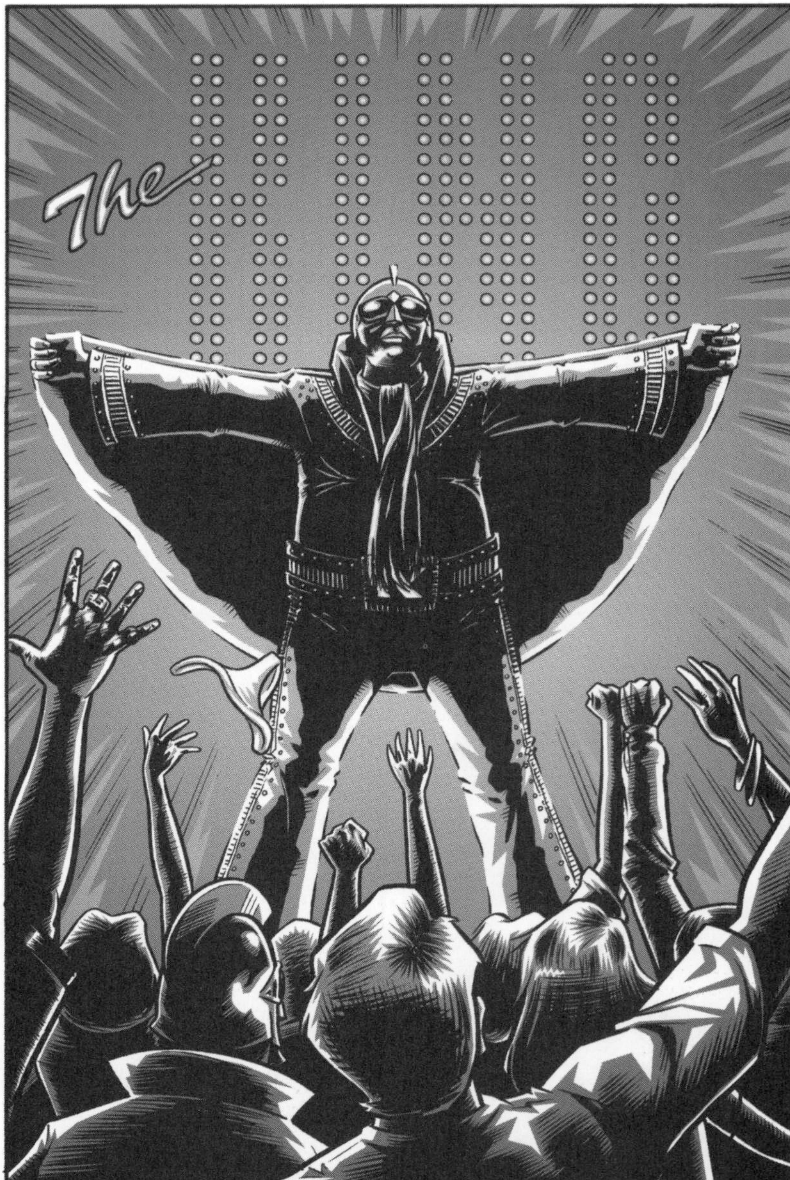
The

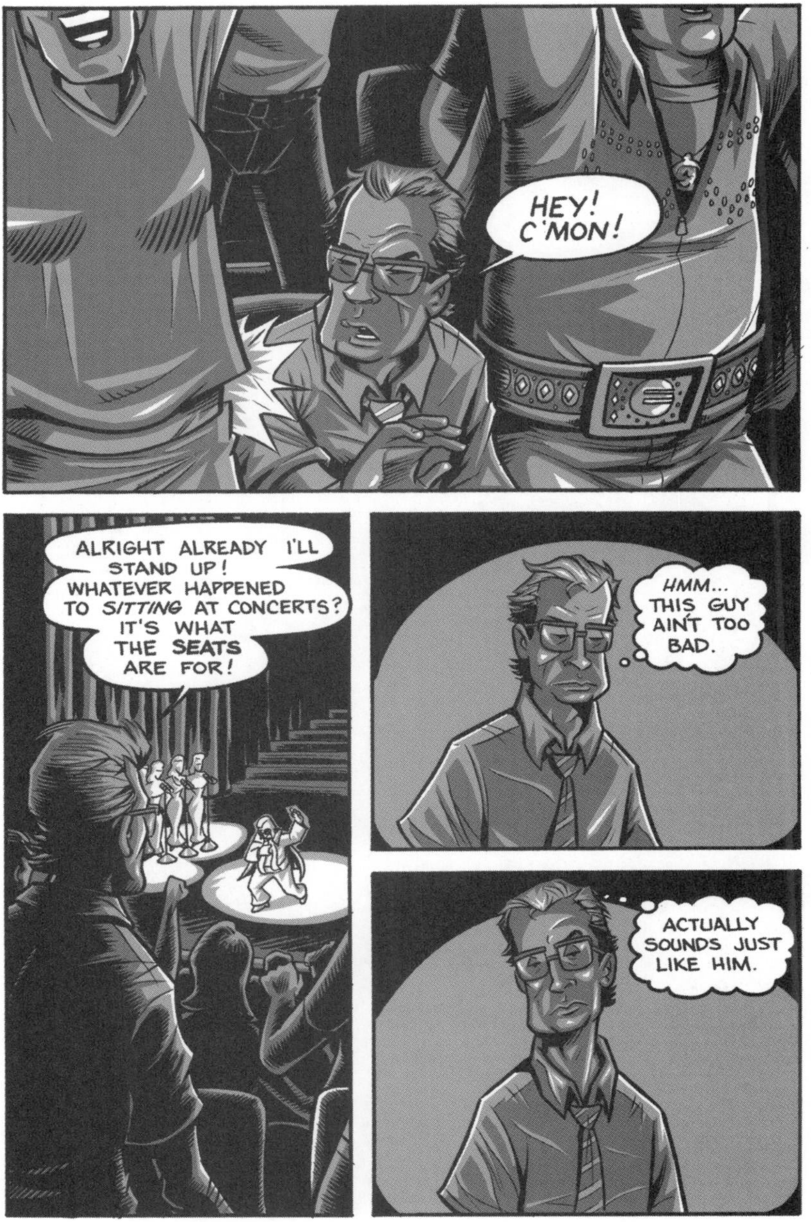
HEY! C'MON!
ALRIGHT ALREADY I'LL STAND UP! WHATEVER HAPPENED TO *SITTING* AT CONCERTS? IT'S WHAT THE **SEATS** ARE FOR!
HMM... THIS GUY AIN'T TOO BAD.
ACTUALLY SOUNDS JUST LIKE HIM.

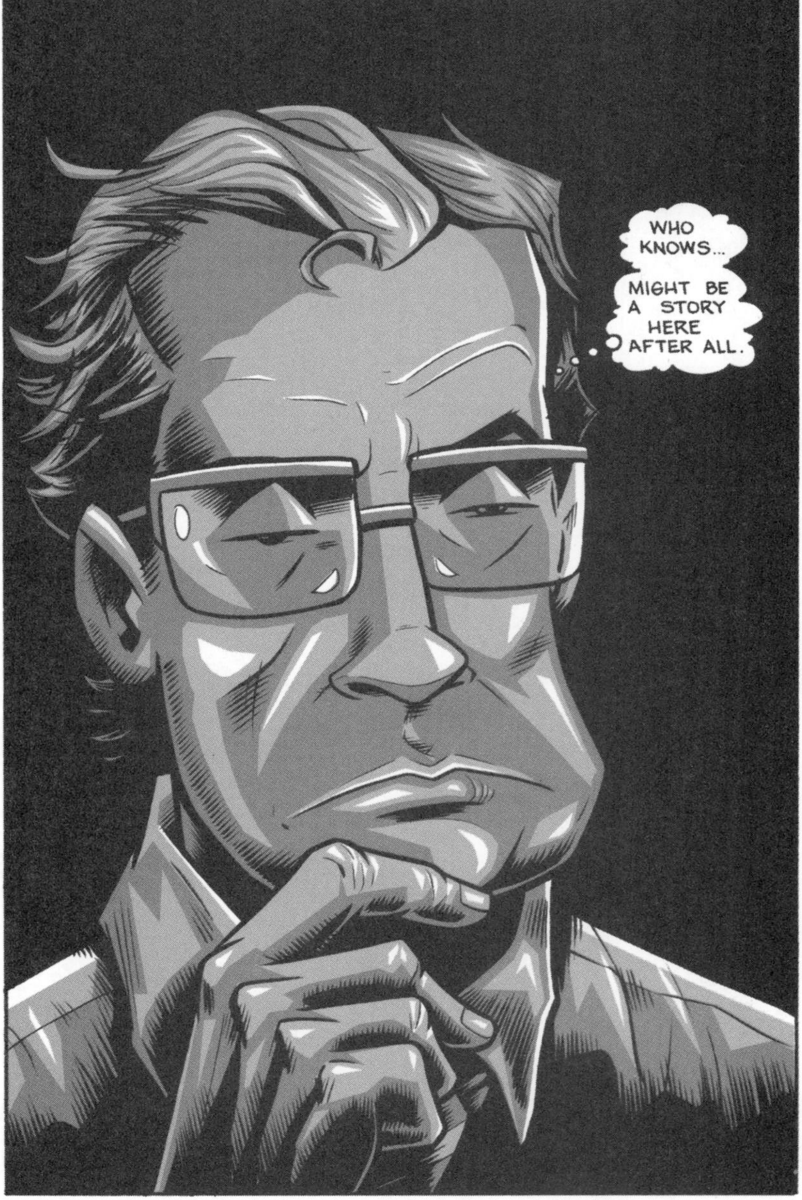
WHO KNOWS...
MIGHT BE A STORY HERE AFTER ALL.

"HE IS THE DEITY SUPREME OF
ROCK AND ROLL RELIGION AS IT EXISTS
IN TODAY'S FORM."

—BOB DYLAN

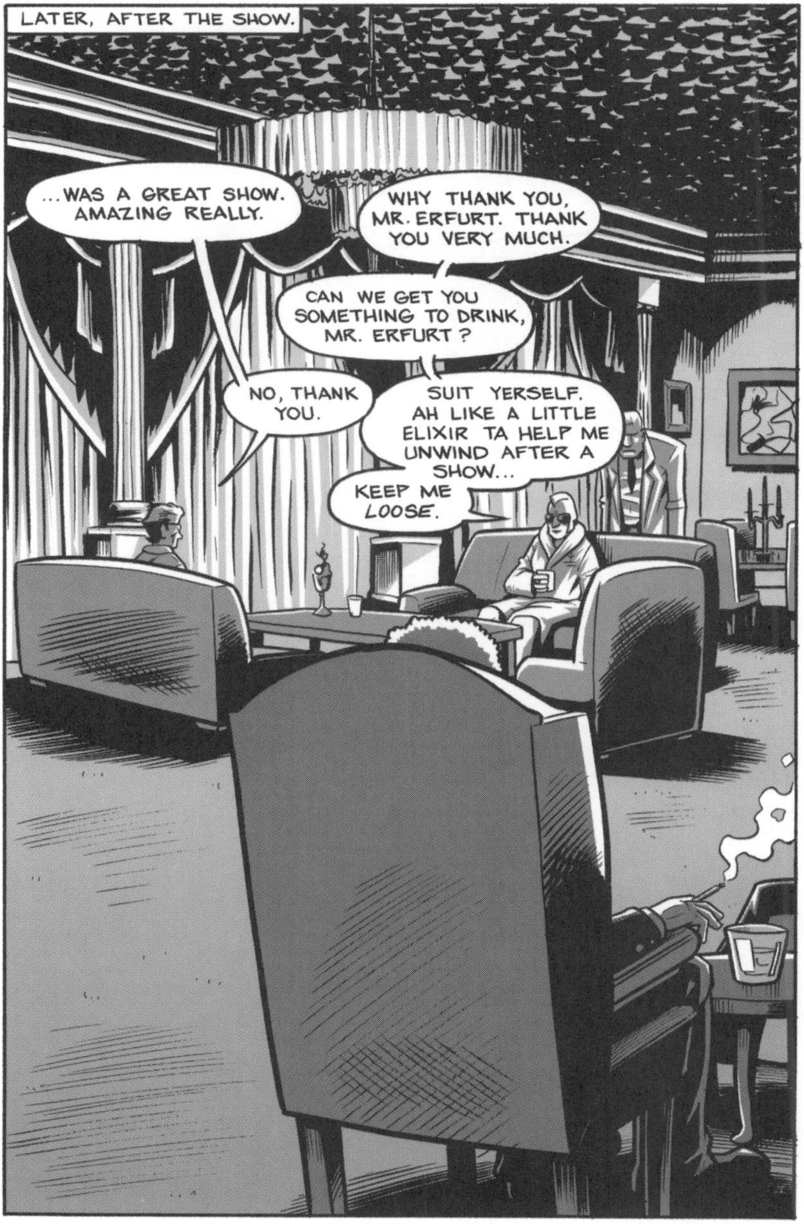
LATER, AFTER THE SHOW.
...WAS A GREAT SHOW. AMAZING REALLY.
WHY THANK YOU, MR. ERFURT. THANK YOU VERY MUCH.
CAN WE GET YOU SOMETHING TO DRINK, MR. ERFURT?
NO, THANK YOU.
SUIT YERSELF. AH LIKE A LITTLE ELIXIR TA HELP ME UNWIND AFTER A SHOW...
KEEP ME LOOSE.

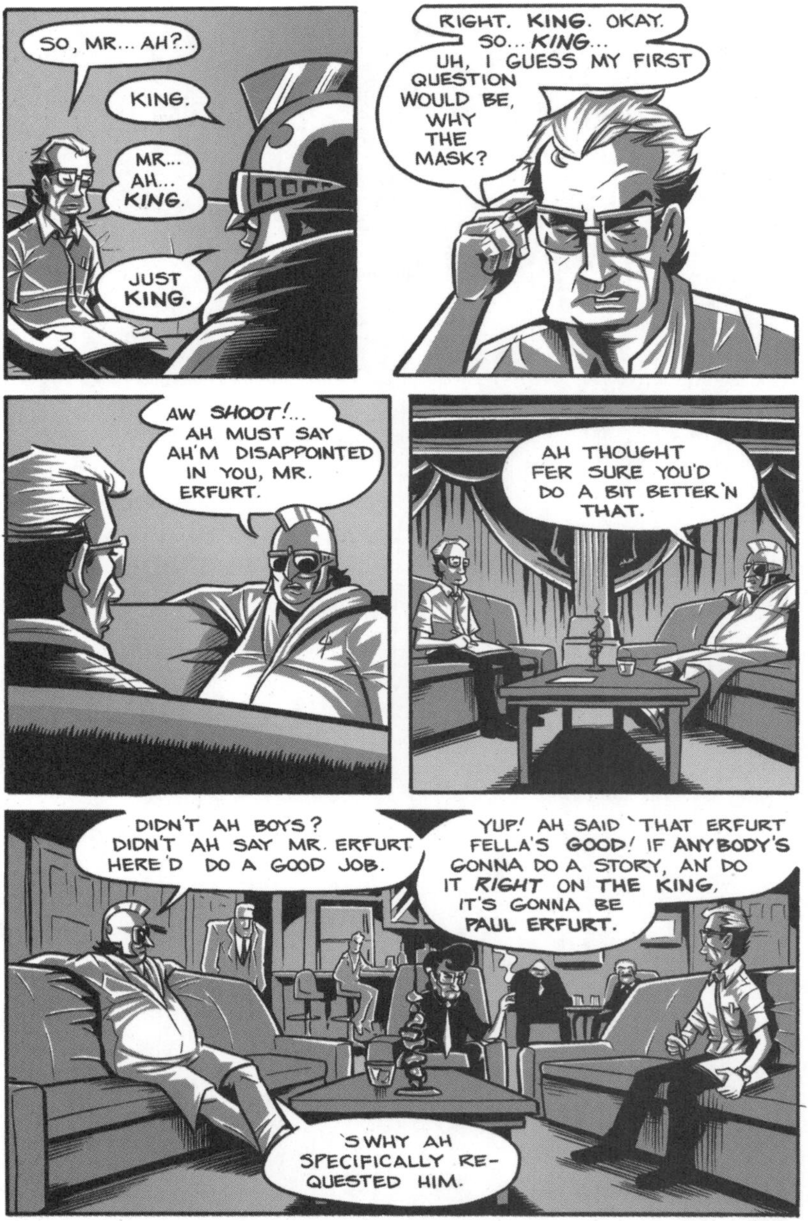
SO, MR... AH?...
KING.
MR... AH... KING.
JUST KING.
RIGHT. KING. OKAY. SO... KING... UH, I GUESS MY FIRST QUESTION WOULD BE, WHY THE MASK?
AW SHOOT!... AH MUST SAY AH'M DISAPPOINTED IN YOU, MR. ERFURT.
AH THOUGHT FER SURE YOU'D DO A BIT BETTER'N THAT.
DIDN'T AH BOYS? DIDN'T AH SAY MR. ERFURT HERE'D DO A GOOD JOB.
YUP! AH SAID `THAT ERFURT FELLA'S GOOD! IF ANYBODY'S GONNA DO A STORY, AN' DO IT RIGHT ON THE KING, IT'S GONNA BE PAUL ERFURT.
`S WHY AH SPECIFICALLY RE-QUESTED HIM.

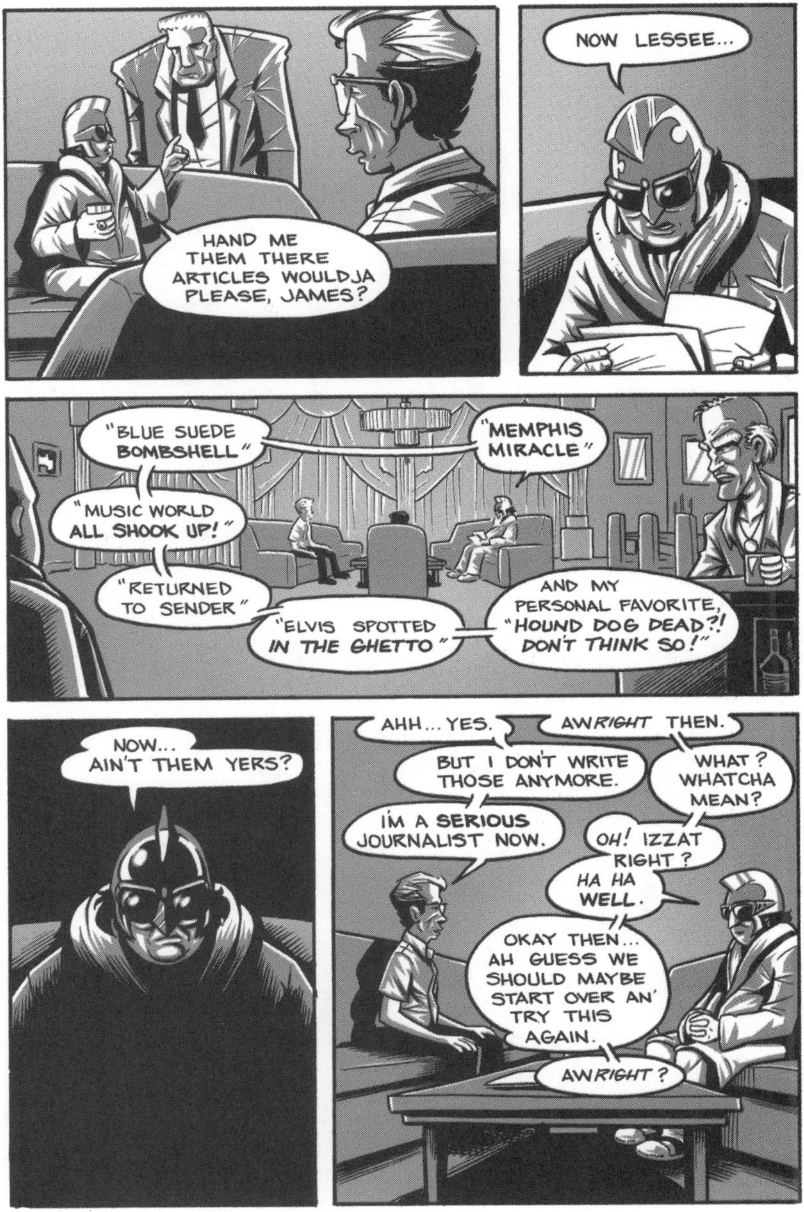
HAND ME THEM THERE ARTICLES WOULDJA PLEASE, JAMES?
NOW LESSEE...
"BLUE SUEDE BOMBSHELL"
"MEMPHIS MIRACLE"
"MUSIC WORLD ALL SHOOK UP!"
"RETURNED TO SENDER"
"ELVIS SPOTTED IN THE GHETTO"
AND MY PERSONAL FAVORITE, "HOUND DOG DEAD?! DON'T THINK SO!"
NOW... AIN'T THEM YERS?
AHH... YES.
BUT I DON'T WRITE THOSE ANYMORE.
I'M A SERIOUS JOURNALIST NOW.
AWRIGHT THEN.
WHAT? WHATCHA MEAN?
OH! IZZAT RIGHT?
HA HA WELL.
OKAY THEN... AH GUESS WE SHOULD MAYBE START OVER AN' TRY THIS AGAIN.
AWRIGHT?

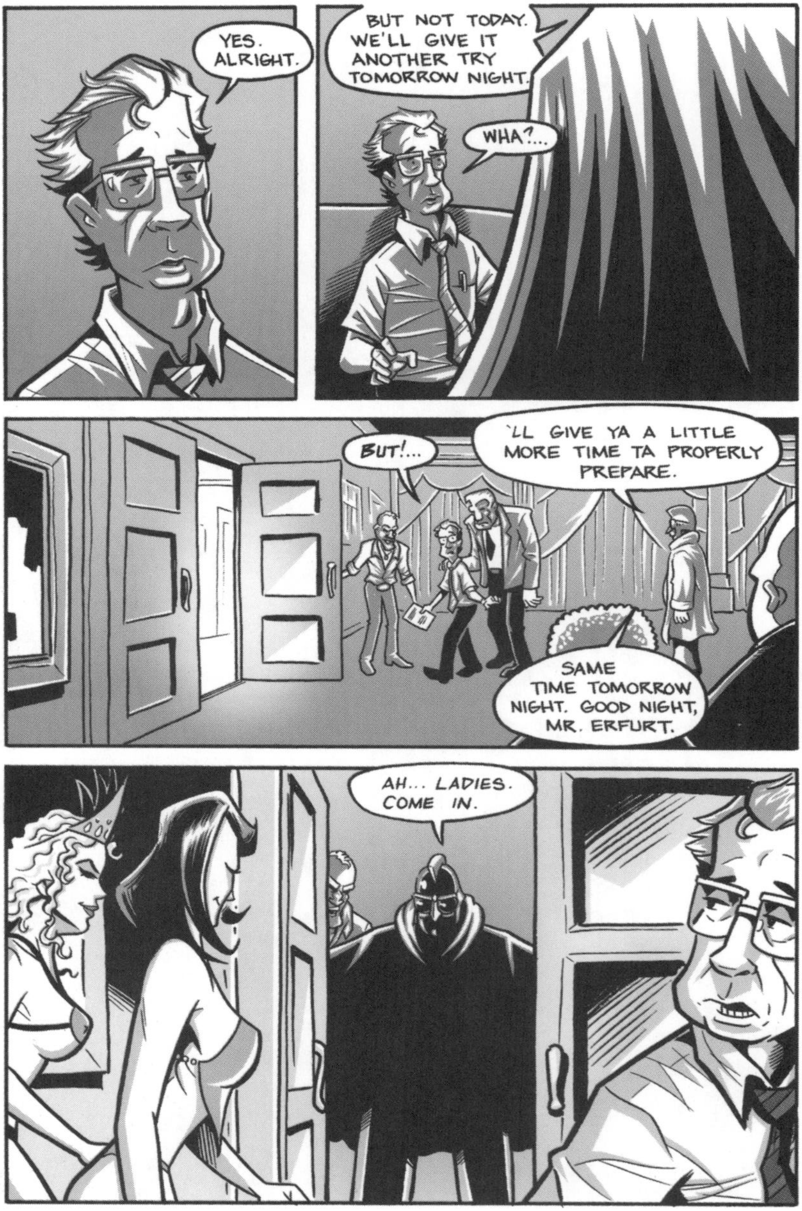
YES. ALRIGHT.
BUT NOT TODAY. WE'LL GIVE IT ANOTHER TRY TOMORROW NIGHT.
WHA?...
BUT!...
'LL GIVE YA A LITTLE MORE TIME TA PROPERLY PREPARE.
SAME TIME TOMORROW NIGHT. GOOD NIGHT, MR. ERFURT.
AH... LADIES. COME IN.

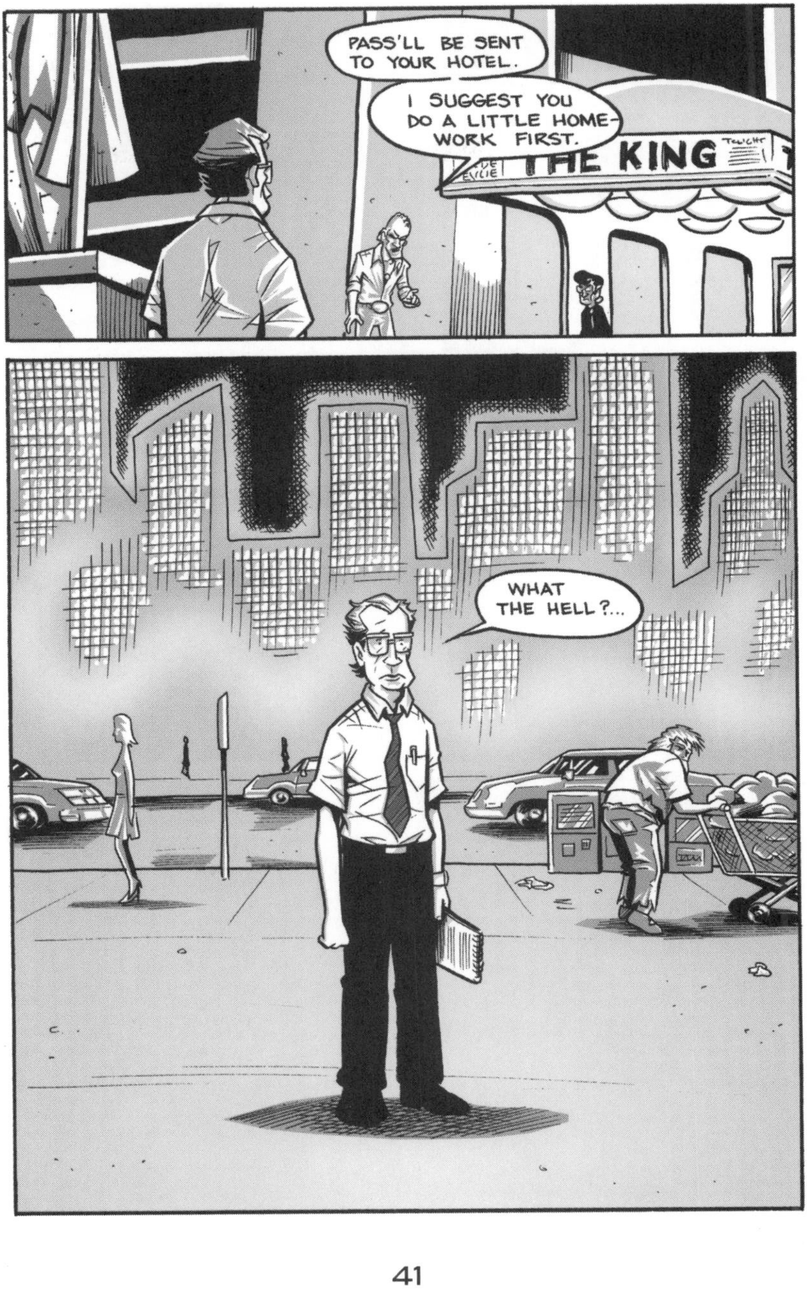
PASS'LL BE SENT TO YOUR HOTEL.
I SUGGEST YOU DO A LITTLE HOME-WORK FIRST.
THE KING
WHAT THE HELL?...

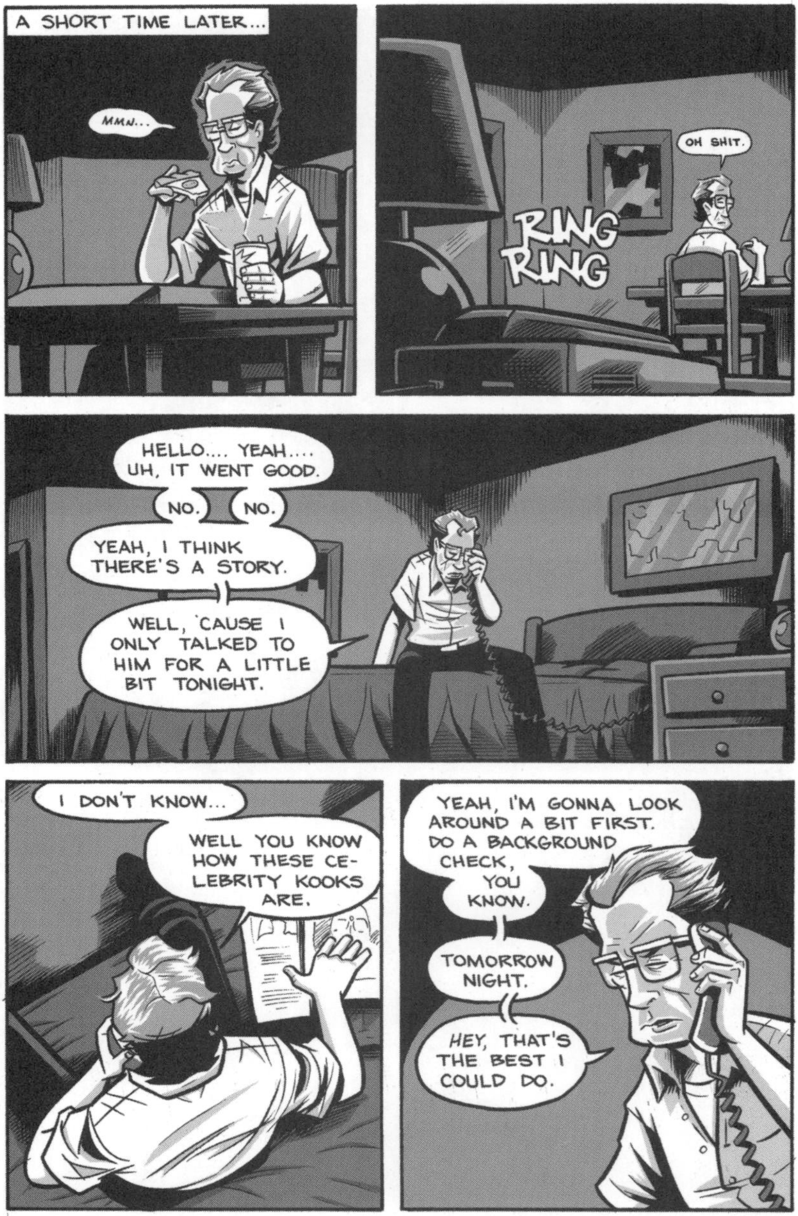
A SHORT TIME LATER...
MMN...
OH SHIT.
RING RING
HELLO.... YEAH.... UH, IT WENT GOOD.
NO.
NO.
YEAH, I THINK THERE'S A STORY.
WELL, 'CAUSE I ONLY TALKED TO HIM FOR A LITTLE BIT TONIGHT.
I DON'T KNOW...
WELL YOU KNOW HOW THESE CE-LEBRITY KOOKS ARE.
YEAH, I'M GONNA LOOK AROUND A BIT FIRST. DO A BACKGROUND CHECK,
YOU KNOW.
TOMORROW NIGHT.
HEY, THAT'S THE BEST I COULD DO.

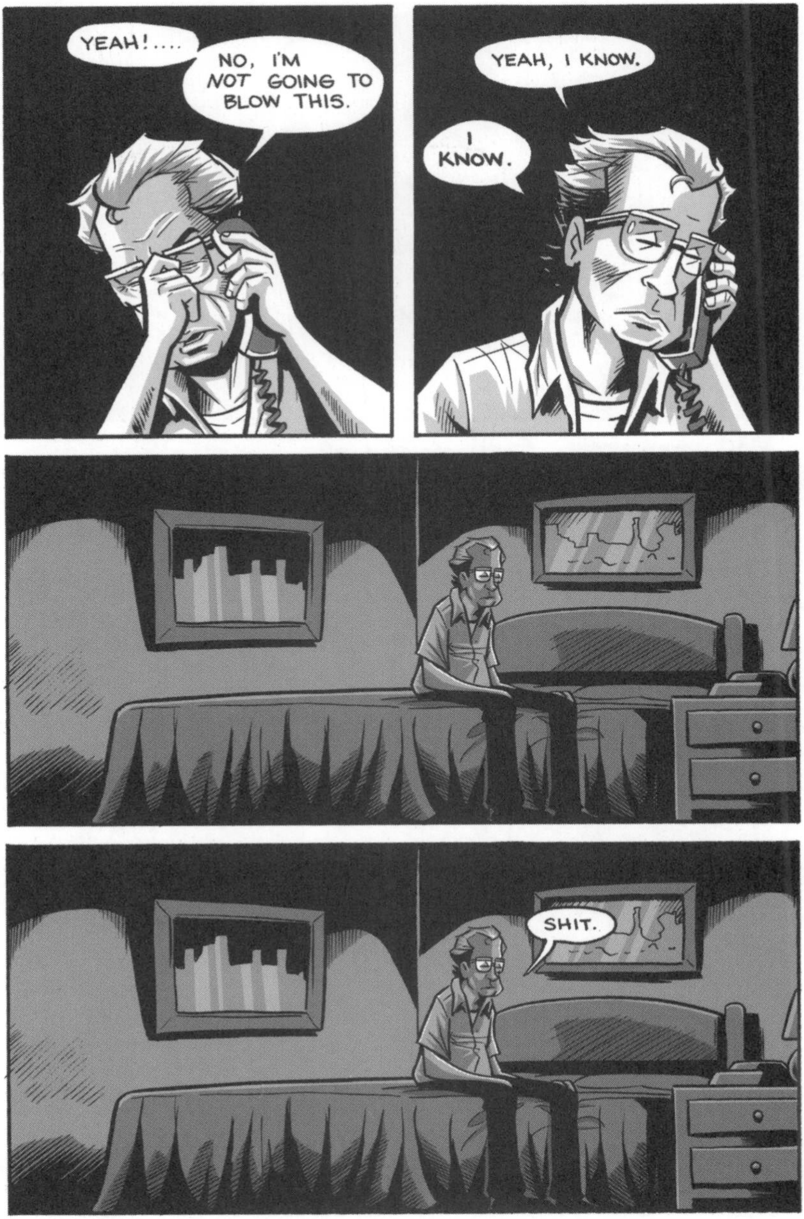
YEAH!....
NO, I'M *NOT* GOING TO BLOW THIS.
YEAH, I KNOW.
I KNOW.
SHIT.

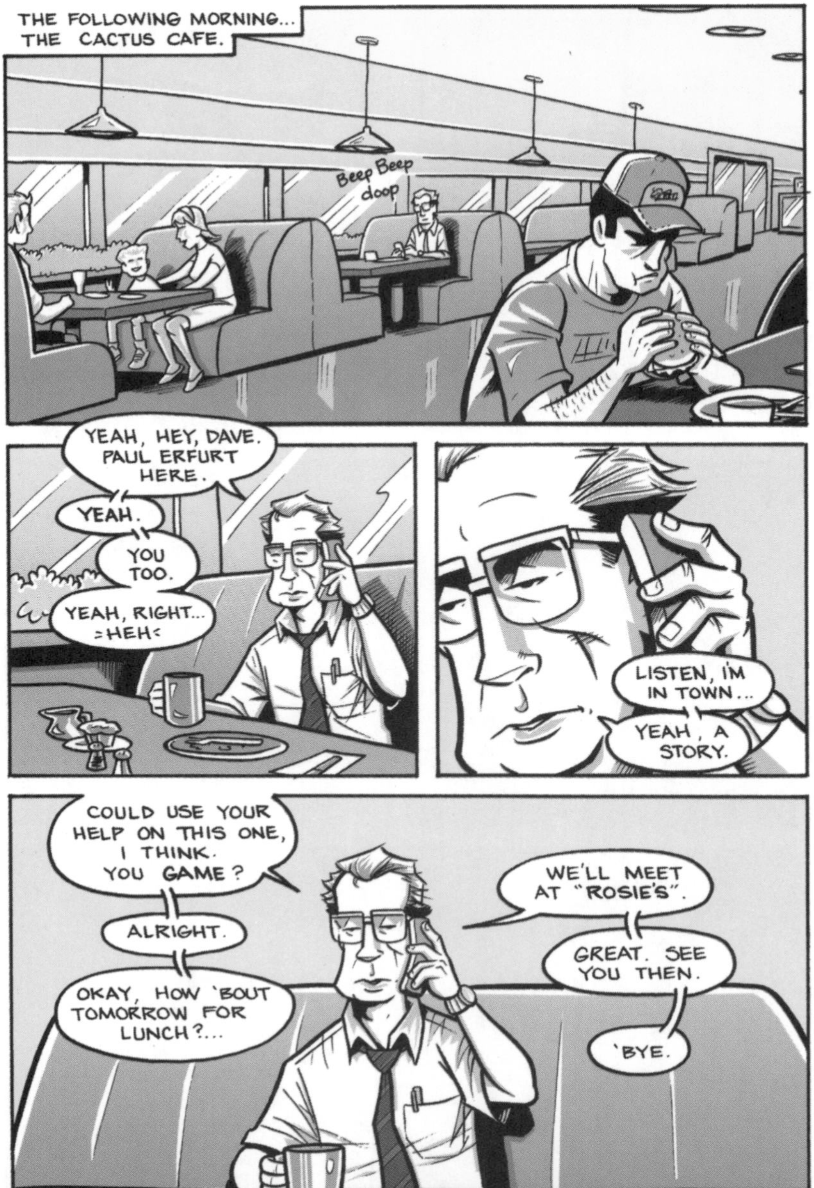

THE FOLLOWING MORNING... THE CACTUS CAFE.
Beep Beep doop
YEAH, HEY, DAVE. PAUL ERFURT HERE.
YEAH.
YOU TOO.
YEAH, RIGHT... >HEH<
LISTEN, I'M IN TOWN...
YEAH, A STORY.
COULD USE YOUR HELP ON THIS ONE, I THINK. YOU GAME?
ALRIGHT.
OKAY, HOW 'BOUT TOMORROW FOR LUNCH?...
WE'LL MEET AT "ROSIE'S".
GREAT. SEE YOU THEN.
'BYE.

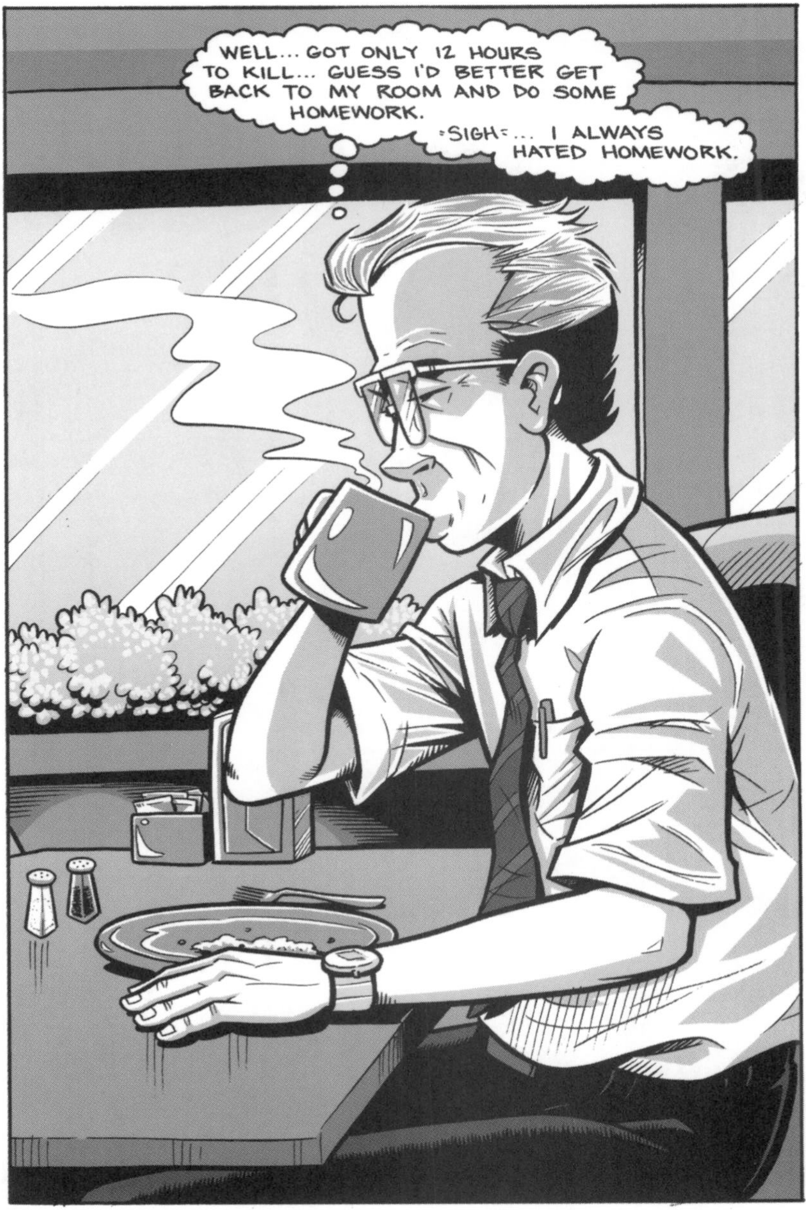
WELL... GOT ONLY 12 HOURS TO KILL... GUESS I'D BETTER GET BACK TO MY ROOM AND DO SOME HOMEWORK.
=SIGH=... I ALWAYS HATED HOMEWORK.

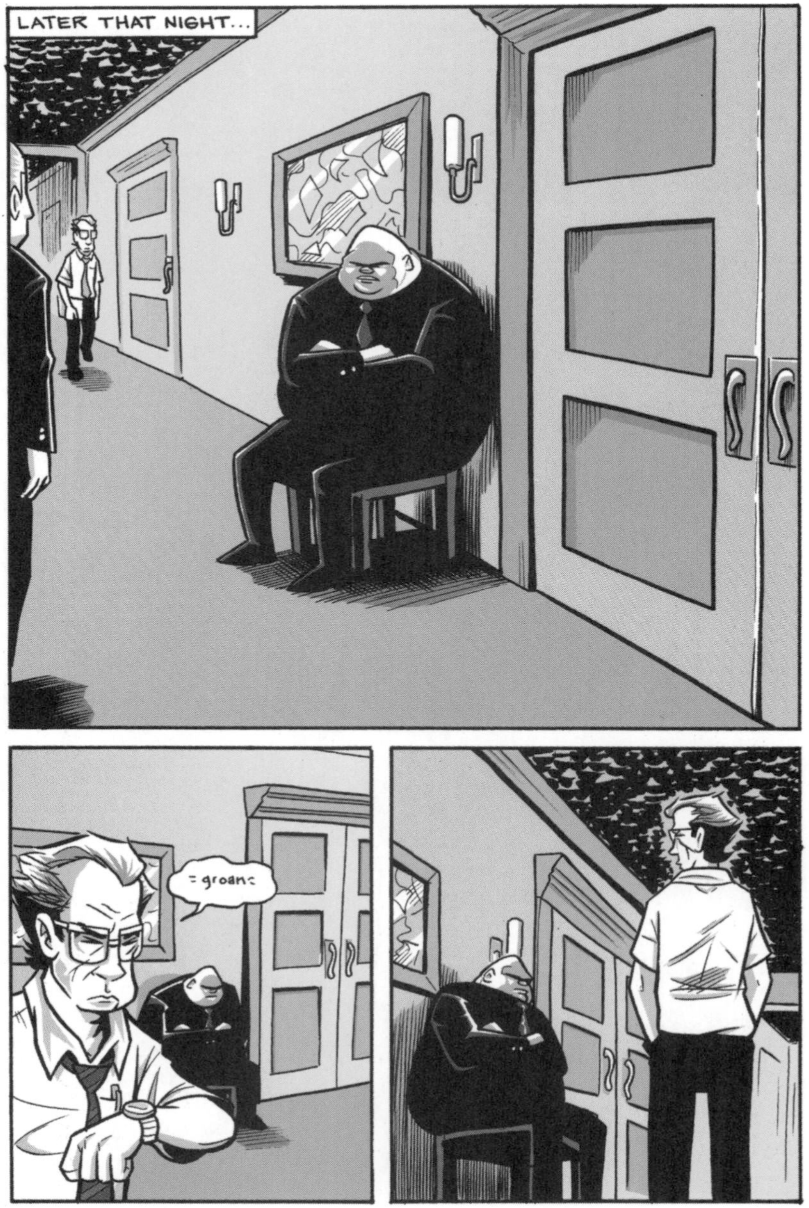
LATER THAT NIGHT...
=groan=

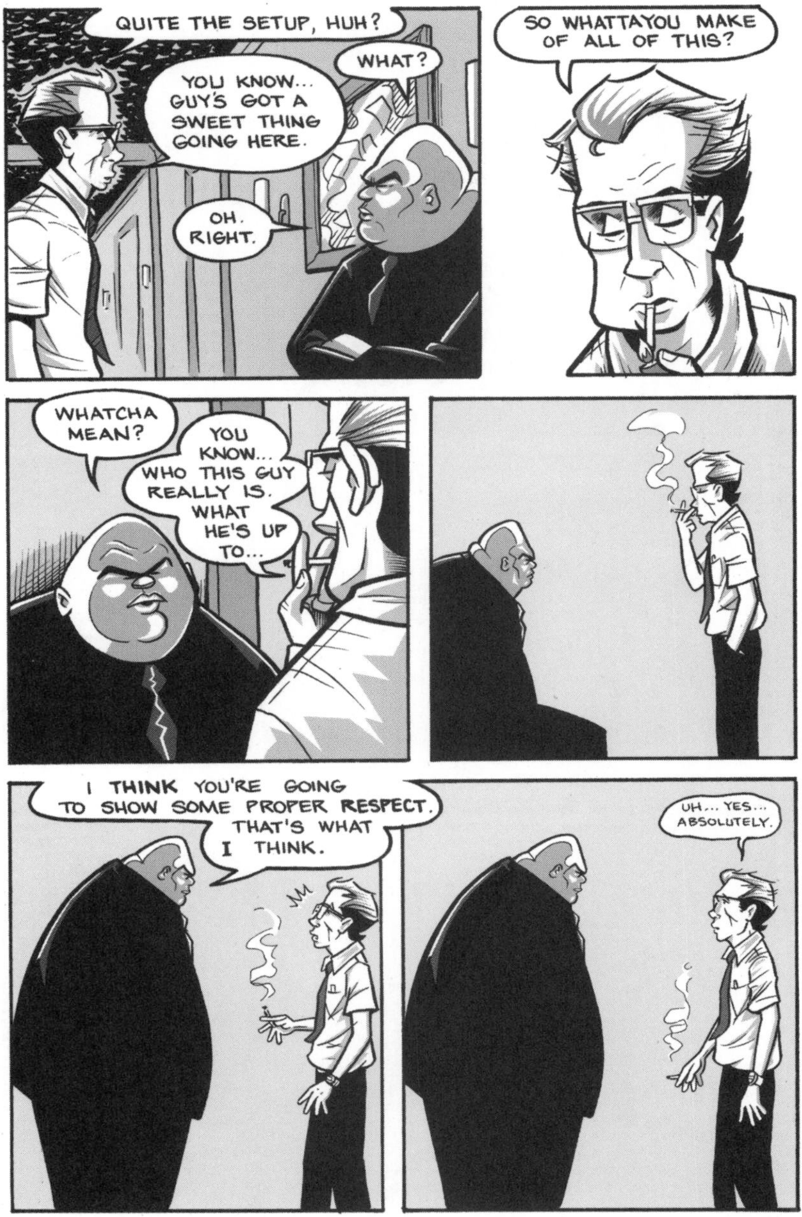
QUITE THE SETUP, HUH?
WHAT?
YOU KNOW... GUY'S GOT A SWEET THING GOING HERE.
OH. RIGHT.
SO WHATTAYOU MAKE OF ALL OF THIS?
WHATCHA MEAN?
YOU KNOW... WHO THIS GUY REALLY IS. WHAT HE'S UP TO...
I THINK YOU'RE GOING TO SHOW SOME PROPER RESPECT. THAT'S WHAT I THINK.
UH... YES... ABSOLUTELY.

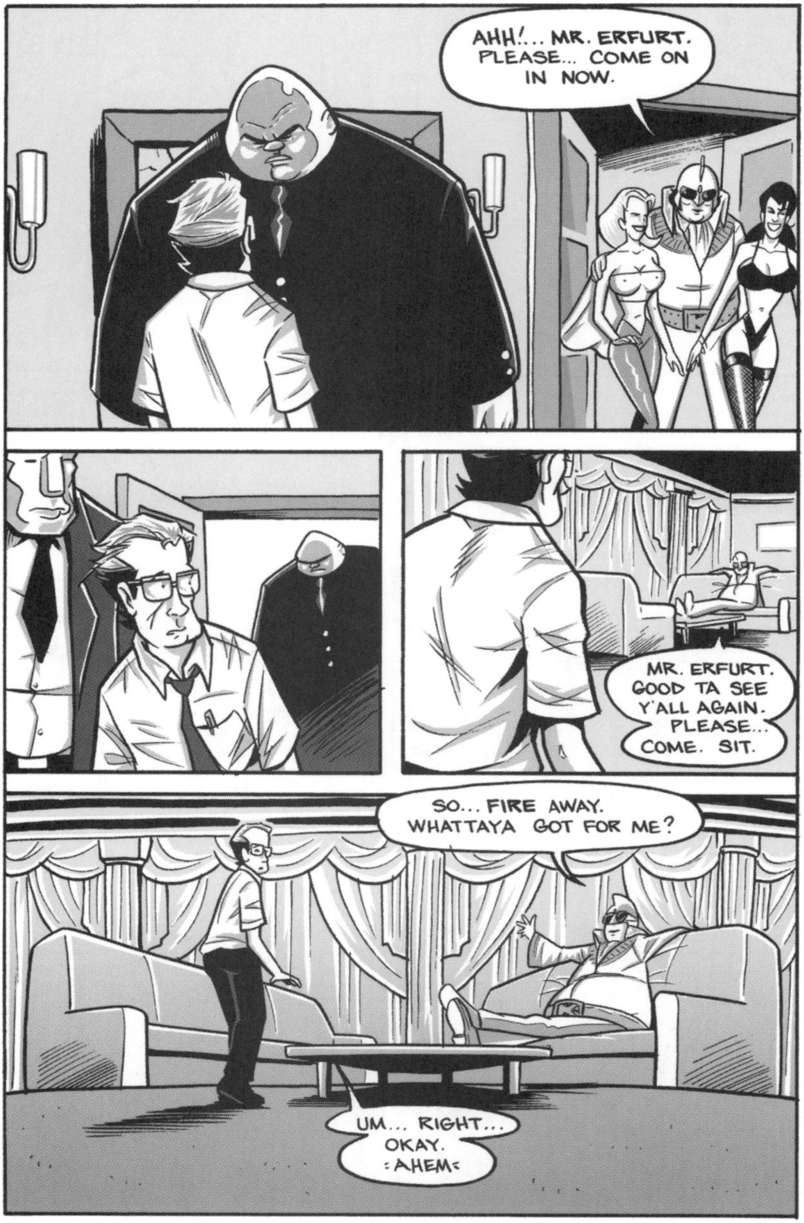
AHH!... MR. ERFURT. PLEASE... COME ON IN NOW.
MR. ERFURT. GOOD TA SEE Y'ALL AGAIN. PLEASE... COME. SIT.
SO... FIRE AWAY. WHATTAYA GOT FOR ME?
UM... RIGHT... OKAY. :AHEM:

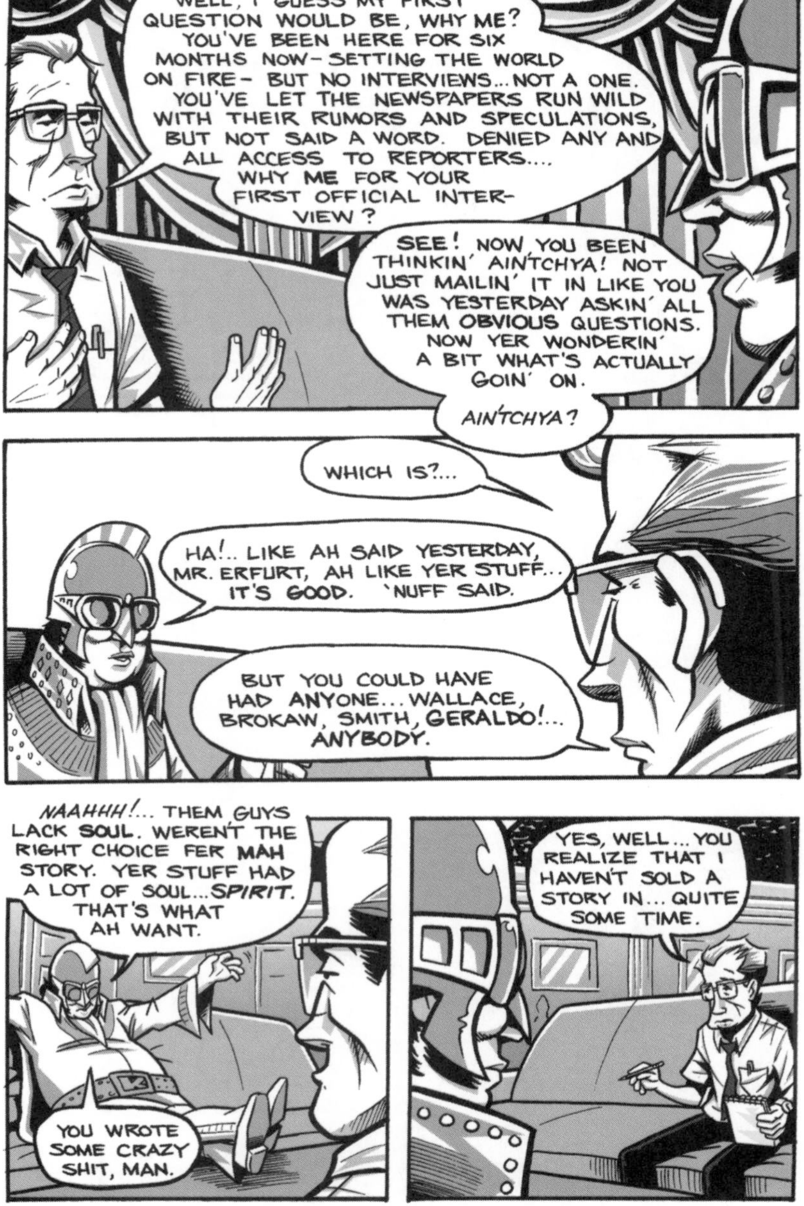
WELL, I GUESS MY FIRST QUESTION WOULD BE, WHY ME? YOU'VE BEEN HERE FOR SIX MONTHS NOW- SETTING THE WORLD ON FIRE- BUT NO INTERVIEWS... NOT A ONE. YOU'VE LET THE NEWSPAPERS RUN WILD WITH THEIR RUMORS AND SPECULATIONS, BUT NOT SAID A WORD. DENIED ANY AND ALL ACCESS TO REPORTERS.... WHY ME FOR YOUR FIRST OFFICIAL INTER-VIEW?
SEE! NOW YOU BEEN THINKIN' AIN'TCHYA! NOT JUST MAILIN' IT IN LIKE YOU WAS YESTERDAY ASKIN' ALL THEM OBVIOUS QUESTIONS. NOW YER WONDERIN' A BIT WHAT'S ACTUALLY GOIN' ON.
AIN'TCHYA?
WHICH IS?...
HA!.. LIKE AH SAID YESTERDAY, MR. ERFURT, AH LIKE YER STUFF... IT'S GOOD. 'NUFF SAID.
BUT YOU COULD HAVE HAD ANYONE... WALLACE, BROKAW, SMITH, GERALDO!... ANYBODY.
NAAHHH!... THEM GUYS LACK SOUL. WEREN'T THE RIGHT CHOICE FER MAH STORY. YER STUFF HAD A LOT OF SOUL... SPIRIT. THAT'S WHAT AH WANT.
YOU WROTE SOME CRAZY SHIT, MAN.
YES, WELL... YOU REALIZE THAT I HAVEN'T SOLD A STORY IN... QUITE SOME TIME.

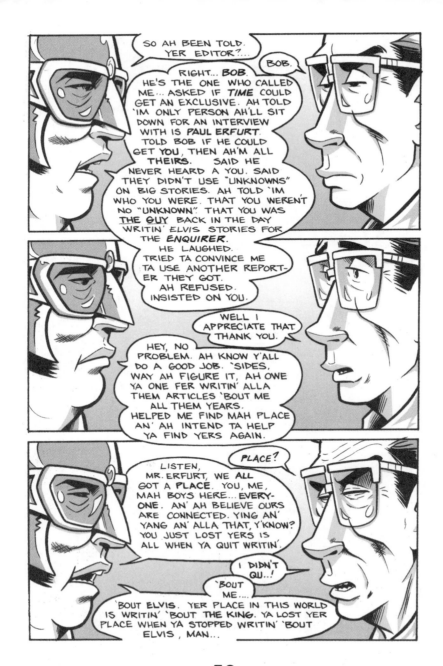

SO AH BEEN TOLD. YER EDITOR?...

BOB.

RIGHT... **BOB**. HE'S THE ONE WHO CALLED ME... ASKED IF **TIME** COULD GET AN EXCLUSIVE. AH TOLD 'IM ONLY PERSON AH'LL SIT DOWN FOR AN INTERVIEW WITH IS **PAUL ERFURT**. TOLD BOB IF HE COULD GET **YOU**, THEN AH'M ALL **THEIRS**. SAID HE NEVER HEARD A YOU. SAID THEY DIDN'T USE "UNKNOWNS" ON BIG STORIES. AH TOLD 'IM WHO YOU WERE. THAT YOU WEREN'T NO "UNKNOWN". THAT YOU WAS **THE GUY** BACK IN THE DAY WRITIN' ELVIS STORIES FOR THE **ENQUIRER**.

HE LAUGHED. TRIED TA CONVINCE ME TA USE ANOTHER REPORTER THEY GOT. AH REFUSED. INSISTED ON YOU.

WELL I APPRECIATE THAT. THANK YOU.

HEY, NO PROBLEM. AH KNOW Y'ALL DO A GOOD JOB. 'SIDES, WAY AH FIGURE IT, AH OWE YA ONE FER WRITIN' ALLA THEM ARTICLES 'BOUT ME ALL THEM YEARS. HELPED ME FIND MAH PLACE AN' AH INTEND TA HELP YA FIND YERS AGAIN.

PLACE?

LISTEN, MR. ERFURT, WE ALL GOT A **PLACE**. YOU, ME, MAH BOYS HERE... EVERY-ONE. AN' AH BELIEVE OURS ARE CONNECTED. YING AN' YANG AN' ALLA THAT, Y'KNOW? YOU JUST LOST YERS IS ALL WHEN YA QUIT WRITIN'.

I DIDN'T QU..!

'BOUT ME....

'BOUT ELVIS. YER PLACE IN THIS WORLD IS WRITIN' 'BOUT **THE KING**. YA LOST YER PLACE WHEN YA STOPPED WRITIN' 'BOUT ELVIS, MAN...

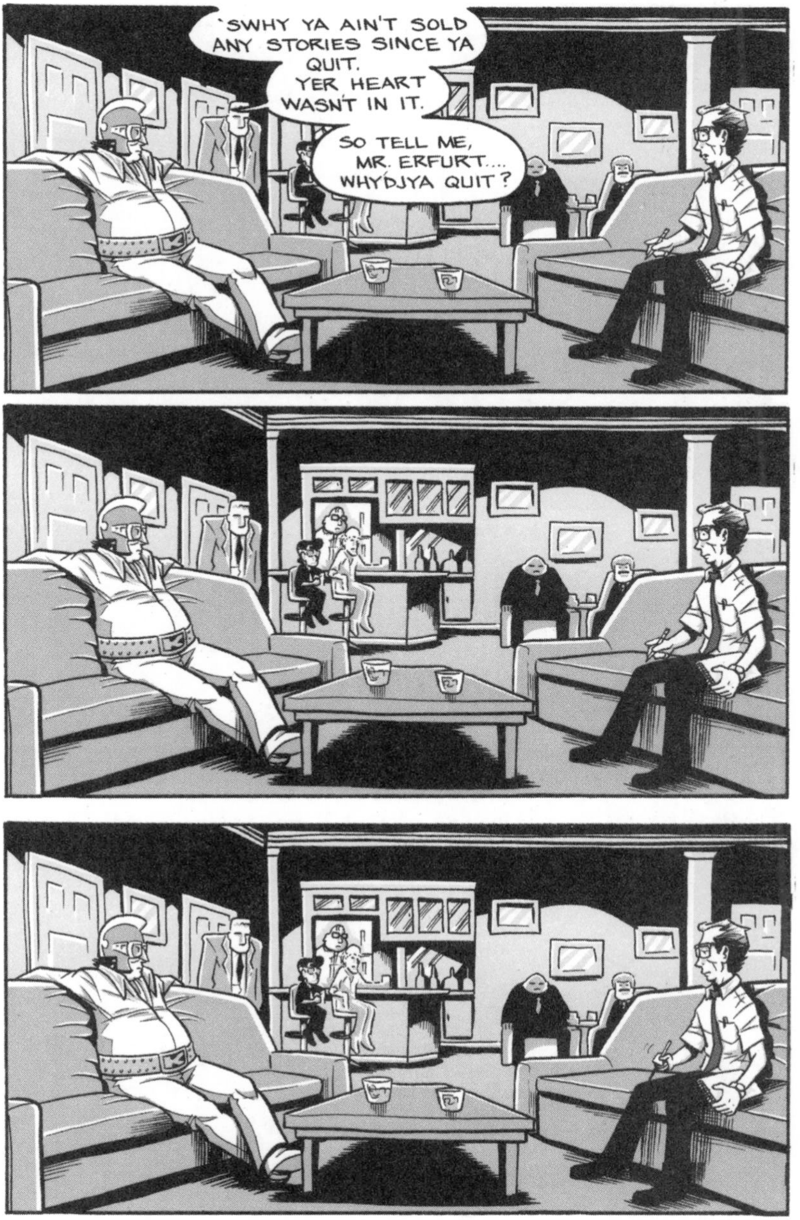

'SWHY YA AIN'T SOLD ANY STORIES SINCE YA QUIT.
YER HEART WASN'T IN IT.
SO TELL ME, MR. ERFURT.... WHY'DJYA QUIT?

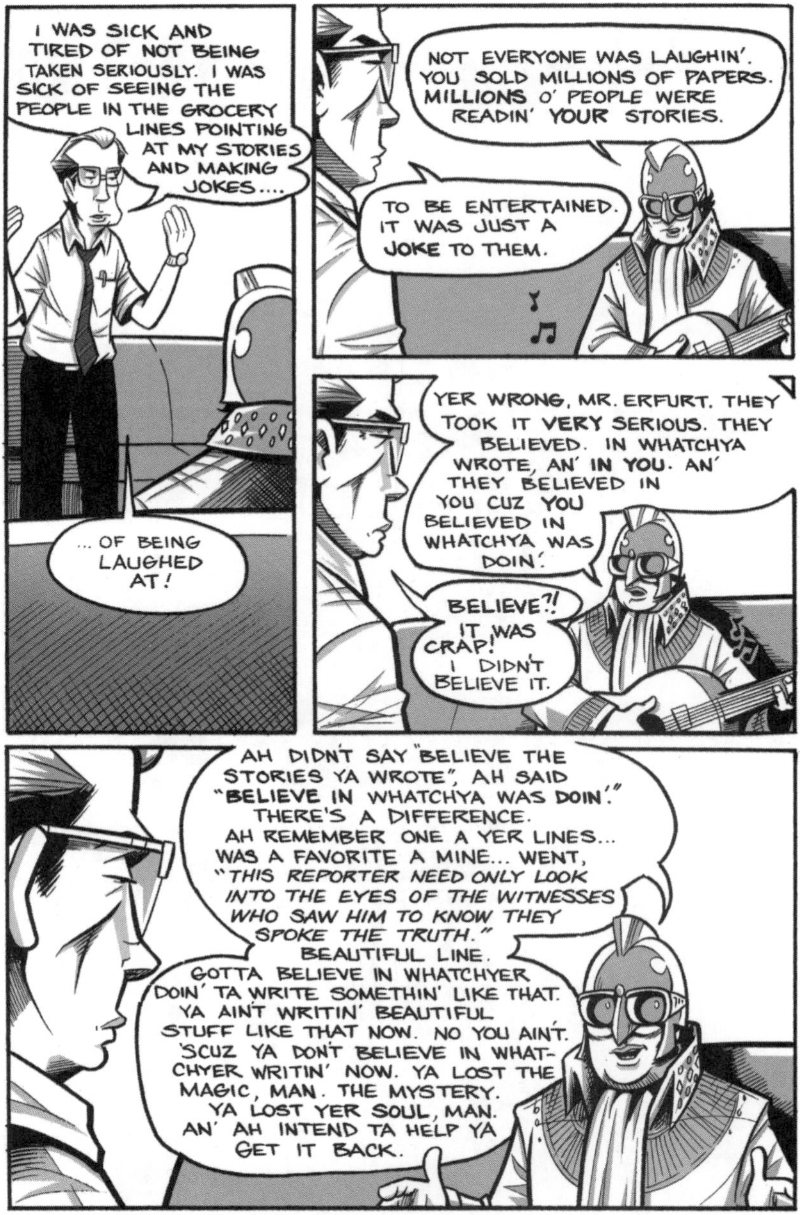
I WAS SICK AND TIRED OF NOT BEING TAKEN SERIOUSLY. I WAS SICK OF SEEING THE PEOPLE IN THE GROCERY LINES POINTING AT MY STORIES AND MAKING JOKES....
... OF BEING LAUGHED AT!
NOT EVERYONE WAS LAUGHIN'. YOU SOLD MILLIONS OF PAPERS. MILLIONS O' PEOPLE WERE READIN' YOUR STORIES.
TO BE ENTERTAINED. IT WAS JUST A JOKE TO THEM.
YER WRONG, MR. ERFURT. THEY TOOK IT VERY SERIOUS. THEY BELIEVED. IN WHATCHYA WROTE, AN' IN YOU. AN' THEY BELIEVED IN YOU CUZ YOU BELIEVED IN WHATCHYA WAS DOIN'.
BELIEVE?! IT WAS CRAP! I DIDN'T BELIEVE IT.
AH DIDN'T SAY "BELIEVE THE STORIES YA WROTE", AH SAID "BELIEVE IN WHATCHYA WAS DOIN'." THERE'S A DIFFERENCE. AH REMEMBER ONE A YER LINES... WAS A FAVORITE A MINE... WENT, "THIS REPORTER NEED ONLY LOOK INTO THE EYES OF THE WITNESSES WHO SAW HIM TO KNOW THEY SPOKE THE TRUTH." BEAUTIFUL LINE. GOTTA BELIEVE IN WHATCHYER DOIN' TA WRITE SOMETHIN' LIKE THAT. YA AIN'T WRITIN' BEAUTIFUL STUFF LIKE THAT NOW. NO YOU AIN'T. 'SCUZ YA DON'T BELIEVE IN WHATCHYER WRITIN' NOW. YA LOST THE MAGIC, MAN. THE MYSTERY. YA LOST YER SOUL, MAN. AN' AH INTEND TA HELP YA GET IT BACK.

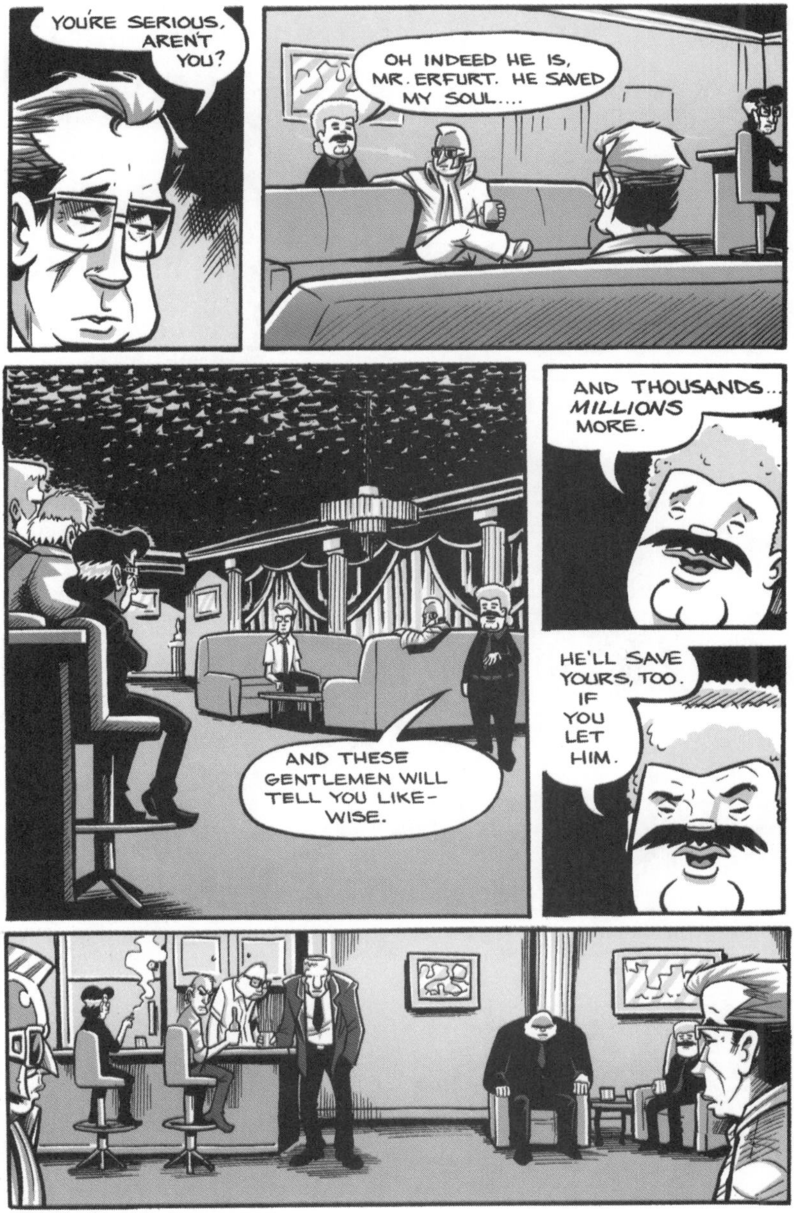
YOU'RE SERIOUS, AREN'T YOU?
OH INDEED HE IS, MR. ERFURT. HE SAVED MY SOUL....
AND THOUSANDS... MILLIONS MORE.
AND THESE GENTLEMEN WILL TELL YOU LIKE-WISE.
HE'LL SAVE YOURS, TOO. IF YOU LET HIM.

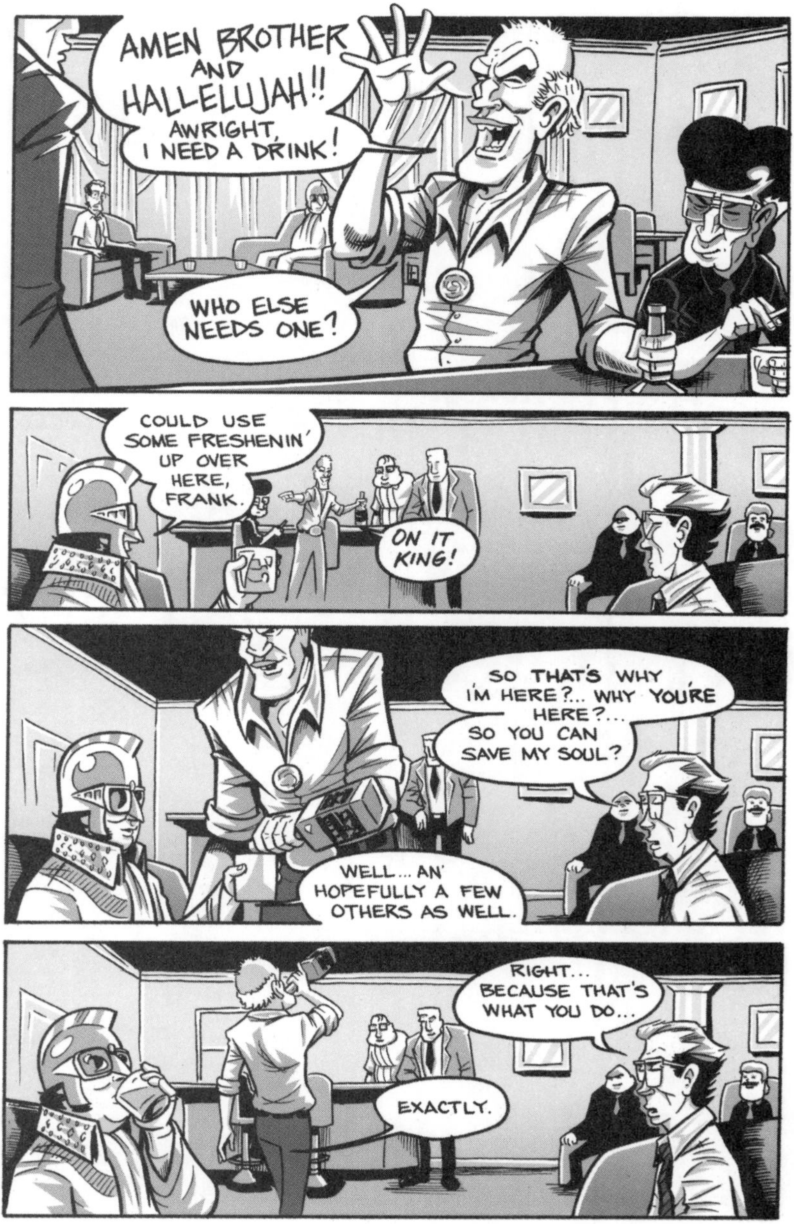
AMEN BROTHER AND HALLELUJAH!!
AWRIGHT, I NEED A DRINK!
WHO ELSE NEEDS ONE?
COULD USE SOME FRESHENIN' UP OVER HERE, FRANK.
ON IT KING!
SO THAT'S WHY I'M HERE?... WHY YOU'RE HERE?...
SO YOU CAN SAVE MY SOUL?
WELL... AN' HOPEFULLY A FEW OTHERS AS WELL.
RIGHT... BECAUSE THAT'S WHAT YOU DO...
EXACTLY.

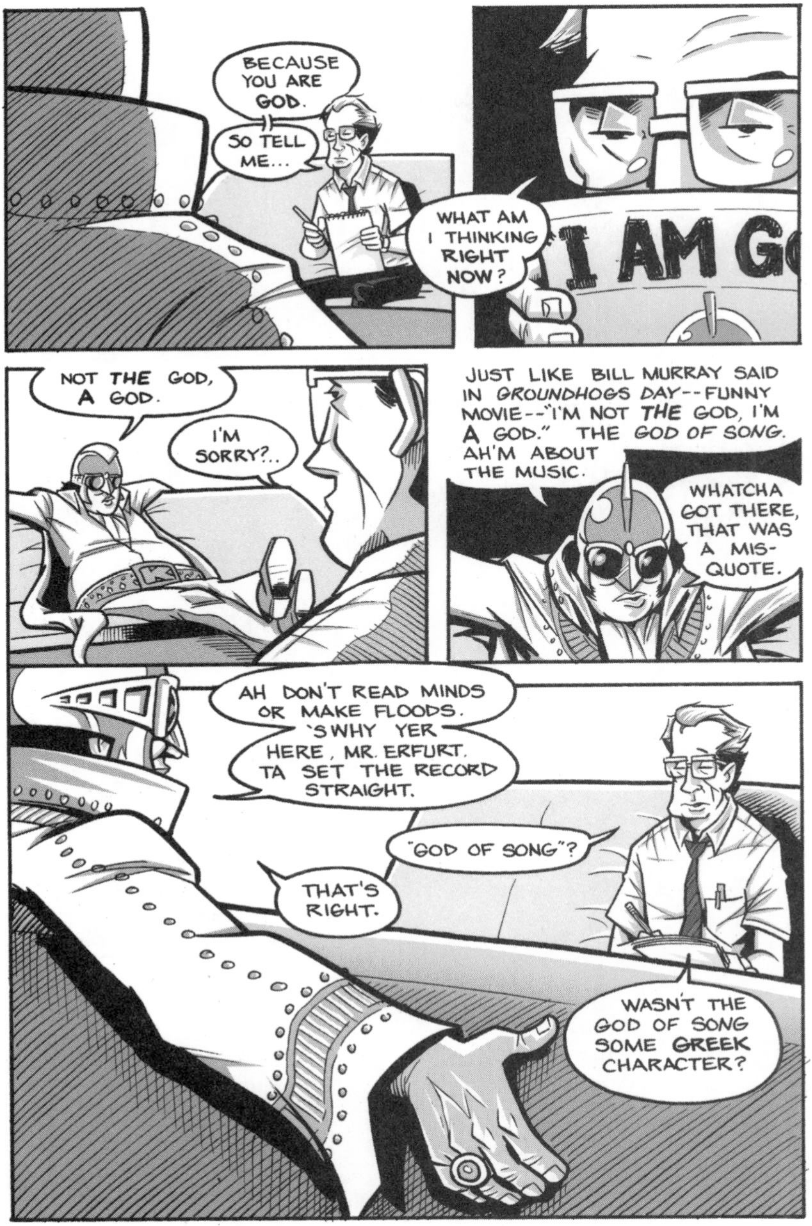
BECAUSE YOU ARE GOD.
SO TELL ME...
WHAT AM I THINKING RIGHT NOW?
I AM G
NOT THE GOD, A GOD.
I'M SORRY?..
JUST LIKE BILL MURRAY SAID IN GROUNDHOGS DAY--FUNNY MOVIE--"I'M NOT THE GOD, I'M A GOD." THE GOD OF SONG. AH'M ABOUT THE MUSIC.
WHATCHA GOT THERE, THAT WAS A MIS-QUOTE.
AH DON'T READ MINDS OR MAKE FLOODS. 'S WHY YER HERE, MR. ERFURT. TA SET THE RECORD STRAIGHT.
"GOD OF SONG"?
THAT'S RIGHT.
WASN'T THE GOD OF SONG SOME GREEK CHARACTER?

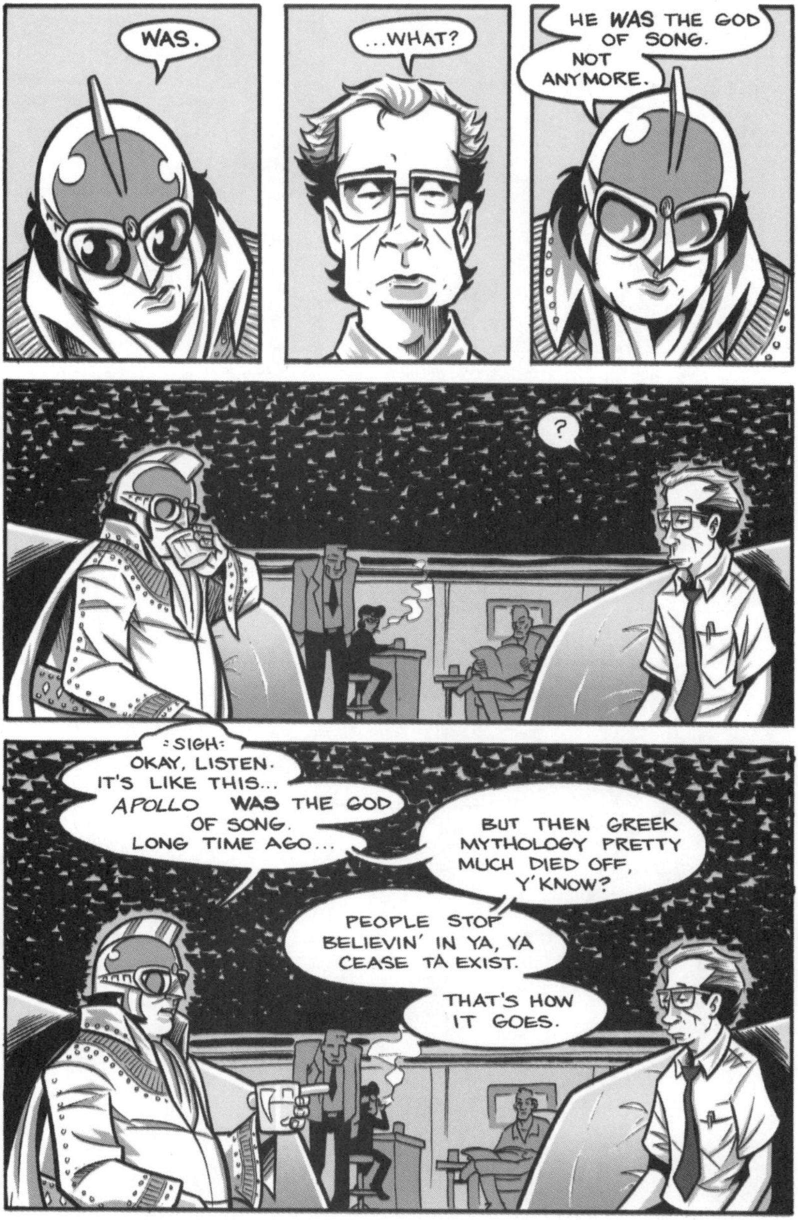
WAS.
...WHAT?
HE WAS THE GOD OF SONG.
NOT ANYMORE.
?
:SIGH: OKAY, LISTEN. IT'S LIKE THIS... APOLLO WAS THE GOD OF SONG. LONG TIME AGO...
BUT THEN GREEK MYTHOLOGY PRETTY MUCH DIED OFF, Y'KNOW?
PEOPLE STOP BELIEVIN' IN YA, YA CEASE TA EXIST.
THAT'S HOW IT GOES.

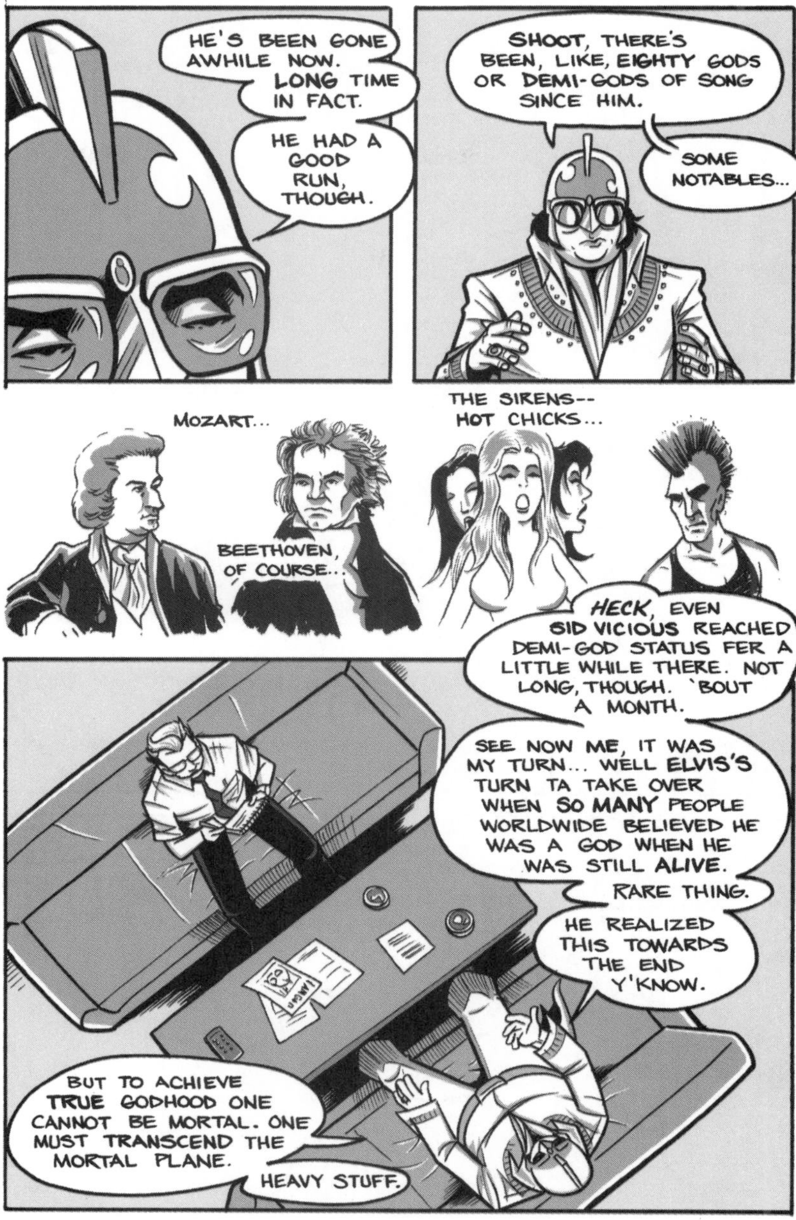

HE'S BEEN GONE AWHILE NOW.
LONG TIME IN FACT.
HE HAD A GOOD RUN, THOUGH.
SHOOT, THERE'S BEEN, LIKE, EIGHTY GODS OR DEMI-GODS OF SONG SINCE HIM.
SOME NOTABLES...
MOZART...
BEETHOVEN, OF COURSE...
THE SIRENS-- HOT CHICKS...
HECK, EVEN SID VICIOUS REACHED DEMI-GOD STATUS FER A LITTLE WHILE THERE. NOT LONG, THOUGH. `BOUT A MONTH.
SEE NOW ME, IT WAS MY TURN... WELL ELVIS'S TURN TA TAKE OVER WHEN SO MANY PEOPLE WORLDWIDE BELIEVED HE WAS A GOD WHEN HE WAS STILL ALIVE.
RARE THING.
HE REALIZED THIS TOWARDS THE END Y'KNOW.
BUT TO ACHIEVE TRUE GODHOOD ONE CANNOT BE MORTAL. ONE MUST TRANSCEND THE MORTAL PLANE.
HEAVY STUFF.

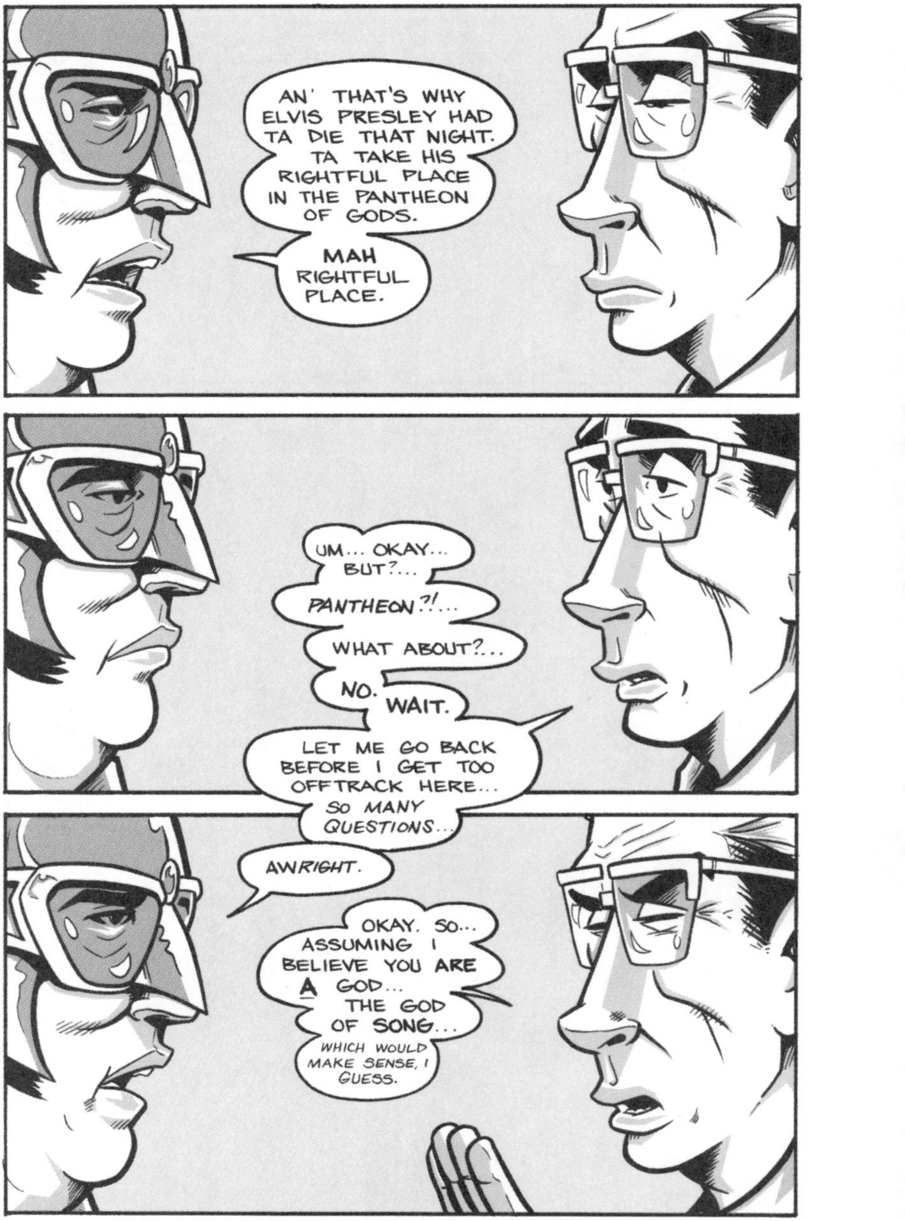
AN' THAT'S WHY ELVIS PRESLEY HAD TA DIE THAT NIGHT. TA TAKE HIS RIGHTFUL PLACE IN THE PANTHEON OF GODS.
MAH RIGHTFUL PLACE.
UM... OKAY... BUT?...
PANTHEON?!...
WHAT ABOUT?...
NO. WAIT.
LET ME GO BACK BEFORE I GET TOO OFFTRACK HERE... SO MANY QUESTIONS...
AWRIGHT.
OKAY. SO... ASSUMING I BELIEVE YOU ARE A GOD... THE GOD OF SONG... WHICH WOULD MAKE SENSE, I GUESS.

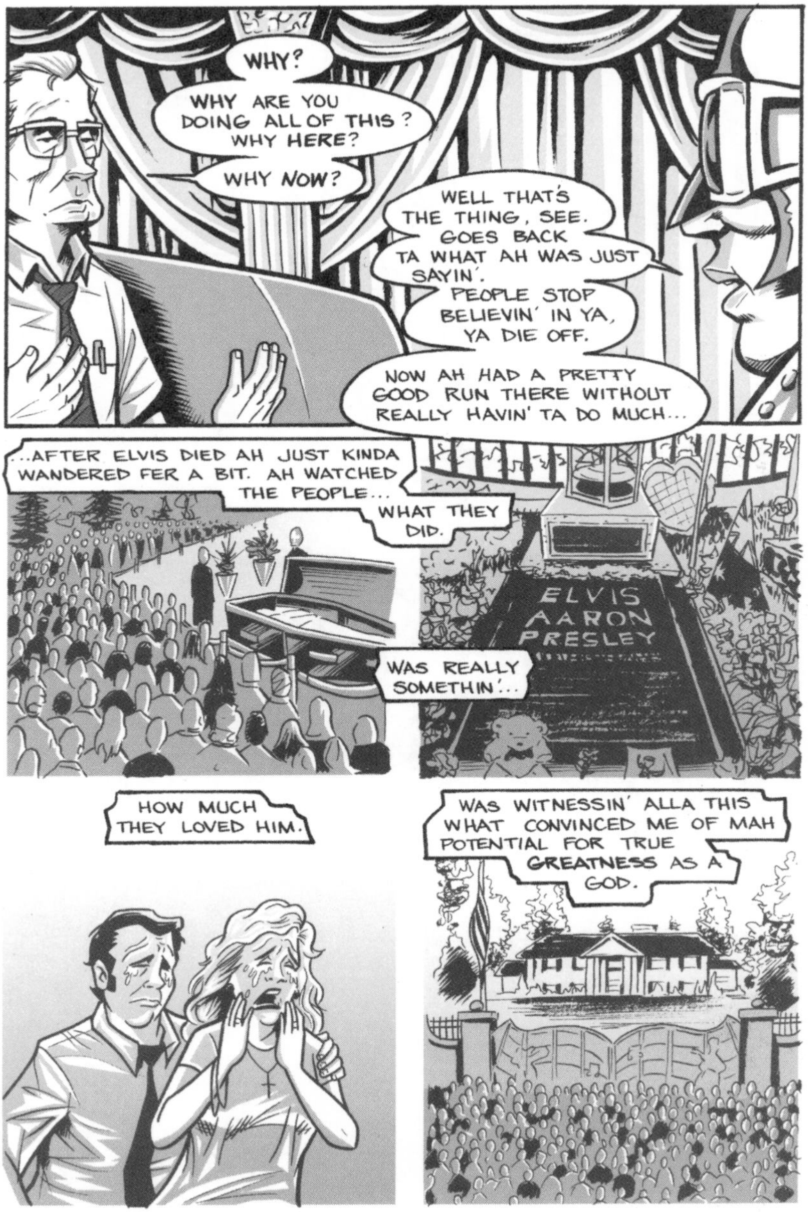

WHY?
WHY ARE YOU DOING ALL OF THIS? WHY HERE?
WHY NOW?
WELL THAT'S THE THING, SEE. GOES BACK TA WHAT AH WAS JUST SAYIN'.
PEOPLE STOP BELIEVIN' IN YA, YA DIE OFF.
NOW AH HAD A PRETTY GOOD RUN THERE WITHOUT REALLY HAVIN' TA DO MUCH...
...AFTER ELVIS DIED AH JUST KINDA WANDERED FER A BIT. AH WATCHED THE PEOPLE...
WHAT THEY DID.
ELVIS AARON PRESLEY
WAS REALLY SOMETHIN'...
HOW MUCH THEY LOVED HIM.
WAS WITNESSIN' ALLA THIS WHAT CONVINCED ME OF MAH POTENTIAL FOR TRUE GREATNESS AS A GOD.

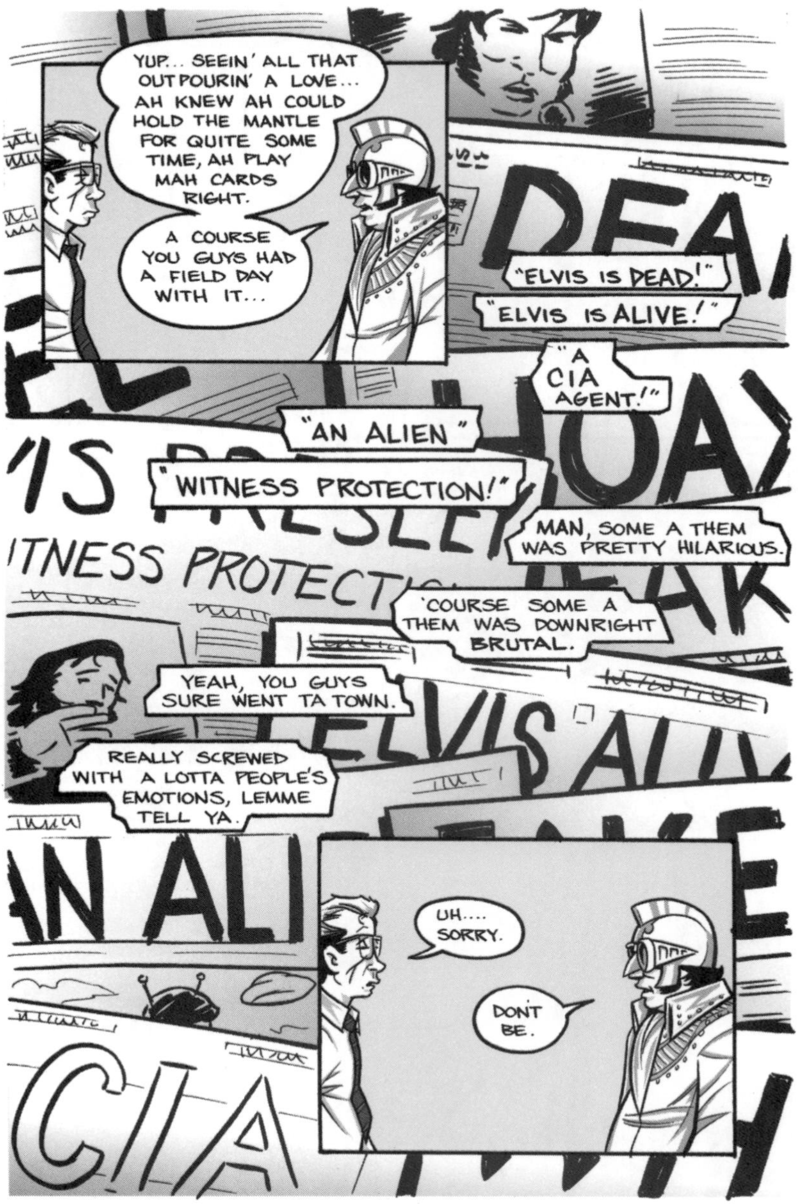
YUP... SEEIN' ALL THAT OUTPOURIN' A LOVE... AH KNEW AH COULD HOLD THE MANTLE FOR QUITE SOME TIME, AH PLAY MAH CARDS RIGHT.
A COURSE YOU GUYS HAD A FIELD DAY WITH IT...
"ELVIS IS DEAD!"
"ELVIS IS ALIVE!"
"A CIA AGENT!"
"AN ALIEN"
"WITNESS PROTECTION!"
MAN, SOME A THEM WAS PRETTY HILARIOUS.
'COURSE SOME A THEM WAS DOWNRIGHT BRUTAL.
YEAH, YOU GUYS SURE WENT TA TOWN.
REALLY SCREWED WITH A LOTTA PEOPLE'S EMOTIONS, LEMME TELL YA.
UH.... SORRY.
DON'T BE.
DEA
HOAX
PRESLEY
WITNESS PROTECTI
ELVIS ALIV
AN ALI
CIA

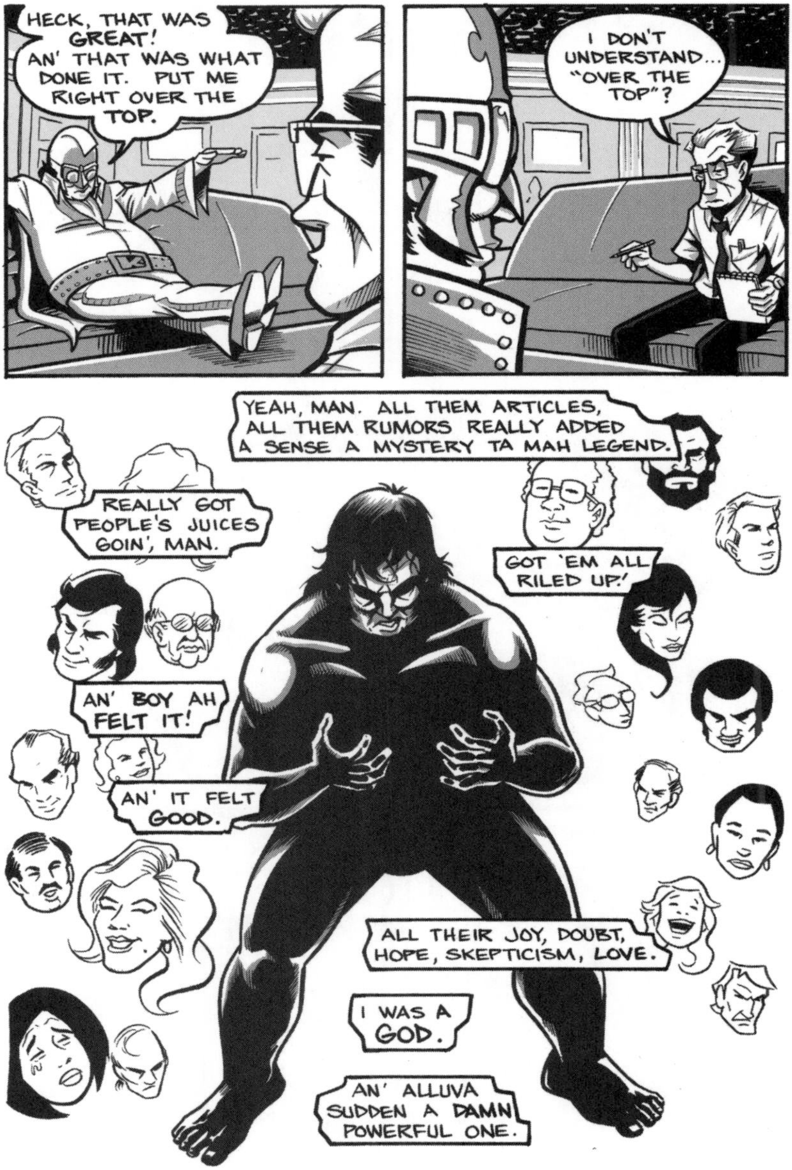
HECK, THAT WAS GREAT! AN' THAT WAS WHAT DONE IT. PUT ME RIGHT OVER THE TOP.
I DON'T UNDERSTAND... "OVER THE TOP"?
YEAH, MAN. ALL THEM ARTICLES, ALL THEM RUMORS REALLY ADDED A SENSE A MYSTERY TA MAH LEGEND.
REALLY GOT PEOPLE'S JUICES GOIN', MAN.
GOT 'EM ALL RILED UP!
AN' BOY AH FELT IT!
AN' IT FELT GOOD.
ALL THEIR JOY, DOUBT, HOPE, SKEPTICISM, LOVE.
I WAS A GOD.
AN' ALLUVA SUDDEN A DAMN POWERFUL ONE.

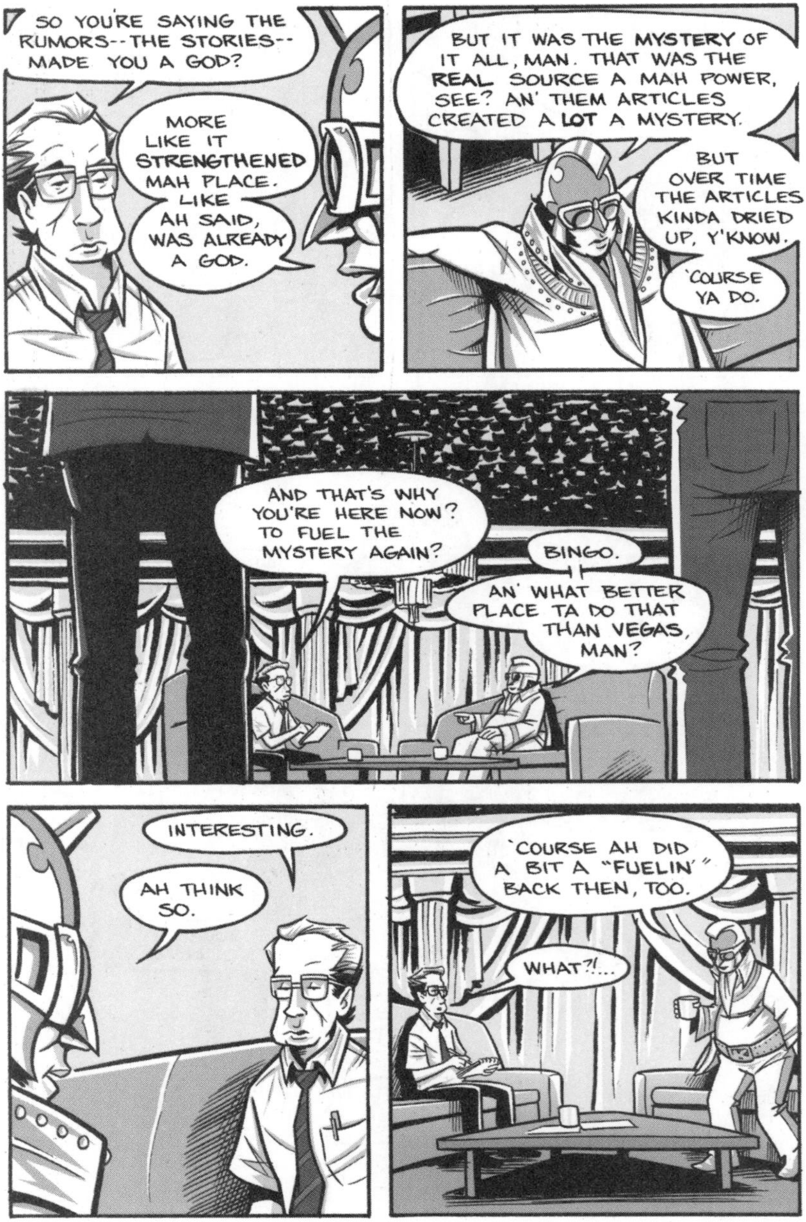
SO YOU'RE SAYING THE RUMORS--THE STORIES--MADE YOU A GOD?
MORE LIKE IT STRENGTHENED MAH PLACE. LIKE AH SAID, WAS ALREADY A GOD.
BUT IT WAS THE MYSTERY OF IT ALL, MAN. THAT WAS THE REAL SOURCE A MAH POWER, SEE? AN' THEM ARTICLES CREATED A LOT A MYSTERY.
BUT OVER TIME THE ARTICLES KINDA DRIED UP, Y'KNOW.
`COURSE YA DO.
AND THAT'S WHY YOU'RE HERE NOW? TO FUEL THE MYSTERY AGAIN?
BINGO.
AN' WHAT BETTER PLACE TA DO THAT THAN VEGAS, MAN?
INTERESTING.
AH THINK SO.
`COURSE AH DID A BIT A "FUELIN'" BACK THEN, TOO.
WHAT?!...

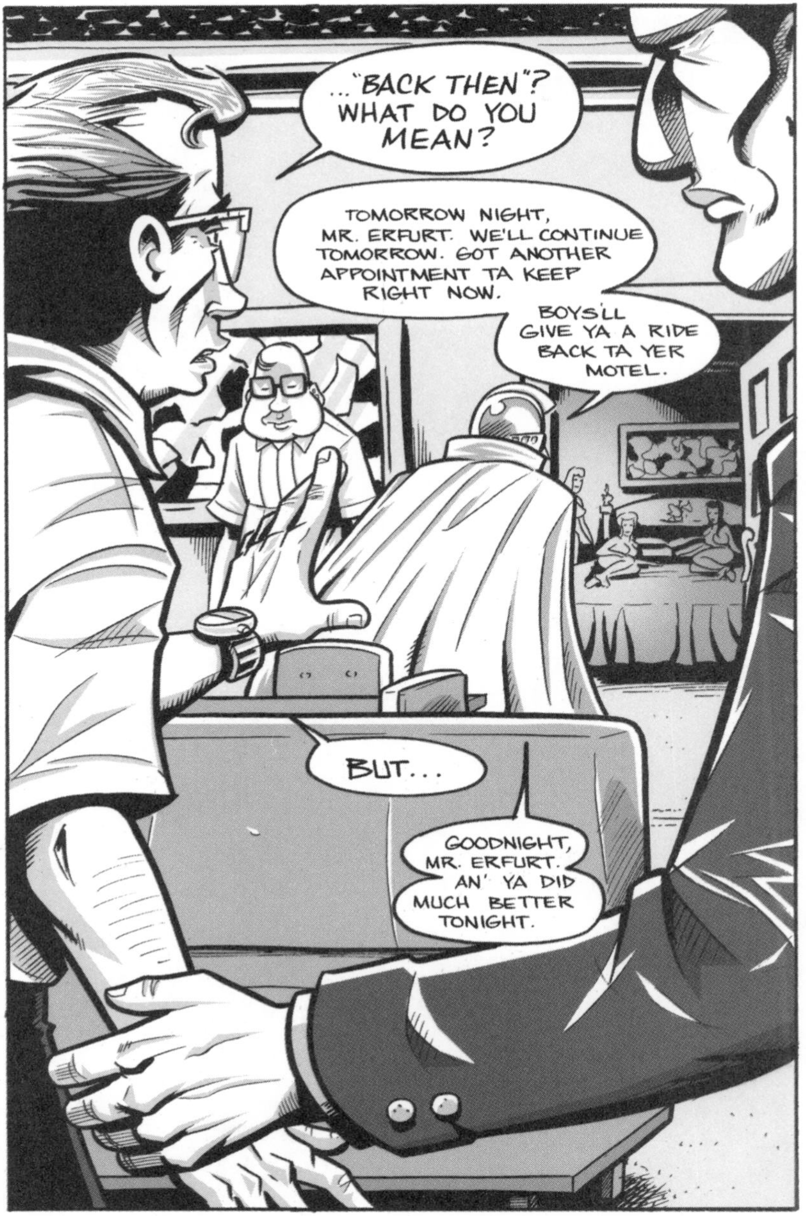
..."BACK THEN"? WHAT DO YOU MEAN?
TOMORROW NIGHT, MR. ERFURT. WE'LL CONTINUE TOMORROW. GOT ANOTHER APPOINTMENT TA KEEP RIGHT NOW.
BOYS'LL GIVE YA A RIDE BACK TA YER MOTEL.
BUT...
GOODNIGHT, MR. ERFURT. AN' YA DID MUCH BETTER TONIGHT.

"ELVIS IS NOT A GOD, BUT WE WORSHIP
HIM BECAUSE HE IS ELVIS."

—SAM PHILLIPS
ELVIS' FIRST RECORD PRODUCER

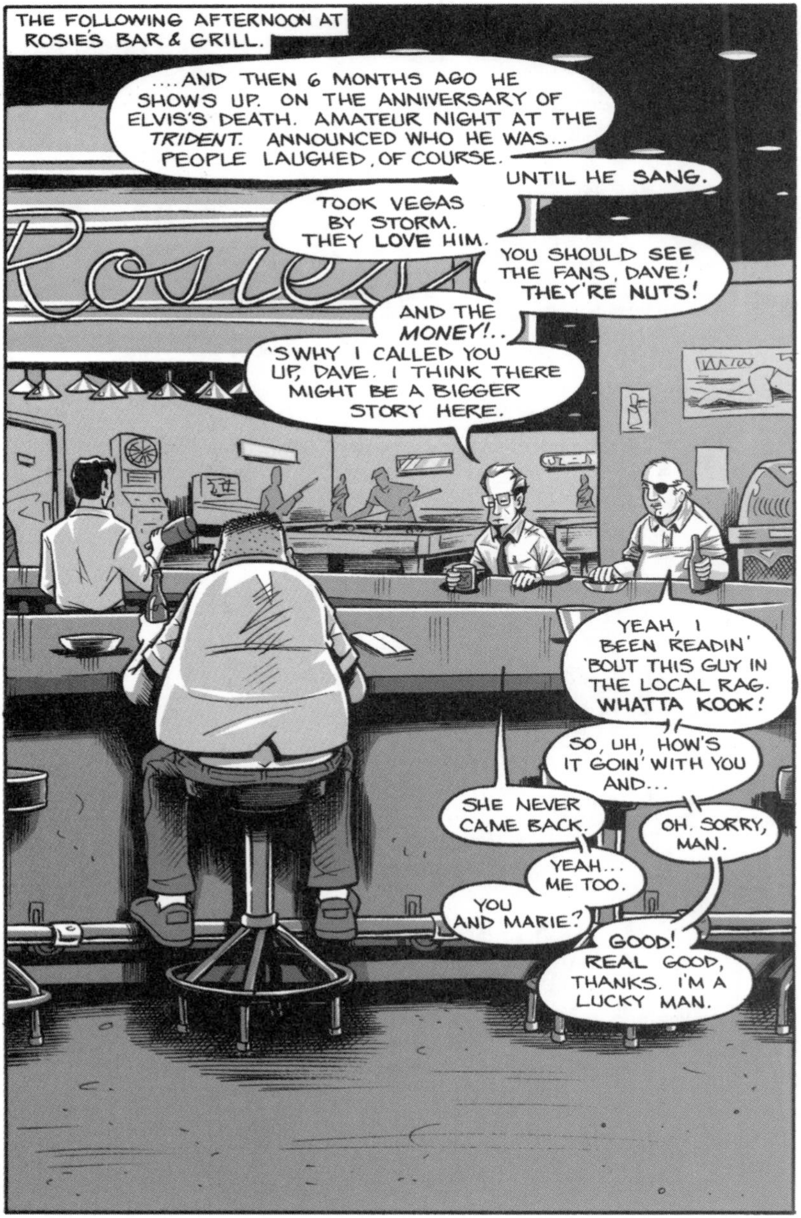
THE FOLLOWING AFTERNOON AT ROSIE'S BAR & GRILL.
....AND THEN 6 MONTHS AGO HE SHOWS UP. ON THE ANNIVERSARY OF ELVIS'S DEATH. AMATEUR NIGHT AT THE TRIDENT. ANNOUNCED WHO HE WAS... PEOPLE LAUGHED, OF COURSE.
UNTIL HE SANG.
TOOK VEGAS BY STORM. THEY LOVE HIM.
YOU SHOULD SEE THE FANS, DAVE! THEY'RE NUTS!
AND THE MONEY!..
'SWHY I CALLED YOU UP, DAVE. I THINK THERE MIGHT BE A BIGGER STORY HERE.
Rosie's
YEAH, I BEEN READIN' 'BOUT THIS GUY IN THE LOCAL RAG. WHATTA KOOK!
SO, UH, HOW'S IT GOIN' WITH YOU AND...
SHE NEVER CAME BACK.
OH. SORRY, MAN.
YEAH... ME TOO.
YOU AND MARIE?
GOOD! REAL GOOD, THANKS. I'M A LUCKY MAN.

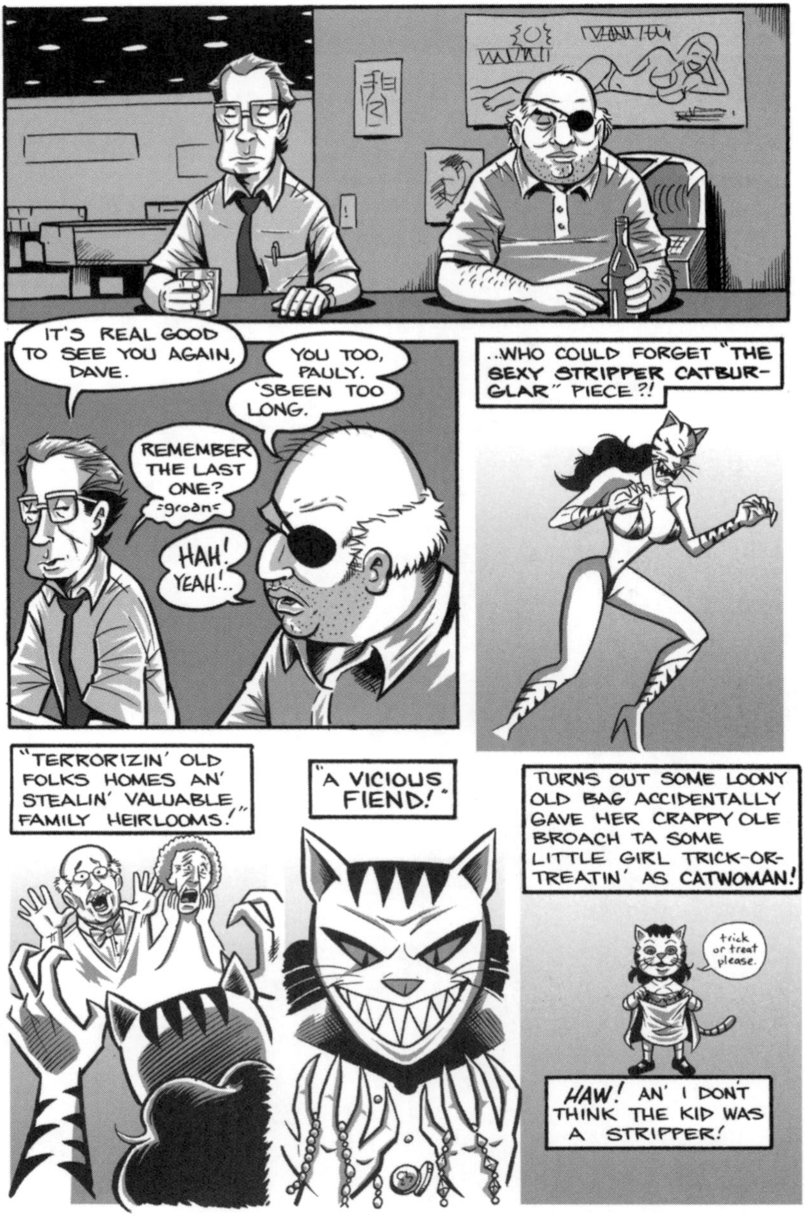
IT'S REAL GOOD TO SEE YOU AGAIN, DAVE.
YOU TOO, PAULY. 'SBEEN TOO LONG.
REMEMBER THE LAST ONE? =groan=
HAH! YEAH!...
...WHO COULD FORGET "THE SEXY STRIPPER CATBURGLAR" PIECE?!
"TERRORIZIN' OLD FOLKS HOMES AN' STEALIN' VALUABLE FAMILY HEIRLOOMS!"
"A VICIOUS FIEND!"
TURNS OUT SOME LOONY OLD BAG ACCIDENTALLY GAVE HER CRAPPY OLE BROACH TA SOME LITTLE GIRL TRICK-OR-TREATIN' AS CATWOMAN!
trick or treat please.
HAW! AN' I DON'T THINK THE KID WAS A STRIPPER!

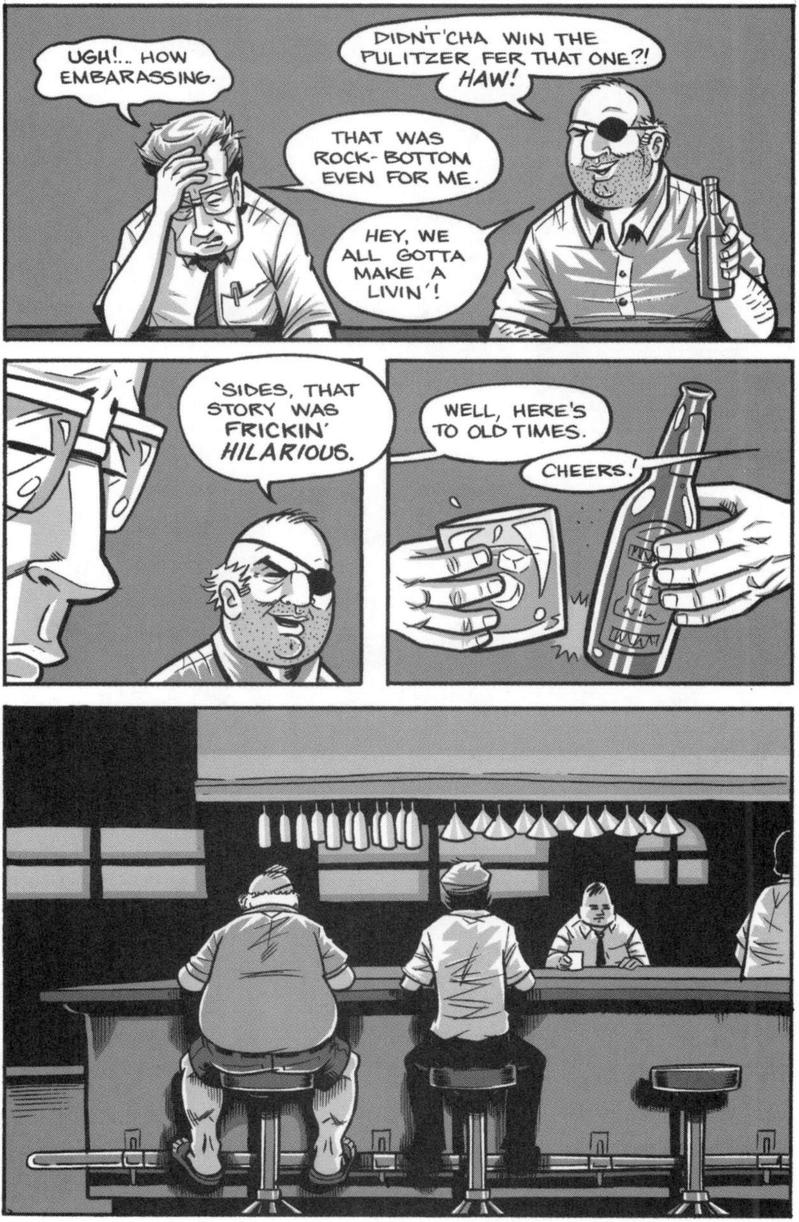
UGH!... HOW EMBARASSING.
DIDN'T'CHA WIN THE PULITZER FER THAT ONE?! HAW!
THAT WAS ROCK-BOTTOM EVEN FOR ME.
HEY, WE ALL GOTTA MAKE A LIVIN'!
'SIDES, THAT STORY WAS FRICKIN' HILARIOUS.
WELL, HERE'S TO OLD TIMES.
CHEERS.!

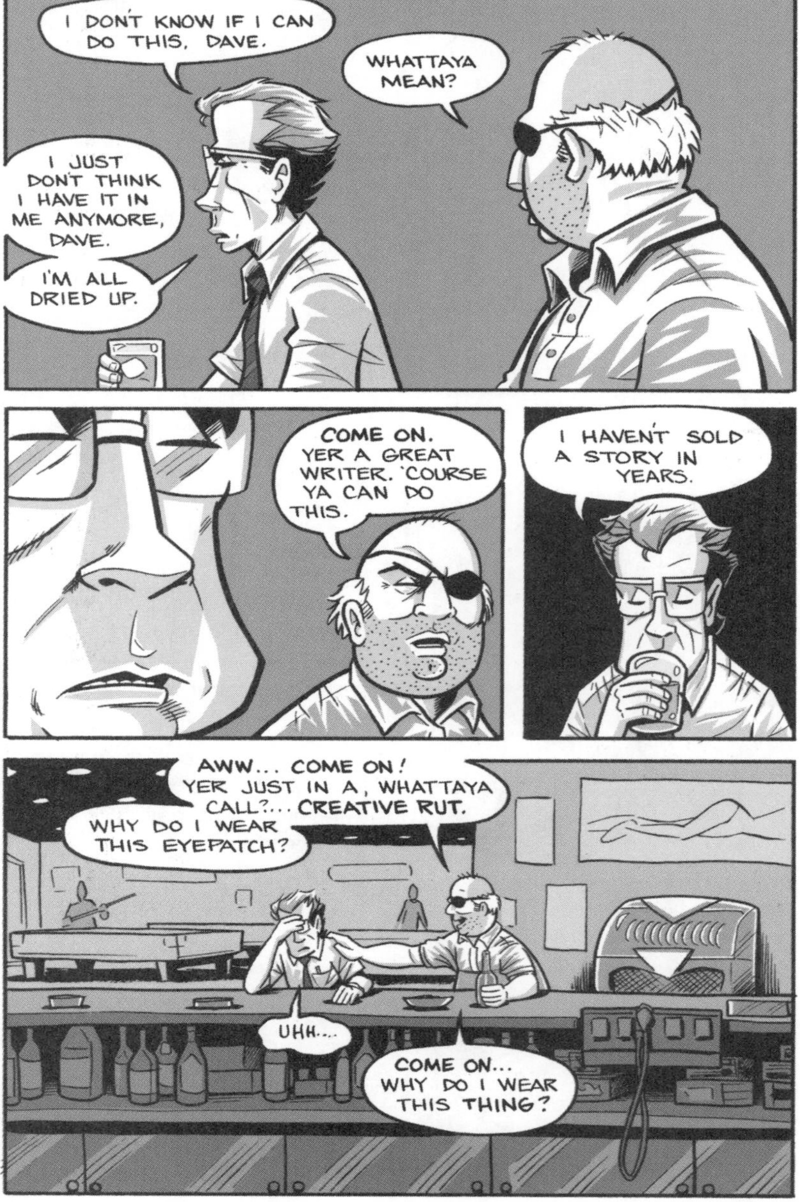
I DON'T KNOW IF I CAN DO THIS, DAVE.
WHATTAYA MEAN?
I JUST DON'T THINK I HAVE IT IN ME ANYMORE, DAVE.
I'M ALL DRIED UP.
COME ON. YER A GREAT WRITER. 'COURSE YA CAN DO THIS.
I HAVEN'T SOLD A STORY IN YEARS.
AWW... COME ON! YER JUST IN A, WHATTAYA CALL?... CREATIVE RUT.
WHY DO I WEAR THIS EYEPATCH?
UHH....
COME ON... WHY DO I WEAR THIS THING?

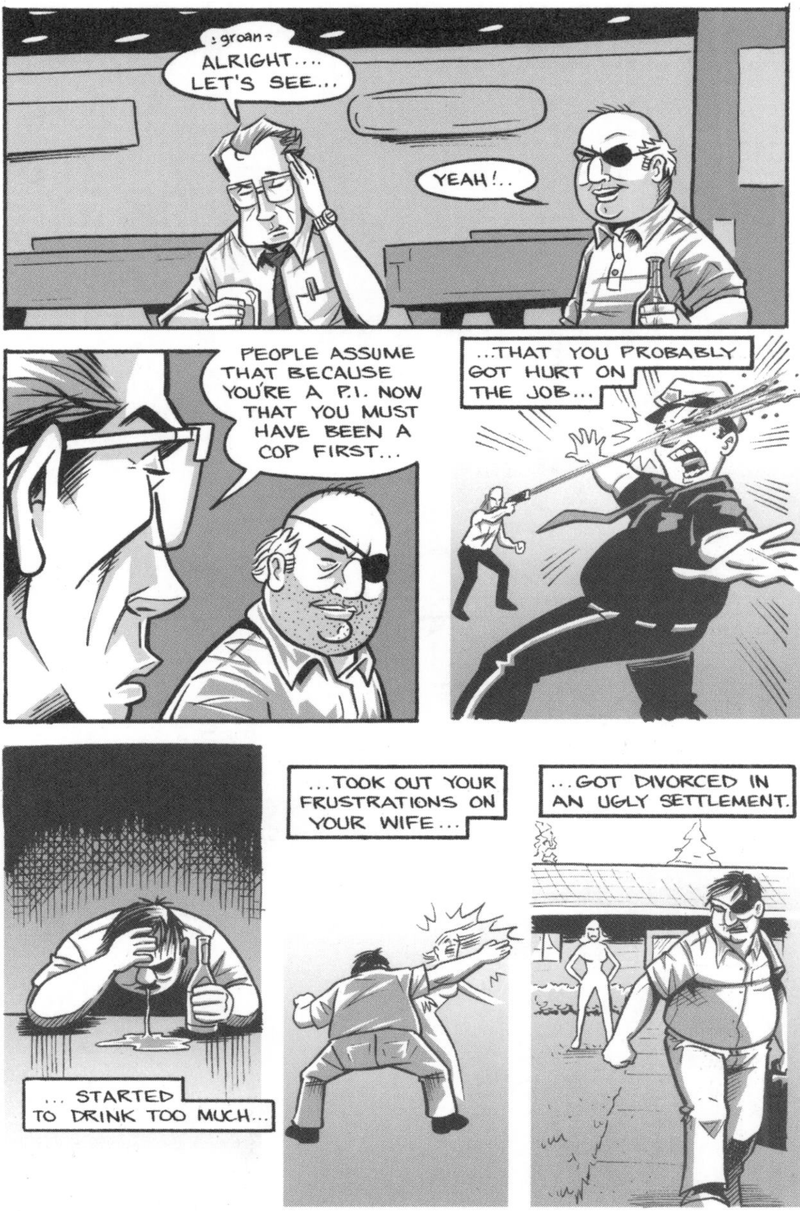
:groan:
ALRIGHT.... LET'S SEE...
YEAH!..
PEOPLE ASSUME THAT BECAUSE YOU'RE A P.I. NOW THAT YOU MUST HAVE BEEN A COP FIRST...
...THAT YOU PROBABLY GOT HURT ON THE JOB...
... STARTED TO DRINK TOO MUCH...
...TOOK OUT YOUR FRUSTRATIONS ON YOUR WIFE...
...GOT DIVORCED IN AN UGLY SETTLEMENT.

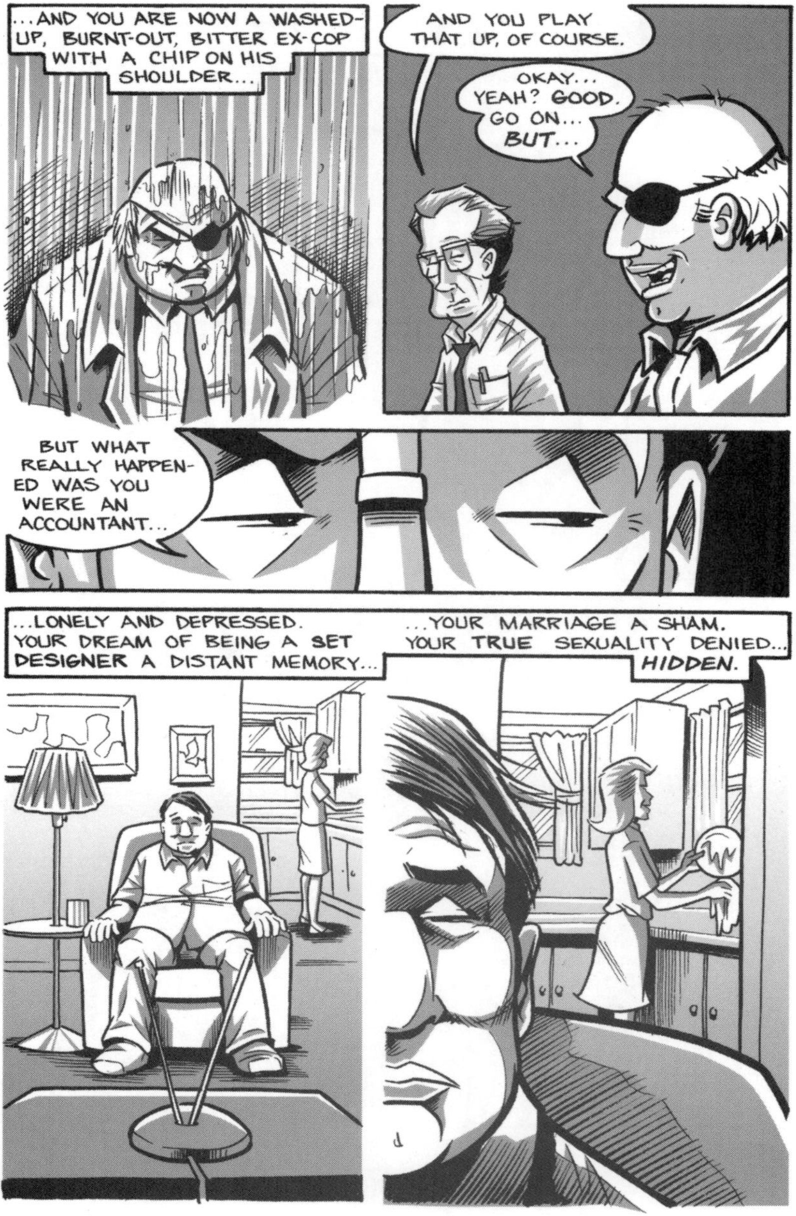
...AND YOU ARE NOW A WASHED-UP, BURNT-OUT, BITTER EX-COP WITH A CHIP ON HIS SHOULDER...
AND YOU PLAY THAT UP, OF COURSE.
OKAY... YEAH? GOOD. GO ON... BUT...
BUT WHAT REALLY HAPPENED WAS YOU WERE AN ACCOUNTANT...
...LONELY AND DEPRESSED. YOUR DREAM OF BEING A SET DESIGNER A DISTANT MEMORY...
...YOUR MARRIAGE A SHAM. YOUR TRUE SEXUALITY DENIED... HIDDEN.

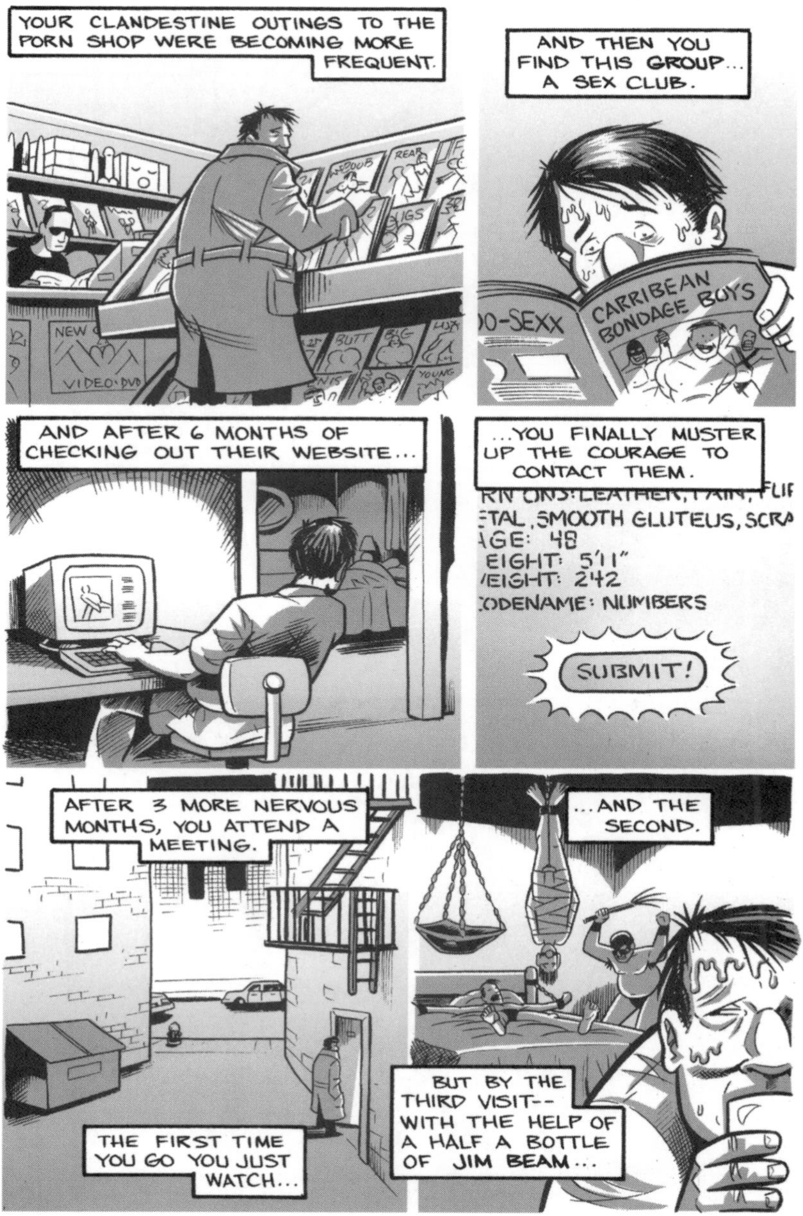

YOUR CLANDESTINE OUTINGS TO THE PORN SHOP WERE BECOMING MORE FREQUENT.
REAR
BUTT
BIG
YOUNG
VIDEO·DVD
AND THEN YOU FIND THIS **GROUP**... A SEX CLUB.
CARRIBEAN BONDAGE BOYS
AND AFTER 6 MONTHS OF CHECKING OUT THEIR WEBSITE...
...YOU FINALLY MUSTER UP THE COURAGE TO CONTACT THEM.
ETAL, SMOOTH GLUTEUS, SCRA
AGE: 48
EIGHT: 5'11"
EIGHT: 242
ODENAME: NUMBERS
SUBMIT!
AFTER 3 MORE NERVOUS MONTHS, YOU ATTEND A MEETING.
THE FIRST TIME YOU GO YOU JUST WATCH...
...AND THE SECOND.
BUT BY THE THIRD VISIT-- WITH THE HELP OF A HALF A BOTTLE OF **JIM BEAM**...

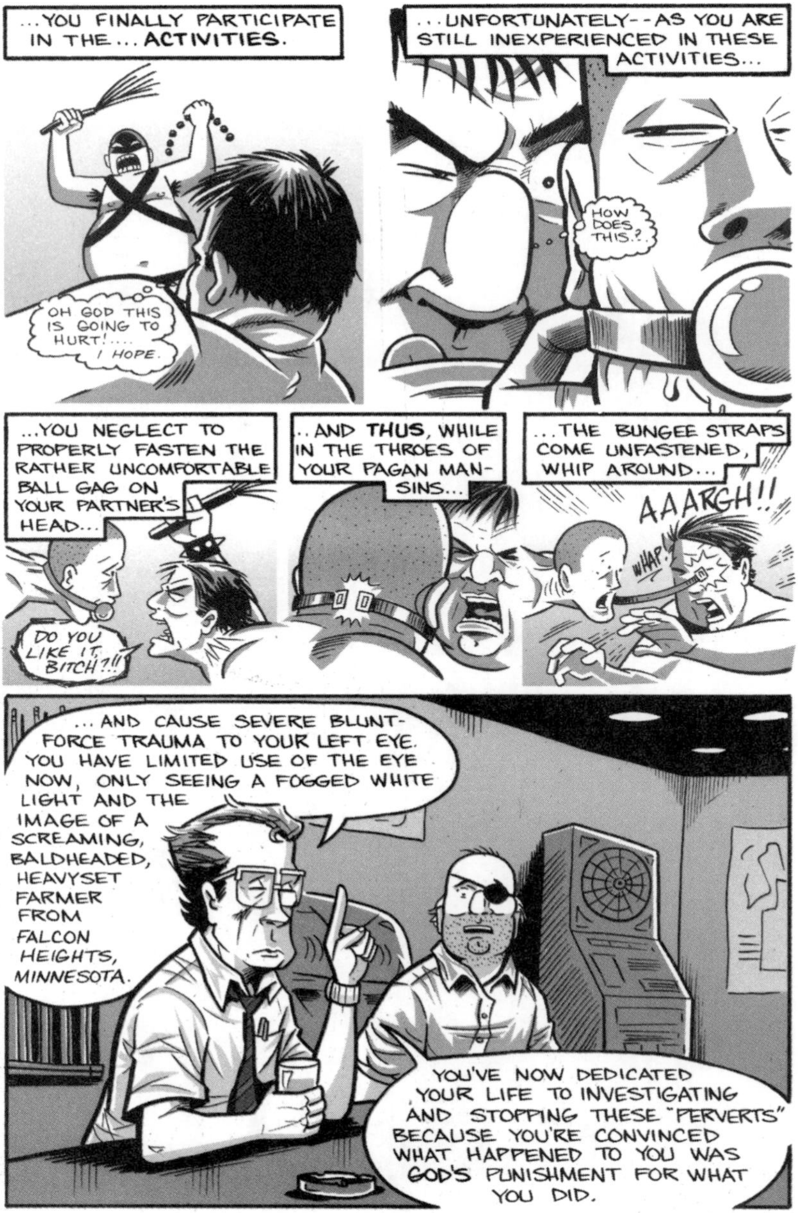
...YOU FINALLY PARTICIPATE IN THE... **ACTIVITIES**.
OH GOD THIS IS GOING TO HURT!.... I HOPE.
...UNFORTUNATELY--AS YOU ARE STILL INEXPERIENCED IN THESE ACTIVITIES...
HOW DOES THIS..?..
...YOU NEGLECT TO PROPERLY FASTEN THE RATHER UNCOMFORTABLE BALL GAG ON YOUR PARTNER'S HEAD...
DO YOU LIKE IT, BITCH?!!
..AND **THUS**, WHILE IN THE THROES OF YOUR PAGAN MAN-SINS...
...THE BUNGEE STRAPS COME UNFASTENED, WHIP AROUND...
AAARGH!!
WHAP!
...AND CAUSE SEVERE BLUNT-FORCE TRAUMA TO YOUR LEFT EYE. YOU HAVE LIMITED USE OF THE EYE NOW, ONLY SEEING A FOGGED WHITE LIGHT AND THE IMAGE OF A SCREAMING, BALDHEADED, HEAVYSET FARMER FROM FALCON HEIGHTS, MINNESOTA.
YOU'VE NOW DEDICATED YOUR LIFE TO INVESTIGATING AND STOPPING THESE "PERVERTS" BECAUSE YOU'RE CONVINCED WHAT HAPPENED TO YOU WAS GOD'S PUNISHMENT FOR WHAT YOU DID.

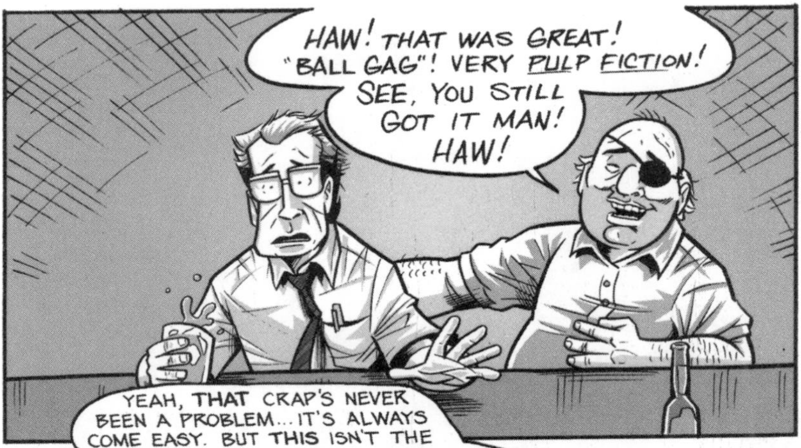
HAW! THAT WAS GREAT! "BALL GAG"! VERY PULP FICTION! SEE, YOU STILL GOT IT MAN! HAW!
YEAH, THAT CRAP'S NEVER BEEN A PROBLEM... IT'S ALWAYS COME EASY. BUT THIS ISN'T THE ENQUIRER... IT'S REAL THIS TIME... LEGITIMATE... TIME MAGAZINE, DAVE. THIS COULD BE THE CHANCE I'VE ALWAYS DREAMED OF. I'VE GOTTA PLAY THIS ONE STRAIGHT. I CAN'T BLOW THIS.

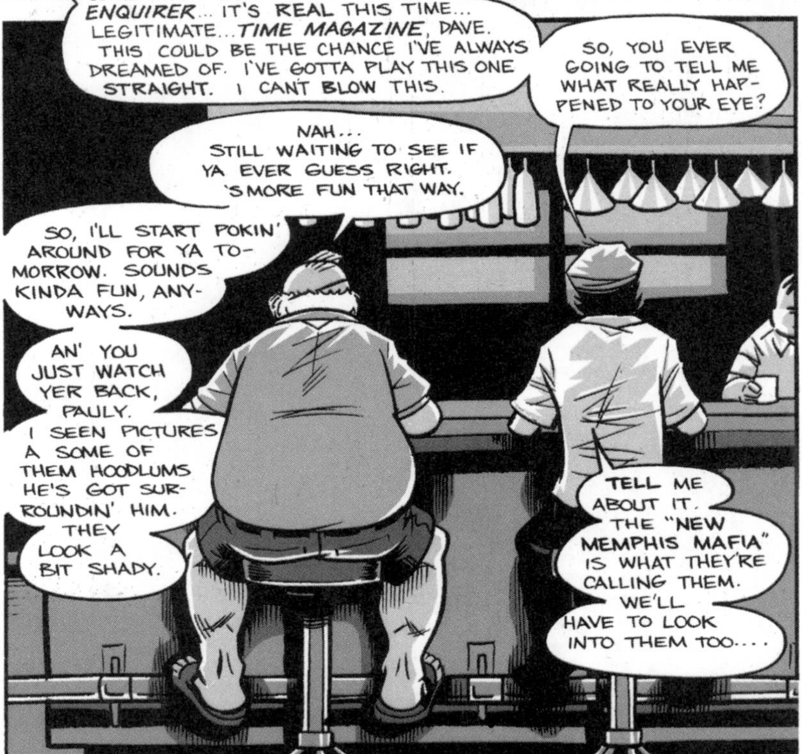
SO, YOU EVER GOING TO TELL ME WHAT REALLY HAPPENED TO YOUR EYE?
NAH... STILL WAITING TO SEE IF YA EVER GUESS RIGHT. 'S MORE FUN THAT WAY.
SO, I'LL START POKIN' AROUND FOR YA TOMORROW. SOUNDS KINDA FUN, ANYWAYS.
AN' YOU JUST WATCH YER BACK, PAULY. I SEEN PICTURES A SOME OF THEM HOODLUMS HE'S GOT SURROUNDIN' HIM. THEY LOOK A BIT SHADY.
TELL ME ABOUT IT. THE "NEW MEMPHIS MAFIA" IS WHAT THEY'RE CALLING THEM. WE'LL HAVE TO LOOK INTO THEM TOO....

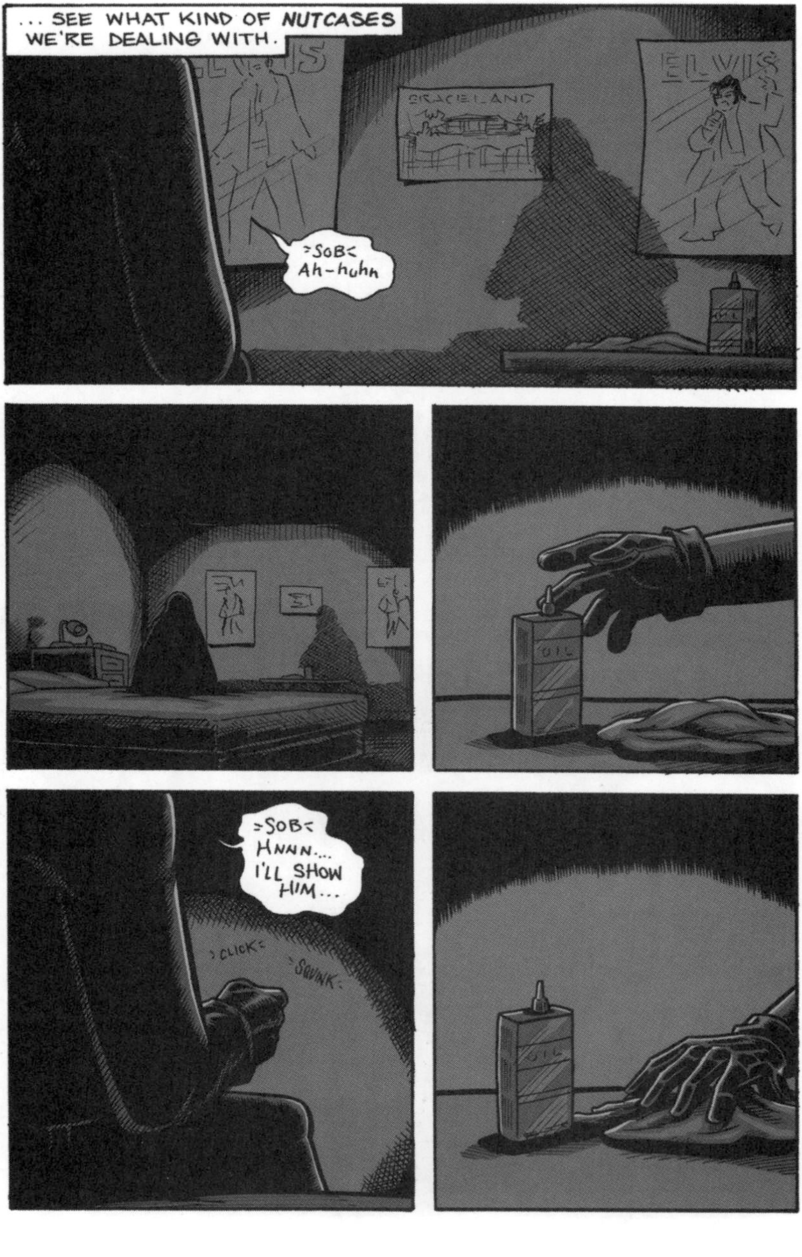
... SEE WHAT KIND OF NUTCASES WE'RE DEALING WITH.
ELVIS
GRACELAND
ELVIS
>SOB< Ah-huhn
OIL
OIL
>SOB< HNNN... I'LL SHOW HIM...
>CLICK<
>SQUINK<
OIL

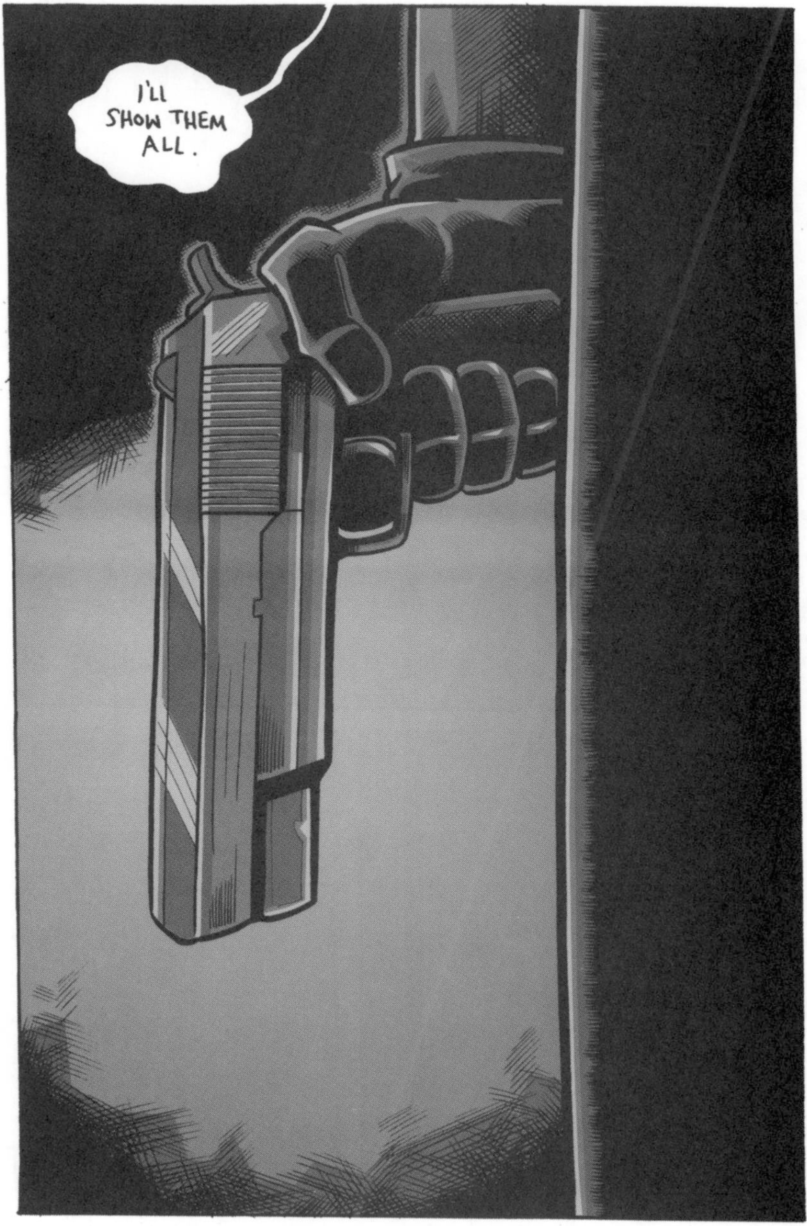
I'LL SHOW THEM ALL.

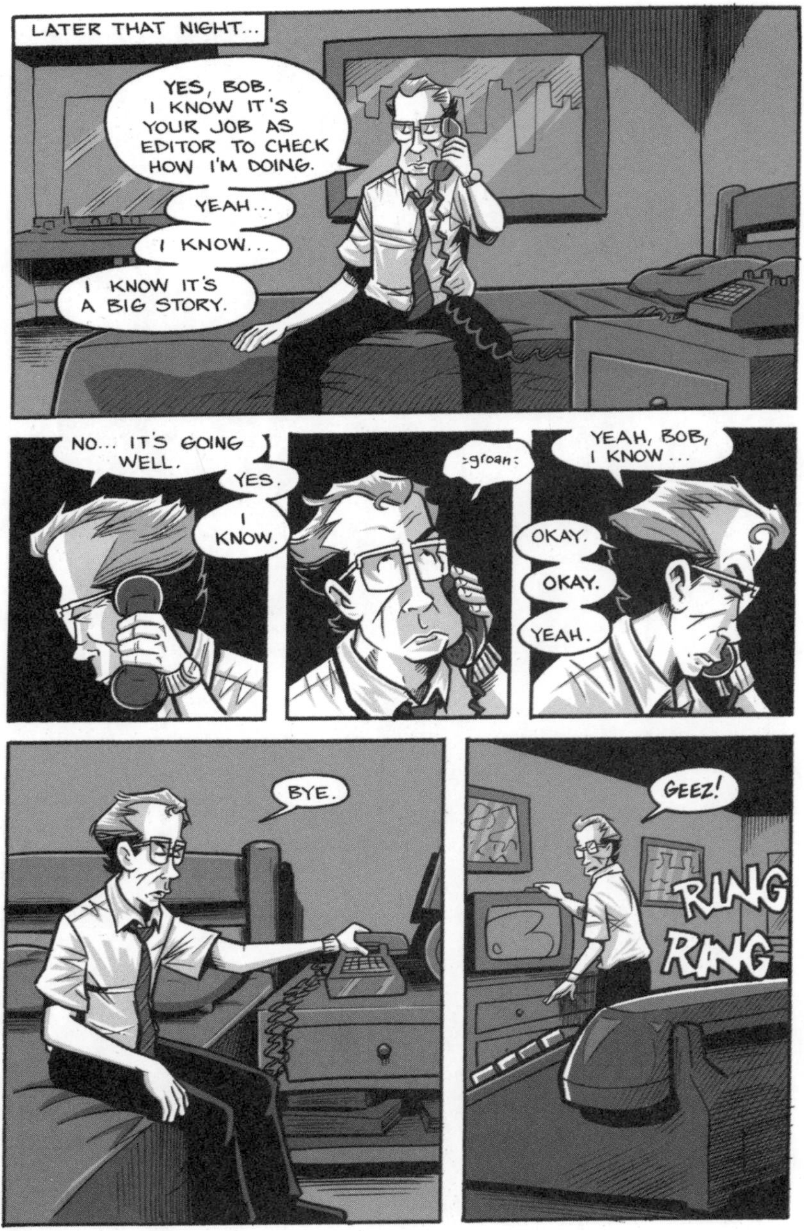
LATER THAT NIGHT...
YES, BOB. I KNOW IT'S YOUR JOB AS EDITOR TO CHECK HOW I'M DOING.
YEAH...
I KNOW...
I KNOW IT'S A BIG STORY.
NO... IT'S GOING WELL.
YES.
I KNOW.
:groan:
YEAH, BOB, I KNOW...
OKAY.
OKAY.
YEAH.
BYE.
GEEZ!
RING
RING

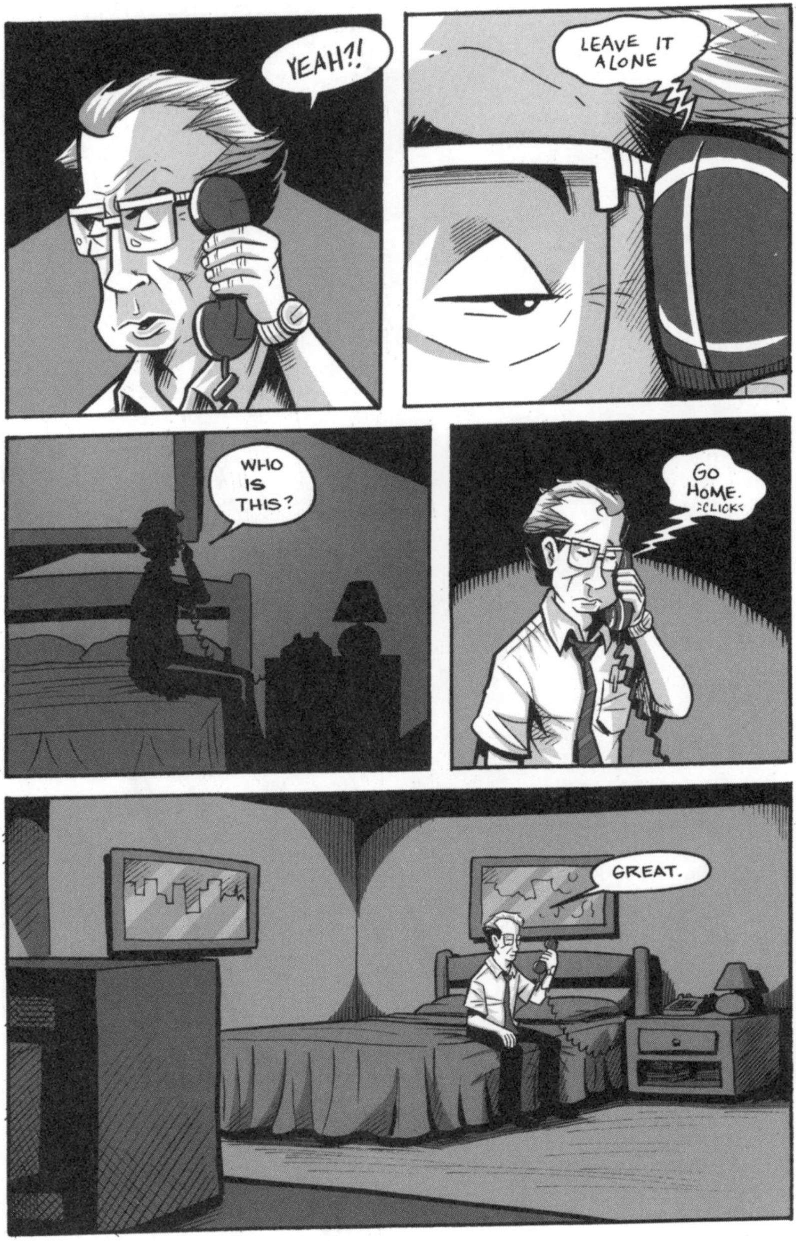
YEAH?!
LEAVE IT ALONE
WHO IS THIS?
GO HOME.
>CLICK<
GREAT.

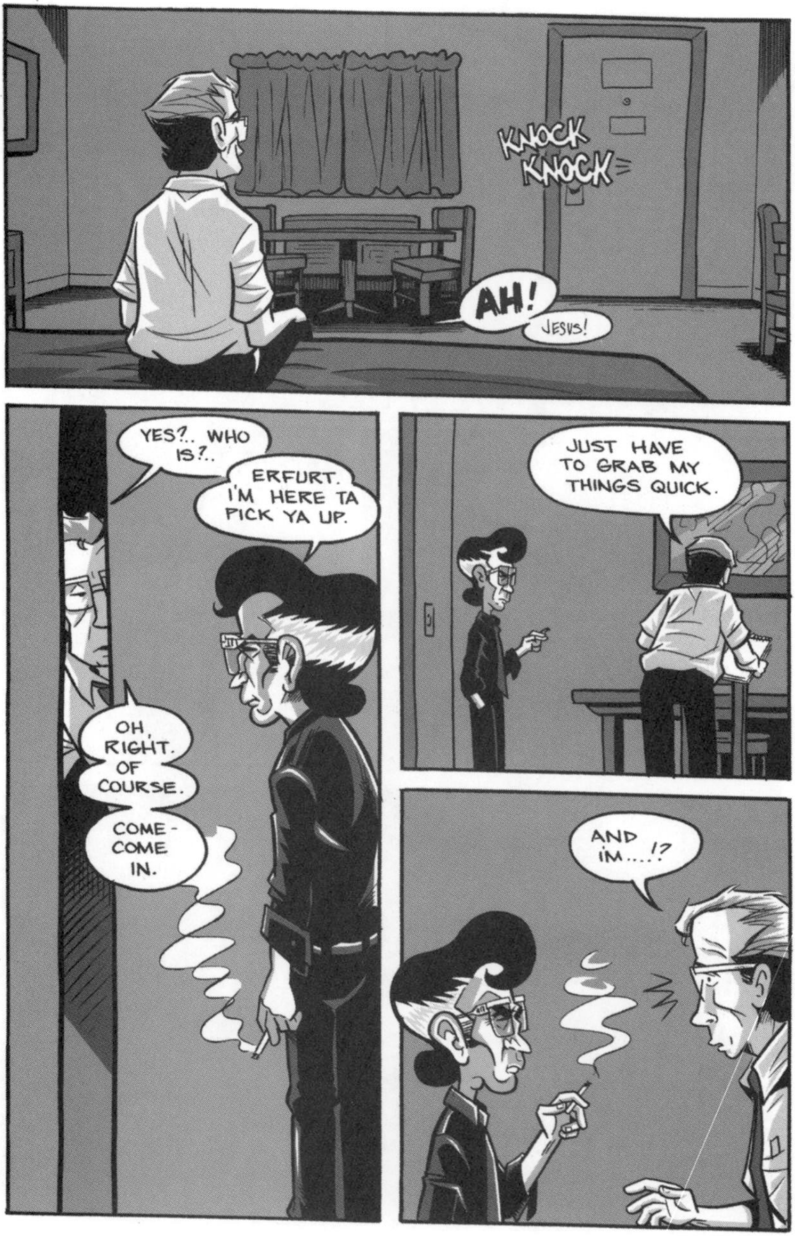
KNOCK KNOCK
AH!
JESUS!
YES?.. WHO IS?..
ERFURT. I'M HERE TA PICK YA UP.
OH, RIGHT. OF COURSE.
COME - COME IN.
JUST HAVE TO GRAB MY THINGS QUICK.
AND IM....!?

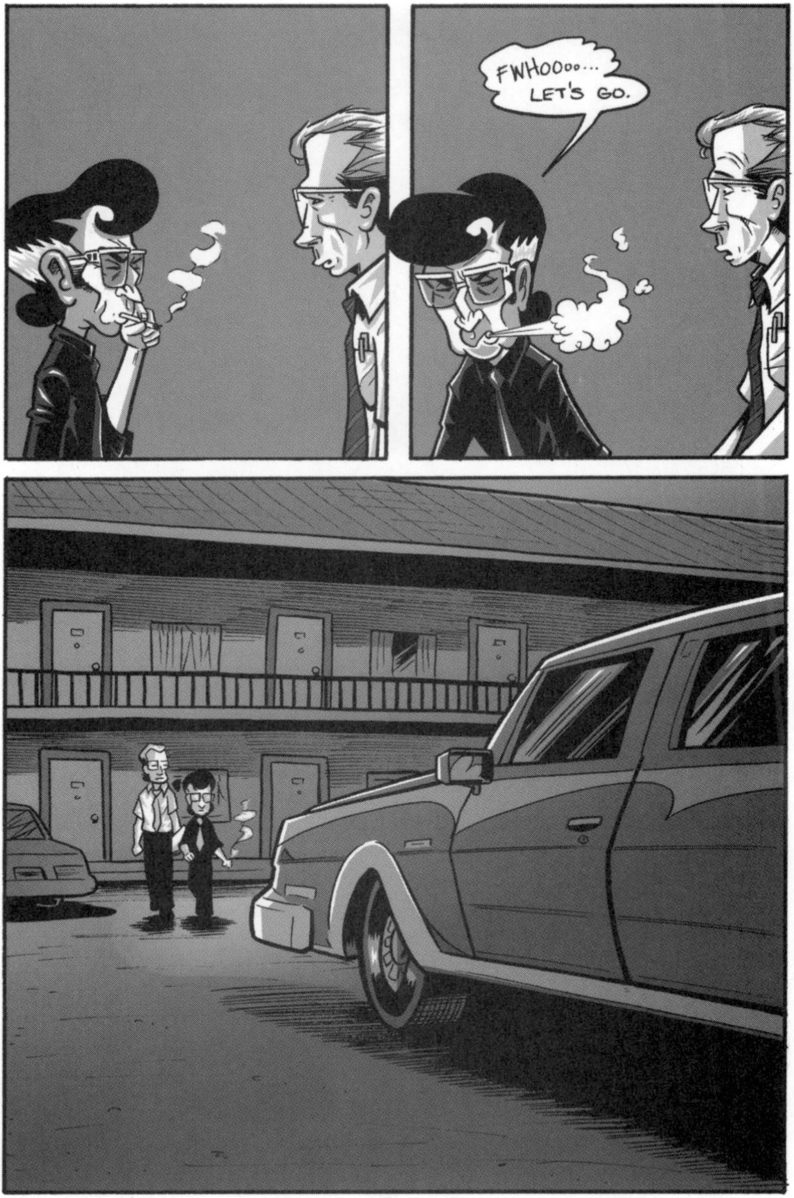
FWHOooo...
LET'S GO.

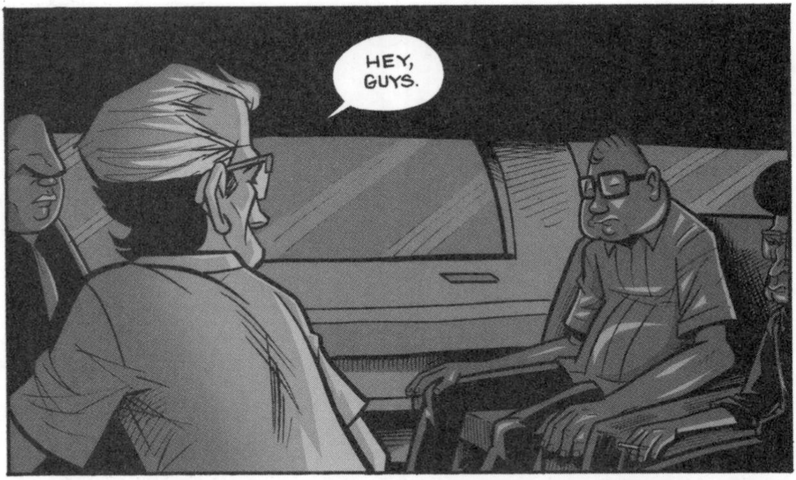
HEY, GUYS.

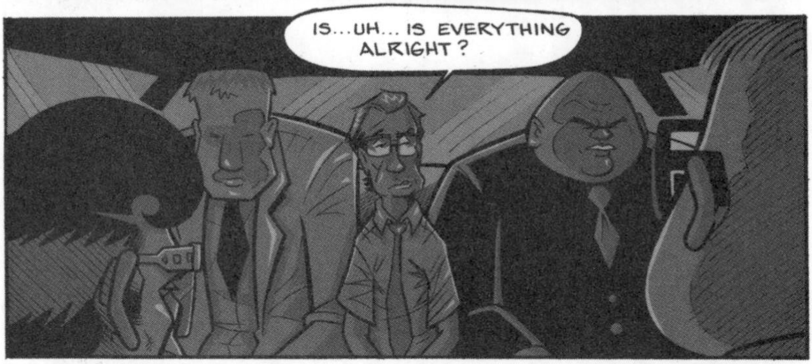
IS...UH... IS EVERYTHING ALRIGHT?

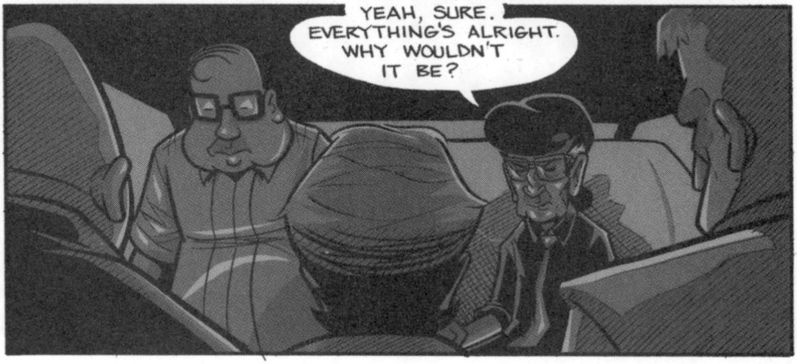
YEAH, SURE. EVERYTHING'S ALRIGHT. WHY WOULDN'T IT BE?

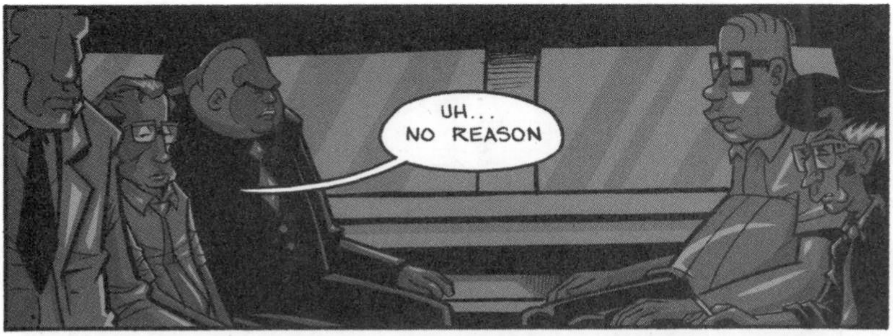
UH...
NO REASON

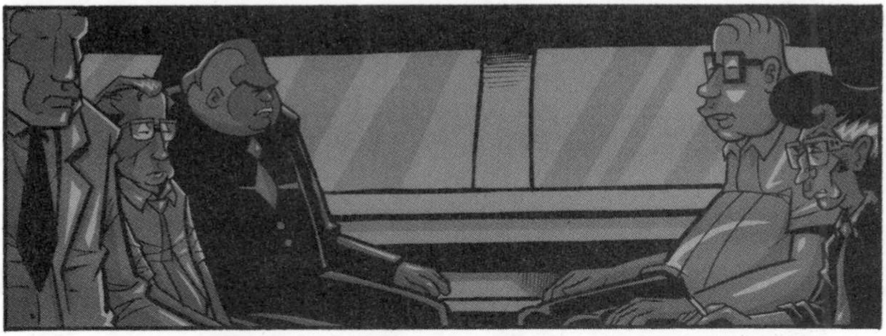

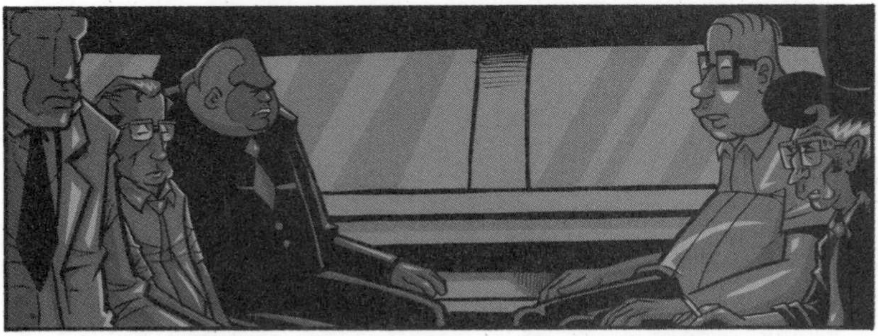

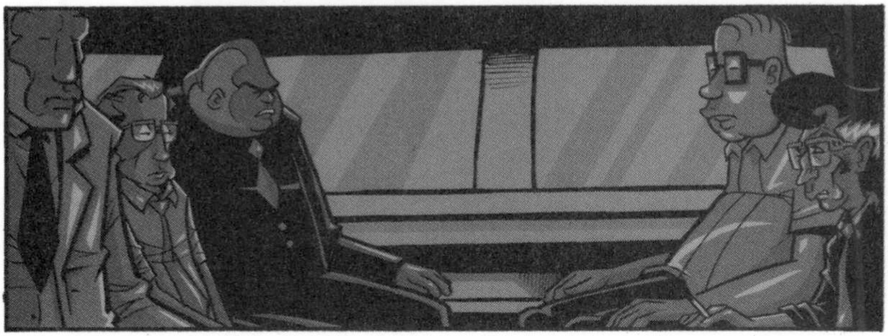

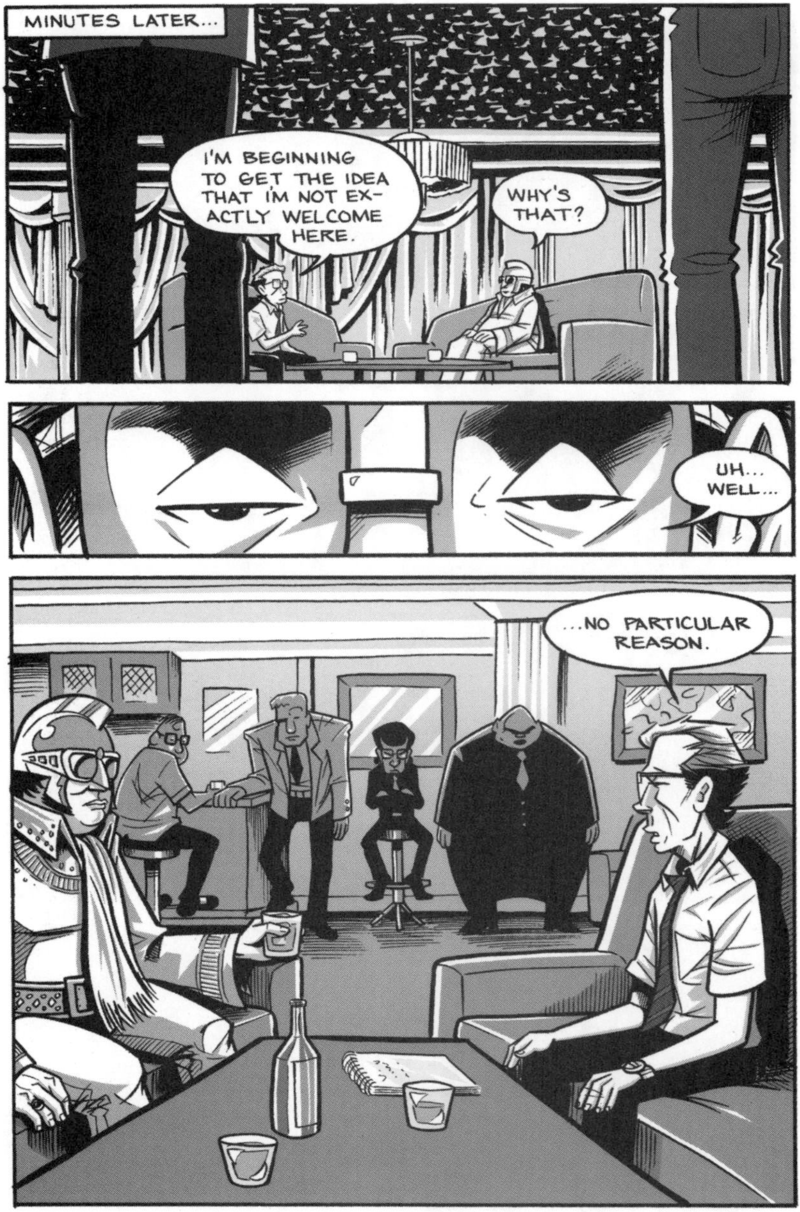
MINUTES LATER...
I'M BEGINNING TO GET THE IDEA THAT I'M NOT EXACTLY WELCOME HERE.
WHY'S THAT?
UH... WELL...
...NO PARTICULAR REASON.

AWW, THEY'S JUST BEIN' A BIT OVERPROTECTIVE IS ALL... AIN'TCHA BOYS? THEY'RE WORRIED 'BOUT WHAT YER GOIN' TA WRITE. BUT AH TOLD 'EM YER GONNA WRITE A FAIR ARTICLE. THAT YER A PROFESSIONAL JOURNALIST, AN' THAT'S WHAT PROFESSIONALS DO.

AIN'T THAT SO, MR. ERFURT?

...YES...YES, OF COURSE.

SEE BOYS! JUST LIKE AH TOLD YA! AN' IF MR. ERFURT HAS ANY QUESTIONS FOR ANY OF YA YOU JUST GO RIGHT ON AHEAD AN' ANSWER 'EM.

ACTUALLY, FIRST I'D LIKE TO...

AH EXPECT NOTHIN LESS THAN FULL COOPERATION.

ALRIGHT FELLAS?

85

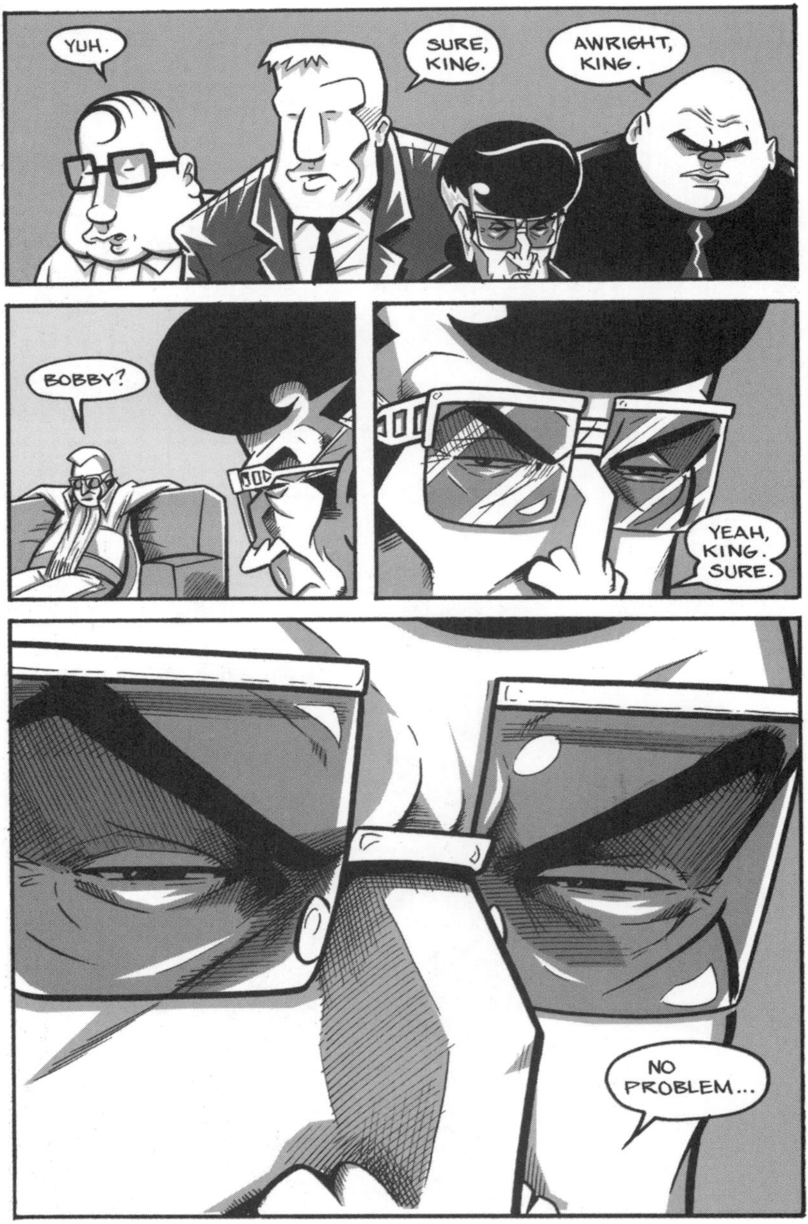
YUH.
SURE, KING.
AWRIGHT, KING.
BOBBY?
YEAH, KING. SURE.
NO PROBLEM...

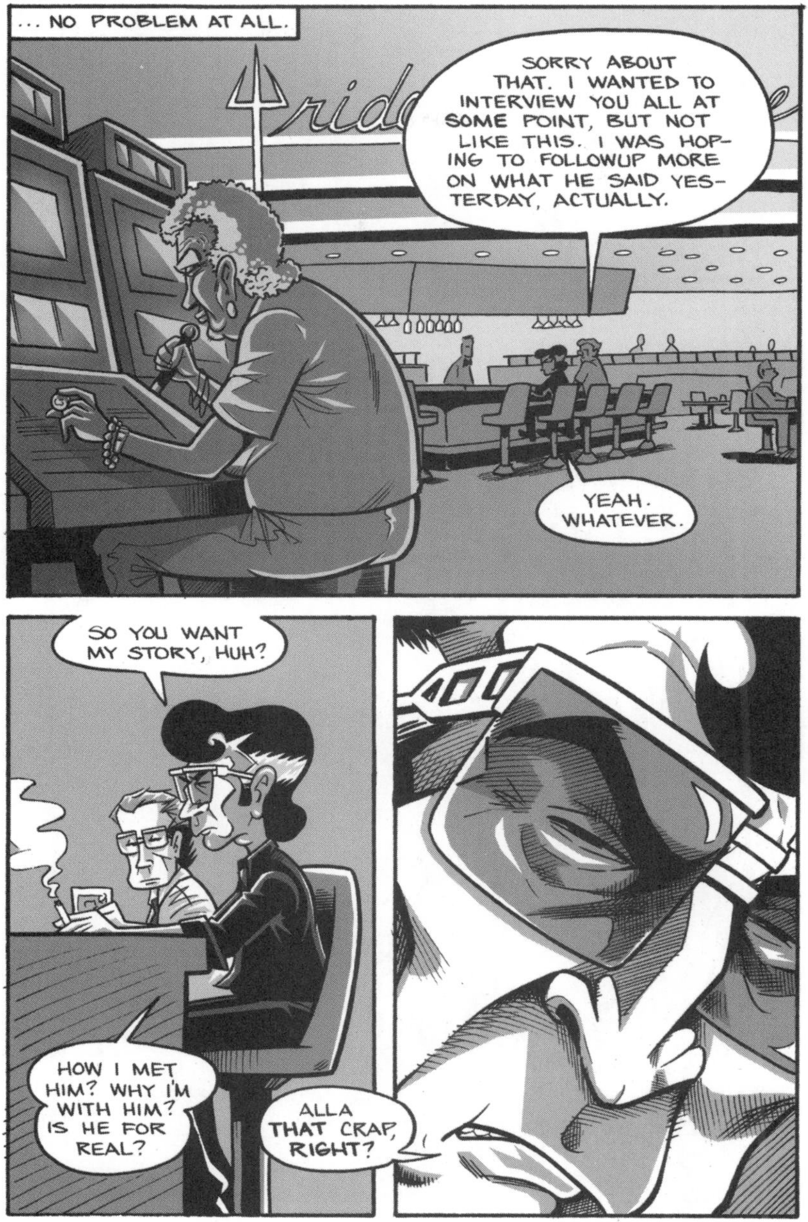
... NO PROBLEM AT ALL.
SORRY ABOUT THAT. I WANTED TO INTERVIEW YOU ALL AT SOME POINT, BUT NOT LIKE THIS. I WAS HOPING TO FOLLOWUP MORE ON WHAT HE SAID YESTERDAY, ACTUALLY.
YEAH. WHATEVER.
SO YOU WANT MY STORY, HUH?
HOW I MET HIM? WHY I'M WITH HIM? IS HE FOR REAL?
ALLA THAT CRAP, RIGHT?

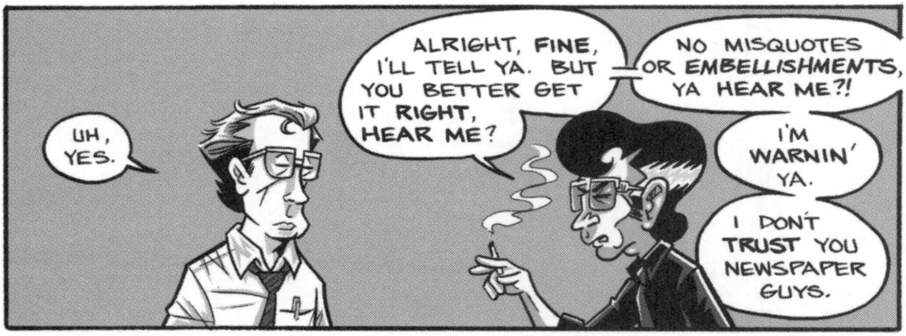
UH, YES.
ALRIGHT, FINE, I'LL TELL YA. BUT YOU BETTER GET IT RIGHT, HEAR ME?
NO MISQUOTES OR EMBELLISHMENTS, YA HEAR ME?!
I'M WARNIN' YA.
I DON'T TRUST YOU NEWSPAPER GUYS.

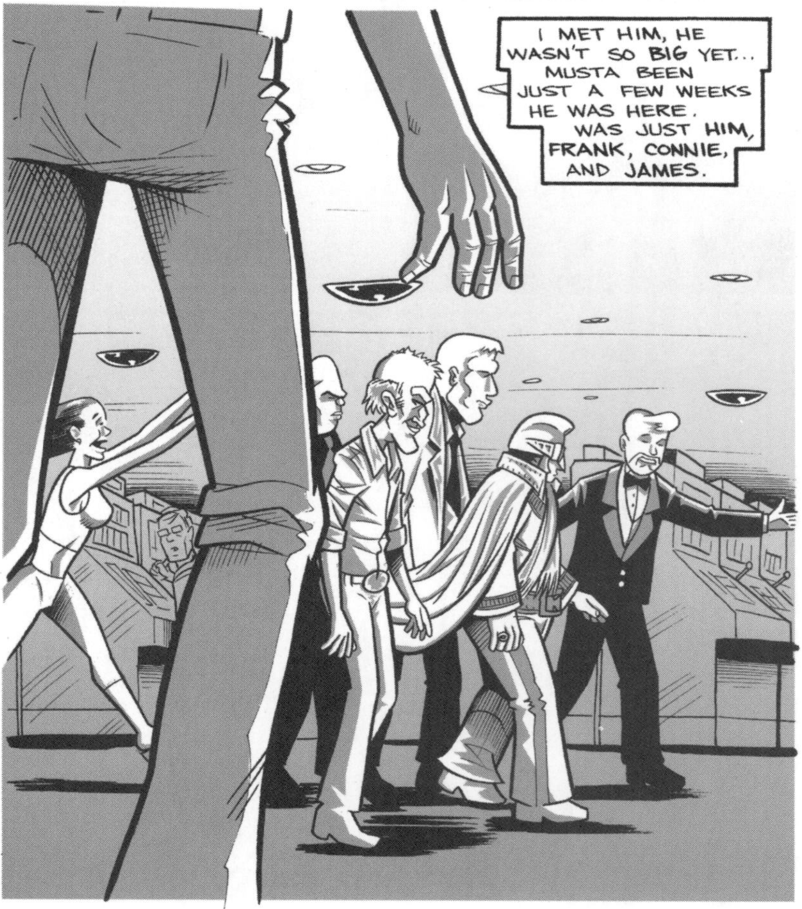
I MET HIM, HE WASN'T SO BIG YET... MUSTA BEEN JUST A FEW WEEKS HE WAS HERE. WAS JUST HIM, FRANK, CONNIE, AND JAMES.

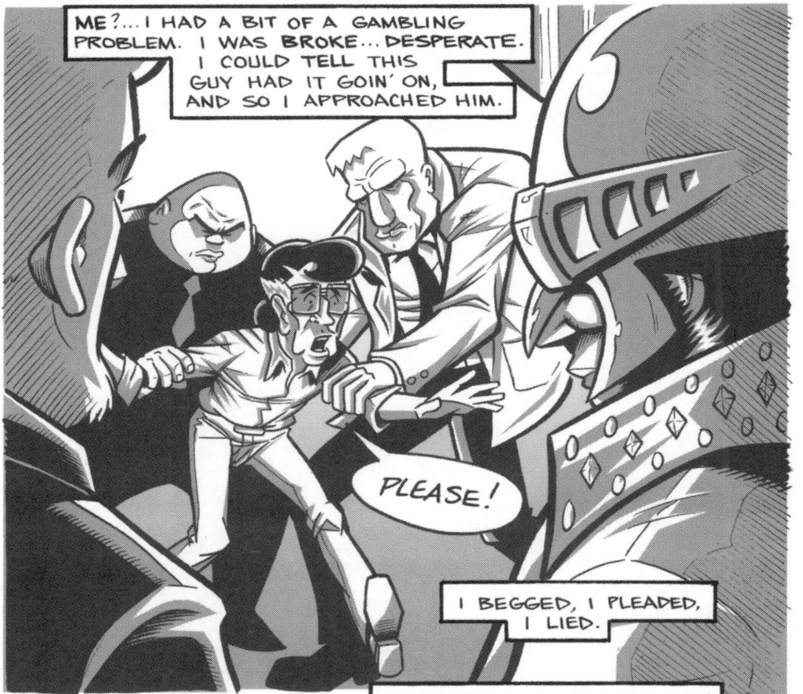
ME?... I HAD A BIT OF A GAMBLING PROBLEM. I WAS BROKE... DESPERATE. I COULD TELL THIS GUY HAD IT GOIN' ON, AND SO I APPROACHED HIM.
PLEASE!
I BEGGED, I PLEADED, I LIED.

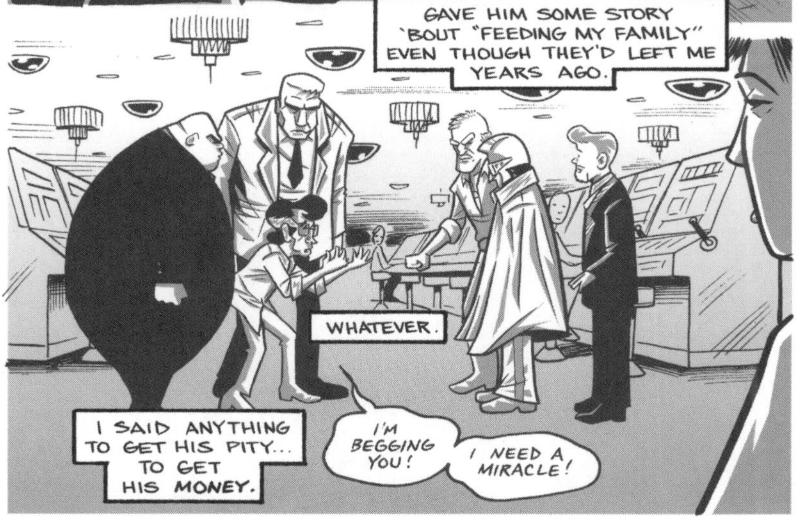
GAVE HIM SOME STORY 'BOUT "FEEDING MY FAMILY" EVEN THOUGH THEY'D LEFT ME YEARS AGO.
WHATEVER.
I SAID ANYTHING TO GET HIS PITY... TO GET HIS MONEY.
I'M BEGGING YOU!
I NEED A MIRACLE!

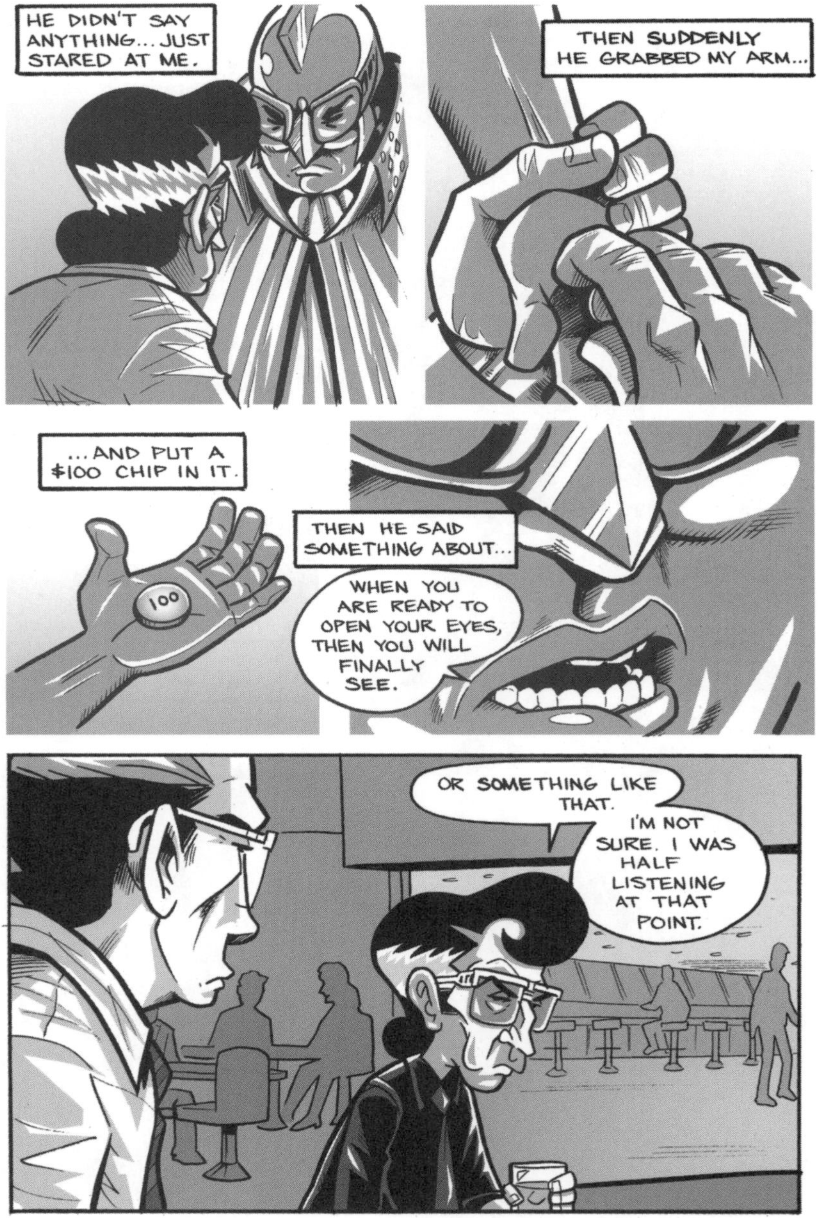
HE DIDN'T SAY ANYTHING... JUST STARED AT ME.
THEN SUDDENLY HE GRABBED MY ARM...
...AND PUT A $100 CHIP IN IT.
100
THEN HE SAID SOMETHING ABOUT...
WHEN YOU ARE READY TO OPEN YOUR EYES, THEN YOU WILL FINALLY SEE.
OR SOMETHING LIKE THAT.
I'M NOT SURE. I WAS HALF LISTENING AT THAT POINT.

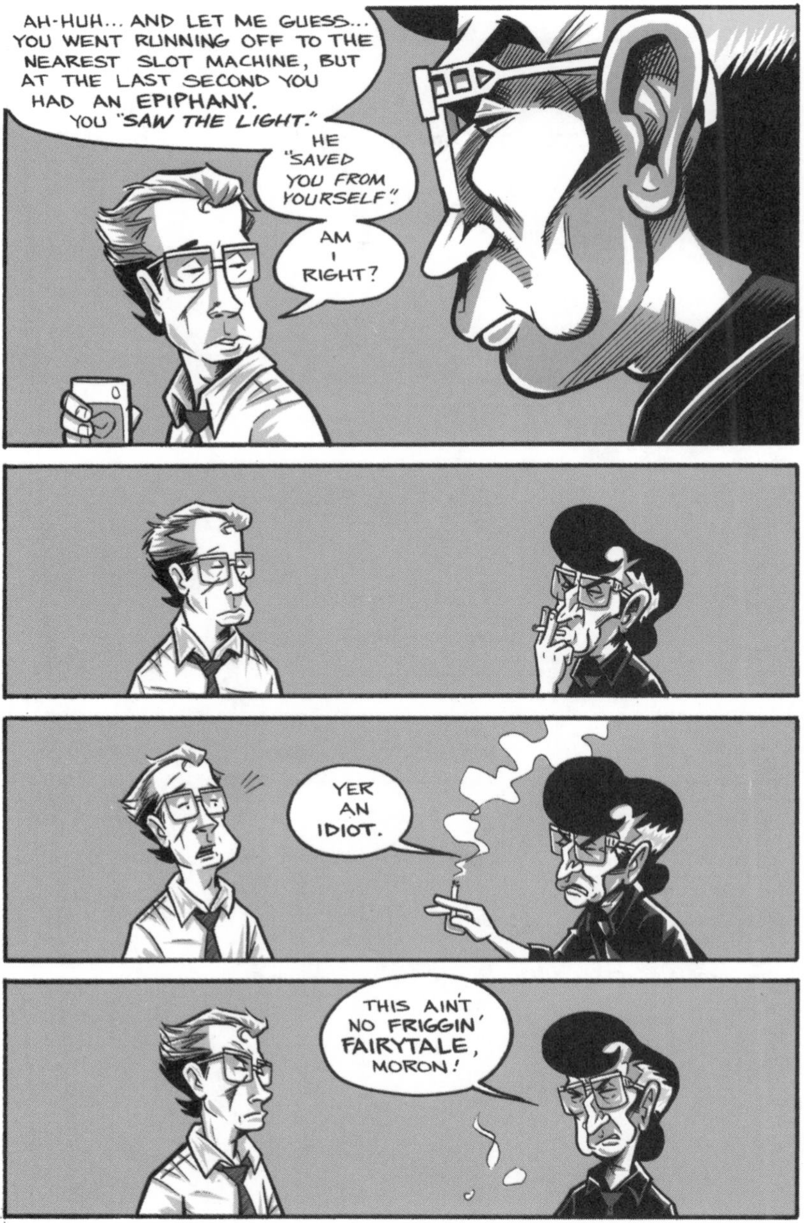
AH-HUH... AND LET ME GUESS... YOU WENT RUNNING OFF TO THE NEAREST SLOT MACHINE, BUT AT THE LAST SECOND YOU HAD AN EPIPHANY. YOU "SAW THE LIGHT."
HE "SAVED YOU FROM YOURSELF"!
AM I RIGHT?
YER AN IDIOT.
THIS AIN'T NO FRIGGIN' FAIRYTALE, MORON!

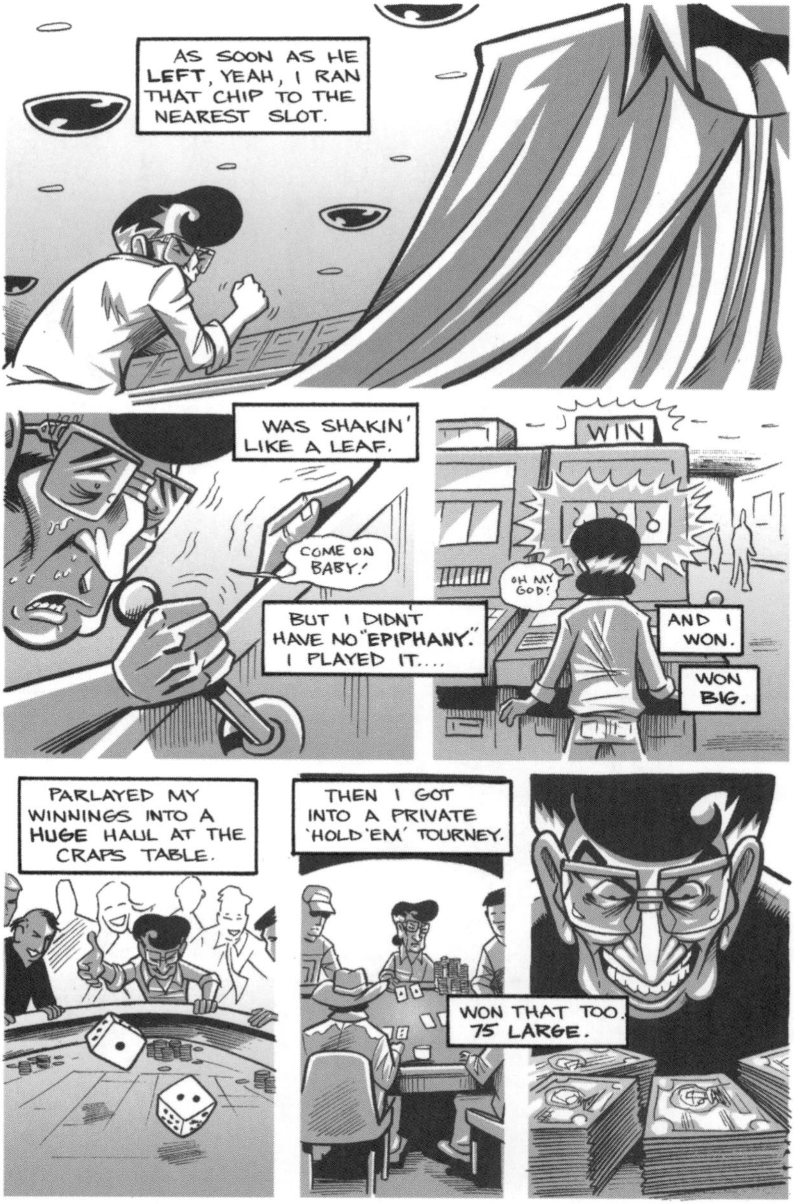
AS SOON AS HE LEFT, YEAH, I RAN THAT CHIP TO THE NEAREST SLOT.
WAS SHAKIN' LIKE A LEAF.
COME ON BABY!
BUT I DIDN'T HAVE NO "EPIPHANY." I PLAYED IT....
WIN
OH MY GOD!
AND I WON.
WON BIG.
PARLAYED MY WINNINGS INTO A HUGE HAUL AT THE CRAPS TABLE.
THEN I GOT INTO A PRIVATE 'HOLD'EM' TOURNEY.
WON THAT TOO. 75 LARGE.

GOT MY "MIRACLE".

SEVENTY-FIVE THOUSAND?!

YUP.

AND THE NEXT DAY I PISSED IT ALL AWAY.

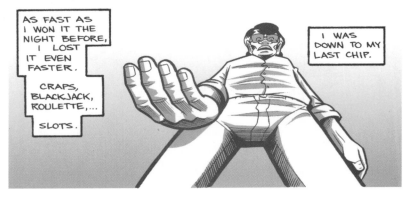

AS FAST AS I WON IT THE NIGHT BEFORE, I LOST IT EVEN FASTER.

CRAPS, BLACKJACK, ROULETTE,...

SLOTS.

I WAS DOWN TO MY LAST CHIP.

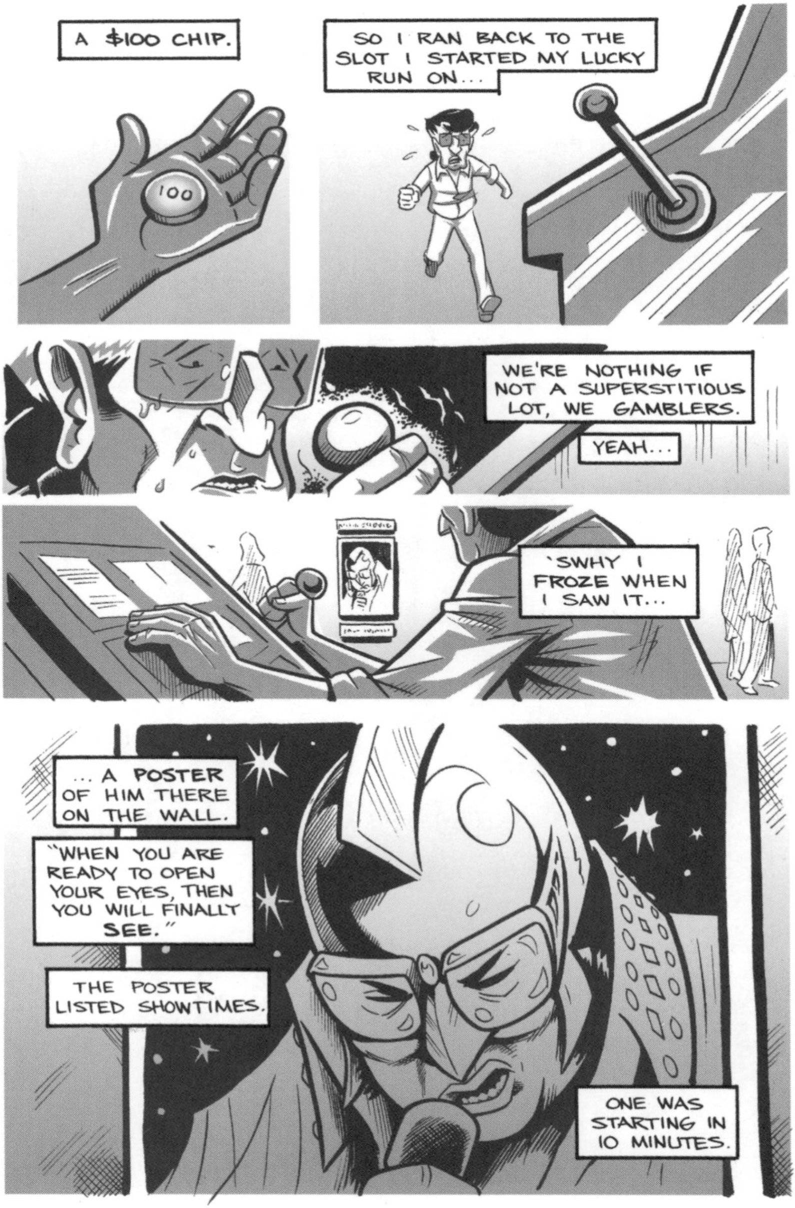
A $100 CHIP.
SO I RAN BACK TO THE SLOT I STARTED MY LUCKY RUN ON...
100
WE'RE NOTHING IF NOT A SUPERSTITIOUS LOT, WE GAMBLERS.
YEAH...
`SWHY I FROZE WHEN I SAW IT...
... A POSTER OF HIM THERE ON THE WALL.
"WHEN YOU ARE READY TO OPEN YOUR EYES, THEN YOU WILL FINALLY SEE."
THE POSTER LISTED SHOWTIMES.
ONE WAS STARTING IN 10 MINUTES.

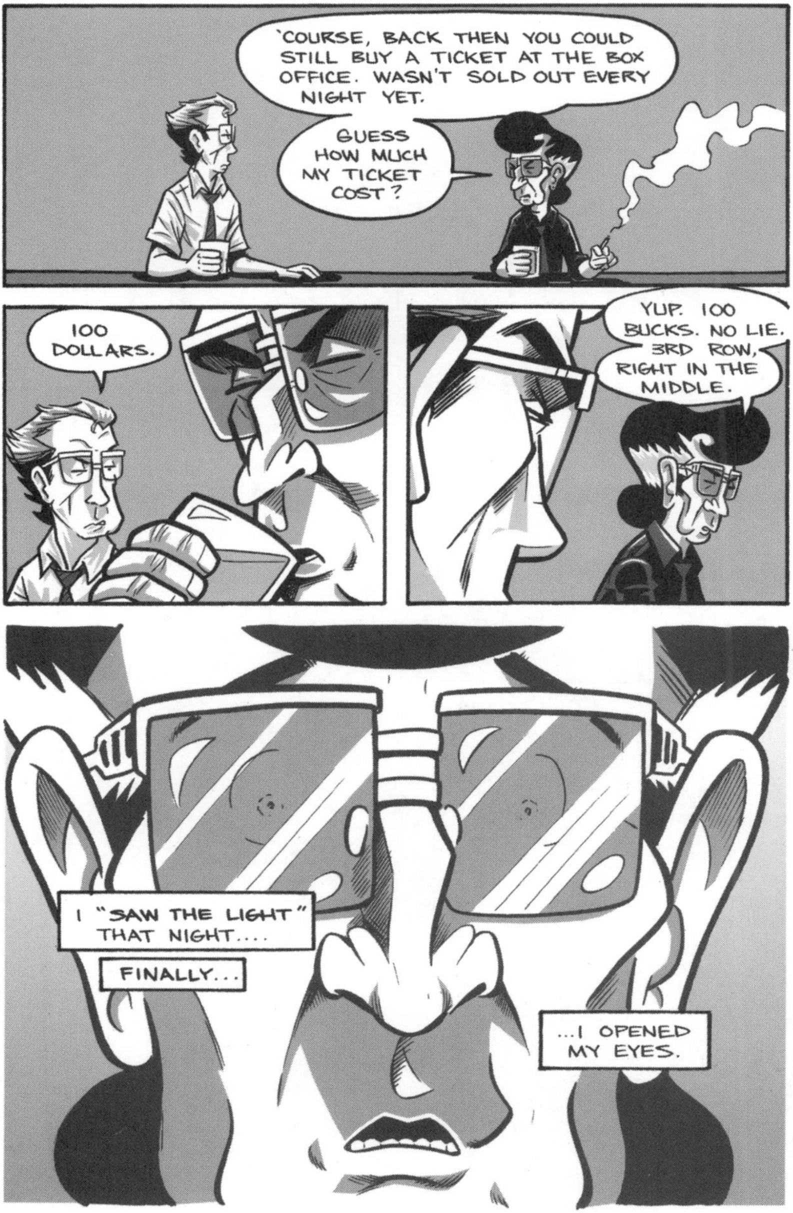
`COURSE, BACK THEN YOU COULD STILL BUY A TICKET AT THE BOX OFFICE. WASN'T SOLD OUT EVERY NIGHT YET.
GUESS HOW MUCH MY TICKET COST?
100 DOLLARS.
YUP. 100 BUCKS. NO LIE. 3RD ROW, RIGHT IN THE MIDDLE.
I "SAW THE LIGHT" THAT NIGHT....
FINALLY...
...I OPENED MY EYES.

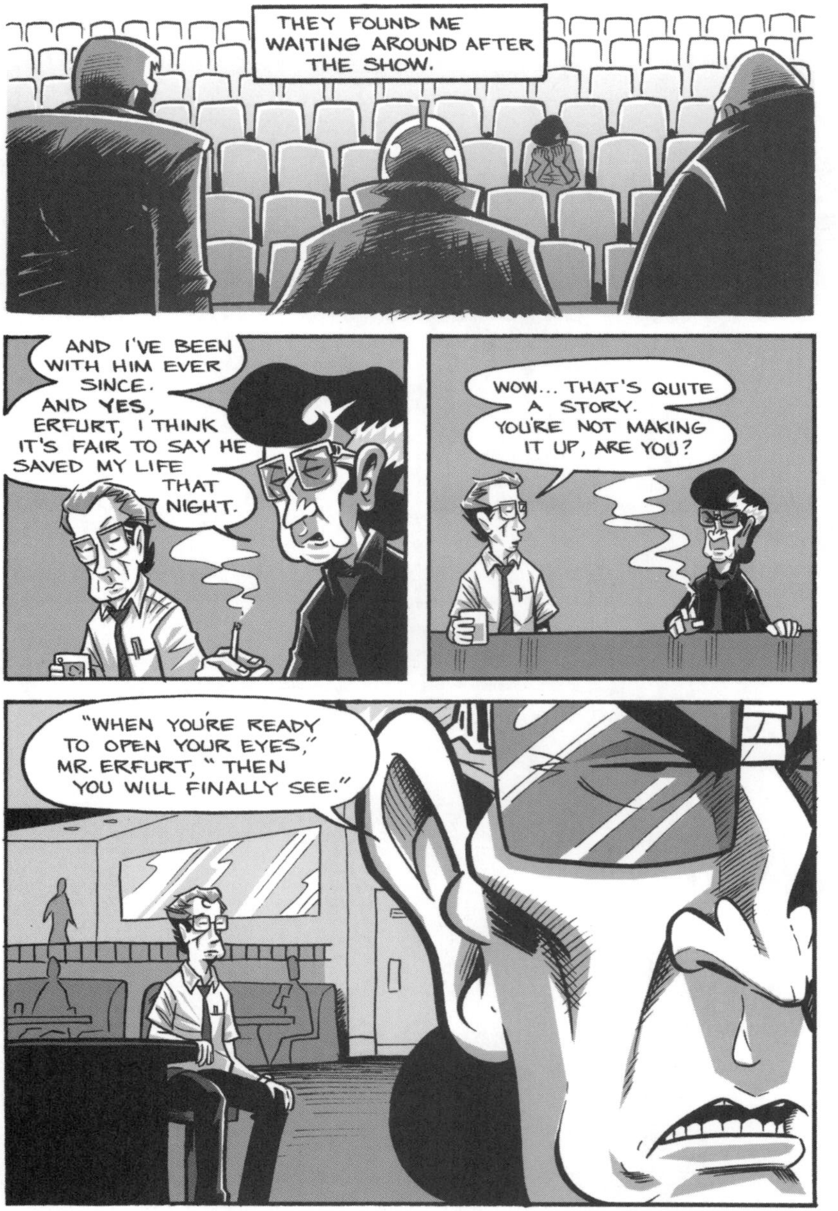
THEY FOUND ME WAITING AROUND AFTER THE SHOW.
AND I'VE BEEN WITH HIM EVER SINCE. AND YES, ERFURT, I THINK IT'S FAIR TO SAY HE SAVED MY LIFE THAT NIGHT.
WOW... THAT'S QUITE A STORY. YOU'RE NOT MAKING IT UP, ARE YOU?
"WHEN YOU'RE READY TO OPEN YOUR EYES," MR. ERFURT, "THEN YOU WILL FINALLY SEE."

LATER, BACK AT THE SUNSET MOTEL.
KLICK KLACKETY KLICK
Blee dee deep
HELLO?
YEAH, HEY DAVE.
NO. NO PROBLEM. JUST WORKING ON THE STORY.
IT'S GOING ALRIGHT, I GUESS.
Delusions of Grandeur
by Paul Erfurt
Upon meeting this man, clad in robes and a gleamin golden helmut, one cannot help but be impressed ...awestruck even. Surrounded by his devoted "followers" and adored by seemingly thousands more, one cannot help but wonder if there is any validity to his claims.
But the moment quickly fades as this impressive figure talks of godhood and power... Then one feels nothing but pity for this delusional soul.
I met "The King" on a very hot Vegas night. After seeing him perform at the Trident's lush Northern Lights Theatre. The performance was, by the way, very impressive. Whoever this man really is there is no denying or disputing the fact that he can sing... Just like Elvis Presley, yes. If one were to close their eyes (which this reporter did) they might even swear they'd been transported back thirty years to a time when the real Elvis walked the Vegas stage. But
THIS IS TURNING INTO A REAL CIRCUS. I INTERVIEWED ONE OF HIS "MEMPHIS MAFIA" GUYS TODAY... BOBBY VARPOSI. REAL PIECE OF WORK. GOT A BIT OF A "NAPOLEON COMPLEX", I THINK.
HAW! YA GOTTA WATCH OUT FOR THOSE SHORT GUYS!
doc.net

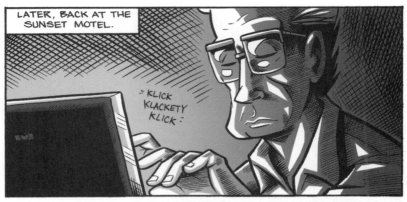

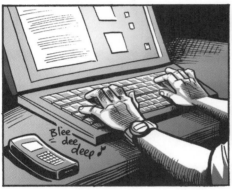

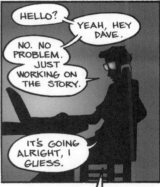

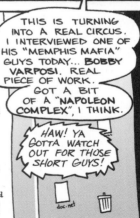

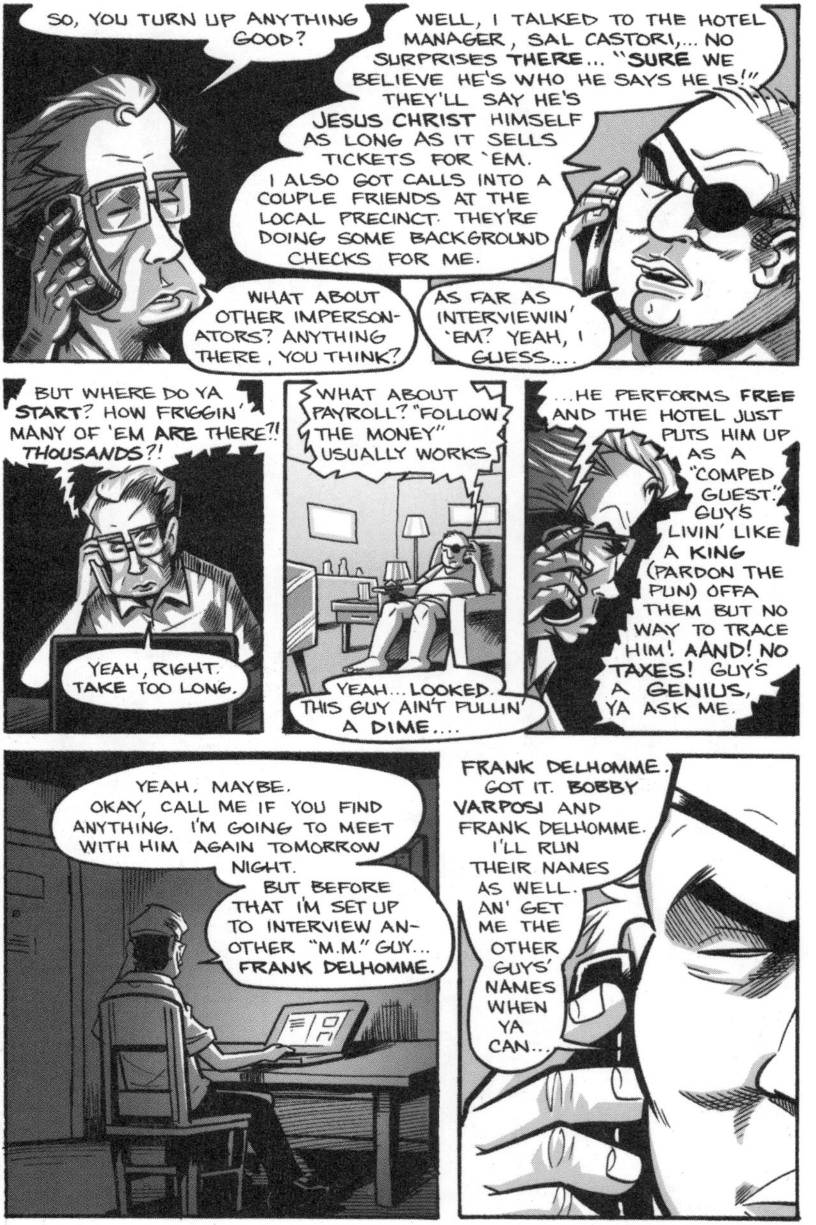
SO, YOU TURN UP ANYTHING GOOD?
WELL, I TALKED TO THE HOTEL MANAGER, SAL CASTORI,... NO SURPRISES THERE... "SURE WE BELIEVE HE'S WHO HE SAYS HE IS!" THEY'LL SAY HE'S JESUS CHRIST HIMSELF AS LONG AS IT SELLS TICKETS FOR 'EM.
I ALSO GOT CALLS INTO A COUPLE FRIENDS AT THE LOCAL PRECINCT. THEY'RE DOING SOME BACKGROUND CHECKS FOR ME.
WHAT ABOUT OTHER IMPERSON-ATORS? ANYTHING THERE, YOU THINK?
AS FAR AS INTERVIEWIN' 'EM? YEAH, I GUESS....
BUT WHERE DO YA START? HOW FRIGGIN' MANY OF 'EM ARE THERE?! THOUSANDS?!
YEAH, RIGHT. TAKE TOO LONG.
WHAT ABOUT PAYROLL? "FOLLOW THE MONEY" USUALLY WORKS.
YEAH... LOOKED. THIS GUY AIN'T PULLIN' A DIME....
...HE PERFORMS FREE AND THE HOTEL JUST PUTS HIM UP AS A "COMPED GUEST." GUY'S LIVIN' LIKE A KING (PARDON THE PUN) OFFA THEM BUT NO WAY TO TRACE HIM! AAND! NO TAXES! GUY'S A GENIUS, YA ASK ME.
YEAH, MAYBE. OKAY, CALL ME IF YOU FIND ANYTHING. I'M GOING TO MEET WITH HIM AGAIN TOMORROW NIGHT.
BUT BEFORE THAT I'M SET UP TO INTERVIEW AN-OTHER "M.M." GUY... FRANK DELHOMME.
FRANK DELHOMME. GOT IT. BOBBY VARPOSI AND FRANK DELHOMME.
I'LL RUN THEIR NAMES AS WELL.
AN' GET ME THE OTHER GUYS' NAMES WHEN YA CAN...

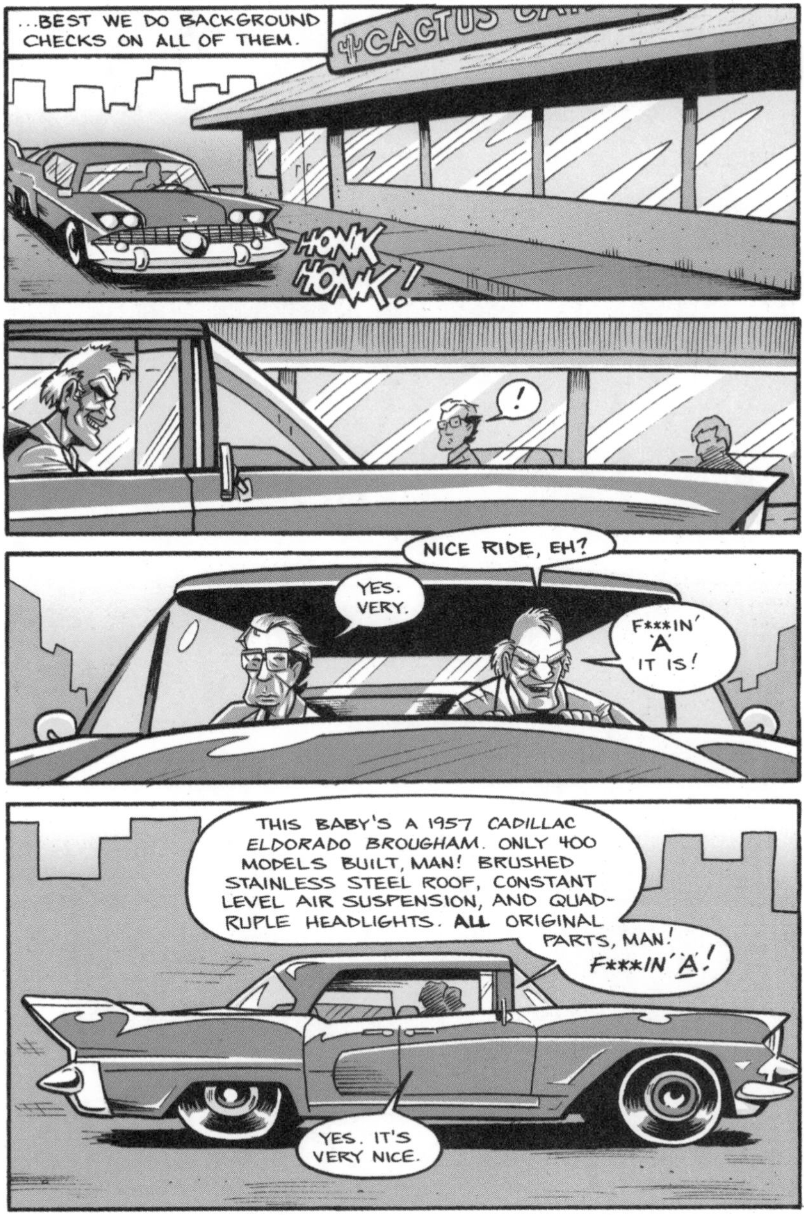
...BEST WE DO BACKGROUND CHECKS ON ALL OF THEM.
CACTUS CA
HONK HONK!
!
NICE RIDE, EH?
YES. VERY.
F***IN' 'A' IT IS!
THIS BABY'S A 1957 CADILLAC ELDORADO BROUGHAM. ONLY 400 MODELS BUILT, MAN! BRUSHED STAINLESS STEEL ROOF, CONSTANT LEVEL AIR SUSPENSION, AND QUADRUPLE HEADLIGHTS. ALL ORIGINAL PARTS, MAN! F***IN' 'A'!
YES. IT'S VERY NICE.

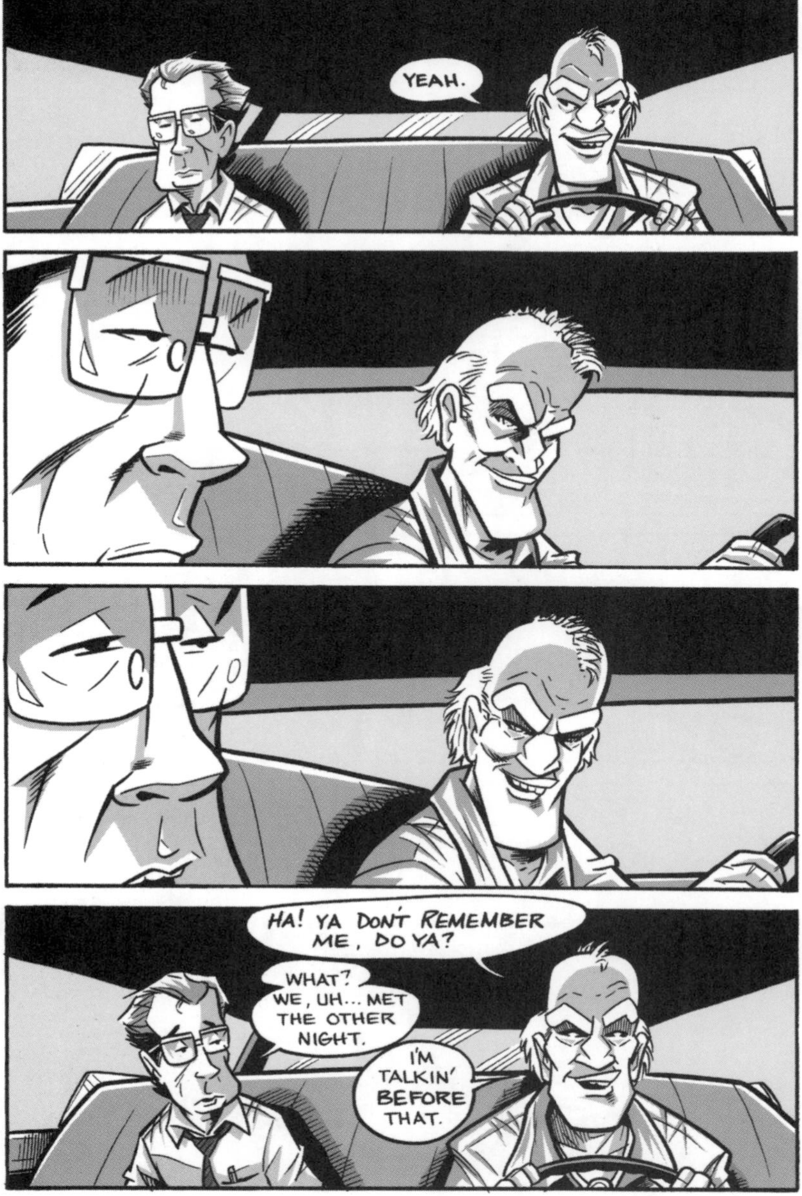
YEAH.
HA! YA DON'T REMEMBER ME, DO YA?
WHAT? WE, UH... MET THE OTHER NIGHT.
I'M TALKIN' BEFORE THAT.

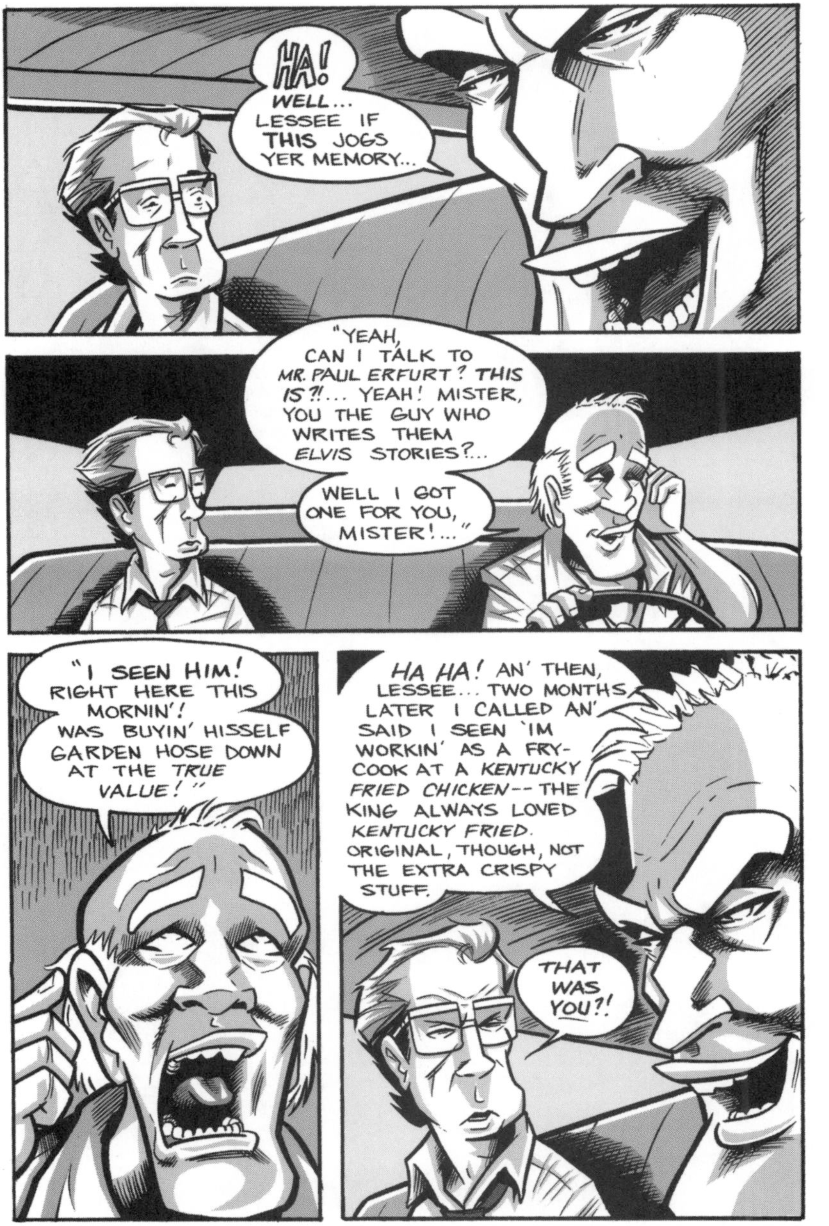
HA! WELL... LESSEE IF THIS JOGS YER MEMORY...
"YEAH, CAN I TALK TO MR. PAUL ERFURT? THIS IS?!... YEAH! MISTER, YOU THE GUY WHO WRITES THEM ELVIS STORIES?...
WELL I GOT ONE FOR YOU, MISTER!..."
"I SEEN HIM! RIGHT HERE THIS MORNIN'! WAS BUYIN' HISSELF GARDEN HOSE DOWN AT THE TRUE VALUE!"
HA HA! AN' THEN, LESSEE... TWO MONTHS LATER I CALLED AN' SAID I SEEN 'IM WORKIN' AS A FRY-COOK AT A KENTUCKY FRIED CHICKEN-- THE KING ALWAYS LOVED KENTUCKY FRIED. ORIGINAL, THOUGH, NOT THE EXTRA CRISPY STUFF.
THAT WAS YOU?!

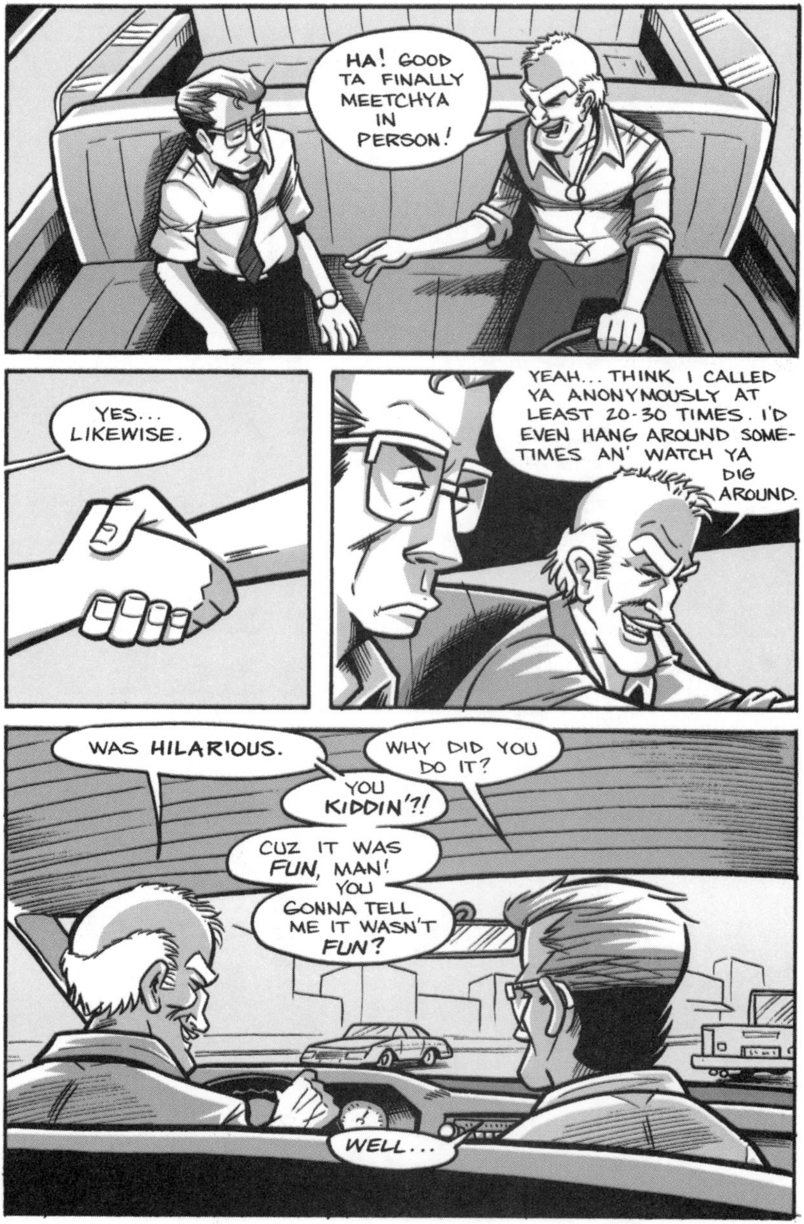
HA! GOOD TA FINALLY MEETCHYA IN PERSON!
YES... LIKEWISE.
YEAH... THINK I CALLED YA ANONYMOUSLY AT LEAST 20-30 TIMES. I'D EVEN HANG AROUND SOMETIMES AN' WATCH YA DIG AROUND.
WAS HILARIOUS.
WHY DID YOU DO IT?
YOU KIDDIN'?!
CUZ IT WAS FUN, MAN! YOU GONNA TELL ME IT WASN'T FUN?
WELL...

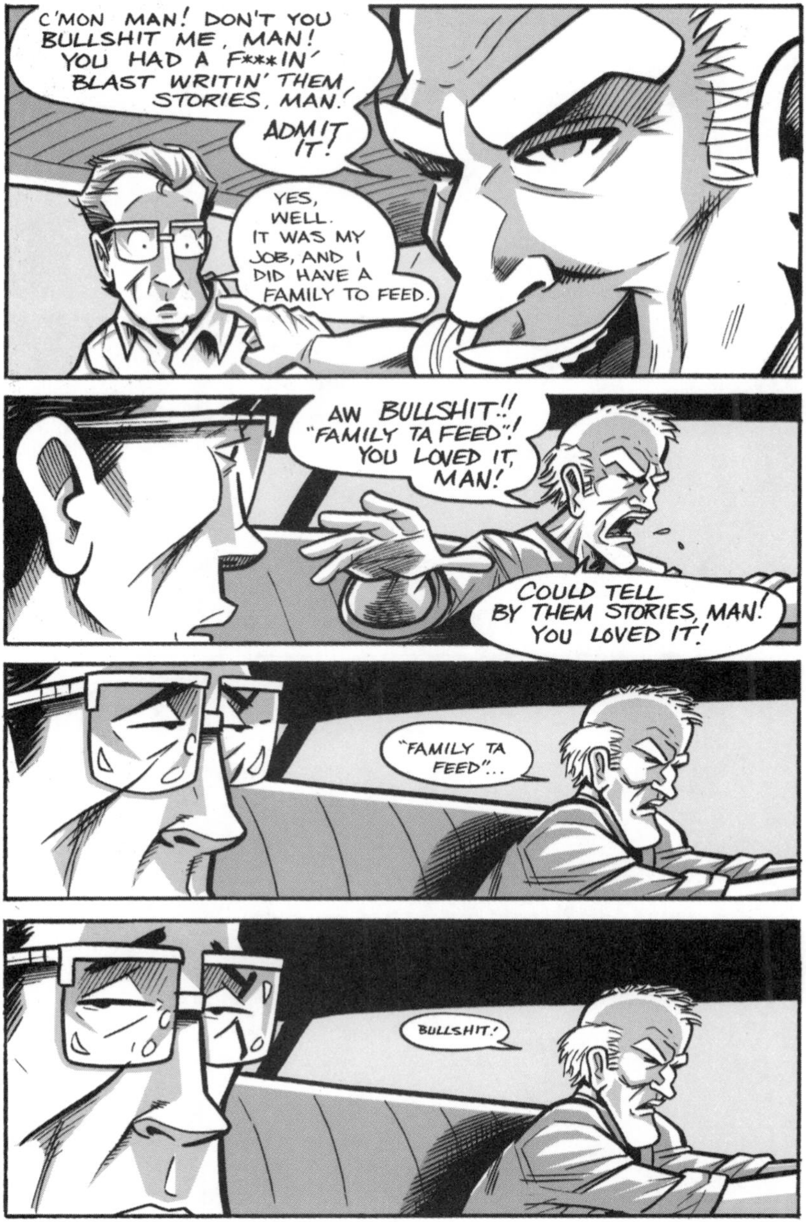
C'MON MAN! DON'T YOU BULLSHIT ME, MAN! YOU HAD A F***IN' BLAST WRITIN' THEM STORIES, MAN!
ADMIT IT!
YES, WELL. IT WAS MY JOB, AND I DID HAVE A FAMILY TO FEED.
AW BULLSHIT!! "FAMILY TA FEED"! YOU LOVED IT, MAN!
COULD TELL BY THEM STORIES, MAN! YOU LOVED IT!
"FAMILY TA FEED"...
BULLSHIT!

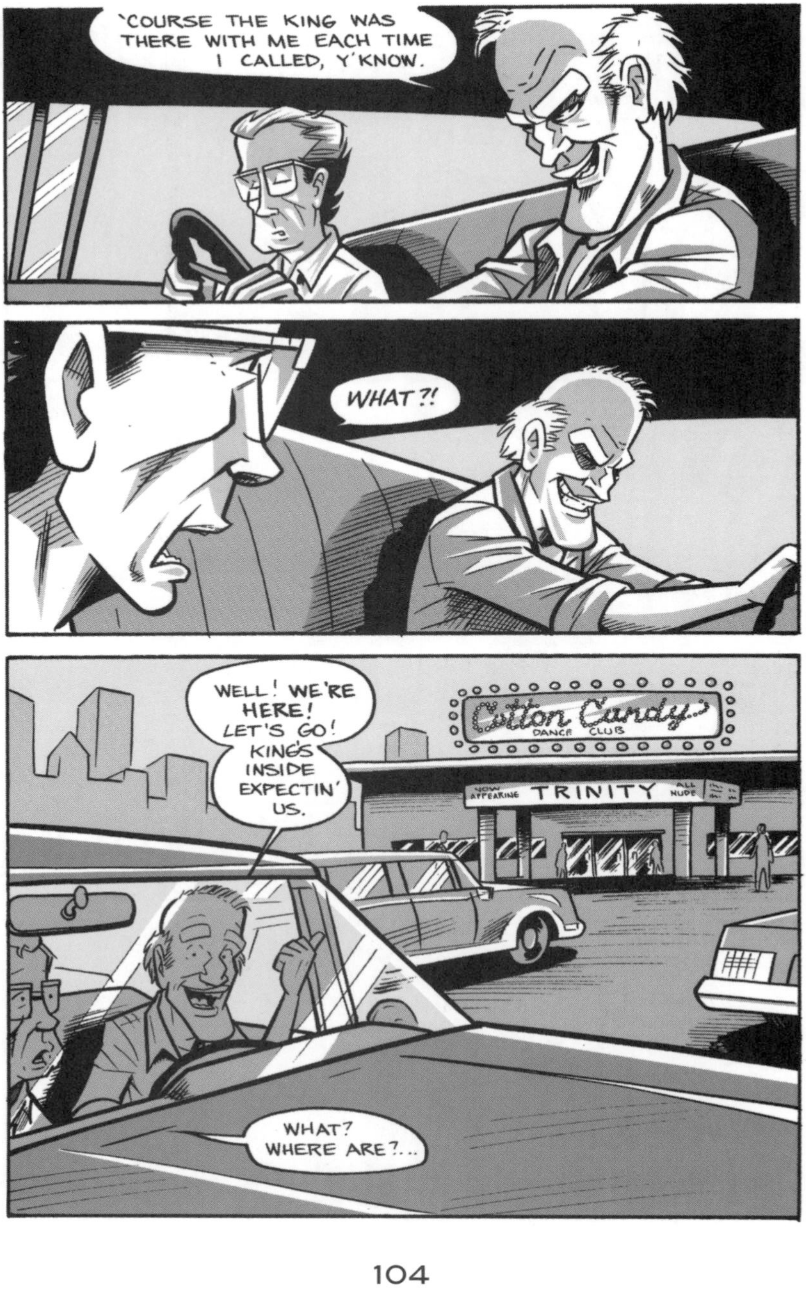

`COURSE THE KING WAS THERE WITH ME EACH TIME I CALLED, Y'KNOW.
WHAT?!
WELL! WE'RE HERE! LET'S GO! KING'S INSIDE EXPECTIN' US.
Cotton Candy
DANCE CLUB
NOW APPEARING TRINITY ALL NUDE
WHAT? WHERE ARE?...

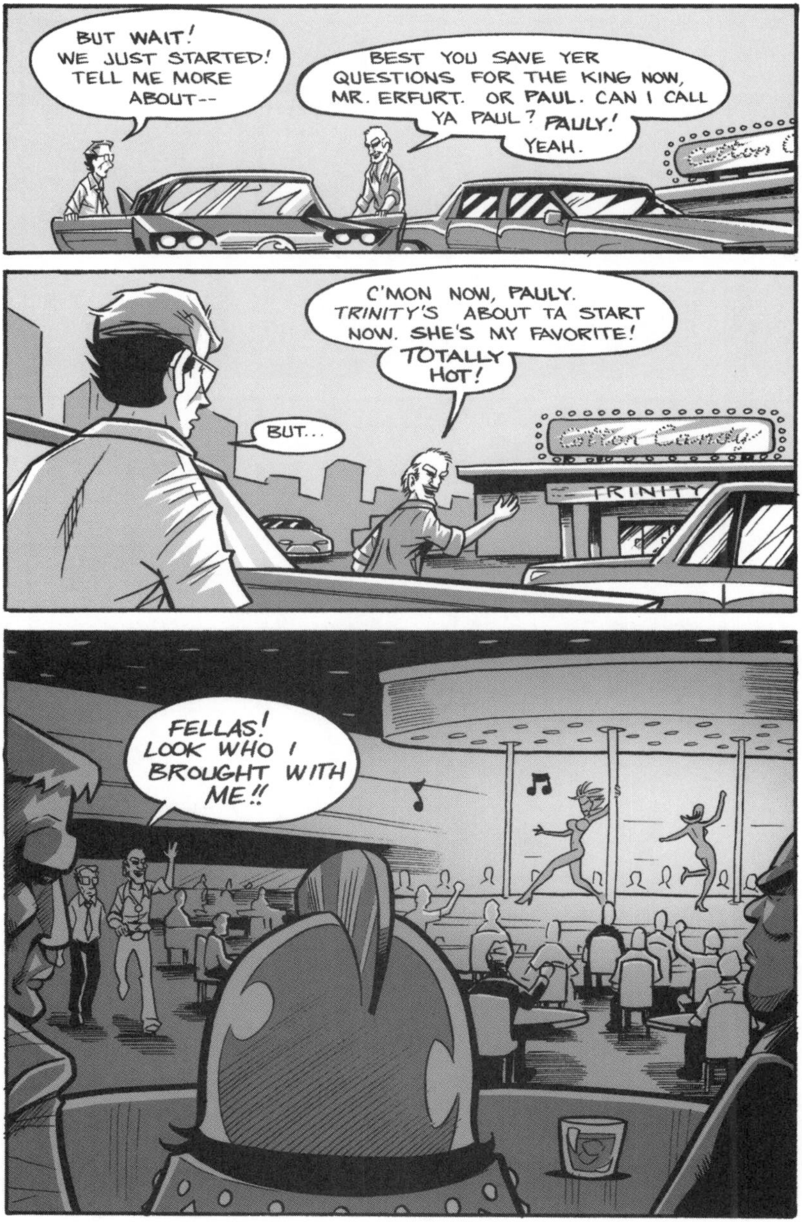
BUT WAIT! WE JUST STARTED! TELL ME MORE ABOUT--
BEST YOU SAVE YER QUESTIONS FOR THE KING NOW, MR. ERFURT. OR PAUL. CAN I CALL YA PAUL? PAULY! YEAH.
C'MON NOW, PAULY. TRINITY'S ABOUT TA START NOW. SHE'S MY FAVORITE!
TOTALLY HOT!
BUT...
TRINITY
FELLAS! LOOK WHO I BROUGHT WITH ME!!

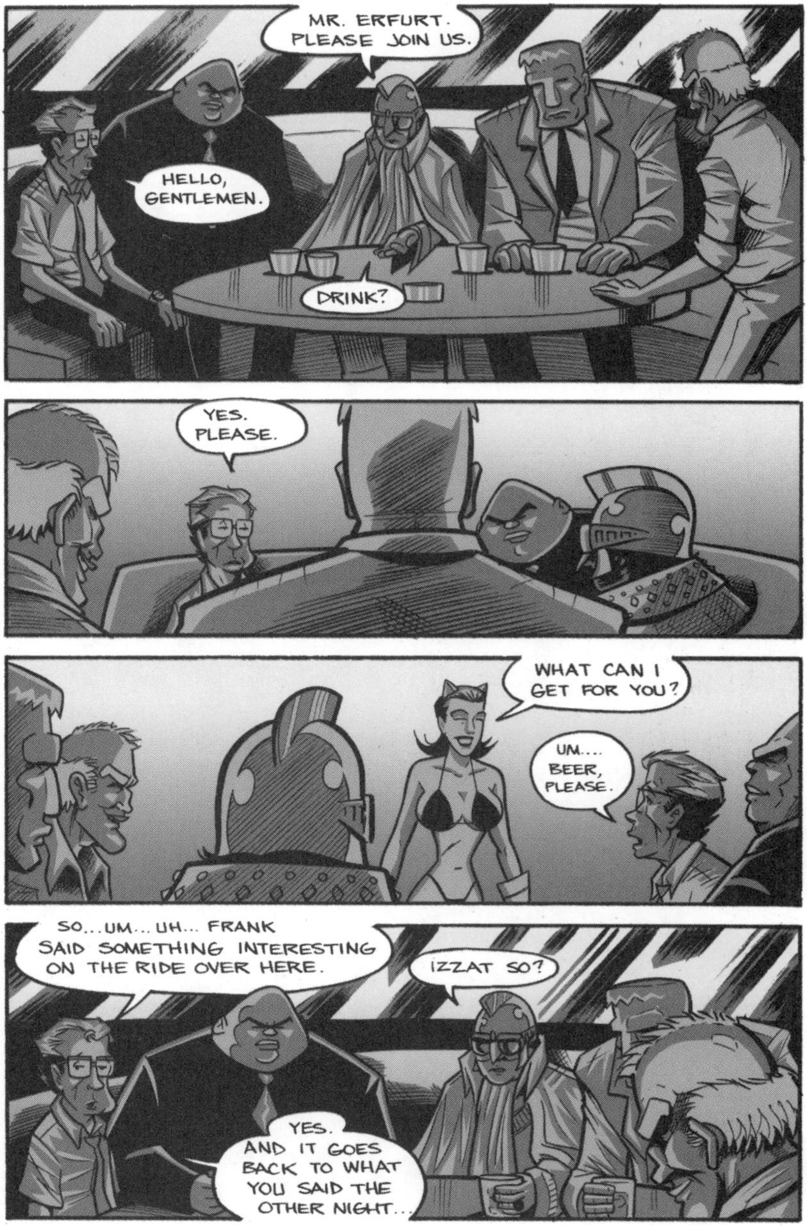
MR. ERFURT. PLEASE JOIN US.
HELLO, GENTLEMEN.
DRINK?
YES. PLEASE.
WHAT CAN I GET FOR YOU?
UM.... BEER, PLEASE.
SO...UM...UH... FRANK SAID SOMETHING INTERESTING ON THE RIDE OVER HERE.
IZZAT SO?
YES. AND IT GOES BACK TO WHAT YOU SAID THE OTHER NIGHT...

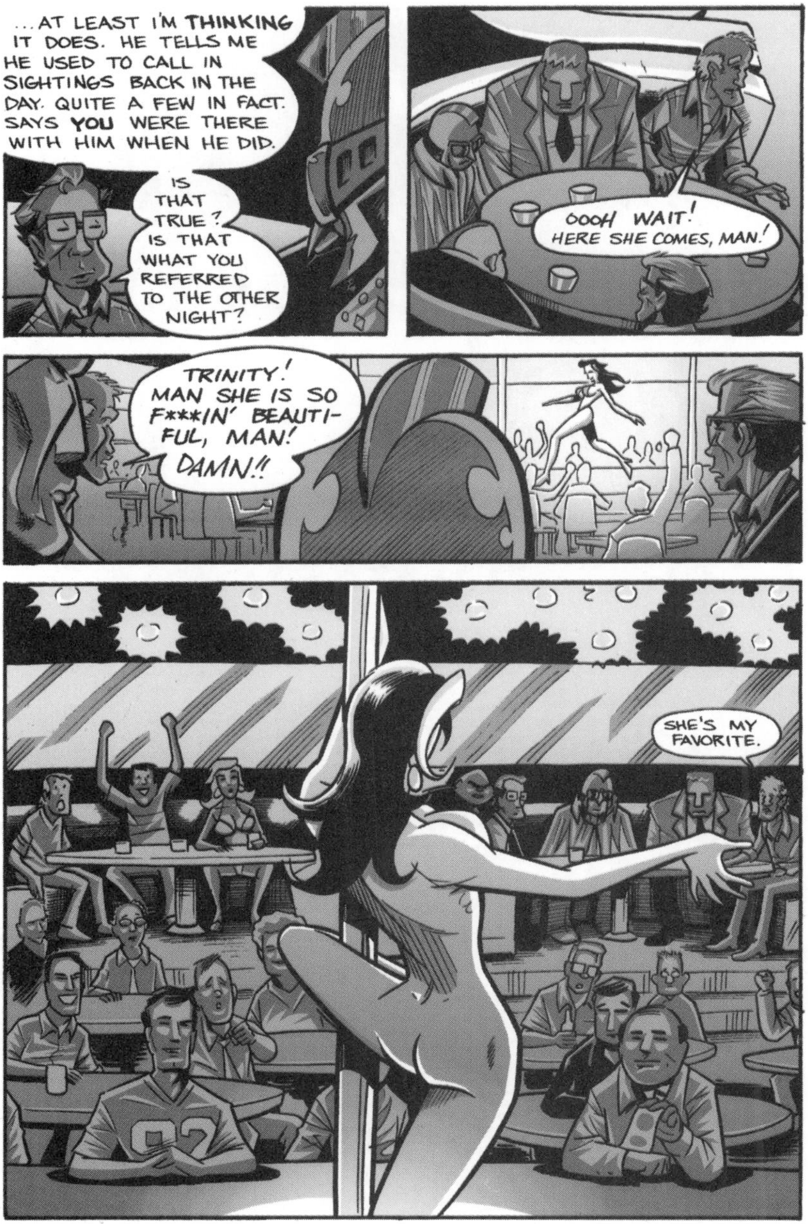
...AT LEAST I'M THINKING IT DOES. HE TELLS ME HE USED TO CALL IN SIGHTINGS BACK IN THE DAY. QUITE A FEW IN FACT. SAYS YOU WERE THERE WITH HIM WHEN HE DID.
IS THAT TRUE? IS THAT WHAT YOU REFERRED TO THE OTHER NIGHT?
OOOH WAIT! HERE SHE COMES, MAN!
TRINITY! MAN SHE IS SO F***IN' BEAUTIFUL, MAN! DAMN!!
SHE'S MY FAVORITE.

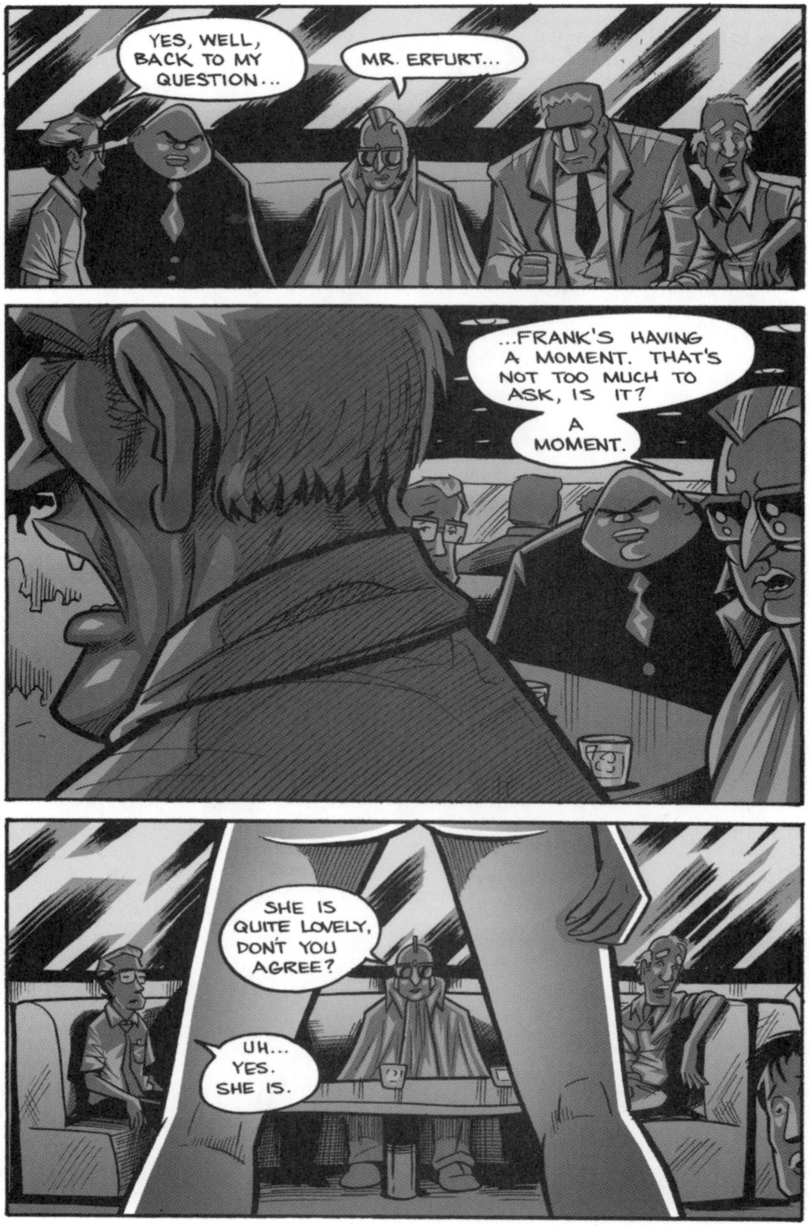
YES, WELL, BACK TO MY QUESTION...
MR. ERFURT...
...FRANK'S HAVING A MOMENT. THAT'S NOT TOO MUCH TO ASK, IS IT?
A MOMENT.
SHE IS QUITE LOVELY, DON'T YOU AGREE?
UH... YES. SHE IS.

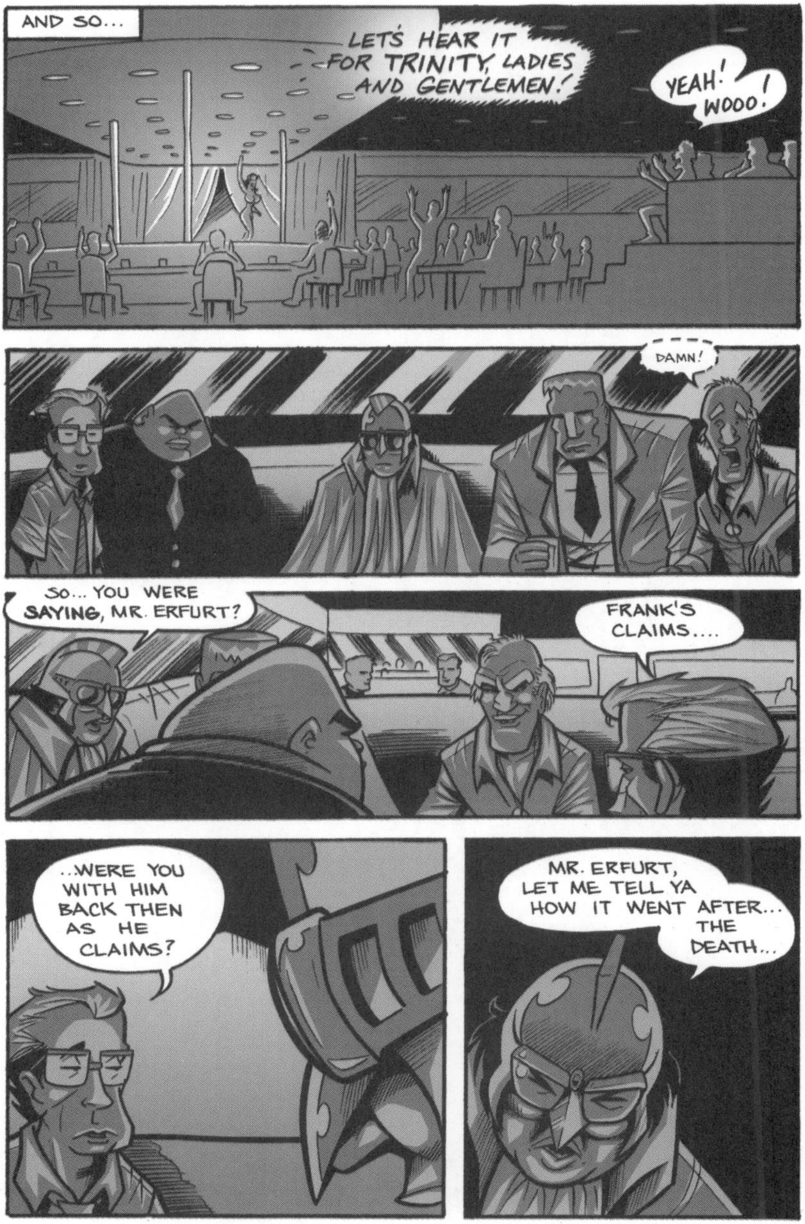
AND SO...
LET'S HEAR IT FOR TRINITY, LADIES AND GENTLEMEN!
YEAH! WOOO!
DAMN!
SO... YOU WERE SAYING, MR. ERFURT?
FRANK'S CLAIMS....
...WERE YOU WITH HIM BACK THEN AS HE CLAIMS?
MR. ERFURT, LET ME TELL YA HOW IT WENT AFTER... THE DEATH...

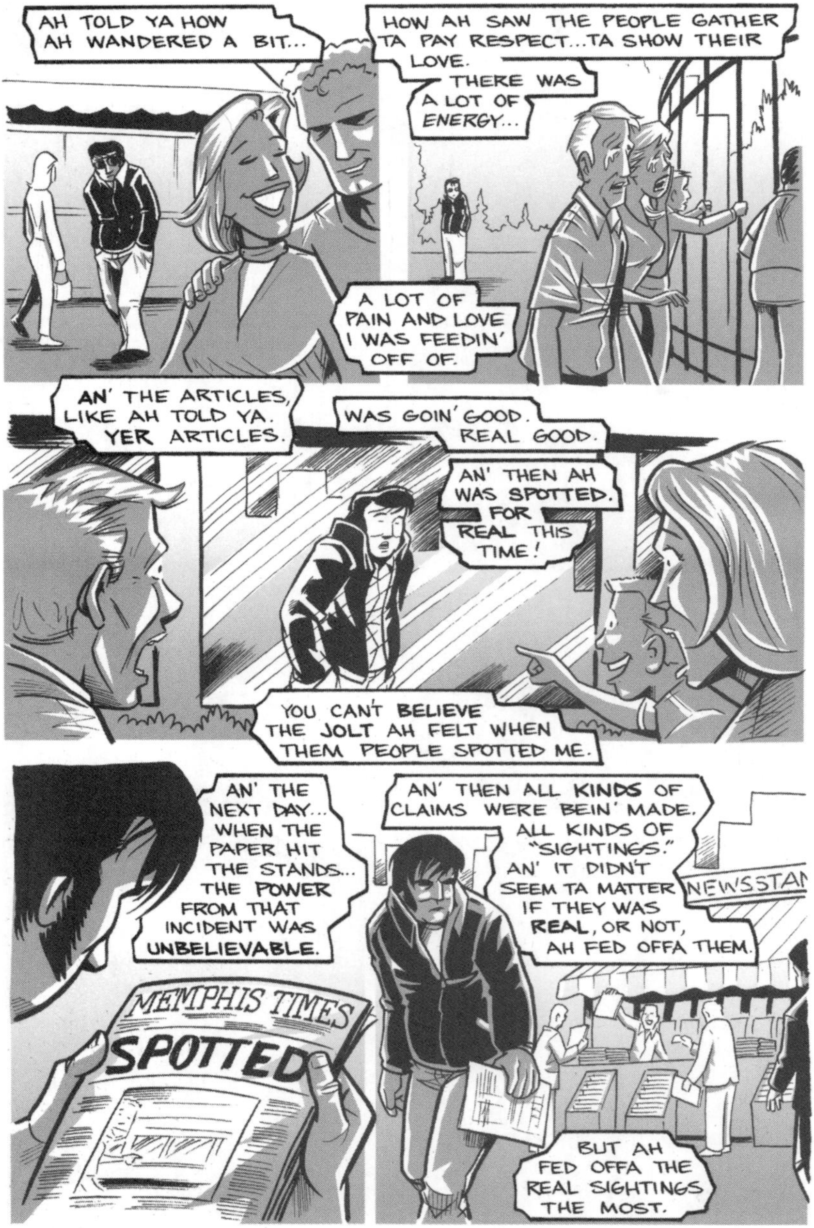
AH TOLD YA HOW AH WANDERED A BIT...
HOW AH SAW THE PEOPLE GATHER TA PAY RESPECT...TA SHOW THEIR LOVE.
THERE WAS A LOT OF ENERGY...
A LOT OF PAIN AND LOVE I WAS FEEDIN' OFF OF.
AN' THE ARTICLES, LIKE AH TOLD YA. YER ARTICLES.
WAS GOIN' GOOD. REAL GOOD.
AN' THEN AH WAS SPOTTED. FOR REAL THIS TIME!
YOU CAN'T BELIEVE THE JOLT AH FELT WHEN THEM PEOPLE SPOTTED ME.
AN' THE NEXT DAY... WHEN THE PAPER HIT THE STANDS... THE POWER FROM THAT INCIDENT WAS UNBELIEVABLE.
AN' THEN ALL KINDS OF CLAIMS WERE BEIN' MADE. ALL KINDS OF "SIGHTINGS." AN' IT DIDN'T SEEM TA MATTER IF THEY WAS REAL, OR NOT, AH FED OFFA THEM.
NEWSSTAN
MEMPHIS TIMES
SPOTTED
BUT AH FED OFFA THE REAL SIGHTINGS THE MOST.

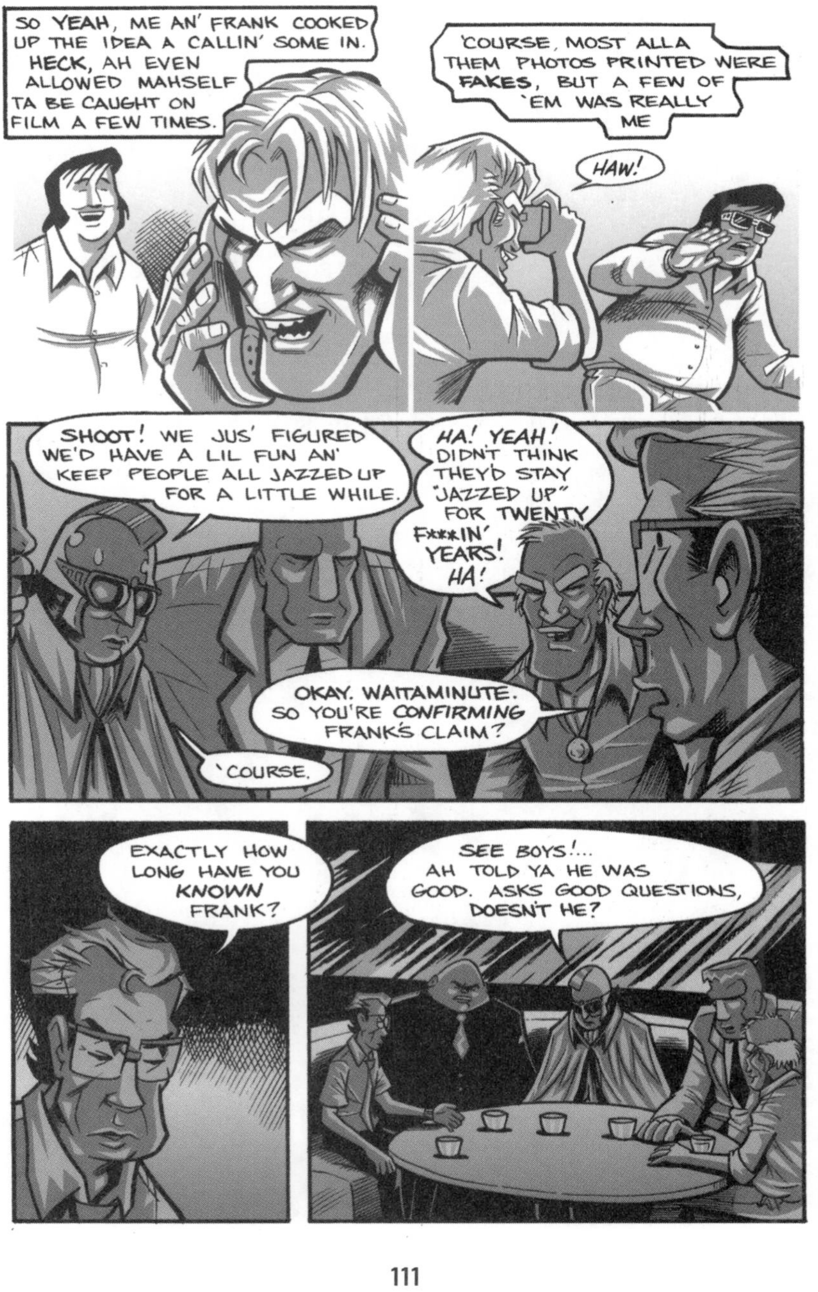
SO YEAH, ME AN' FRANK COOKED UP THE IDEA A CALLIN' SOME IN. HECK, AH EVEN ALLOWED MAHSELF TA BE CAUGHT ON FILM A FEW TIMES.
'COURSE, MOST ALLA THEM PHOTOS PRINTED WERE FAKES, BUT A FEW OF 'EM WAS REALLY ME
HAW!
SHOOT! WE JUS' FIGURED WE'D HAVE A LIL FUN AN' KEEP PEOPLE ALL JAZZED UP FOR A LITTLE WHILE.
HA! YEAH! DIDN'T THINK THEY'D STAY "JAZZED UP" FOR TWENTY F***IN' YEARS! HA!
OKAY. WAITAMINUTE. SO YOU'RE CONFIRMING FRANK'S CLAIM?
'COURSE.
EXACTLY HOW LONG HAVE YOU KNOWN FRANK?
SEE BOYS!... AH TOLD YA HE WAS GOOD. ASKS GOOD QUESTIONS, DOESN'T HE?

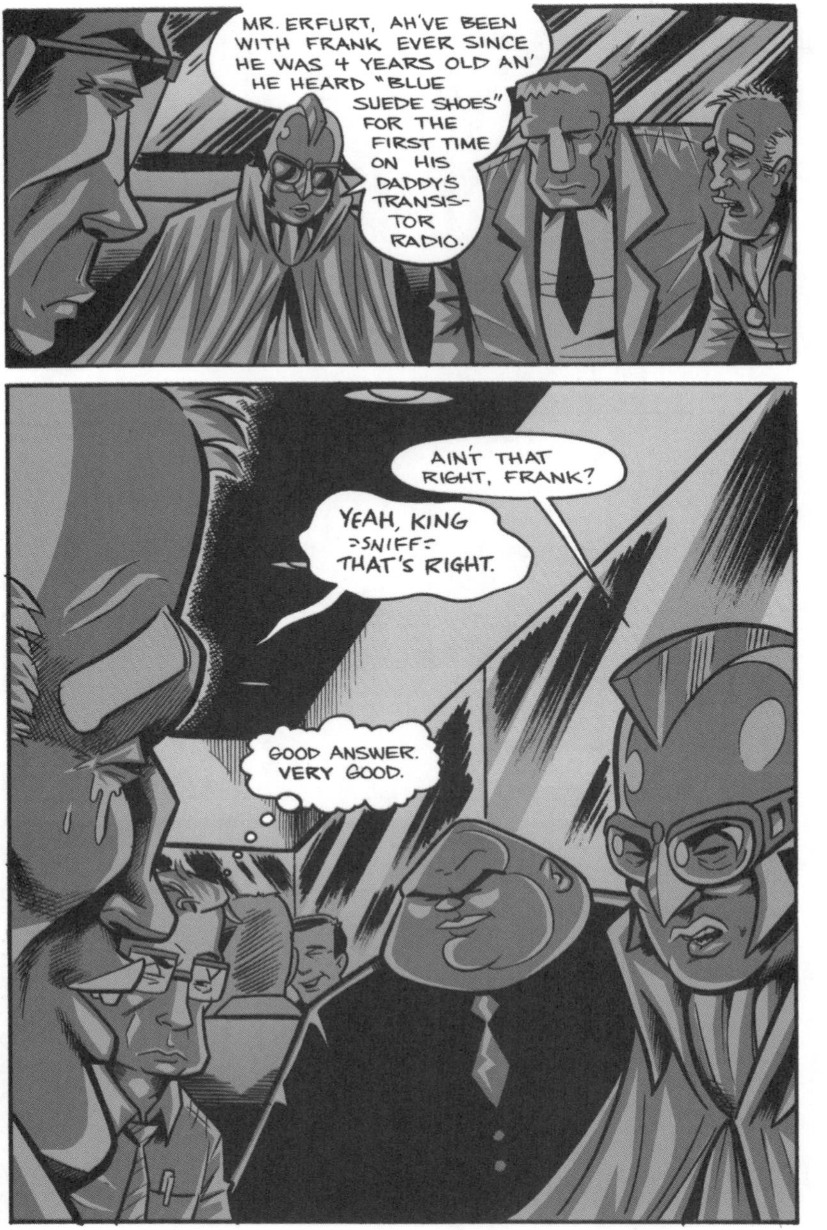
MR. ERFURT, AH'VE BEEN WITH FRANK EVER SINCE HE WAS 4 YEARS OLD AN' HE HEARD "BLUE SUEDE SHOES" FOR THE FIRST TIME ON HIS DADDY'S TRANSIS-TOR RADIO.
AIN'T THAT RIGHT, FRANK?
YEAH, KING =SNIFF= THAT'S RIGHT.
GOOD ANSWER. VERY GOOD.

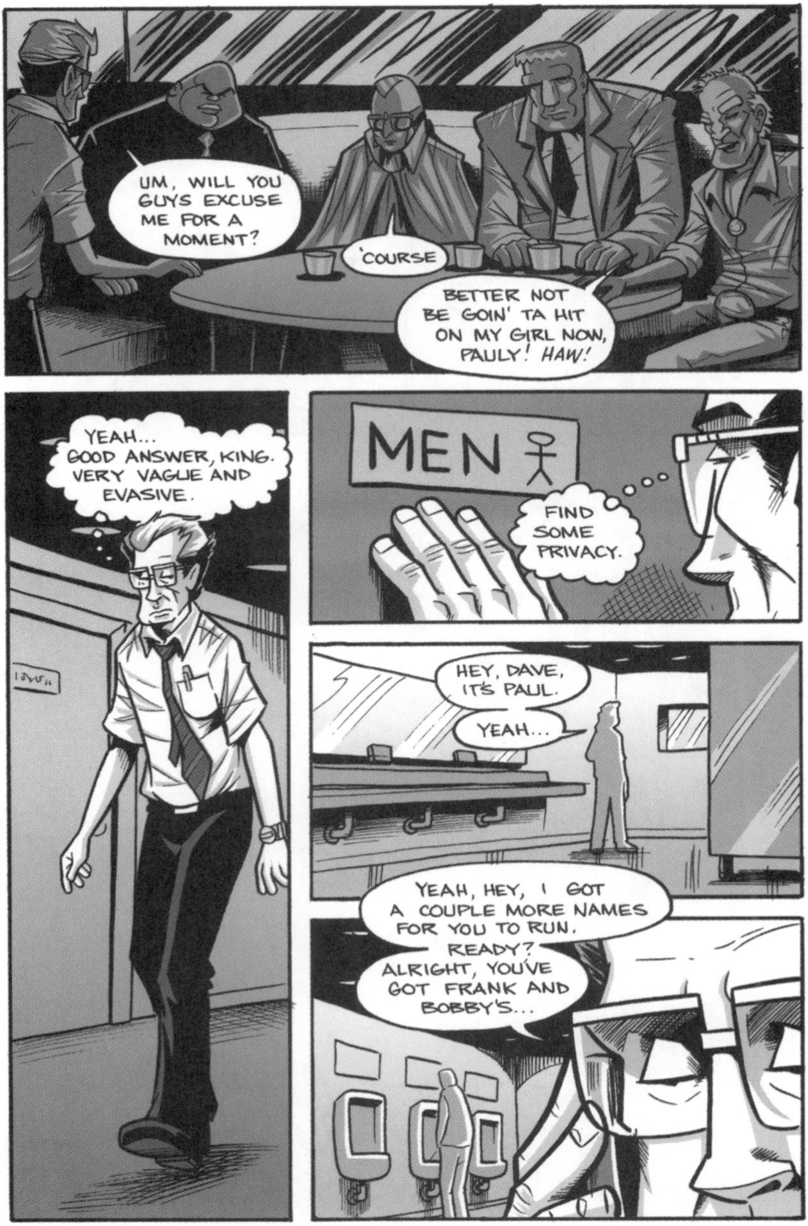
UM, WILL YOU GUYS EXCUSE ME FOR A MOMENT?
'COURSE
BETTER NOT BE GOIN' TA HIT ON MY GIRL NOW, PAULY! HAW!
YEAH... GOOD ANSWER, KING. VERY VAGUE AND EVASIVE.
MEN
FIND SOME PRIVACY.
HEY, DAVE, IT'S PAUL.
YEAH...
YEAH, HEY, I GOT A COUPLE MORE NAMES FOR YOU TO RUN. READY? ALRIGHT, YOU'VE GOT FRANK AND BOBBY'S...

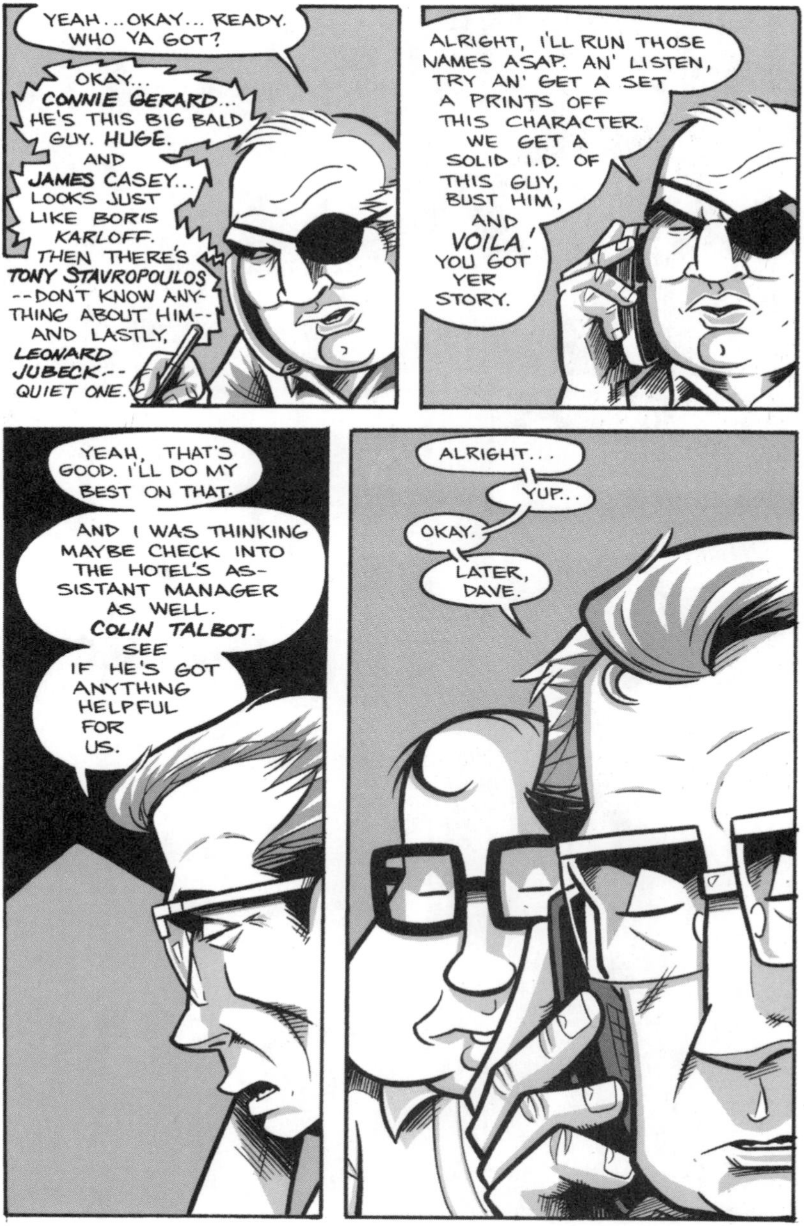
YEAH... OKAY... READY. WHO YA GOT?
OKAY... CONNIE GERARD... HE'S THIS BIG BALD GUY. HUGE. AND JAMES CASEY... LOOKS JUST LIKE BORIS KARLOFF. THEN THERE'S TONY STAVROPOULOS --DON'T KNOW ANYTHING ABOUT HIM-- AND LASTLY, LEONARD JUBECK.-- QUIET ONE.
ALRIGHT, I'LL RUN THOSE NAMES ASAP. AN' LISTEN, TRY AN' GET A SET A PRINTS OFF THIS CHARACTER. WE GET A SOLID I.D. OF THIS GUY, BUST HIM, AND VOILA! YOU GOT YER STORY.
YEAH, THAT'S GOOD. I'LL DO MY BEST ON THAT.
AND I WAS THINKING MAYBE CHECK INTO THE HOTEL'S ASSISTANT MANAGER AS WELL. COLIN TALBOT. SEE IF HE'S GOT ANYTHING HELPFUL FOR US.
ALRIGHT...
YUP...
OKAY.
LATER, DAVE.

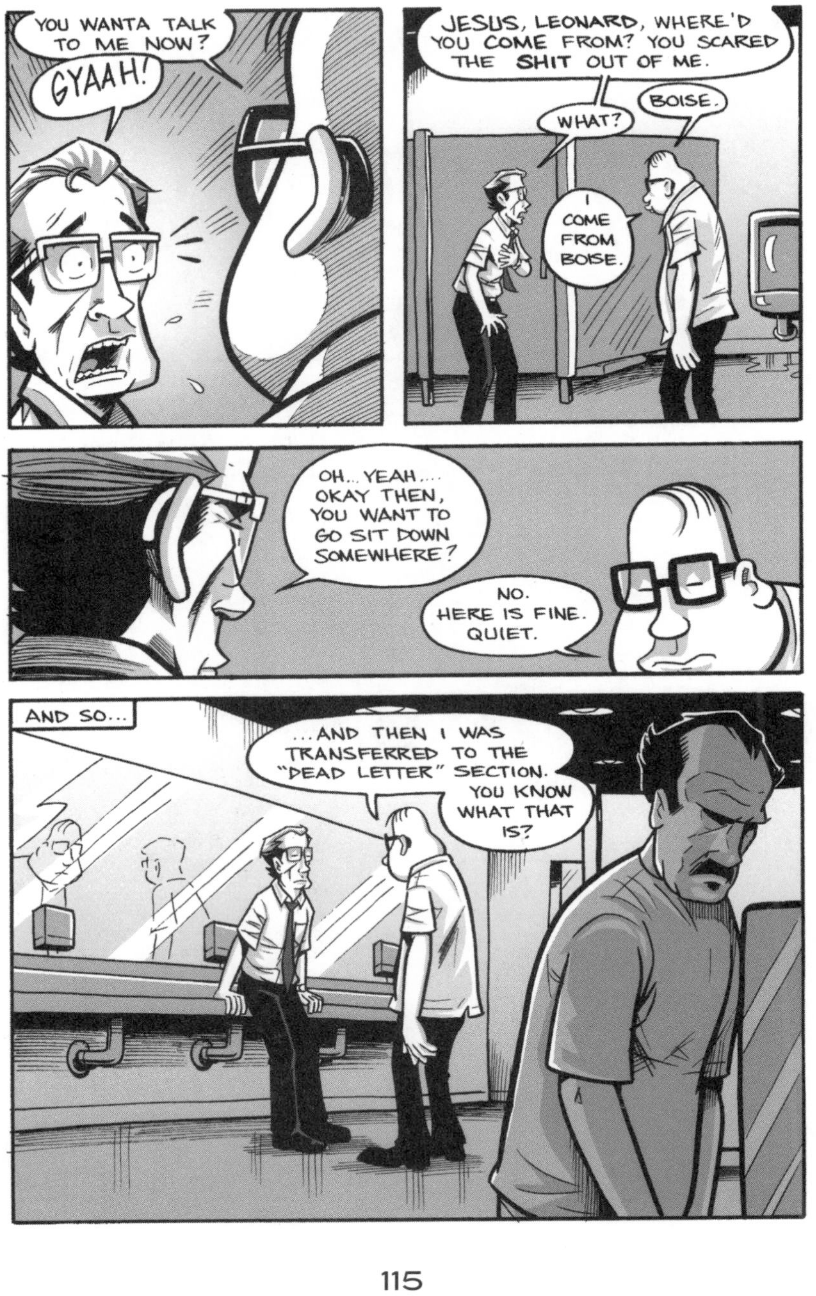
YOU WANTA TALK TO ME NOW?
GYAAH!
JESUS, LEONARD, WHERE'D YOU COME FROM? YOU SCARED THE SHIT OUT OF ME.
WHAT?
BOISE.
I COME FROM BOISE.
OH... YEAH.... OKAY THEN, YOU WANT TO GO SIT DOWN SOMEWHERE?
NO. HERE IS FINE. QUIET.
AND SO...
...AND THEN I WAS TRANSFERRED TO THE "DEAD LETTER" SECTION.
YOU KNOW WHAT THAT IS?

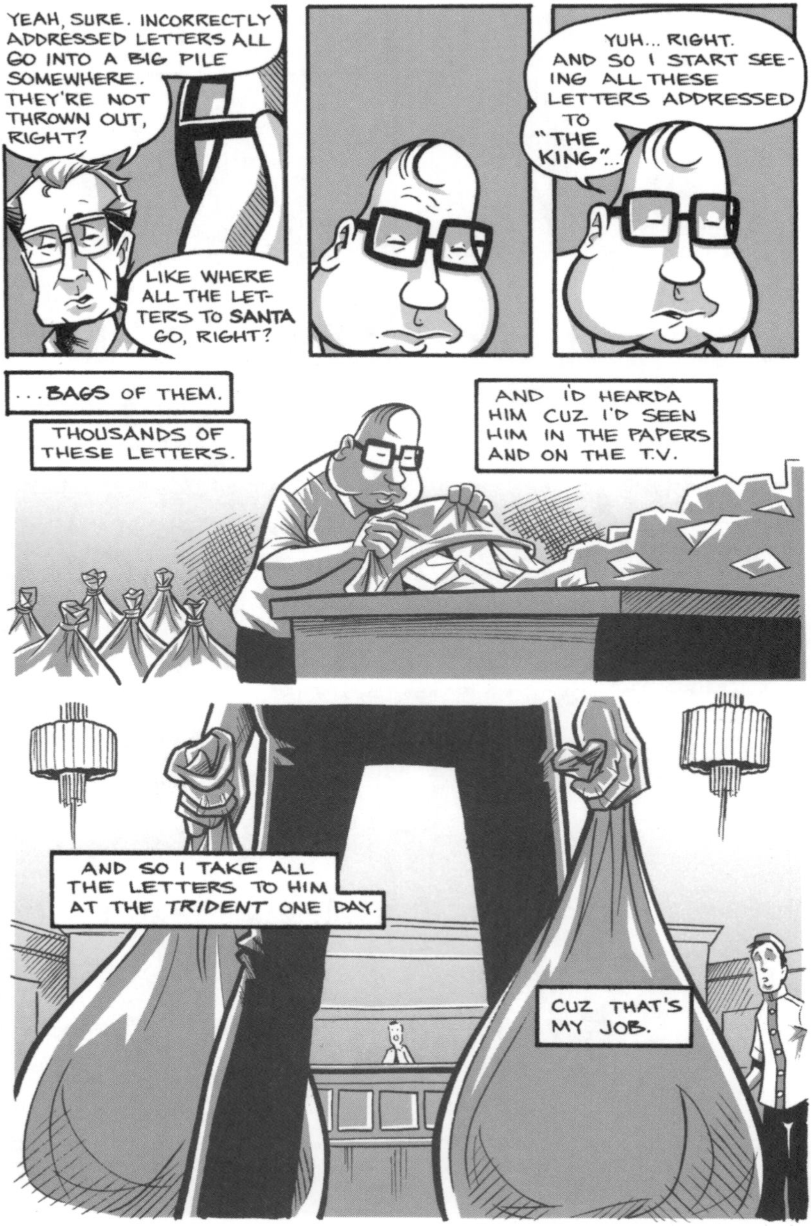
YEAH, SURE. INCORRECTLY ADDRESSED LETTERS ALL GO INTO A BIG PILE SOMEWHERE. THEY'RE NOT THROWN OUT, RIGHT?
LIKE WHERE ALL THE LETTERS TO SANTA GO, RIGHT?
YUH... RIGHT. AND SO I START SEEING ALL THESE LETTERS ADDRESSED TO "THE KING"...
...BAGS OF THEM.
THOUSANDS OF THESE LETTERS.
AND I'D HEARDA HIM CUZ I'D SEEN HIM IN THE PAPERS AND ON THE T.V.
AND SO I TAKE ALL THE LETTERS TO HIM AT THE TRIDENT ONE DAY.
CUZ THAT'S MY JOB.

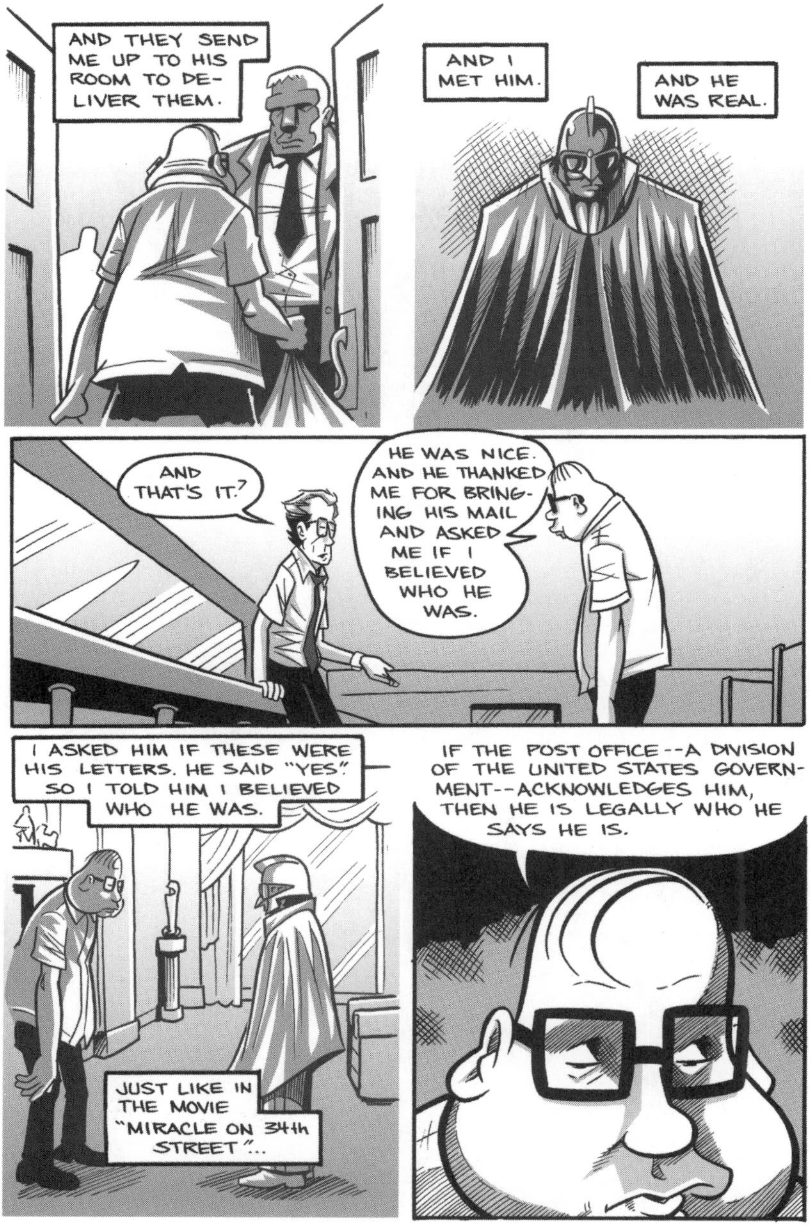
AND THEY SEND ME UP TO HIS ROOM TO DE-LIVER THEM.
AND I MET HIM.
AND HE WAS REAL.
AND THAT'S IT?
HE WAS NICE. AND HE THANKED ME FOR BRING-ING HIS MAIL AND ASKED ME IF I BELIEVED WHO HE WAS.
I ASKED HIM IF THESE WERE HIS LETTERS. HE SAID "YES." SO I TOLD HIM I BELIEVED WHO HE WAS.
JUST LIKE IN THE MOVIE "MIRACLE ON 34th STREET"...
IF THE POST OFFICE--A DIVISION OF THE UNITED STATES GOVERN-MENT--ACKNOWLEDGES HIM, THEN HE IS LEGALLY WHO HE SAYS HE IS.

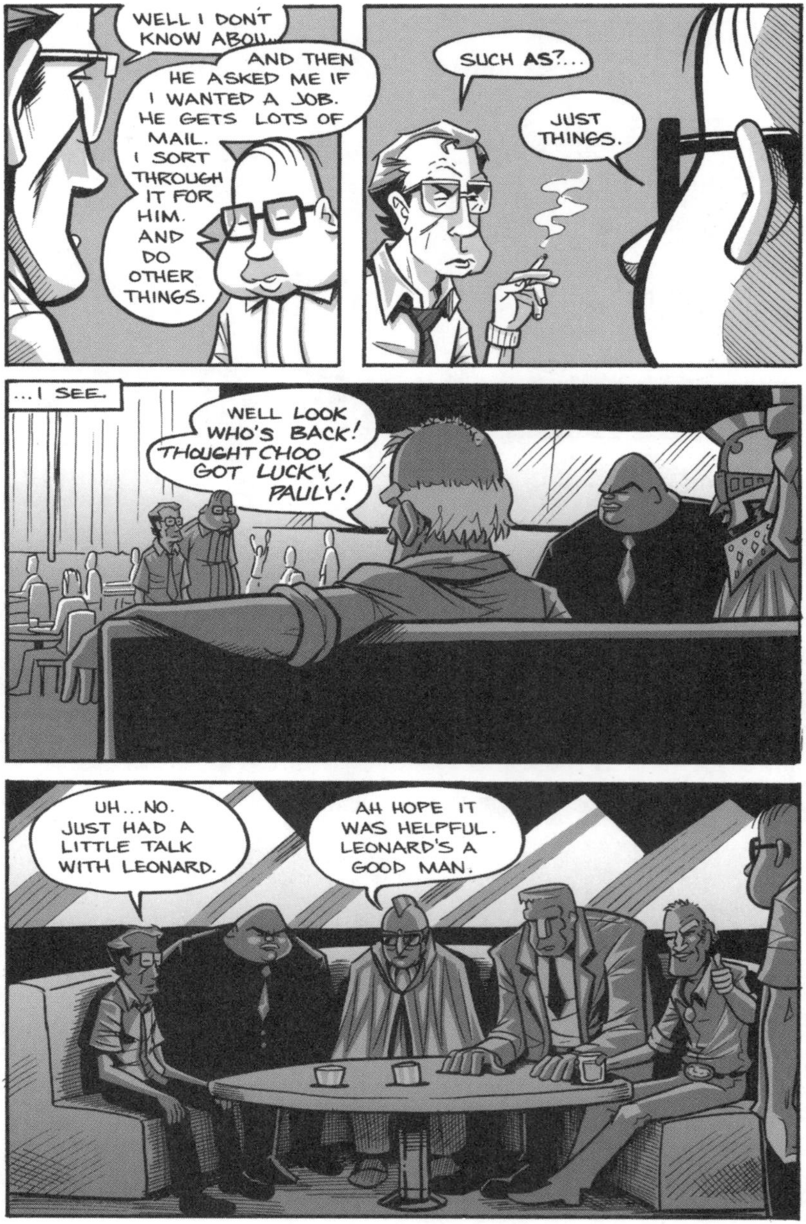
WELL I DON'T KNOW ABOU...
AND THEN HE ASKED ME IF I WANTED A JOB. HE GETS LOTS OF MAIL. I SORT THROUGH IT FOR HIM. AND DO OTHER THINGS.
SUCH AS?...
JUST THINGS.
...I SEE.
WELL LOOK WHO'S BACK! THOUGHT CHOO GOT LUCKY, PAULY!
UH...NO. JUST HAD A LITTLE TALK WITH LEONARD.
AH HOPE IT WAS HELPFUL. LEONARD'S A GOOD MAN.

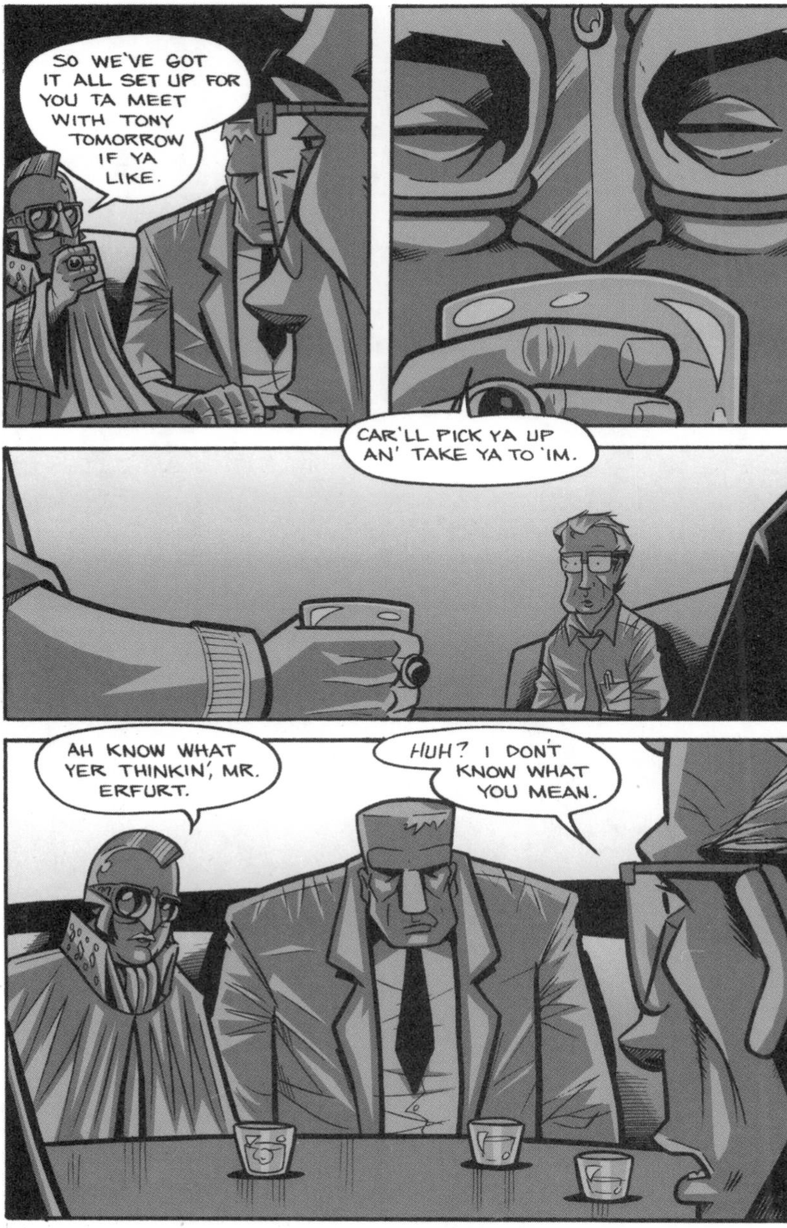
SO WE'VE GOT IT ALL SET UP FOR YOU TA MEET WITH TONY TOMORROW IF YA LIKE.
CAR'LL PICK YA UP AN' TAKE YA TO 'IM.
AH KNOW WHAT YER THINKIN', MR. ERFURT.
HUH? I DON'T KNOW WHAT YOU MEAN.

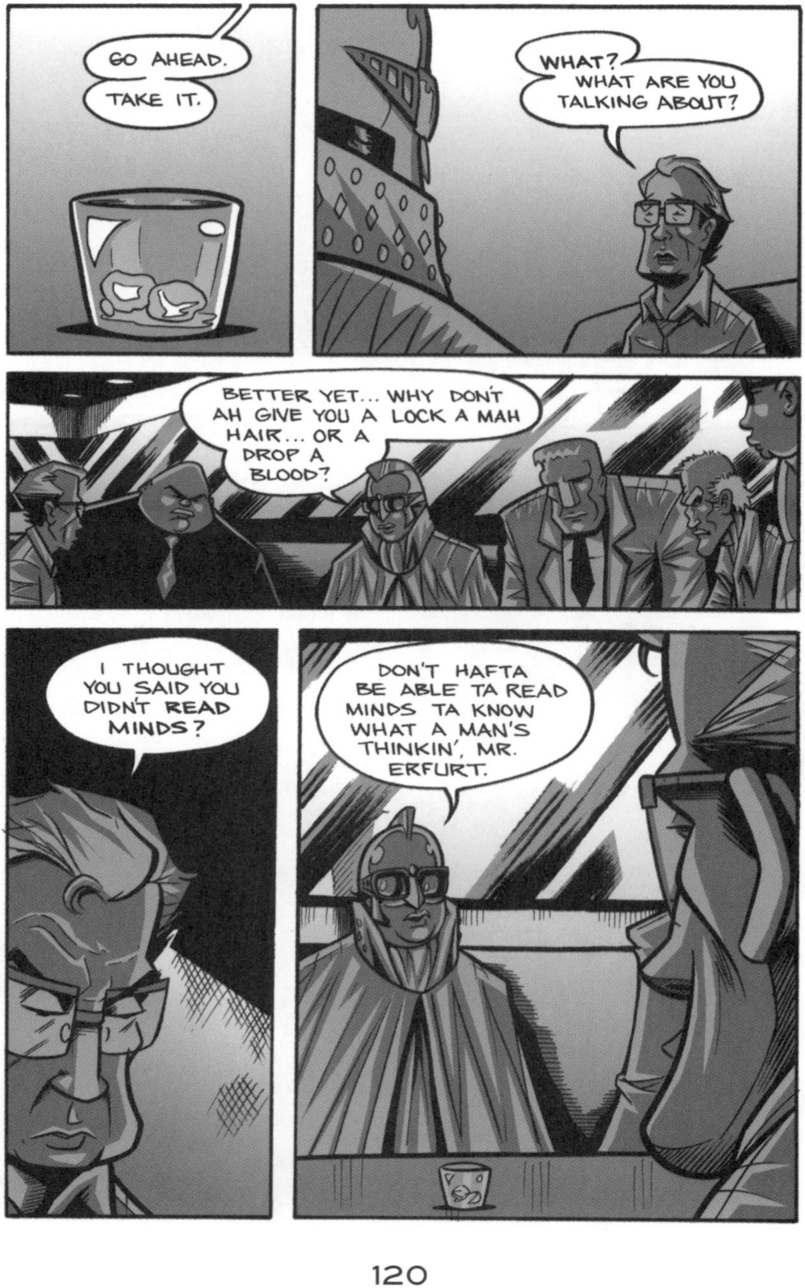
GO AHEAD.
TAKE IT.
WHAT? WHAT ARE YOU TALKING ABOUT?
BETTER YET... WHY DON'T AH GIVE YOU A LOCK A MAH HAIR... OR A DROP A BLOOD?
I THOUGHT YOU SAID YOU DIDN'T READ MINDS?
DON'T HAFTA BE ABLE TA READ MINDS TA KNOW WHAT A MAN'S THINKIN', MR. ERFURT.

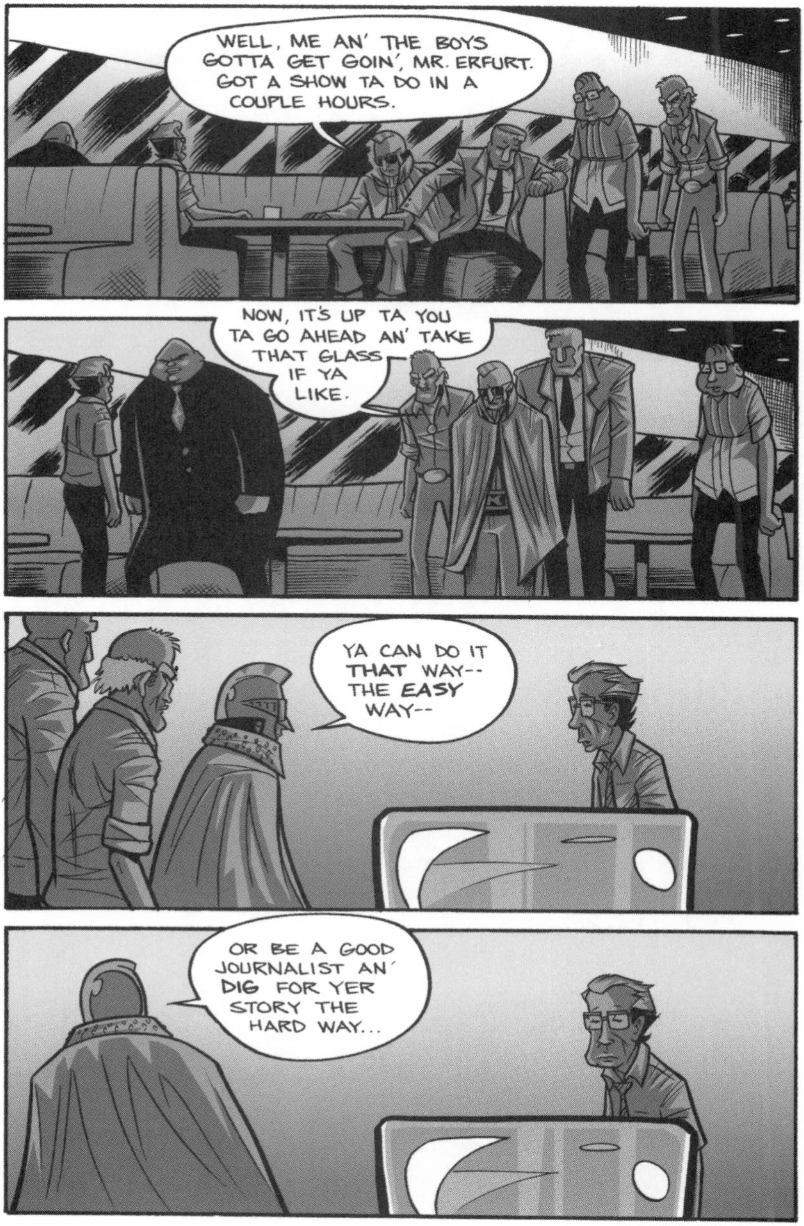
WELL, ME AN' THE BOYS GOTTA GET GOIN', MR. ERFURT. GOT A SHOW TA DO IN A COUPLE HOURS.
NOW, IT'S UP TA YOU TA GO AHEAD AN' TAKE THAT GLASS IF YA LIKE.
YA CAN DO IT THAT WAY-- THE EASY WAY--
OR BE A GOOD JOURNALIST AN' DIG FOR YER STORY THE HARD WAY...

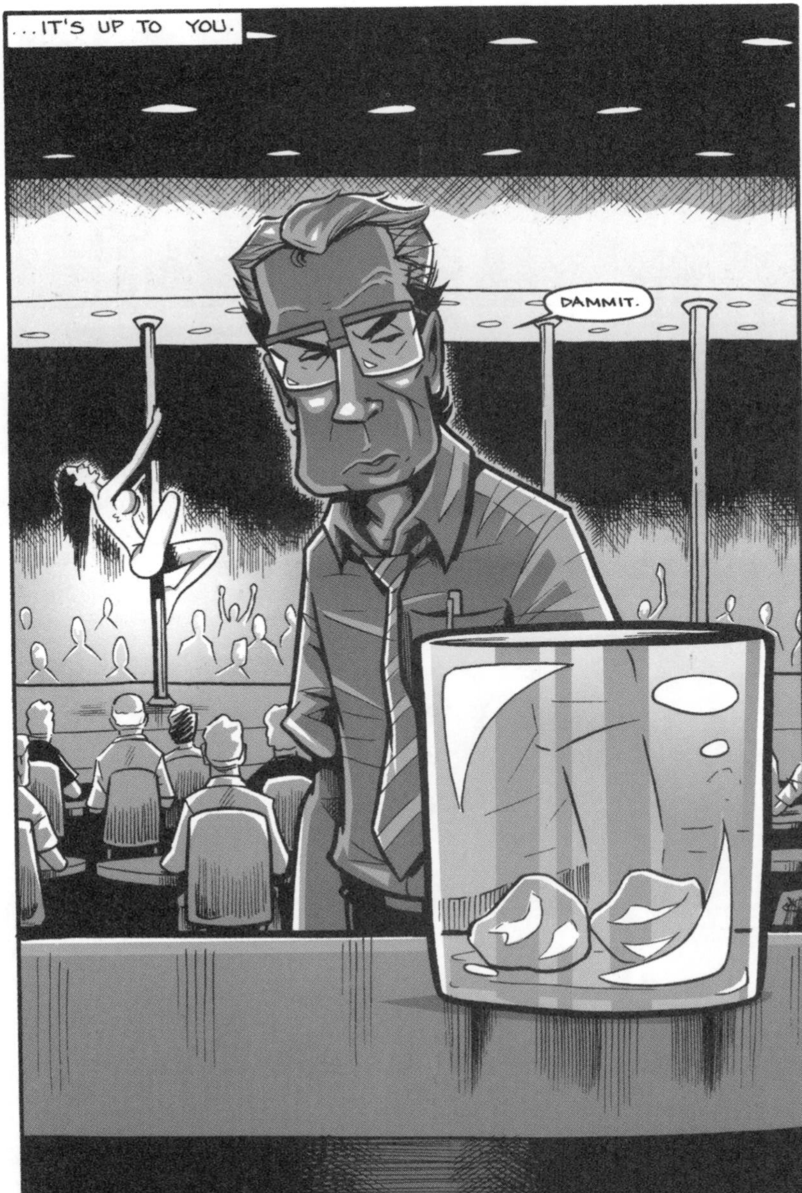
...IT'S UP TO YOU.
DAMMIT.

"BEFORE ELVIS THERE WAS NOTHING."

— JOHN LENNON

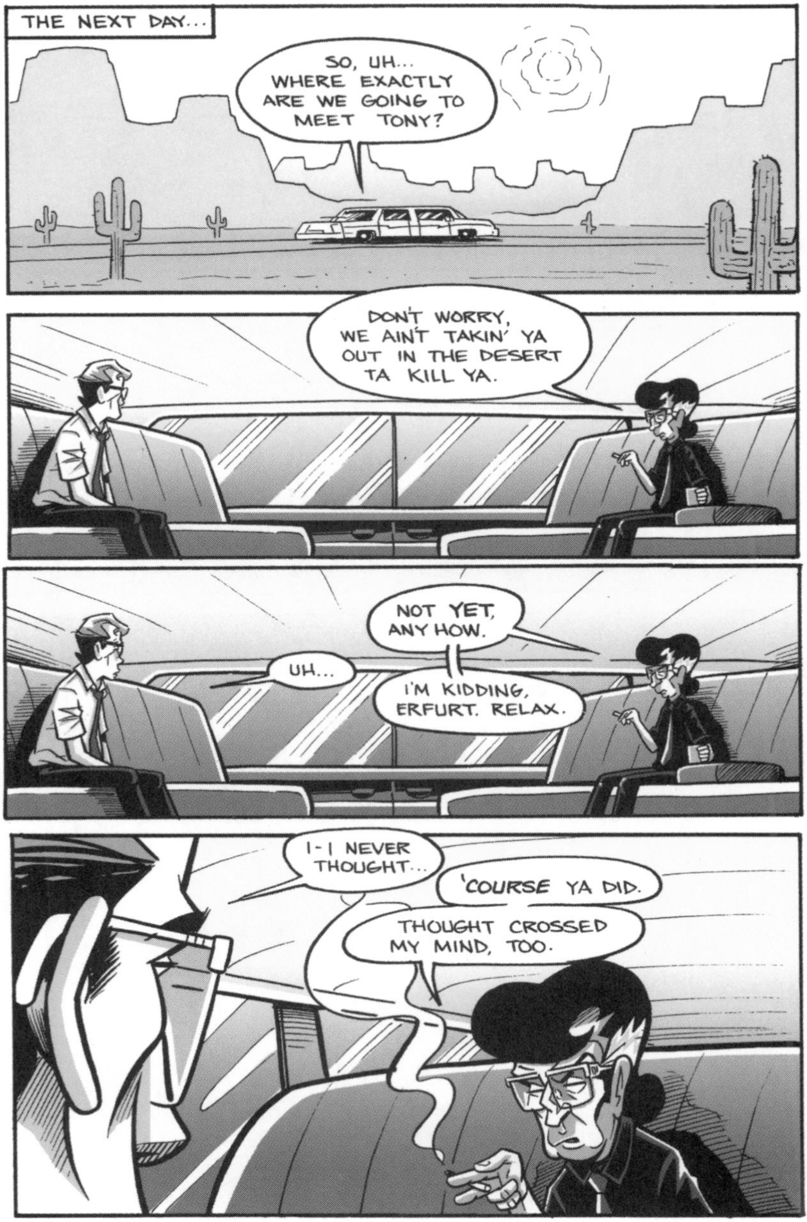
THE NEXT DAY...
SO, UH... WHERE EXACTLY ARE WE GOING TO MEET TONY?
DON'T WORRY, WE AIN'T TAKIN' YA OUT IN THE DESERT TA KILL YA.
NOT YET, ANY HOW.
UH...
I'M KIDDING, ERFURT. RELAX.
I-I NEVER THOUGHT...
'COURSE YA DID.
THOUGHT CROSSED MY MIND, TOO.

BUT TONY DON'T STAY AT THE HOTEL WITH THE REST OF US. GOT HIS OWN PLACE.
LOOK OUT THE WINDOW.
JESUS!
NOT EXACTLY.

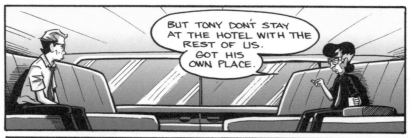

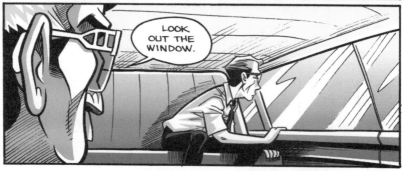

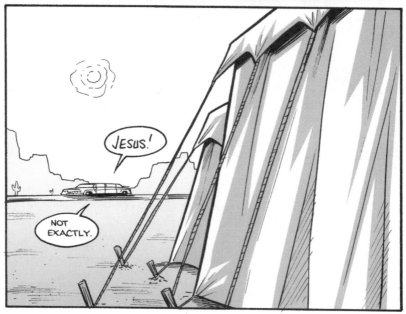

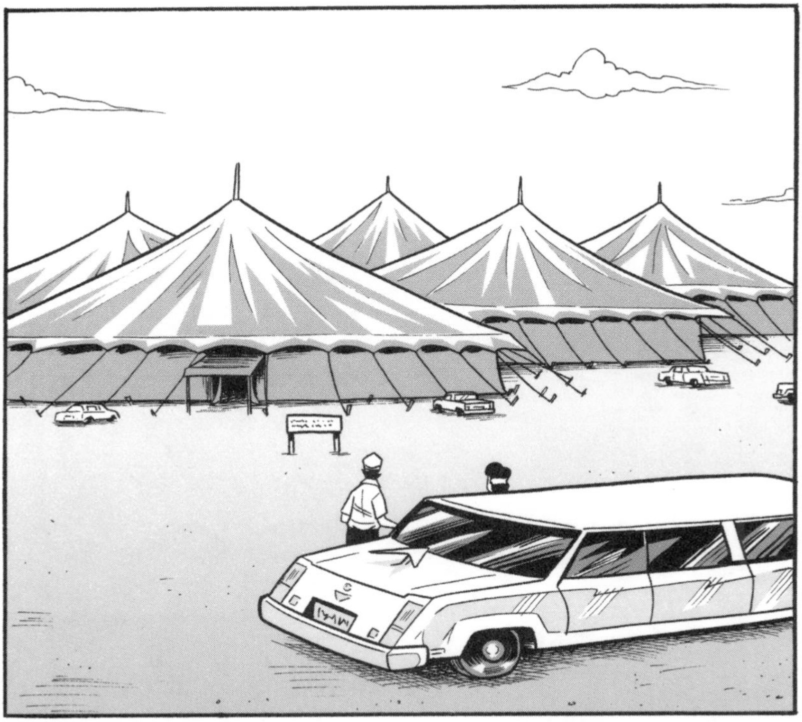

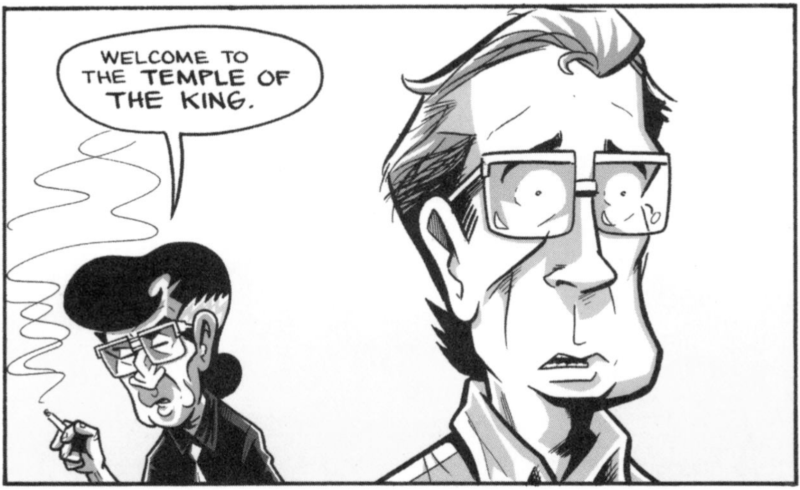
WELCOME TO THE TEMPLE OF THE KING.

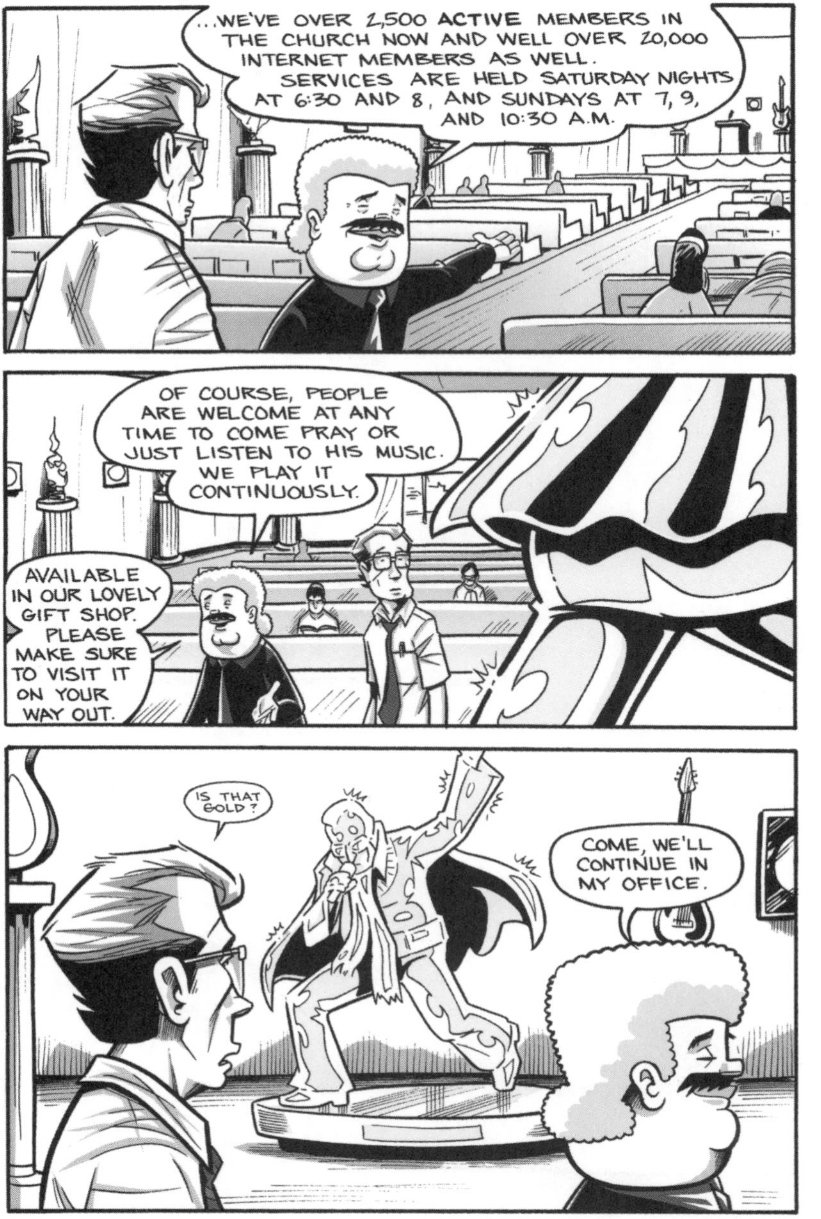
...WE'VE OVER 2,500 ACTIVE MEMBERS IN THE CHURCH NOW AND WELL OVER 20,000 INTERNET MEMBERS AS WELL. SERVICES ARE HELD SATURDAY NIGHTS AT 6:30 AND 8, AND SUNDAYS AT 7, 9, AND 10:30 A.M.
OF COURSE, PEOPLE ARE WELCOME AT ANY TIME TO COME PRAY OR JUST LISTEN TO HIS MUSIC. WE PLAY IT CONTINUOUSLY.
AVAILABLE IN OUR LOVELY GIFT SHOP. PLEASE MAKE SURE TO VISIT IT ON YOUR WAY OUT.
IS THAT GOLD?
COME, WE'LL CONTINUE IN MY OFFICE.

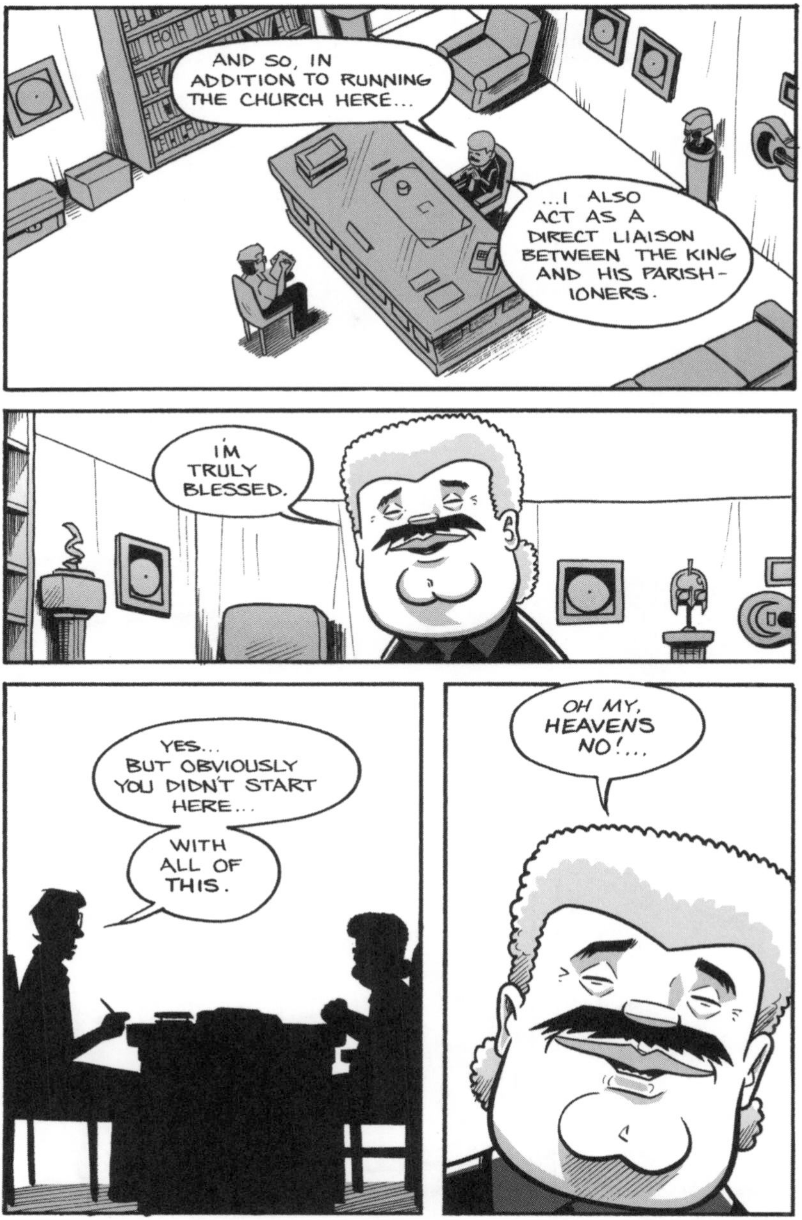
AND SO, IN ADDITION TO RUNNING THE CHURCH HERE...
...I ALSO ACT AS A DIRECT LIAISON BETWEEN THE KING AND HIS PARISH-IONERS.
I'M TRULY BLESSED.
YES... BUT OBVIOUSLY YOU DIDN'T START HERE...
WITH ALL OF THIS.
OH MY, HEAVENS NO!...

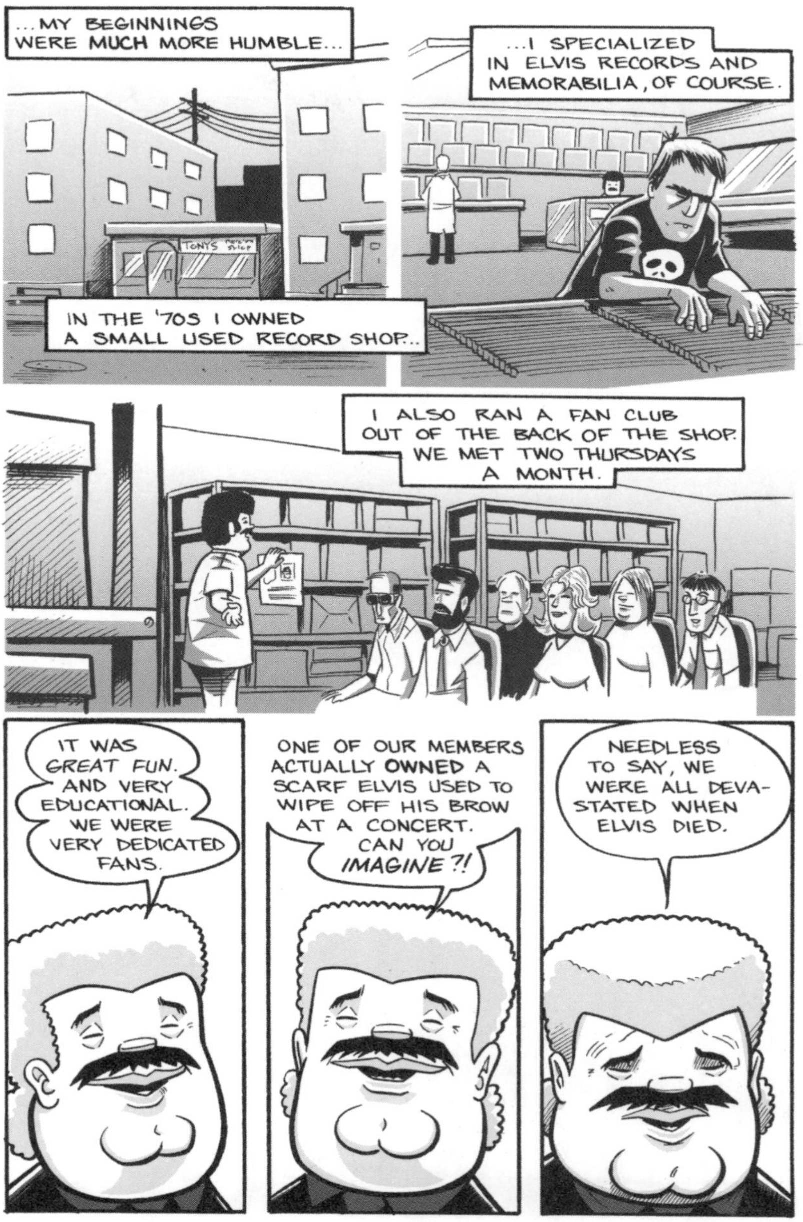

...MY BEGINNINGS WERE MUCH MORE HUMBLE...
IN THE '70S I OWNED A SMALL USED RECORD SHOP...
TONY'S
...I SPECIALIZED IN ELVIS RECORDS AND MEMORABILIA, OF COURSE.
I ALSO RAN A FAN CLUB OUT OF THE BACK OF THE SHOP. WE MET TWO THURSDAYS A MONTH.
IT WAS GREAT FUN. AND VERY EDUCATIONAL. WE WERE VERY DEDICATED FANS.
ONE OF OUR MEMBERS ACTUALLY OWNED A SCARF ELVIS USED TO WIPE OFF HIS BROW AT A CONCERT. CAN YOU IMAGINE?!
NEEDLESS TO SAY, WE WERE ALL DEVA-STATED WHEN ELVIS DIED.

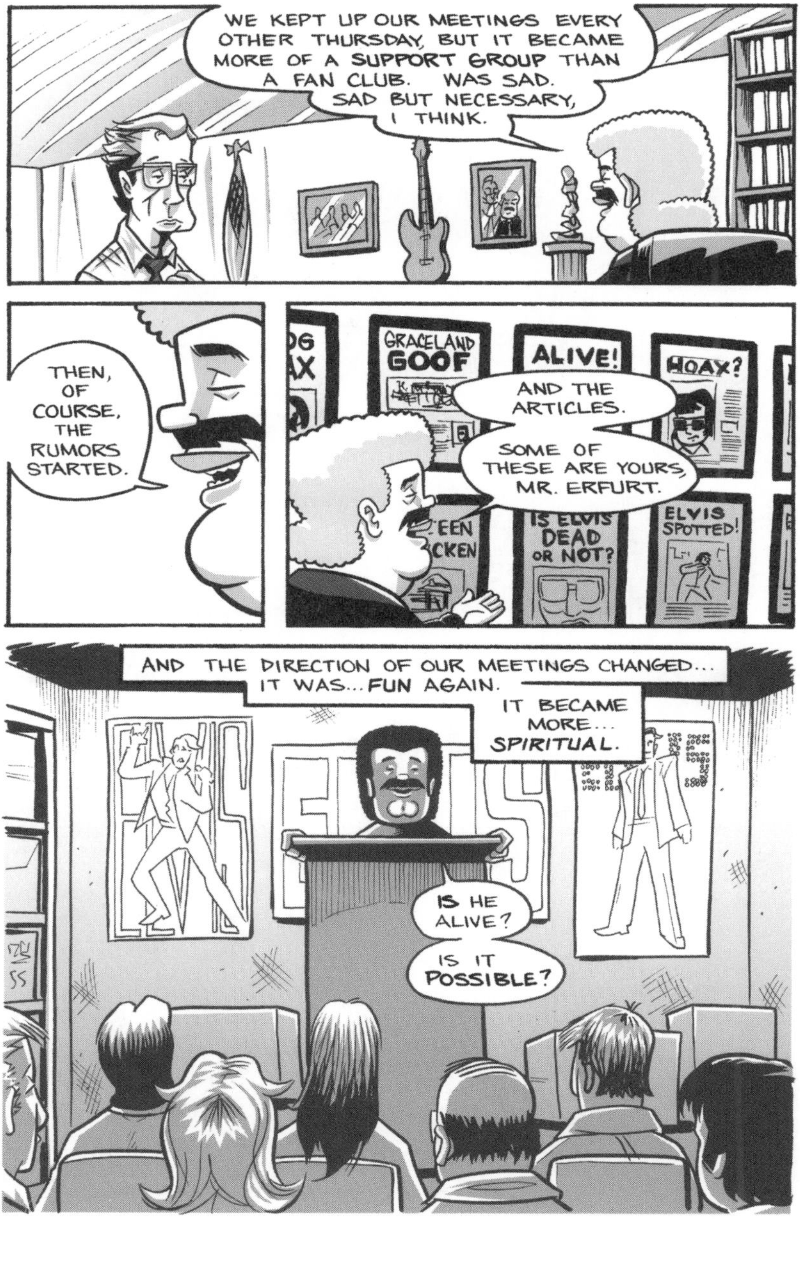
WE KEPT UP OUR MEETINGS EVERY OTHER THURSDAY, BUT IT BECAME MORE OF A SUPPORT GROUP THAN A FAN CLUB. WAS SAD. SAD BUT NECESSARY, I THINK.
THEN, OF COURSE, THE RUMORS STARTED.
GRACELAND GOOF
ALIVE!
HOAX?
AND THE ARTICLES.
SOME OF THESE ARE YOURS, MR. ERFURT.
IS ELVIS DEAD OR NOT?
ELVIS SPOTTED!
AND THE DIRECTION OF OUR MEETINGS CHANGED... IT WAS... FUN AGAIN.
IT BECAME MORE... SPIRITUAL.
IS HE ALIVE?
IS IT POSSIBLE?

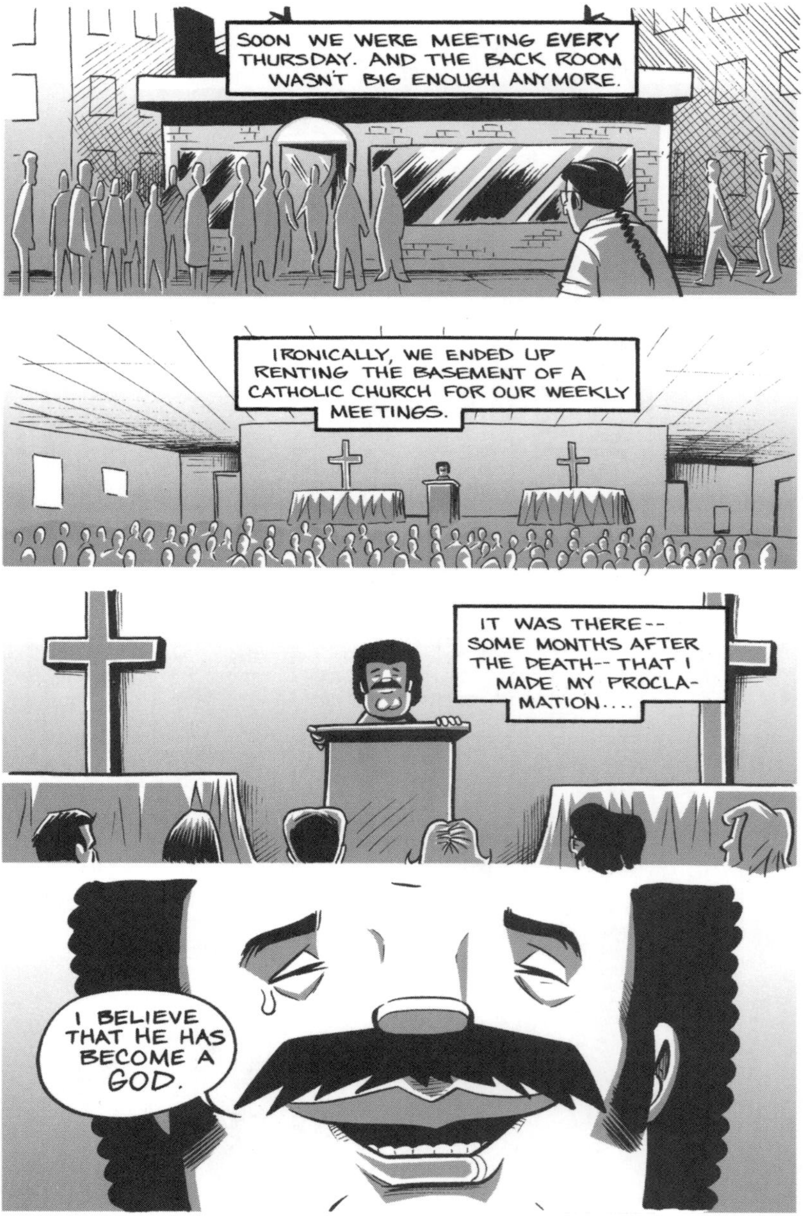
SOON WE WERE MEETING EVERY THURSDAY. AND THE BACK ROOM WASN'T BIG ENOUGH ANYMORE.
IRONICALLY, WE ENDED UP RENTING THE BASEMENT OF A CATHOLIC CHURCH FOR OUR WEEKLY MEETINGS.
IT WAS THERE-- SOME MONTHS AFTER THE DEATH-- THAT I MADE MY PROCLA-MATION....
I BELIEVE THAT HE HAS BECOME A GOD.

WE BECAME THE FIRST OFFICIAL CHURCH OF ELVIS PRESLEY.

WHAT IN THE NAME OF JESUS?!!

WELCOME TO THE FIRST CHURCH OF ELVIS PRESLEY

SERVICES THU. 7-8

'COURSE WHEN THE CHURCH FOUND OUT THEY WEREN'T TOO HAPPY.

WE FLOUNDERED AROUND FROM PLACE TO PLACE FOR A WHILE AFTER THAT... BOWLING ALLEYS, LEGION HALLS, EVEN A FUNERAL HOME--TOO CREEPY--'TIL WE DECIDED TO GET A TENT AND TAKE OUR CHURCH ON THE ROAD.

WE'D MOSTLY SET UP IN FARMERS' FIELDS FOR A FEW WEEKS AT A TIME AND THEN MOVE ON.

REV. STAVROPOULOS

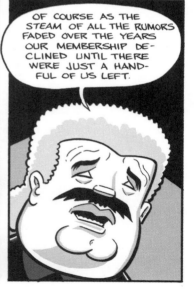

OF COURSE AS THE STEAM OF ALL THE RUMORS FADED OVER THE YEARS OUR MEMBERSHIP DE- CLINED UNTIL THERE WERE JUST A HAND- FUL OF US LEFT.

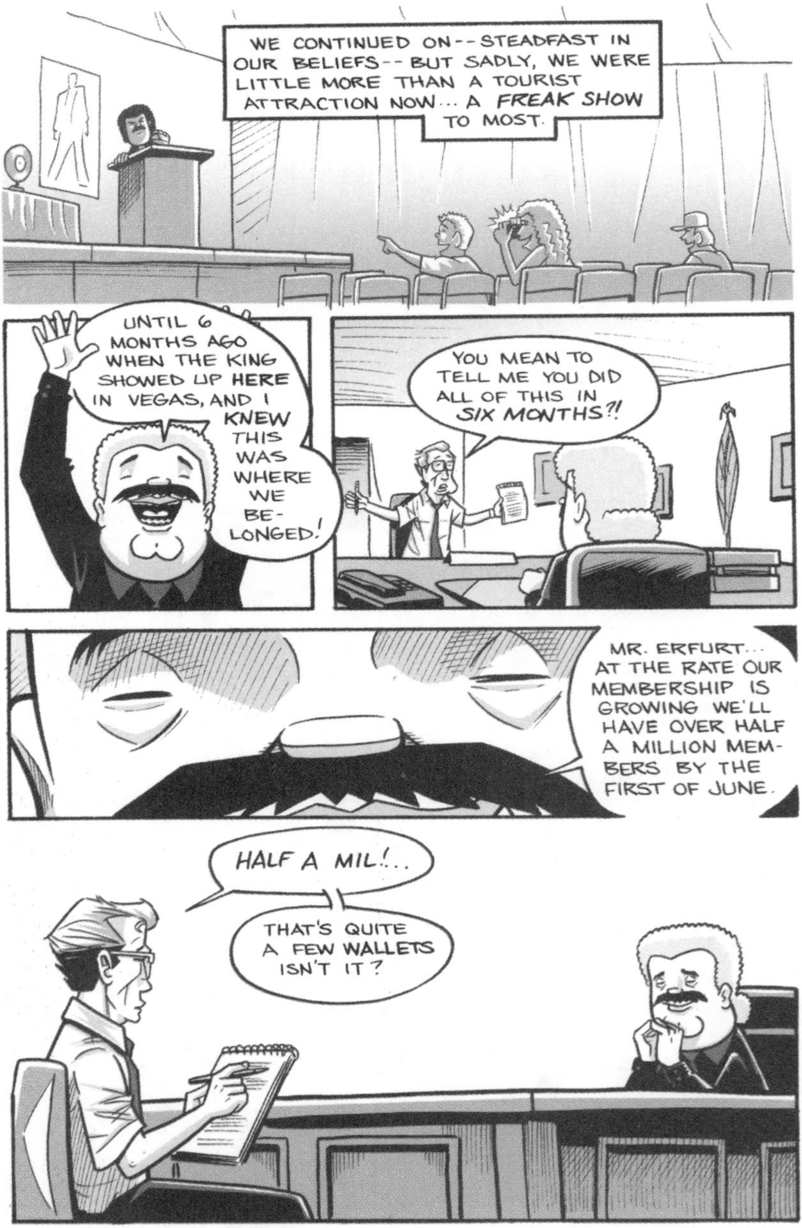
WE CONTINUED ON--STEADFAST IN OUR BELIEFS--BUT SADLY, WE WERE LITTLE MORE THAN A TOURIST ATTRACTION NOW... A FREAK SHOW TO MOST.
UNTIL 6 MONTHS AGO WHEN THE KING SHOWED UP HERE IN VEGAS, AND I KNEW THIS WAS WHERE WE BE-LONGED!
YOU MEAN TO TELL ME YOU DID ALL OF THIS IN SIX MONTHS?!
MR. ERFURT... AT THE RATE OUR MEMBERSHIP IS GROWING WE'LL HAVE OVER HALF A MILLION MEM-BERS BY THE FIRST OF JUNE.
HALF A MIL!...
THAT'S QUITE A FEW WALLETS ISN'T IT?

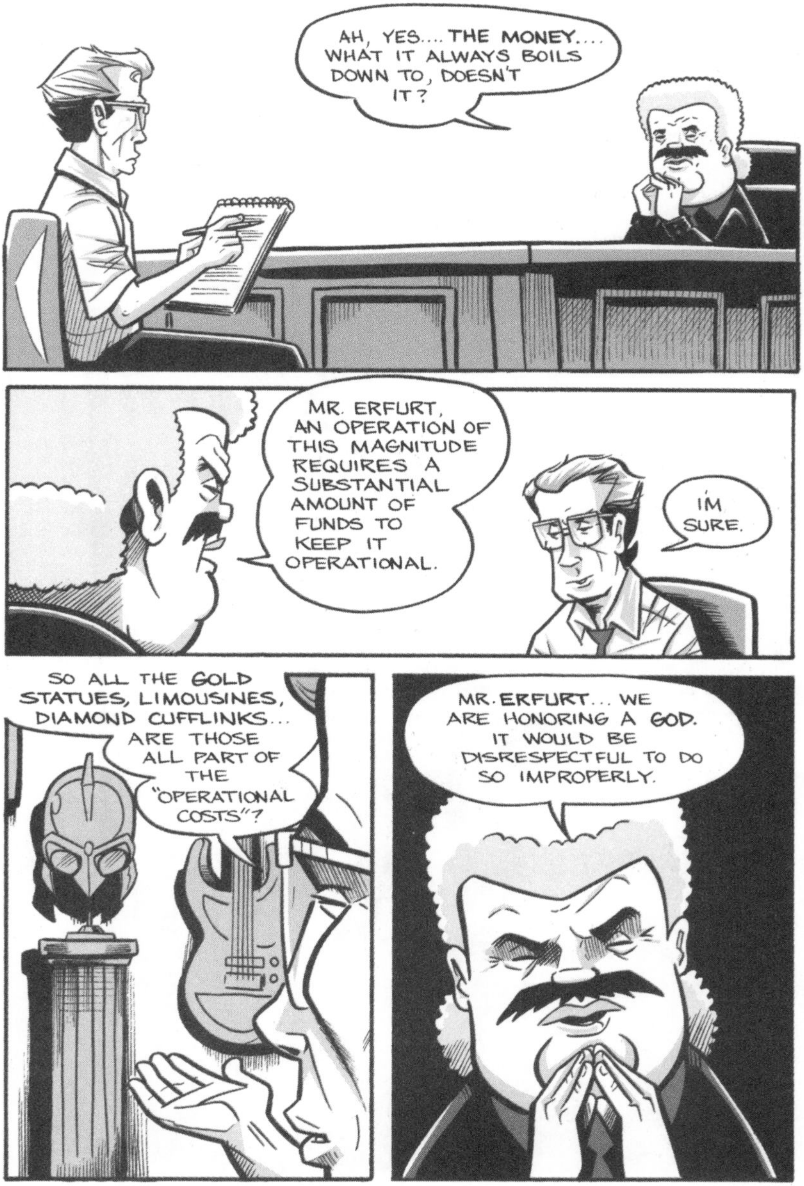
AH, YES.... THE MONEY.... WHAT IT ALWAYS BOILS DOWN TO, DOESN'T IT?
MR. ERFURT, AN OPERATION OF THIS MAGNITUDE REQUIRES A SUBSTANTIAL AMOUNT OF FUNDS TO KEEP IT OPERATIONAL.
I'M SURE.
SO ALL THE GOLD STATUES, LIMOUSINES, DIAMOND CUFFLINKS... ARE THOSE ALL PART OF THE "OPERATIONAL COSTS"?
MR. ERFURT... WE ARE HONORING A GOD. IT WOULD BE DISRESPECTFUL TO DO SO IMPROPERLY.

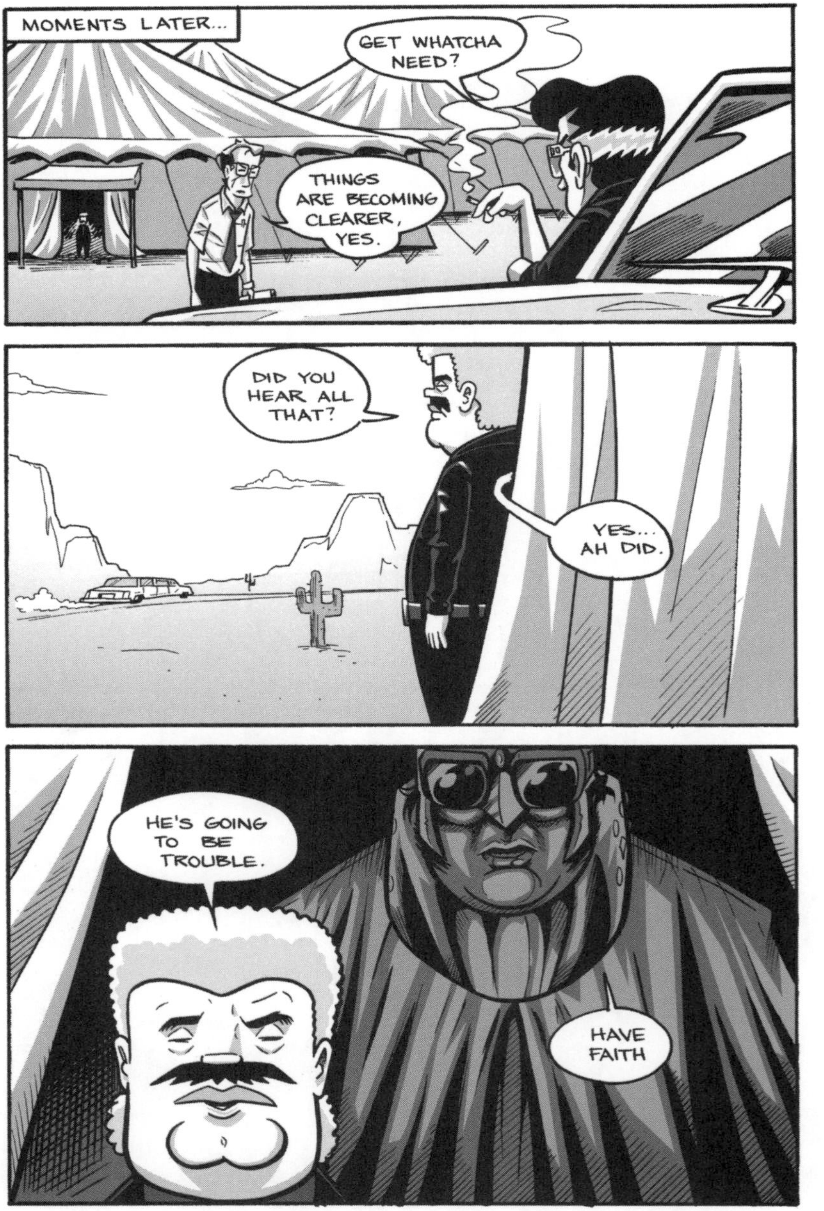
MOMENTS LATER...
GET WHATCHA NEED?
THINGS ARE BECOMING CLEARER, YES.
DID YOU HEAR ALL THAT?
YES... AH DID.
HE'S GOING TO BE TROUBLE.
HAVE FAITH

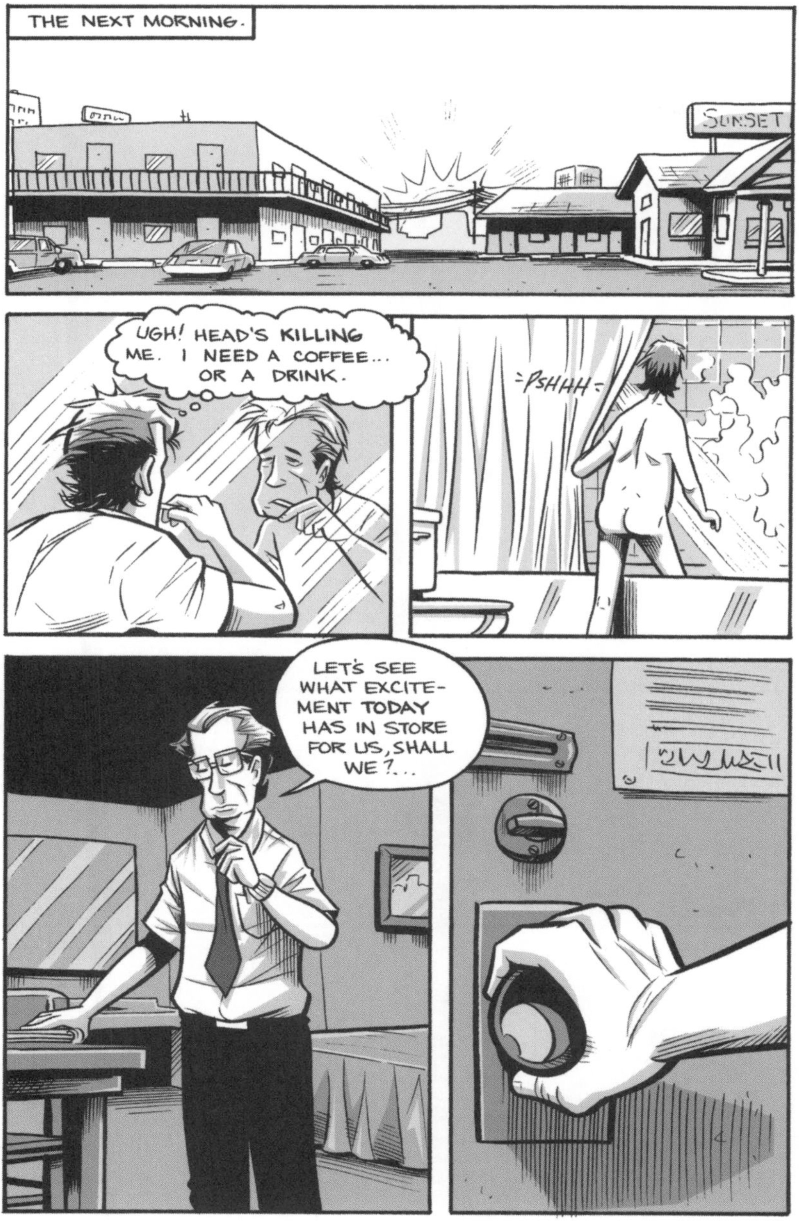
THE NEXT MORNING.
SUNSET
UGH! HEAD'S KILLING ME. I NEED A COFFEE... OR A DRINK.
PSHHH
LET'S SEE WHAT EXCITEMENT TODAY HAS IN STORE FOR US, SHALL WE?...

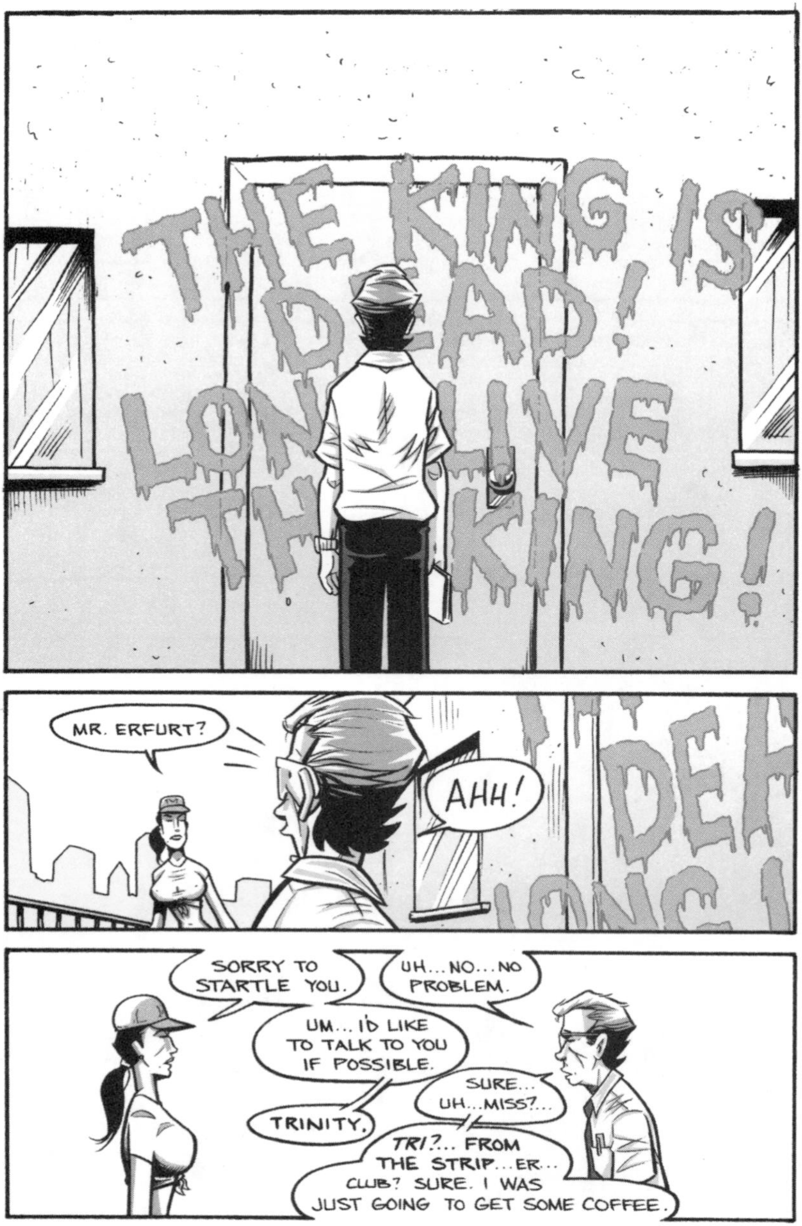
THE KING IS DEAD! LONG LIVE THE KING!
MR. ERFURT?
AHH!
SORRY TO STARTLE YOU.
UH... NO... NO PROBLEM.
UM... I'D LIKE TO TALK TO YOU IF POSSIBLE.
SURE... UH... MISS?...
TRINITY.
TRI?... FROM THE STRIP... ER... CLUB? SURE. I WAS JUST GOING TO GET SOME COFFEE.

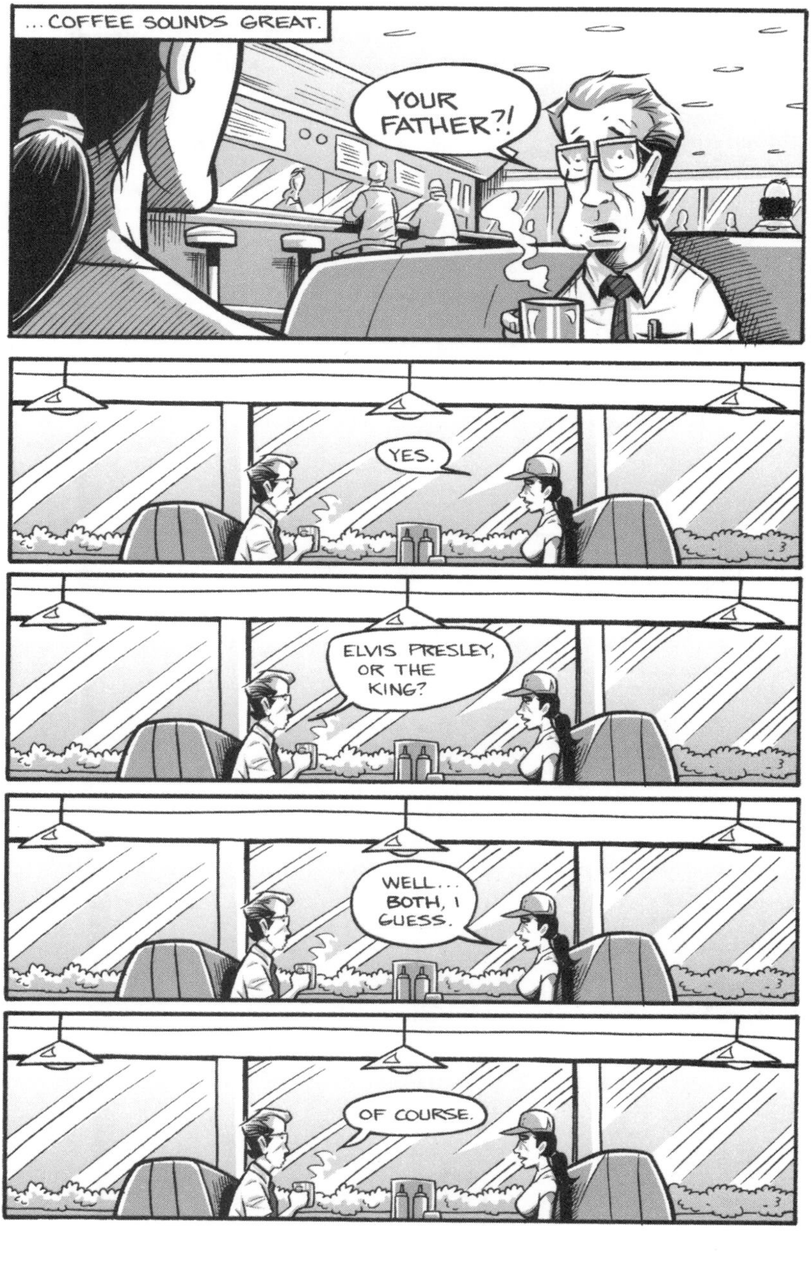
...COFFEE SOUNDS GREAT.
YOUR FATHER?!
YES.
ELVIS PRESLEY, OR THE KING?
WELL... BOTH, I GUESS.
OF COURSE.

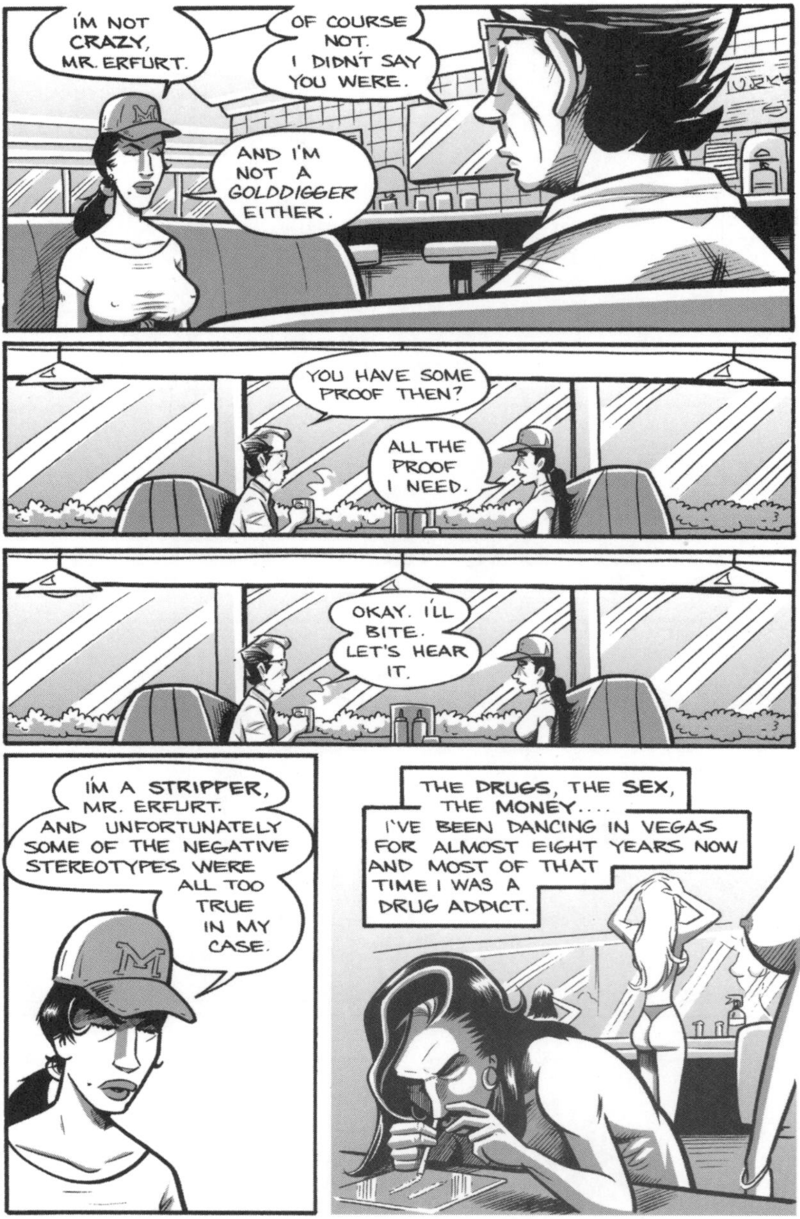
I'M NOT CRAZY, MR. ERFURT.
OF COURSE NOT. I DIDN'T SAY YOU WERE.
AND I'M NOT A GOLDDIGGER EITHER.
YOU HAVE SOME PROOF THEN?
ALL THE PROOF I NEED.
OKAY. I'LL BITE. LET'S HEAR IT.
I'M A STRIPPER, MR. ERFURT. AND UNFORTUNATELY SOME OF THE NEGATIVE STEREOTYPES WERE ALL TOO TRUE IN MY CASE.
THE DRUGS, THE SEX, THE MONEY....
I'VE BEEN DANCING IN VEGAS FOR ALMOST EIGHT YEARS NOW AND MOST OF THAT TIME I WAS A DRUG ADDICT.

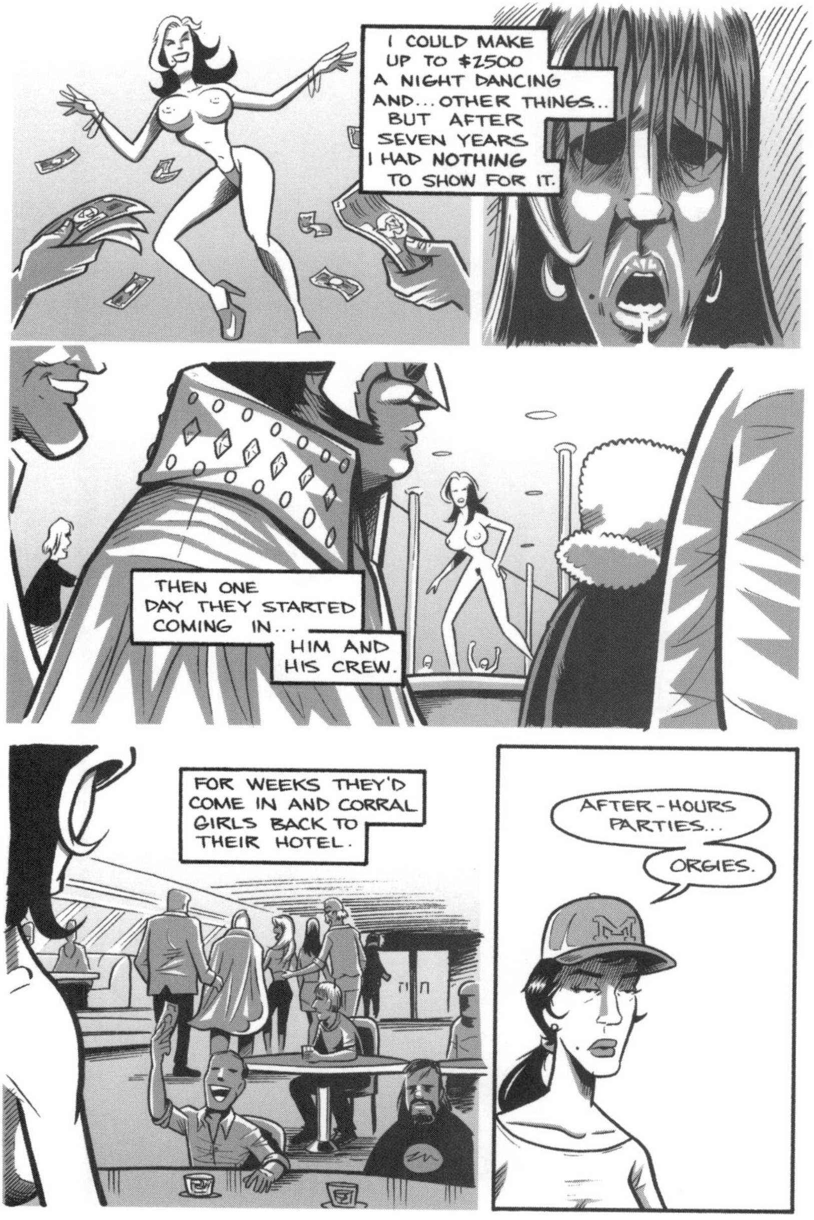
I COULD MAKE UP TO $2500 A NIGHT DANCING AND... OTHER THINGS... BUT AFTER SEVEN YEARS I HAD NOTHING TO SHOW FOR IT.
THEN ONE DAY THEY STARTED COMING IN...
HIM AND HIS CREW.
FOR WEEKS THEY'D COME IN AND CORRAL GIRLS BACK TO THEIR HOTEL.
AFTER-HOURS PARTIES...
ORGIES.

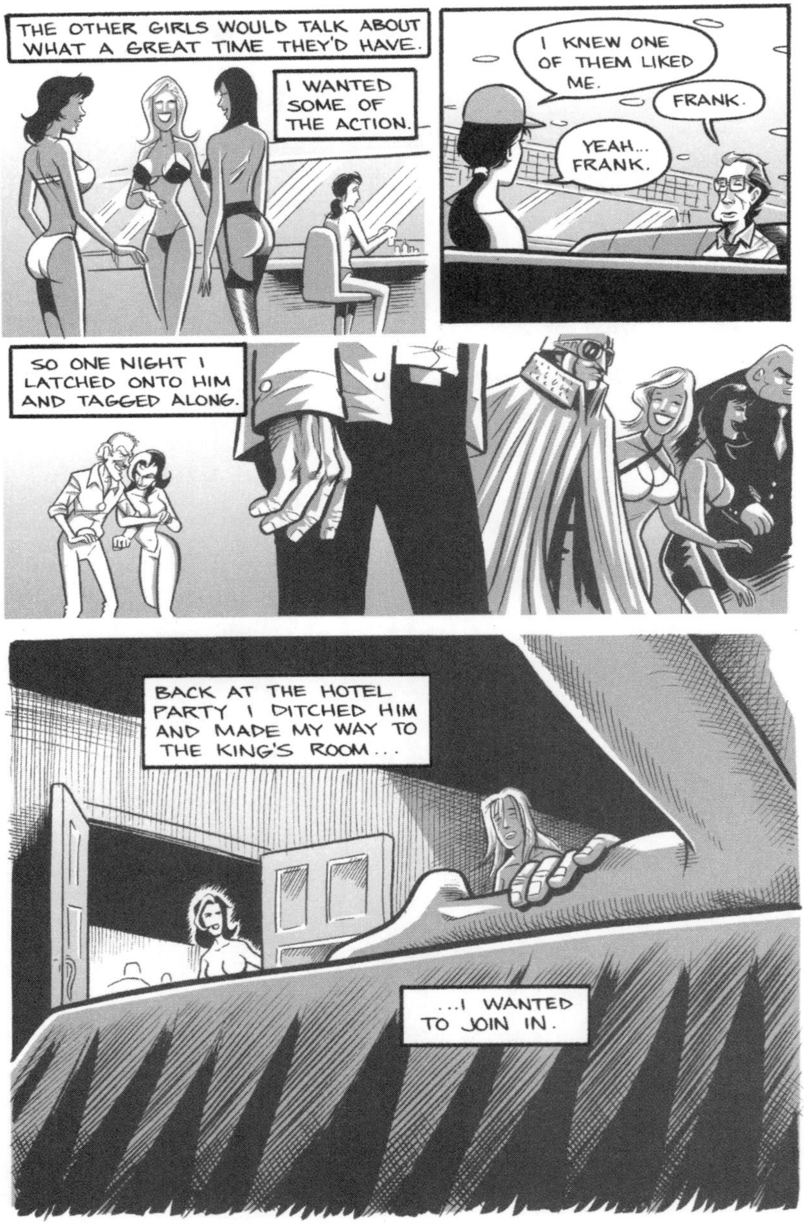
THE OTHER GIRLS WOULD TALK ABOUT WHAT A GREAT TIME THEY'D HAVE.
I WANTED SOME OF THE ACTION.
I KNEW ONE OF THEM LIKED ME.
FRANK.
YEAH... FRANK.
SO ONE NIGHT I LATCHED ONTO HIM AND TAGGED ALONG.
BACK AT THE HOTEL PARTY I DITCHED HIM AND MADE MY WAY TO THE KING'S ROOM...
...I WANTED TO JOIN IN.

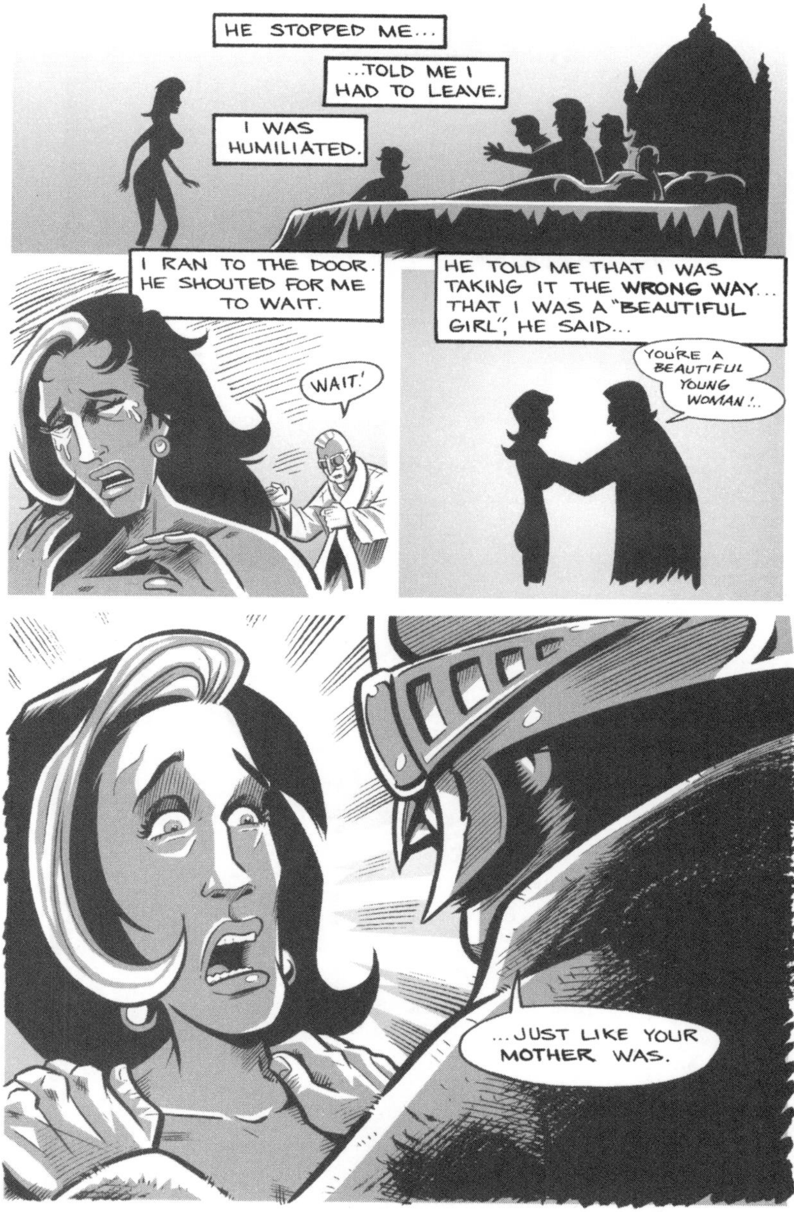
HE STOPPED ME...
...TOLD ME I HAD TO LEAVE.
I WAS HUMILIATED.
I RAN TO THE DOOR. HE SHOUTED FOR ME TO WAIT.
WAIT!
HE TOLD ME THAT I WAS TAKING IT THE WRONG WAY... THAT I WAS A "BEAUTIFUL GIRL", HE SAID...
YOU'RE A BEAUTIFUL YOUNG WOMAN!..
...JUST LIKE YOUR MOTHER WAS.

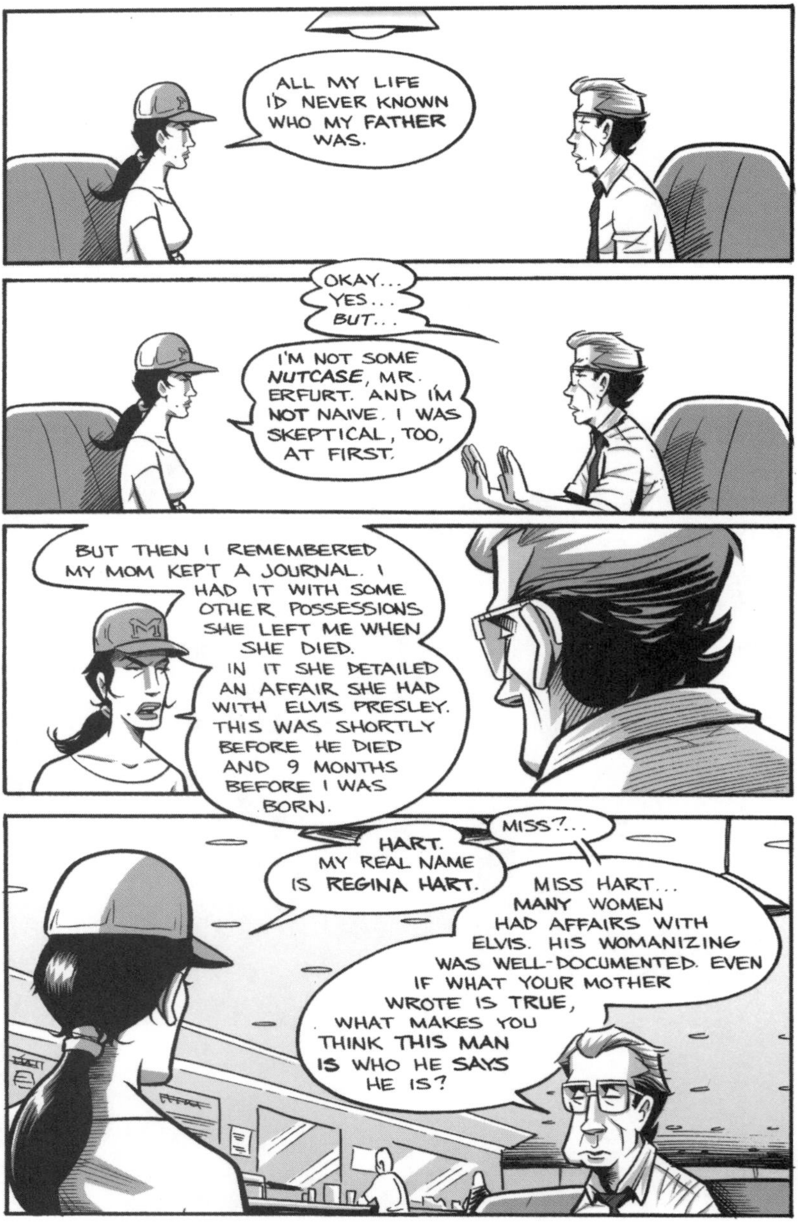
ALL MY LIFE I'D NEVER KNOWN WHO MY FATHER WAS.
OKAY... YES... BUT...
I'M NOT SOME NUTCASE, MR. ERFURT. AND I'M NOT NAIVE. I WAS SKEPTICAL, TOO, AT FIRST.
BUT THEN I REMEMBERED MY MOM KEPT A JOURNAL. I HAD IT WITH SOME OTHER POSSESSIONS SHE LEFT ME WHEN SHE DIED. IN IT SHE DETAILED AN AFFAIR SHE HAD WITH ELVIS PRESLEY. THIS WAS SHORTLY BEFORE HE DIED AND 9 MONTHS BEFORE I WAS BORN.
MISS?...
HART. MY REAL NAME IS REGINA HART.
MISS HART... MANY WOMEN HAD AFFAIRS WITH ELVIS. HIS WOMANIZING WAS WELL-DOCUMENTED. EVEN IF WHAT YOUR MOTHER WROTE IS TRUE, WHAT MAKES YOU THINK THIS MAN IS WHO HE SAYS HE IS?

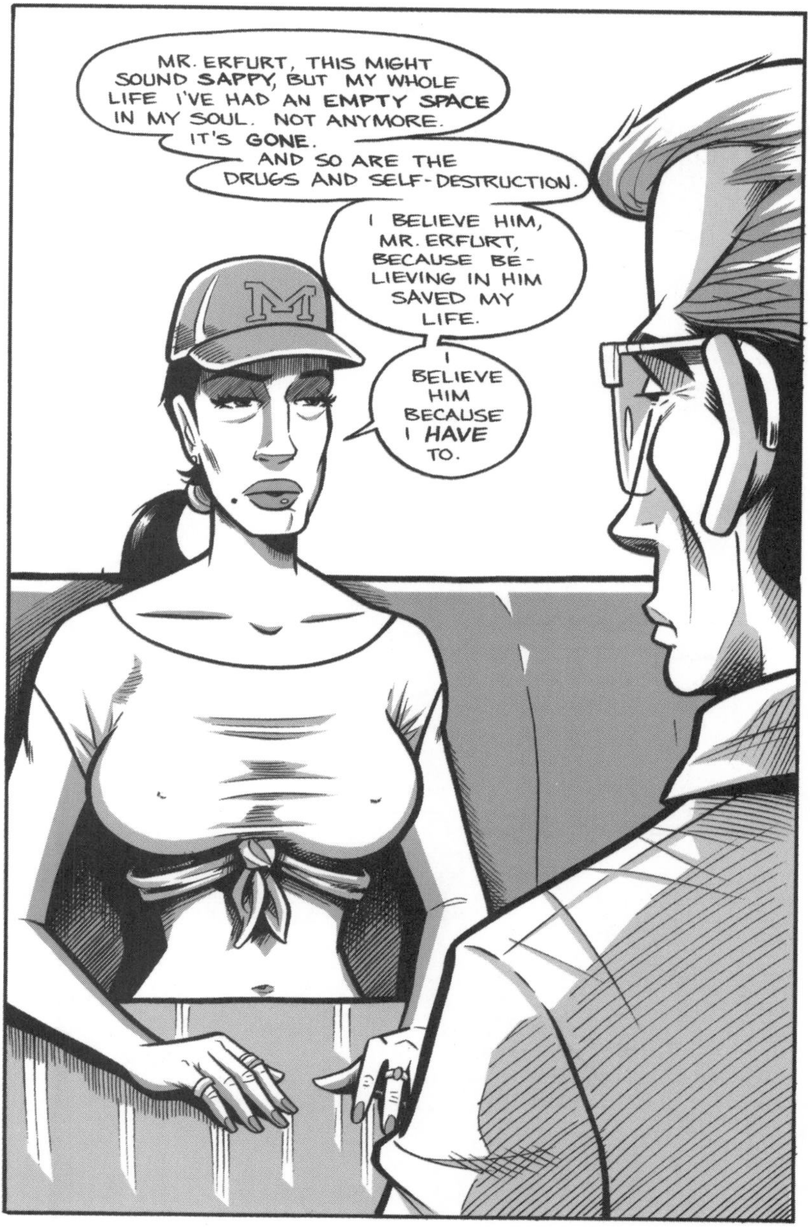
MR. ERFURT, THIS MIGHT SOUND SAPPY, BUT MY WHOLE LIFE I'VE HAD AN EMPTY SPACE IN MY SOUL. NOT ANYMORE. IT'S GONE.
AND SO ARE THE DRUGS AND SELF-DESTRUCTION.
I BELIEVE HIM, MR. ERFURT, BECAUSE BE-LIEVING IN HIM SAVED MY LIFE.
I BELIEVE HIM BECAUSE I HAVE TO.

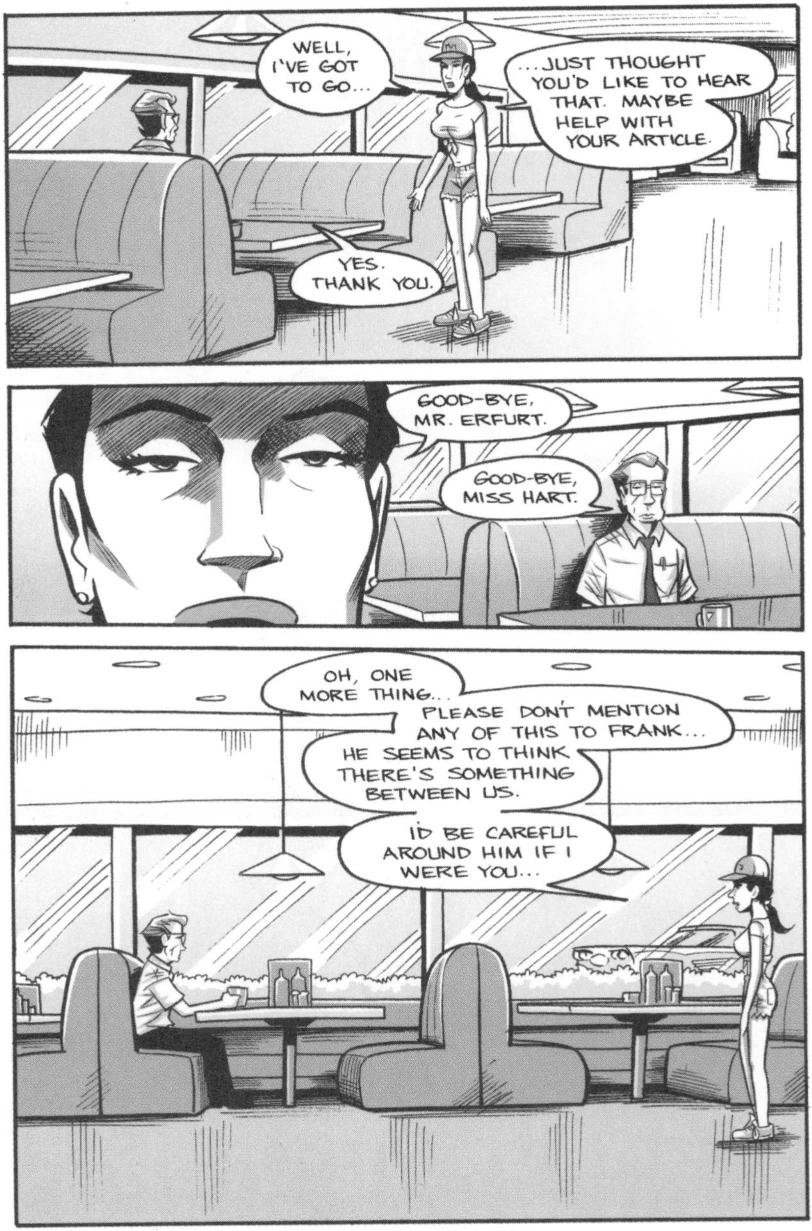
WELL, I'VE GOT TO GO...
...JUST THOUGHT YOU'D LIKE TO HEAR THAT. MAYBE HELP WITH YOUR ARTICLE.
YES. THANK YOU.
GOOD-BYE, MR. ERFURT.
GOOD-BYE, MISS HART.
OH, ONE MORE THING...
PLEASE DON'T MENTION ANY OF THIS TO FRANK...
HE SEEMS TO THINK THERE'S SOMETHING BETWEEN US.
I'D BE CAREFUL AROUND HIM IF I WERE YOU...

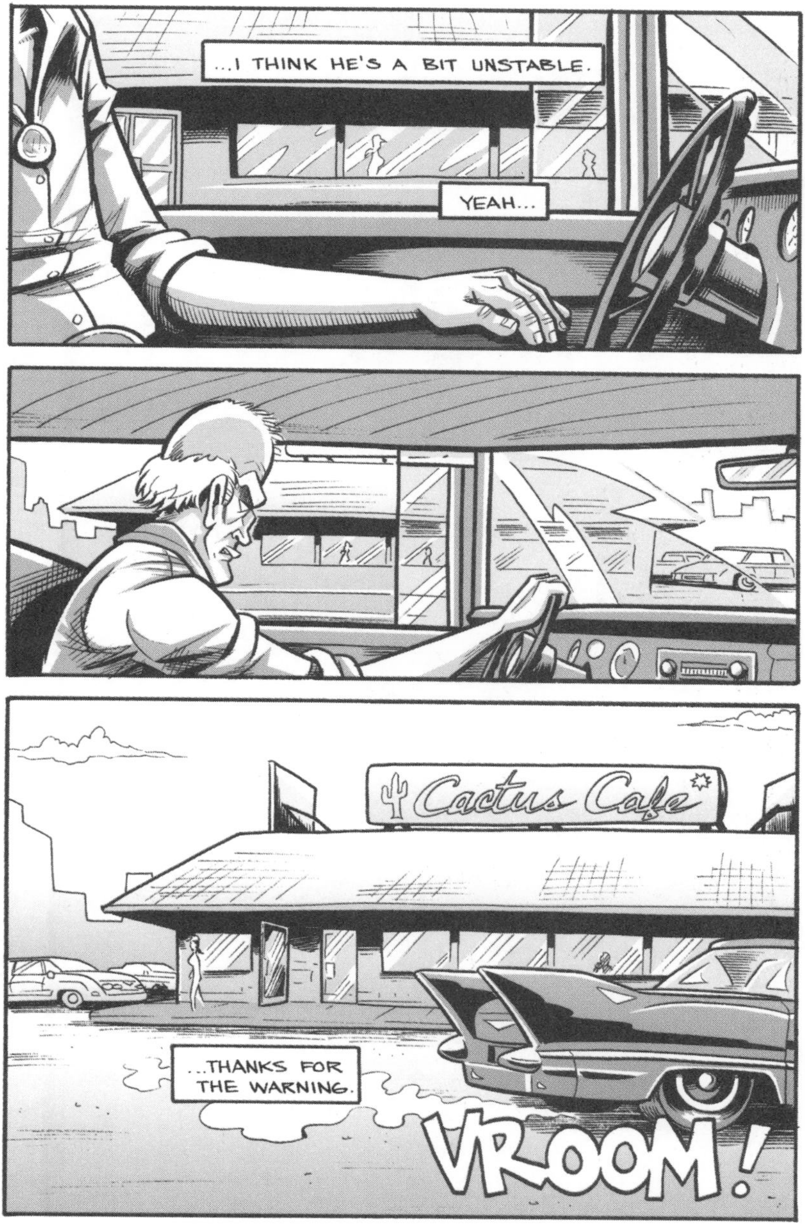
...I THINK HE'S A BIT UNSTABLE.
YEAH...
Cactus Cafe
...THANKS FOR THE WARNING.
VROOM!

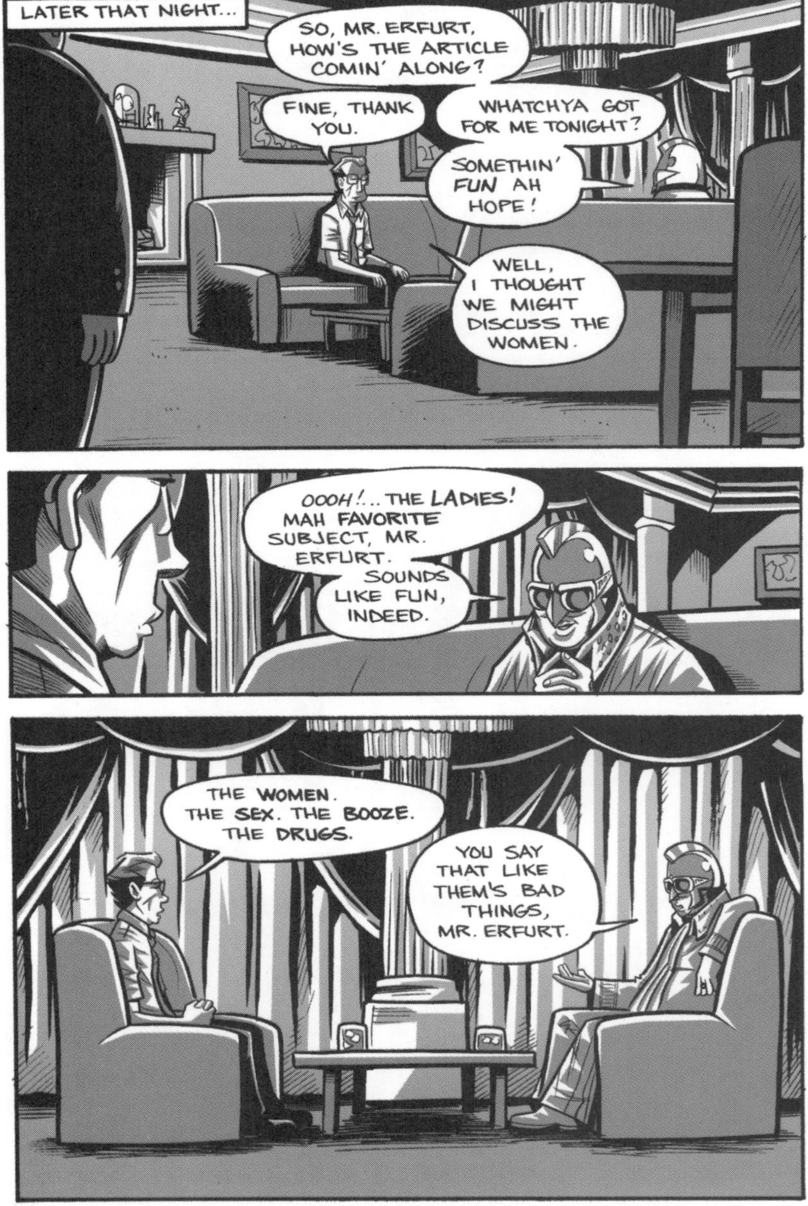
LATER THAT NIGHT...
SO, MR. ERFURT, HOW'S THE ARTICLE COMIN' ALONG?
FINE, THANK YOU.
WHATCHYA GOT FOR ME TONIGHT?
SOMETHIN' FUN AH HOPE!
WELL, I THOUGHT WE MIGHT DISCUSS THE WOMEN.
OOOH!... THE LADIES! MAH FAVORITE SUBJECT, MR. ERFURT.
SOUNDS LIKE FUN, INDEED.
THE WOMEN. THE SEX. THE BOOZE. THE DRUGS.
YOU SAY THAT LIKE THEM'S BAD THINGS, MR. ERFURT.

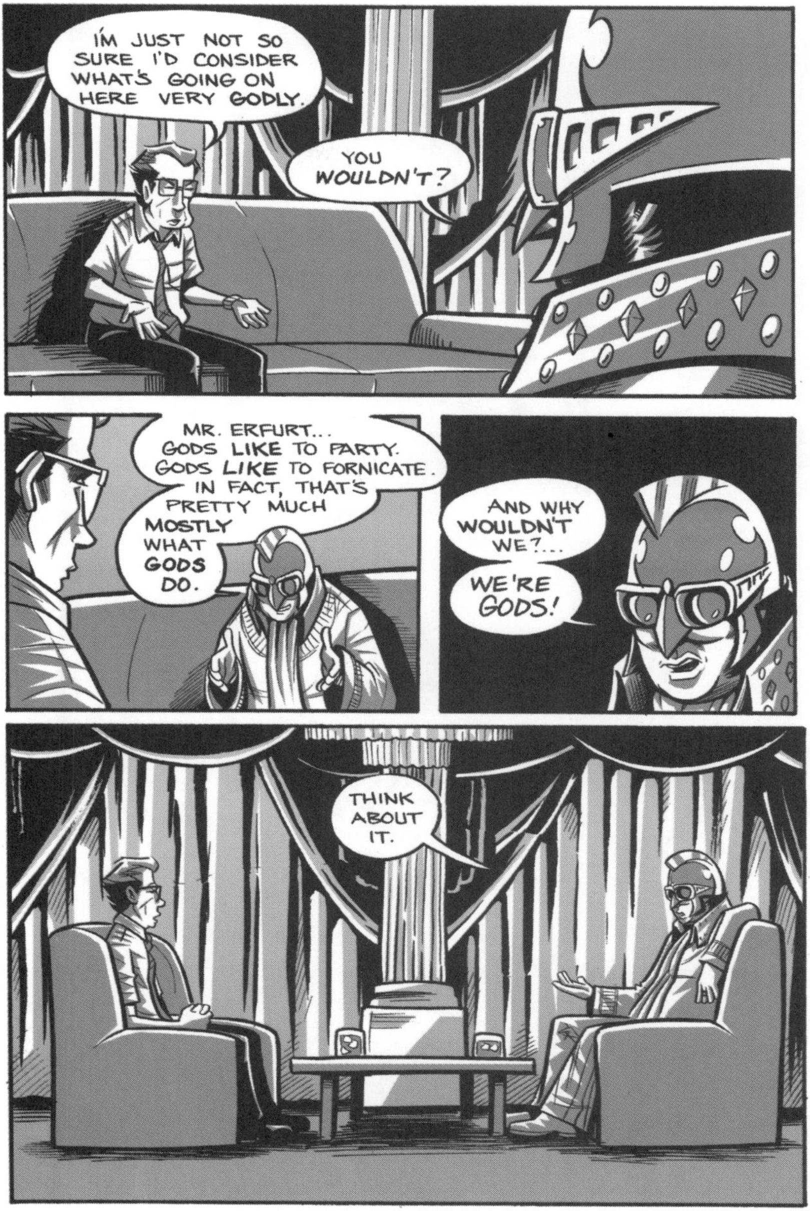
I'M JUST NOT SO SURE I'D CONSIDER WHAT'S GOING ON HERE VERY GODLY.
YOU WOULDN'T?
MR. ERFURT... GODS LIKE TO PARTY. GODS LIKE TO FORNICATE. IN FACT, THAT'S PRETTY MUCH MOSTLY WHAT GODS DO.
AND WHY WOULDN'T WE?...
WE'RE GODS!
THINK ABOUT IT.

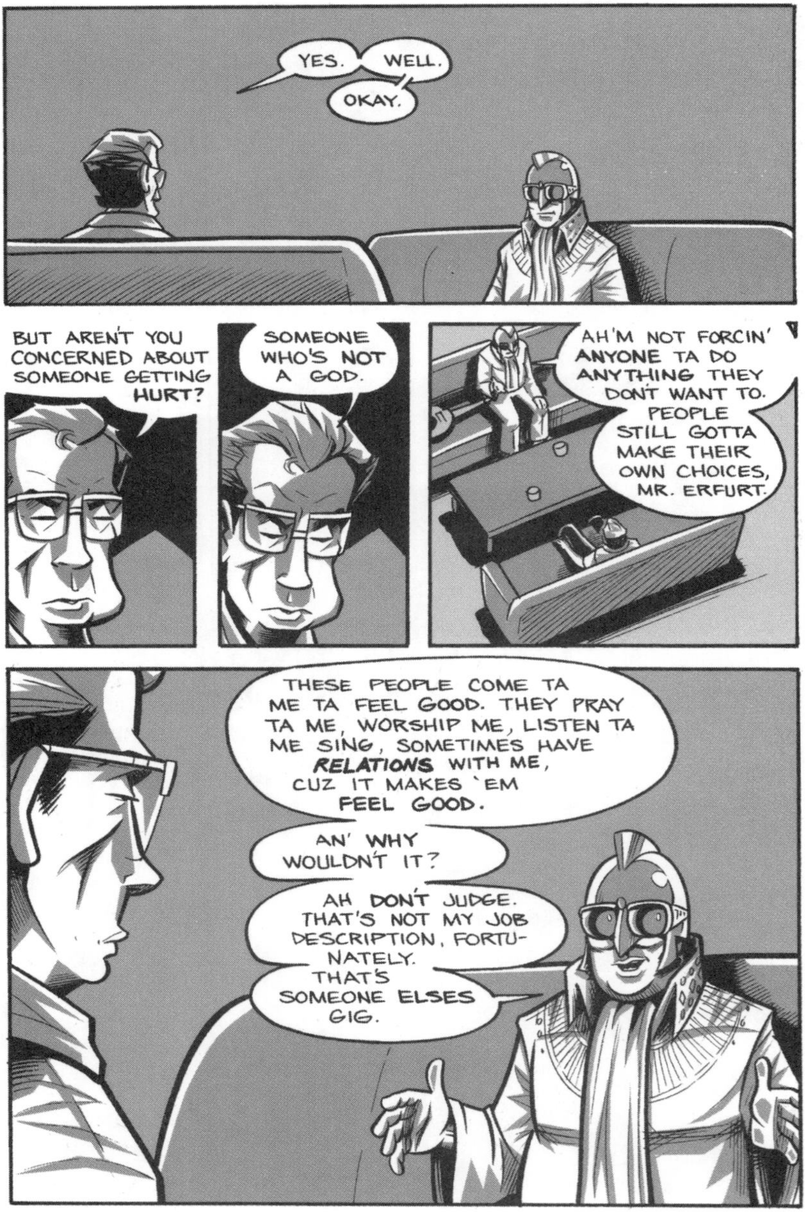
YES.
WELL.
OKAY.
BUT AREN'T YOU CONCERNED ABOUT SOMEONE GETTING HURT?
SOMEONE WHO'S NOT A GOD.
AH'M NOT FORCIN' ANYONE TA DO ANYTHING THEY DON'T WANT TO. PEOPLE STILL GOTTA MAKE THEIR OWN CHOICES, MR. ERFURT.
THESE PEOPLE COME TA ME TA FEEL GOOD. THEY PRAY TA ME, WORSHIP ME, LISTEN TA ME SING, SOMETIMES HAVE RELATIONS WITH ME, CUZ IT MAKES `EM FEEL GOOD.
AN' WHY WOULDN'T IT?
AH DON'T JUDGE. THAT'S NOT MY JOB DESCRIPTION, FORTU-NATELY. THAT'S SOMEONE ELSES GIG.

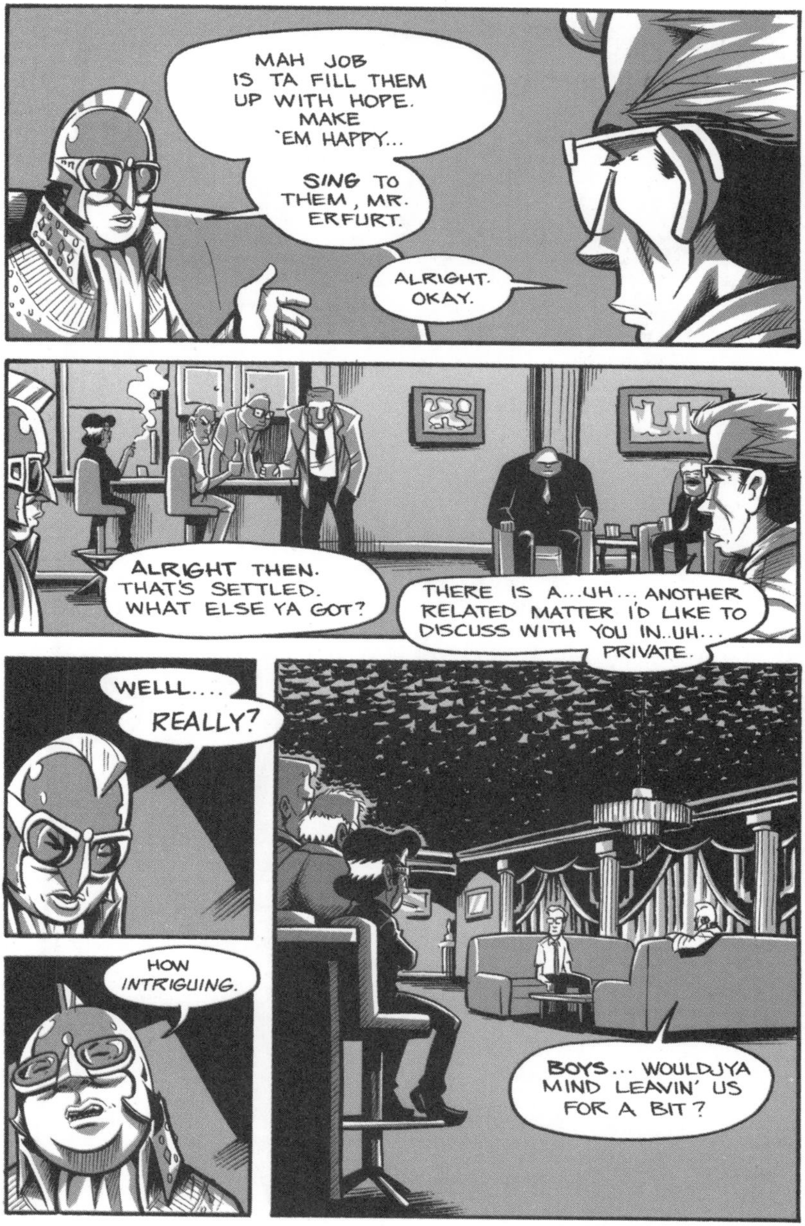
MAH JOB IS TA FILL THEM UP WITH HOPE. MAKE `EM HAPPY...
SING TO THEM, MR. ERFURT.
ALRIGHT. OKAY.
ALRIGHT THEN. THAT'S SETTLED. WHAT ELSE YA GOT?
THERE IS A...UH... ANOTHER RELATED MATTER I'D LIKE TO DISCUSS WITH YOU IN..UH... PRIVATE.
WELLL....
REALLY?
HOW INTRIGUING.
BOYS... WOULDJYA MIND LEAVIN' US FOR A BIT?

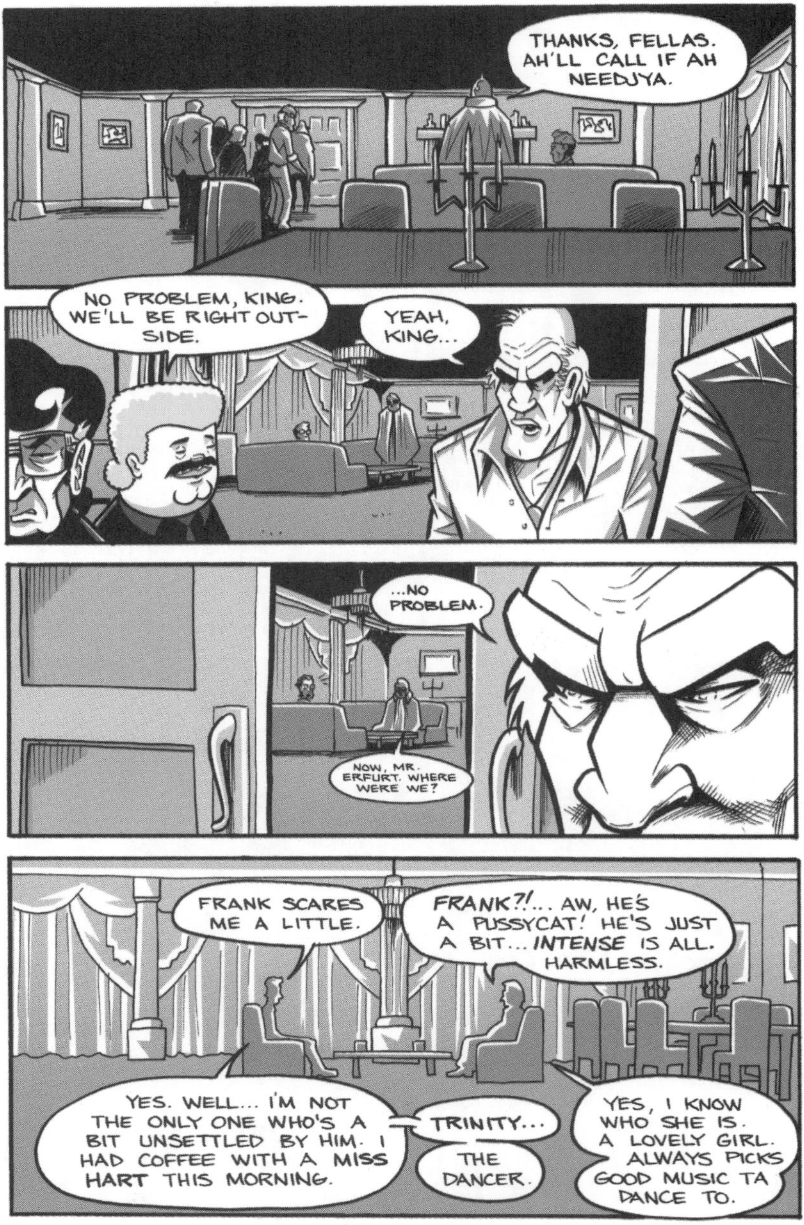
THANKS, FELLAS. AH'LL CALL IF AH NEEDJYA.
NO PROBLEM, KING. WE'LL BE RIGHT OUT-SIDE.
YEAH, KING...
...NO PROBLEM.
NOW, MR. ERFURT. WHERE WERE WE?
FRANK SCARES ME A LITTLE.
FRANK?!... AW, HE'S A PUSSYCAT! HE'S JUST A BIT... INTENSE IS ALL. HARMLESS.
YES. WELL... I'M NOT THE ONLY ONE WHO'S A BIT UNSETTLED BY HIM. I HAD COFFEE WITH A MISS HART THIS MORNING.
TRINITY...
THE DANCER.
YES, I KNOW WHO SHE IS. A LOVELY GIRL. ALWAYS PICKS GOOD MUSIC TA DANCE TO.

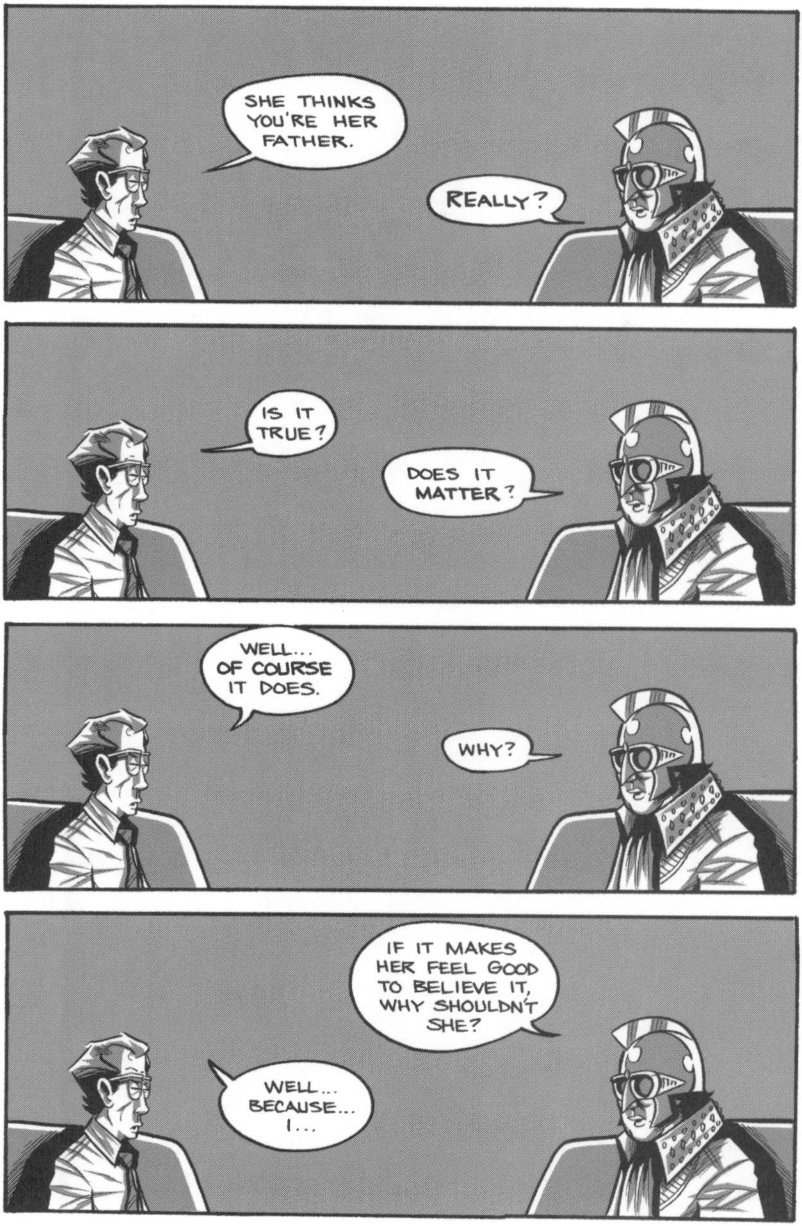
SHE THINKS YOU'RE HER FATHER.
REALLY?
IS IT TRUE?
DOES IT MATTER?
WELL... OF COURSE IT DOES.
WHY?
IF IT MAKES HER FEEL GOOD TO BELIEVE IT, WHY SHOULDN'T SHE?
WELL... BECAUSE... I...

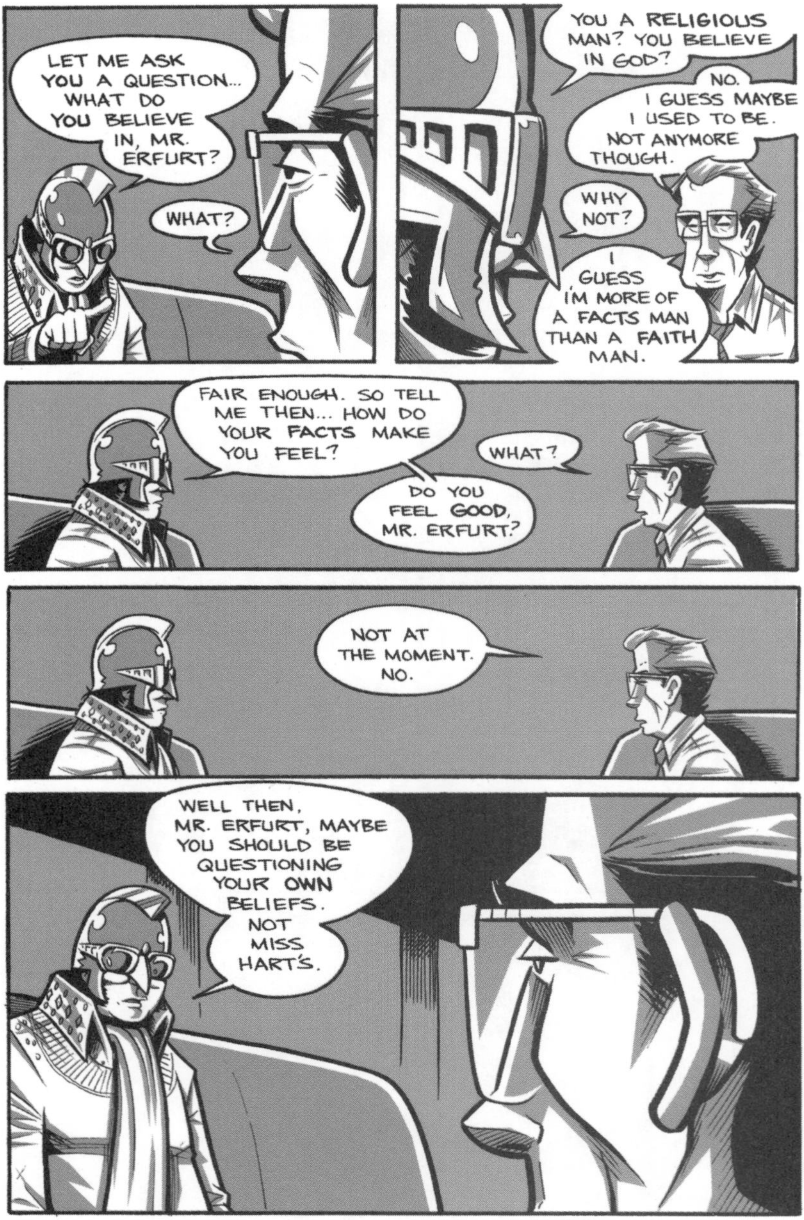
LET ME ASK YOU A QUESTION... WHAT DO YOU BELIEVE IN, MR. ERFURT?
WHAT?
YOU A RELIGIOUS MAN? YOU BELIEVE IN GOD?
NO. I GUESS MAYBE I USED TO BE. NOT ANYMORE THOUGH.
WHY NOT?
I GUESS I'M MORE OF A FACTS MAN THAN A FAITH MAN.
FAIR ENOUGH. SO TELL ME THEN... HOW DO YOUR FACTS MAKE YOU FEEL?
WHAT?
DO YOU FEEL GOOD, MR. ERFURT?
NOT AT THE MOMENT. NO.
WELL THEN, MR. ERFURT, MAYBE YOU SHOULD BE QUESTIONING YOUR OWN BELIEFS. NOT MISS HART'S.

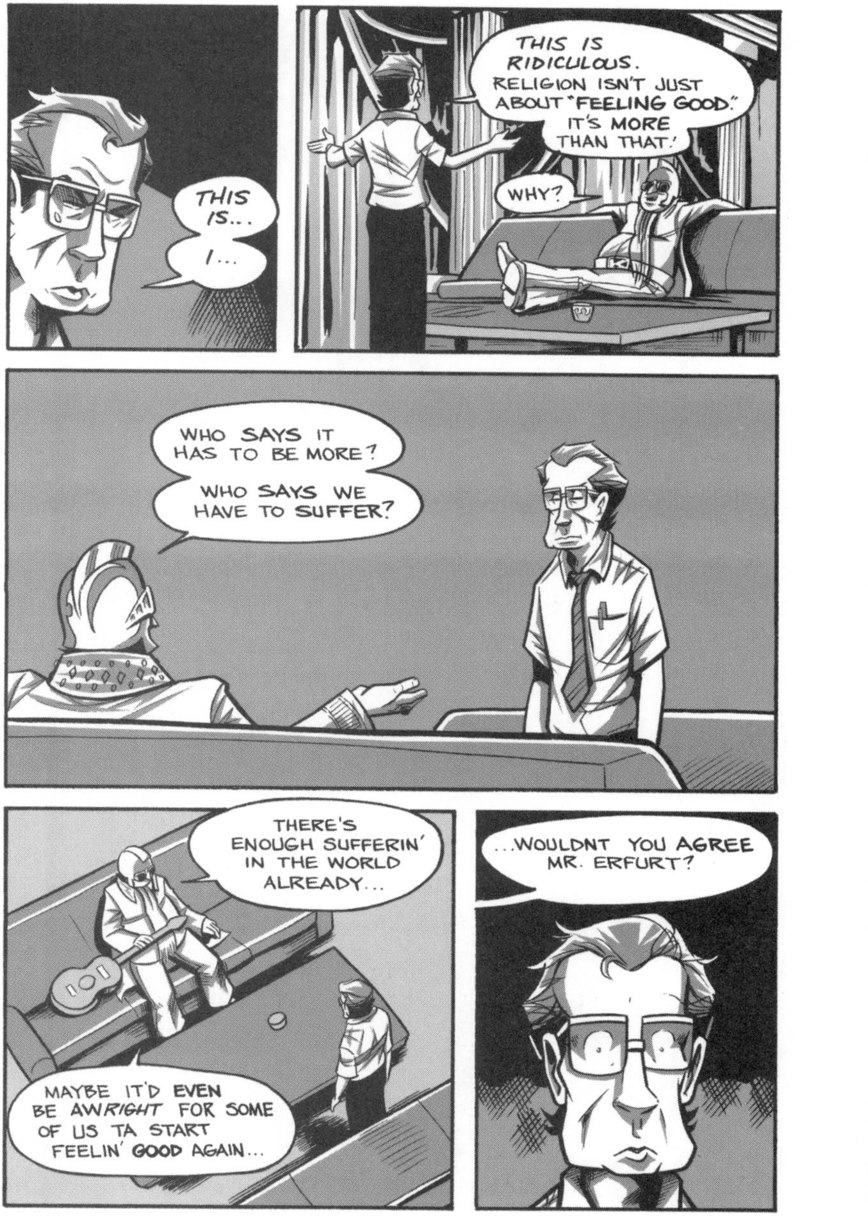
THIS IS...
I...
THIS IS RIDICULOUS. RELIGION ISN'T JUST ABOUT "FEELING GOOD." IT'S MORE THAN THAT!
WHY?
WHO SAYS IT HAS TO BE MORE?
WHO SAYS WE HAVE TO SUFFER?
THERE'S ENOUGH SUFFERIN' IN THE WORLD ALREADY...
MAYBE IT'D EVEN BE AWRIGHT FOR SOME OF US TA START FEELIN' GOOD AGAIN...
...WOULDNT YOU AGREE MR. ERFURT?

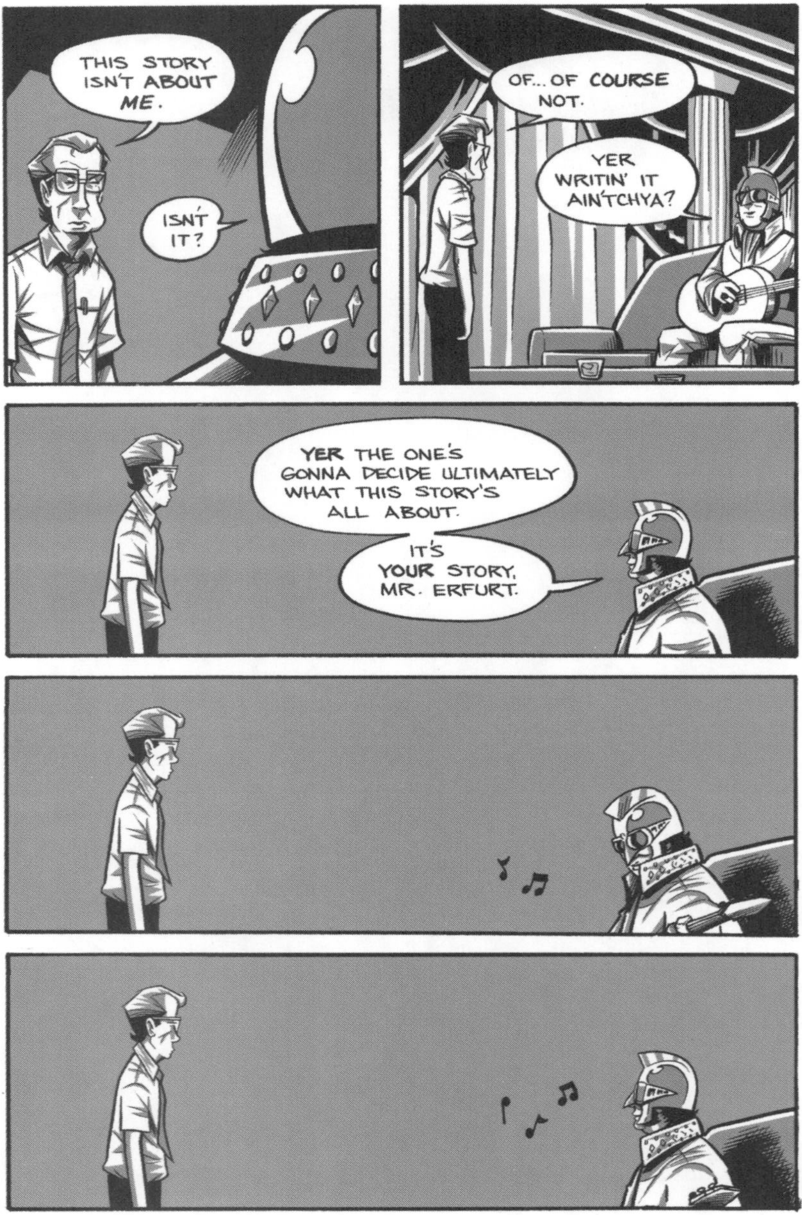
THIS STORY ISN'T ABOUT ME.
ISN'T IT?
OF... OF COURSE NOT.
YER WRITIN' IT AIN'TCHYA?
YER THE ONE'S GONNA DECIDE ULTIMATELY WHAT THIS STORY'S ALL ABOUT.
IT'S YOUR STORY, MR. ERFURT.

LET'S ASSUME I WANT TO BELIEVE...

OKAY.

PROOF. ALL I WANT IS SOME PROOF. SOME FACTS. JUST SOMETHING. ANYTHING.

YOU'VE GOT TO GIVE ME SOMETHING!

MR. ERFURT...

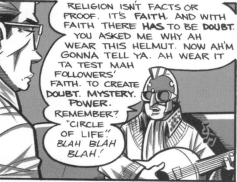

RELIGION ISN'T FACTS OR PROOF. IT'S **FAITH**. AND WITH FAITH THERE **HAS** TO BE **DOUBT**. YOU ASKED ME WHY AH WEAR THIS HELMUT. NOW AH'M GONNA TELL YA. AH WEAR IT TA TEST MAH FOLLOWERS' FAITH. TO CREATE **DOUBT. MYSTERY. POWER.** REMEMBER? "CIRCLE OF LIFE" BLAH BLAH BLAH!

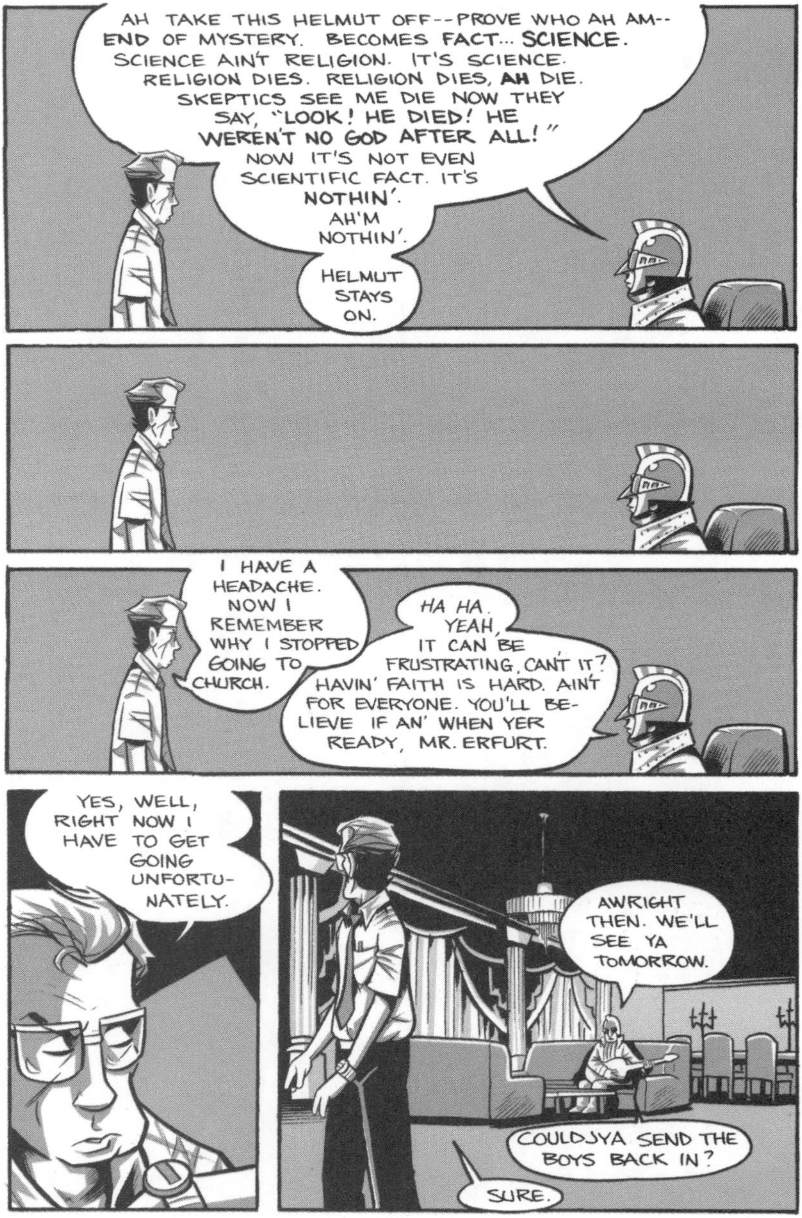
AH TAKE THIS HELMUT OFF--PROVE WHO AH AM-- END OF MYSTERY. BECOMES FACT... SCIENCE. SCIENCE AIN'T RELIGION. IT'S SCIENCE. RELIGION DIES. RELIGION DIES, AH DIE. SKEPTICS SEE ME DIE NOW THEY SAY, "LOOK! HE DIED! HE WEREN'T NO GOD AFTER ALL!" NOW IT'S NOT EVEN SCIENTIFIC FACT. IT'S NOTHIN'. AH'M NOTHIN'.
HELMUT STAYS ON.
I HAVE A HEADACHE. NOW I REMEMBER WHY I STOPPED GOING TO CHURCH.
HA HA. YEAH, IT CAN BE FRUSTRATING, CAN'T IT? HAVIN' FAITH IS HARD. AIN'T FOR EVERYONE. YOU'LL BELIEVE IF AN' WHEN YER READY, MR. ERFURT.
YES, WELL, RIGHT NOW I HAVE TO GET GOING UNFORTUNATELY.
AWRIGHT THEN. WE'LL SEE YA TOMORROW.
COULDJYA SEND THE BOYS BACK IN?
SURE.

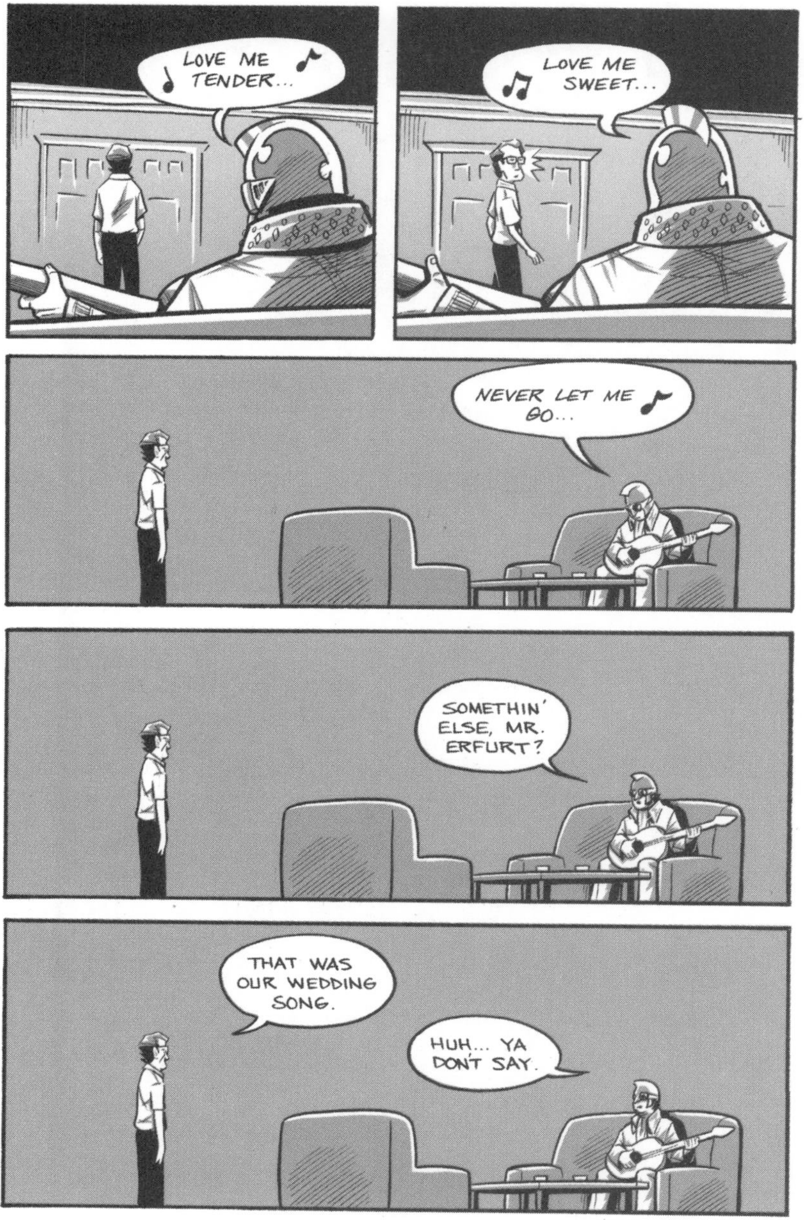
LOVE ME TENDER...
LOVE ME SWEET...
NEVER LET ME GO...
SOMETHIN' ELSE, MR. ERFURT?
THAT WAS OUR WEDDING SONG.
HUH... YA DON'T SAY.

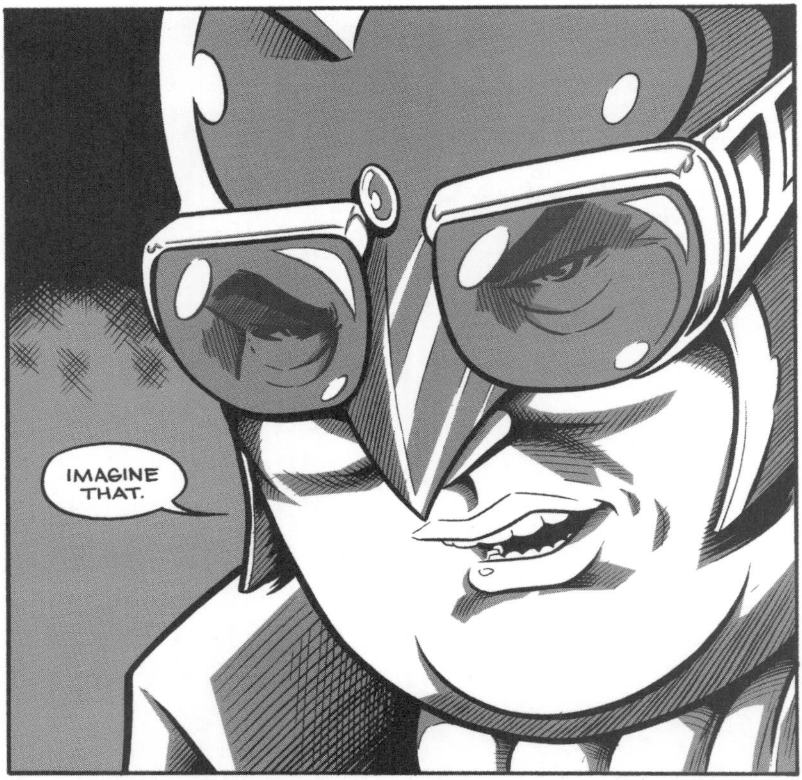
IMAGINE THAT.

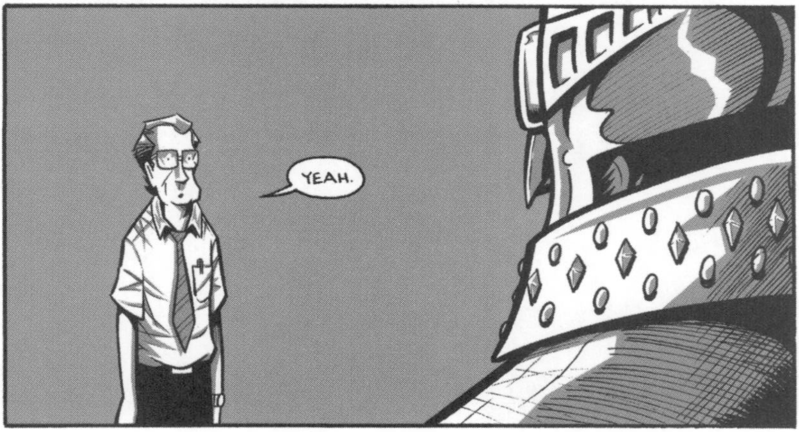
YEAH.

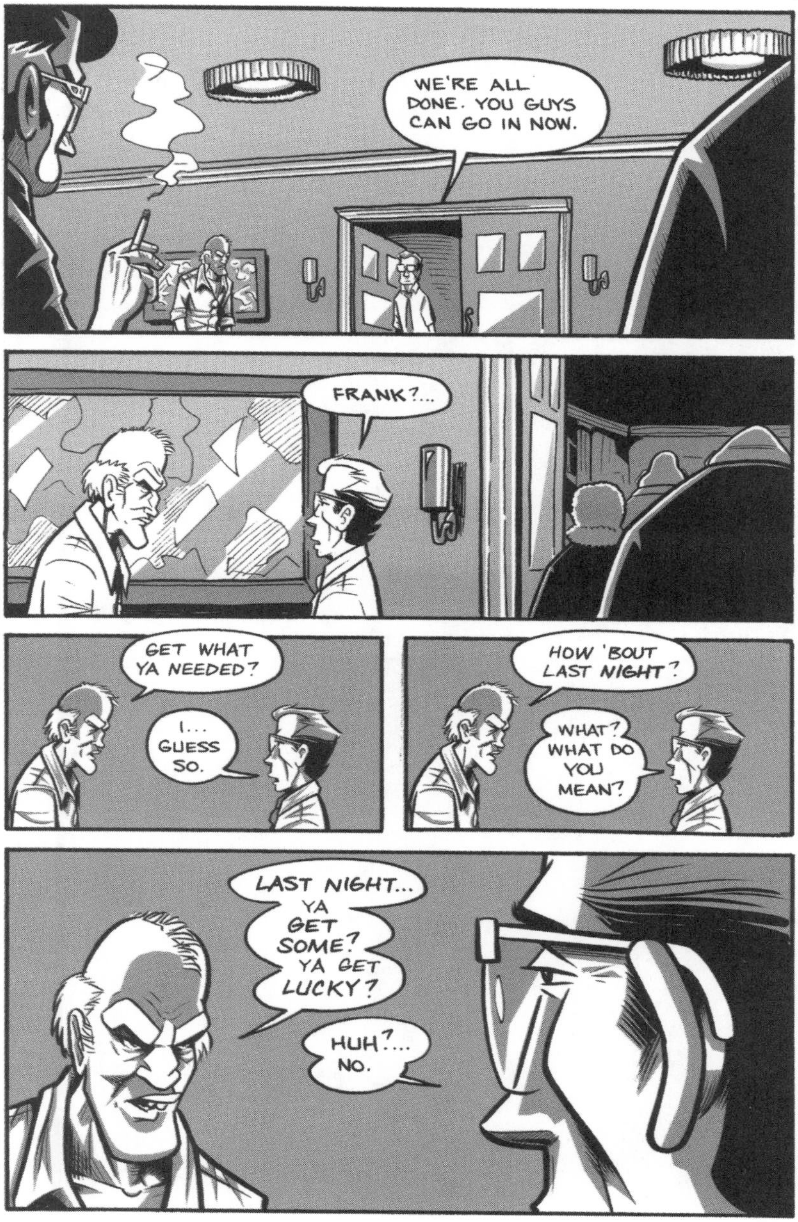
WE'RE ALL DONE. YOU GUYS CAN GO IN NOW.
FRANK?...
GET WHAT YA NEEDED?
I... GUESS SO.
HOW 'BOUT LAST NIGHT?
WHAT? WHAT DO YOU MEAN?
LAST NIGHT... YA GET SOME? YA GET LUCKY?
HUH?.... NO.

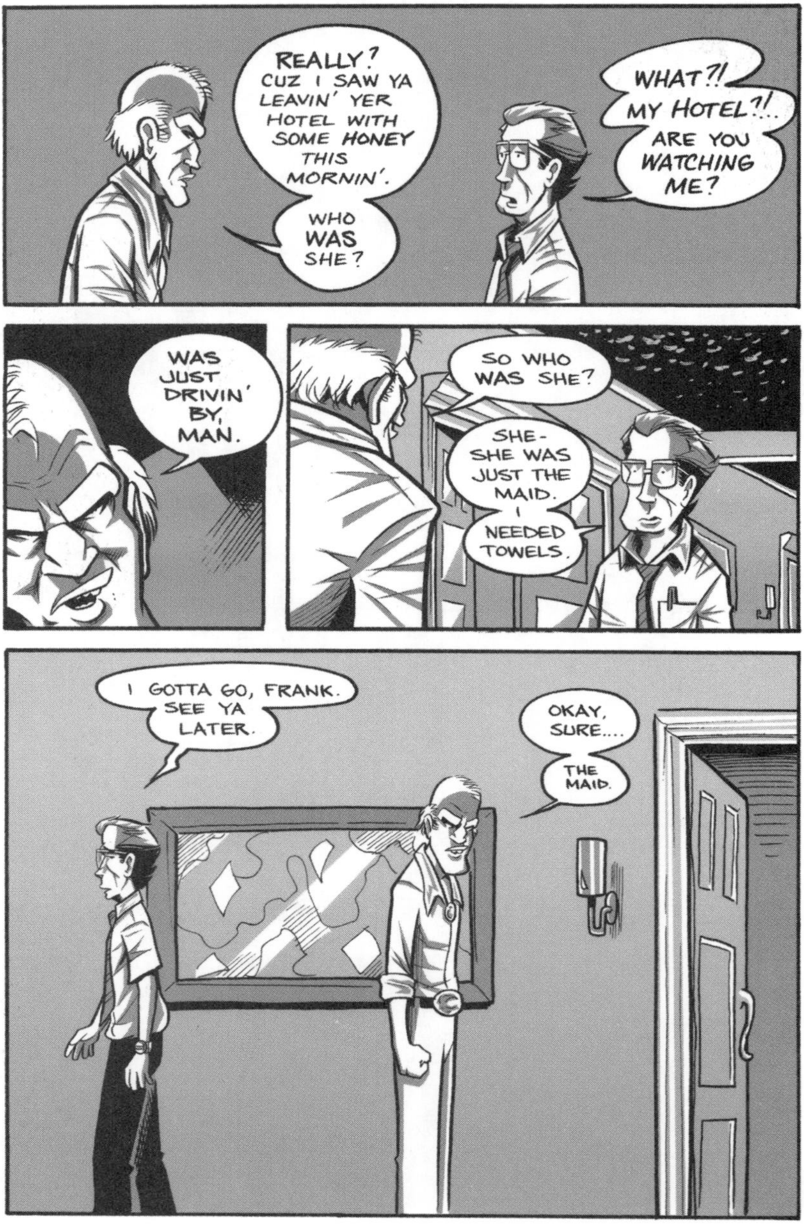
REALLY? CUZ I SAW YA LEAVIN' YER HOTEL WITH SOME HONEY THIS MORNIN'.
WHO WAS SHE?
WHAT?! MY HOTEL?!
ARE YOU WATCHING ME?
WAS JUST DRIVIN' BY, MAN.
SO WHO WAS SHE?
SHE- SHE WAS JUST THE MAID.
I NEEDED TOWELS.
I GOTTA GO, FRANK. SEE YA LATER.
OKAY, SURE....
THE MAID.

"IF THEY FORGET ME, I'LL JUST HAVE TO
DO SOMETHING WORTH REMEMBERING."

— ELVIS

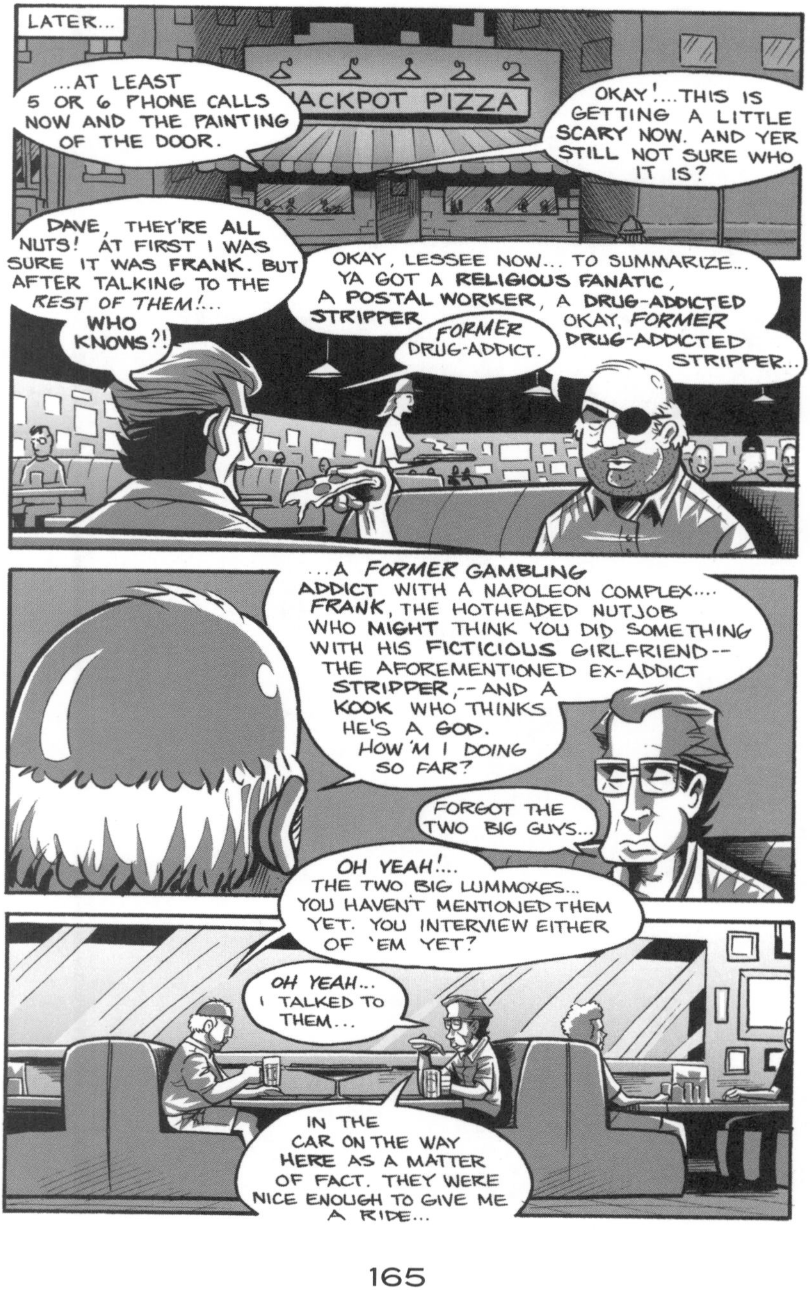
LATER...
...AT LEAST 5 OR 6 PHONE CALLS NOW AND THE PAINTING OF THE DOOR.
ACKPOT PIZZA
OKAY!... THIS IS GETTING A LITTLE SCARY NOW. AND YER STILL NOT SURE WHO IT IS?
DAVE, THEY'RE ALL NUTS! AT FIRST I WAS SURE IT WAS FRANK. BUT AFTER TALKING TO THE REST OF THEM!... WHO KNOWS?!
OKAY, LESSEE NOW... TO SUMMARIZE... YA GOT A RELIGIOUS FANATIC, A POSTAL WORKER, A DRUG-ADDICTED STRIPPER
FORMER DRUG-ADDICT.
OKAY, FORMER DRUG-ADDICTED STRIPPER...
...A FORMER GAMBLING ADDICT WITH A NAPOLEON COMPLEX.... FRANK, THE HOTHEADED NUTJOB WHO MIGHT THINK YOU DID SOMETHING WITH HIS FICTICIOUS GIRLFRIEND-- THE AFOREMENTIONED EX-ADDICT STRIPPER,-- AND A KOOK WHO THINKS HE'S A GOD. HOW 'M I DOING SO FAR?
FORGOT THE TWO BIG GUYS...
OH YEAH!... THE TWO BIG LUMMOXES... YOU HAVEN'T MENTIONED THEM YET. YOU INTERVIEW EITHER OF 'EM YET?
OH YEAH... I TALKED TO THEM...
IN THE CAR ON THE WAY HERE AS A MATTER OF FACT. THEY WERE NICE ENOUGH TO GIVE ME A RIDE...

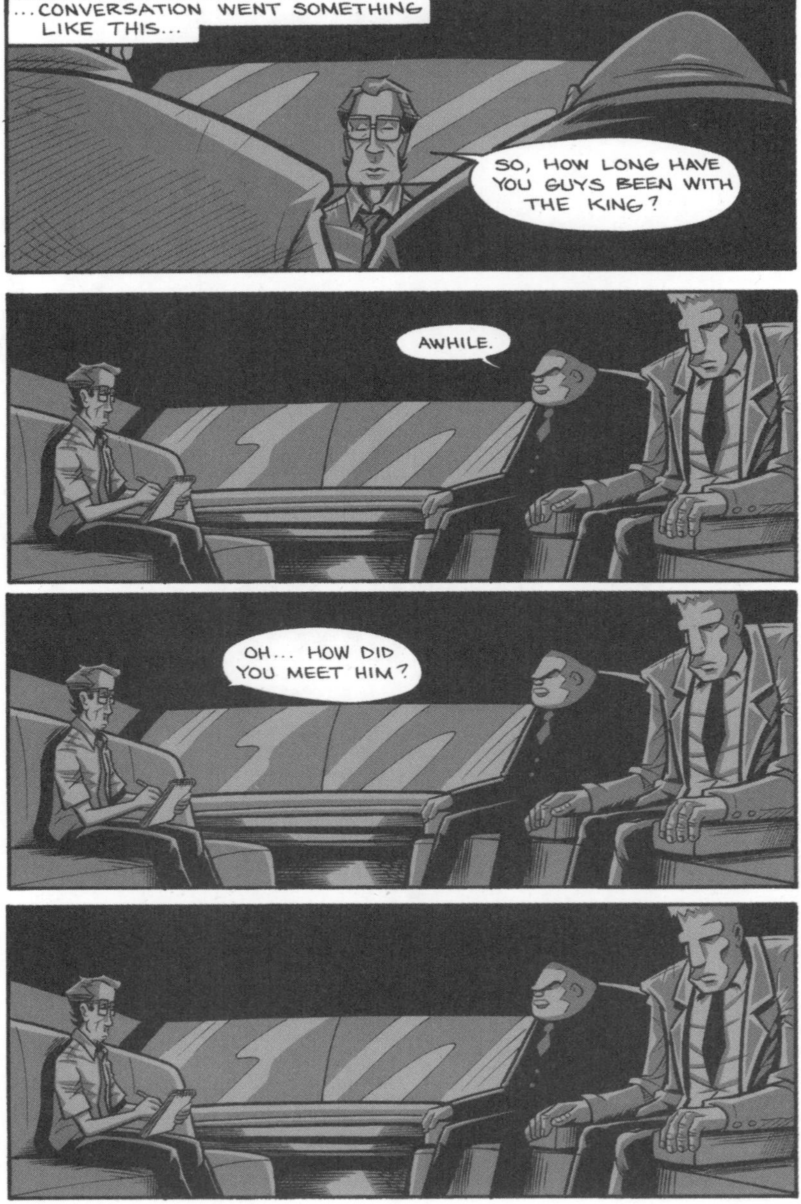
...CONVERSATION WENT SOMETHING LIKE THIS...
SO, HOW LONG HAVE YOU GUYS BEEN WITH THE KING?
AWHILE.
OH... HOW DID YOU MEET HIM?

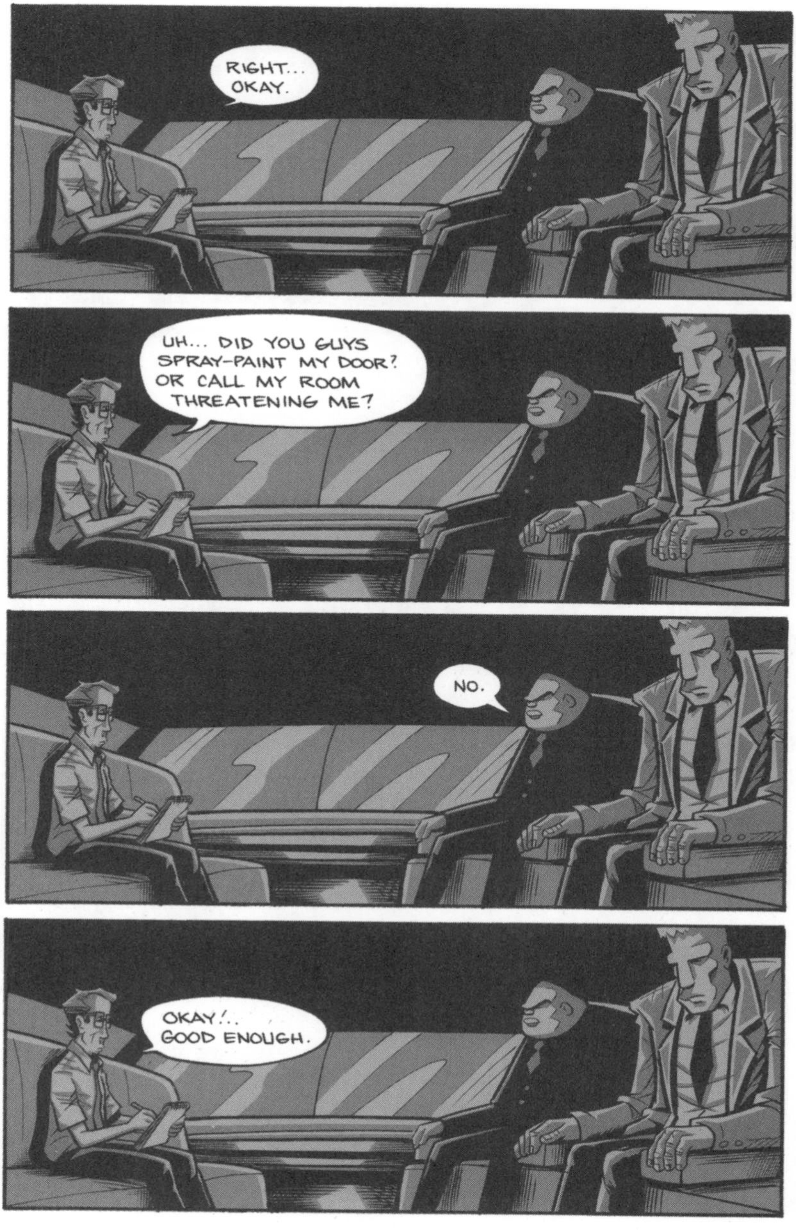
RIGHT... OKAY.
UH... DID YOU GUYS SPRAY-PAINT MY DOOR? OR CALL MY ROOM THREATENING ME?
NO.
OKAY!.. GOOD ENOUGH.

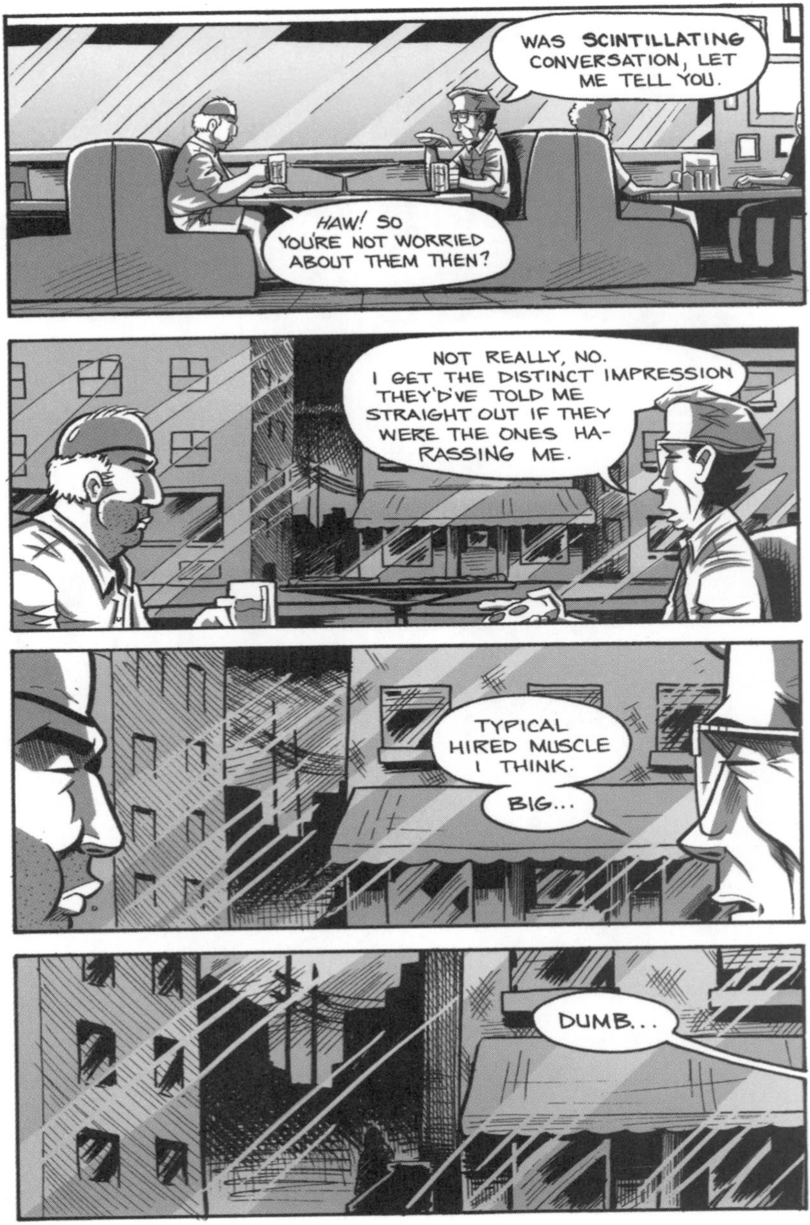
WAS SCINTILLATING CONVERSATION, LET ME TELL YOU.
HAW! SO YOU'RE NOT WORRIED ABOUT THEM THEN?
NOT REALLY, NO. I GET THE DISTINCT IMPRESSION THEY'D'VE TOLD ME STRAIGHT OUT IF THEY WERE THE ONES HA-RASSING ME.
TYPICAL HIRED MUSCLE I THINK.
BIG...
DUMB...

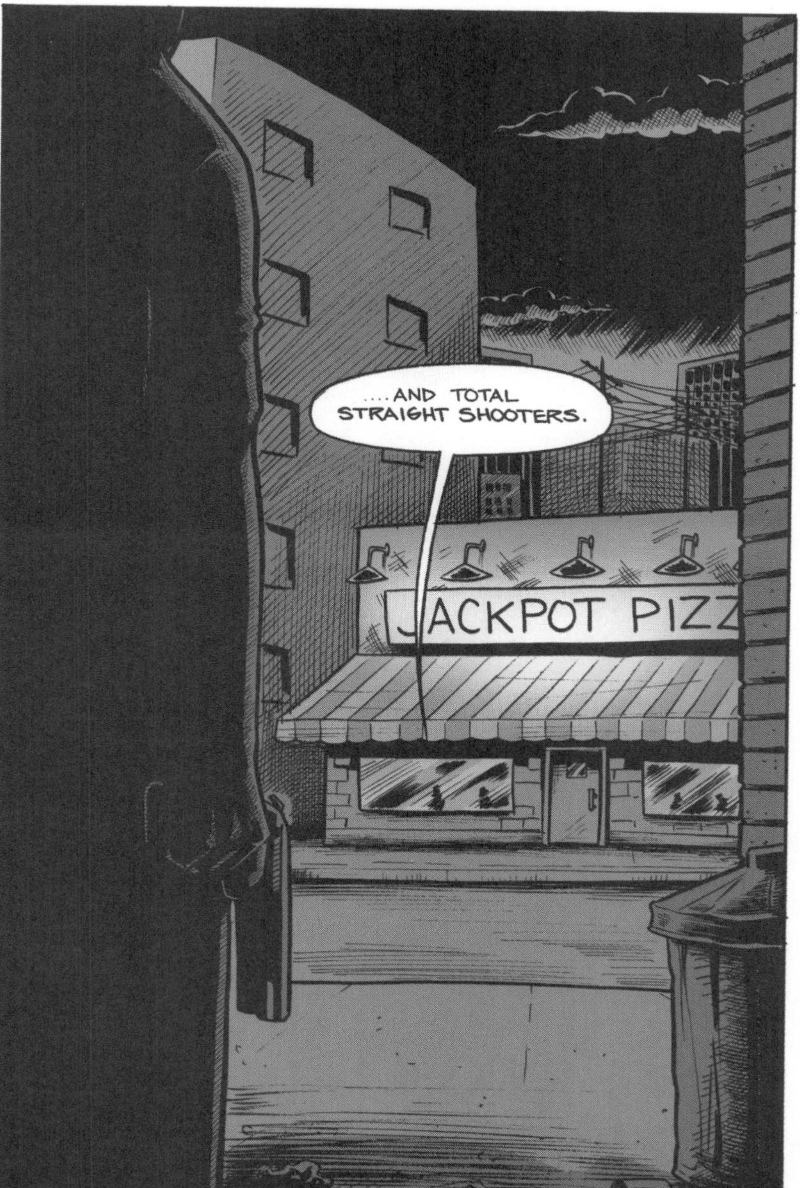
....AND TOTAL STRAIGHT SHOOTERS.
JACKPOT PIZZ

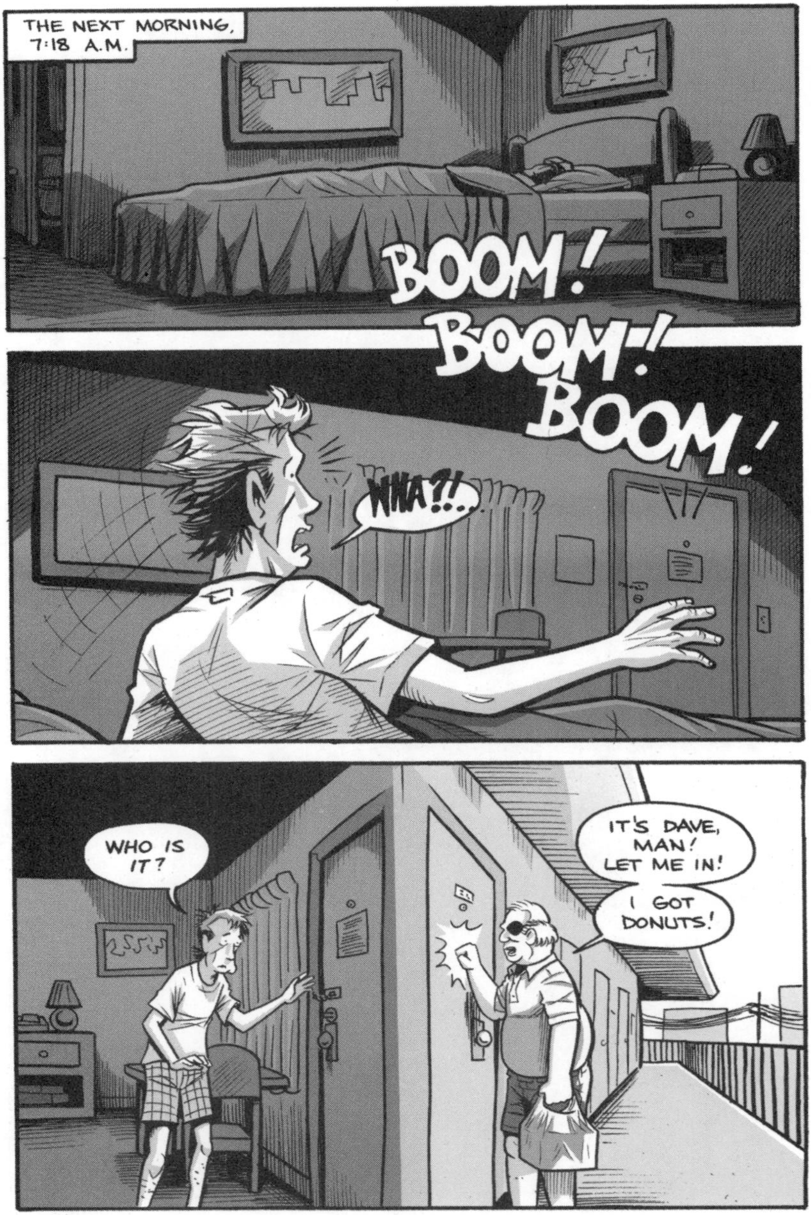
THE NEXT MORNING, 7:18 A.M.
BOOM!
BOOM!
BOOM!
WHA?!!...
WHO IS IT?
IT'S DAVE, MAN! LET ME IN!
I GOT DONUTS!

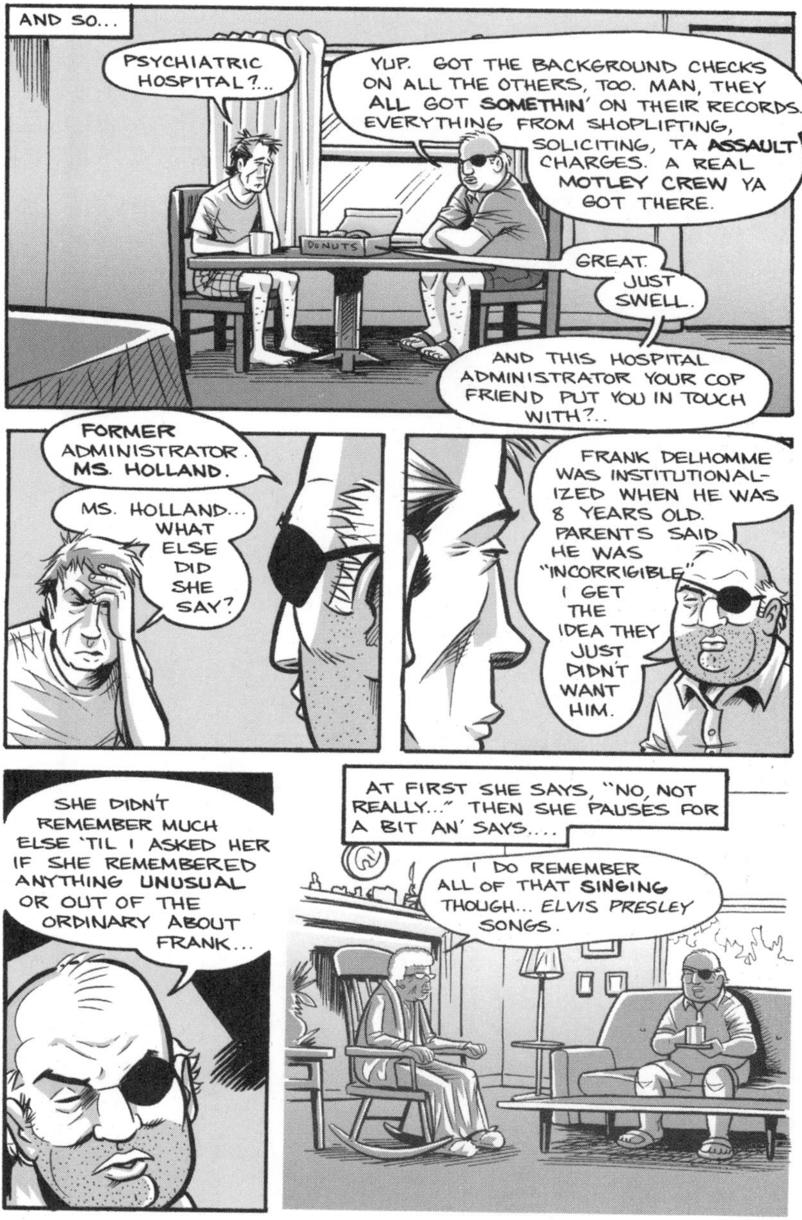

AND SO...
PSYCHIATRIC HOSPITAL?...
YUP. GOT THE BACKGROUND CHECKS ON ALL THE OTHERS, TOO. MAN, THEY ALL GOT SOMETHIN' ON THEIR RECORDS... EVERYTHING FROM SHOPLIFTING, SOLICITING, TA ASSAULT CHARGES. A REAL MOTLEY CREW YA GOT THERE.
DONUTS
GREAT. JUST SWELL.
AND THIS HOSPITAL ADMINISTRATOR YOUR COP FRIEND PUT YOU IN TOUCH WITH?..
FORMER ADMINISTRATOR. MS. HOLLAND.
MS. HOLLAND... WHAT ELSE DID SHE SAY?
FRANK DELHOMME WAS INSTITUTIONAL-IZED WHEN HE WAS 8 YEARS OLD. PARENTS SAID HE WAS "INCORRIGIBLE." I GET THE IDEA THEY JUST DIDN'T WANT HIM.
SHE DIDN'T REMEMBER MUCH ELSE 'TIL I ASKED HER IF SHE REMEMBERED ANYTHING UNUSUAL OR OUT OF THE ORDINARY ABOUT FRANK...
AT FIRST SHE SAYS, "NO, NOT REALLY..." THEN SHE PAUSES FOR A BIT AN' SAYS....
I DO REMEMBER ALL OF THAT SINGING THOUGH... ELVIS PRESLEY SONGS.

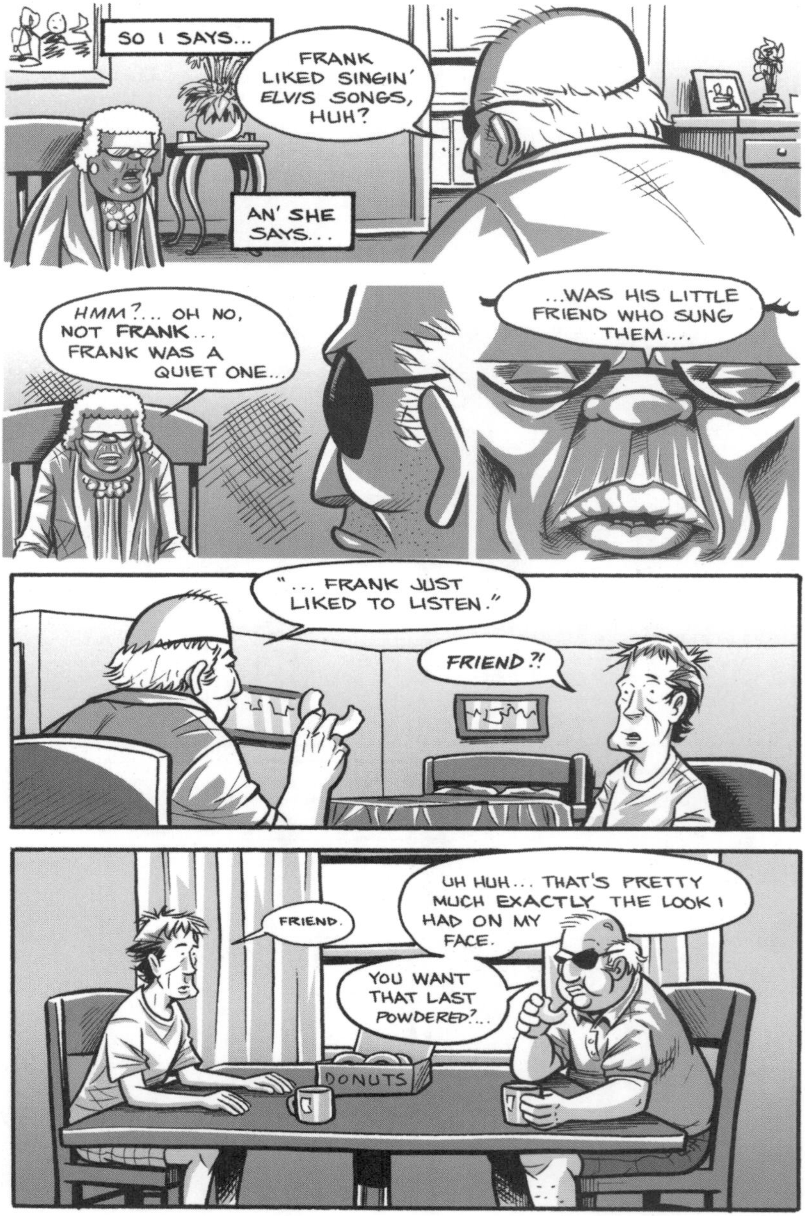
SO I SAYS...
FRANK LIKED SINGIN' ELVIS SONGS, HUH?
AN' SHE SAYS...
HMM?... OH NO, NOT FRANK... FRANK WAS A QUIET ONE...
...WAS HIS LITTLE FRIEND WHO SUNG THEM....
"... FRANK JUST LIKED TO LISTEN."
FRIEND?!
FRIEND.
UH HUH... THAT'S PRETTY MUCH EXACTLY THE LOOK I HAD ON MY FACE.
YOU WANT THAT LAST POWDERED?...
DONUTS

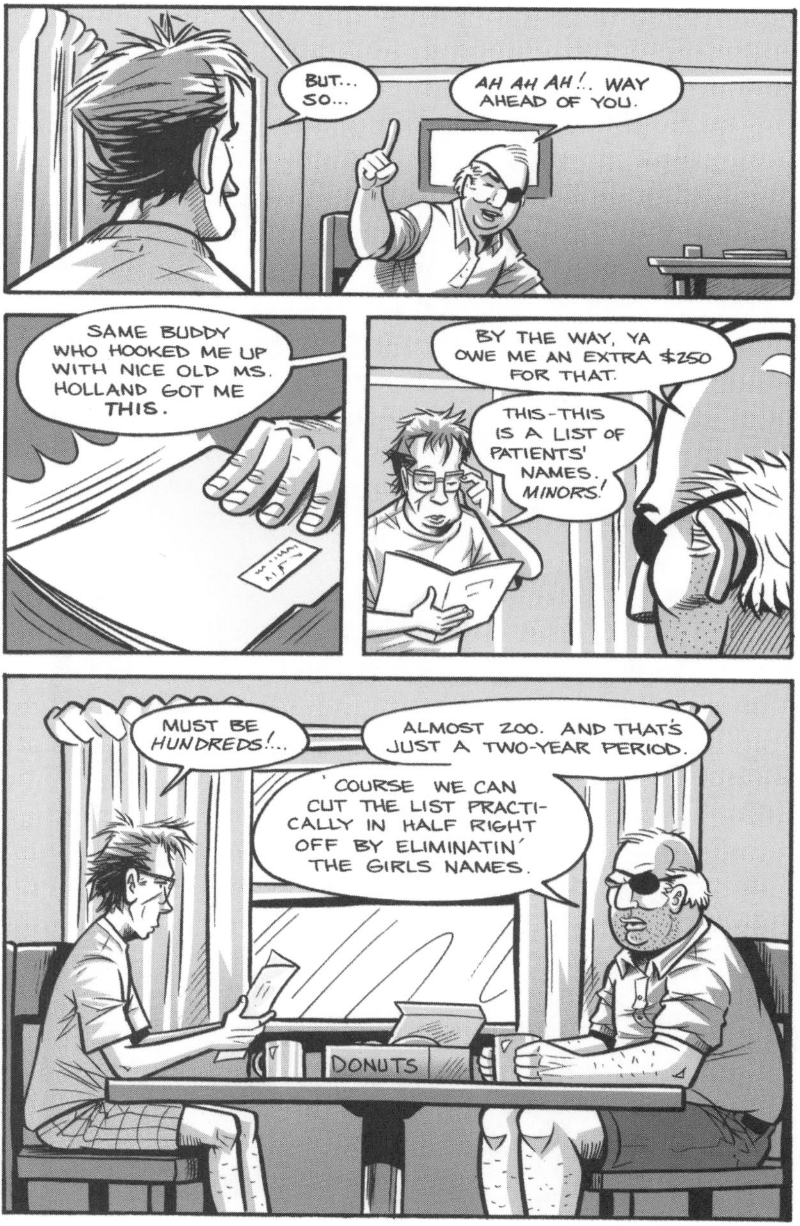
BUT... SO...
AH AH AH!.. WAY AHEAD OF YOU.
SAME BUDDY WHO HOOKED ME UP WITH NICE OLD MS. HOLLAND GOT ME THIS.
BY THE WAY, YA OWE ME AN EXTRA $250 FOR THAT.
THIS-THIS IS A LIST OF PATIENTS' NAMES. MINORS!
MUST BE HUNDREDS!...
ALMOST 200. AND THAT'S JUST A TWO-YEAR PERIOD.
'COURSE WE CAN CUT THE LIST PRACTICALLY IN HALF RIGHT OFF BY ELIMINATIN' THE GIRLS NAMES.
DONUTS

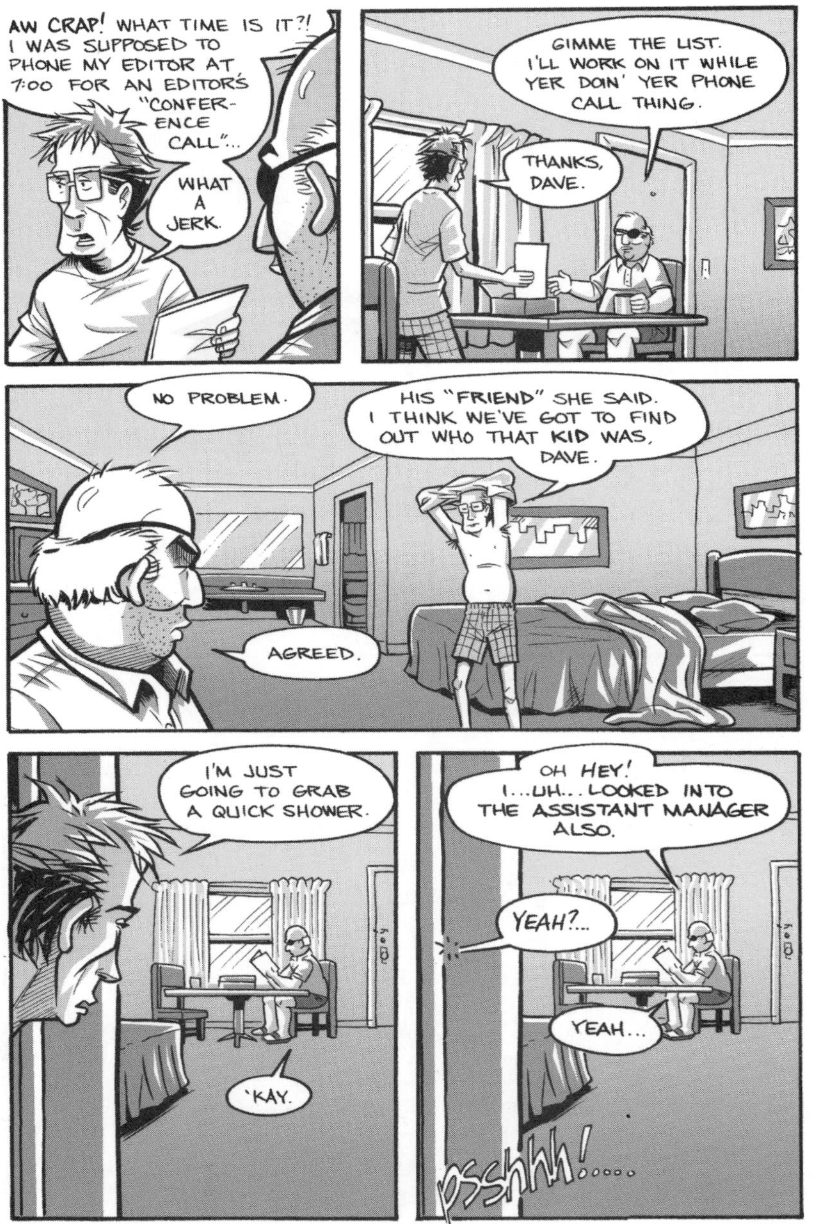
AW CRAP! WHAT TIME IS IT?! I WAS SUPPOSED TO PHONE MY EDITOR AT 7:00 FOR AN EDITOR'S "CONFERENCE CALL"...
WHAT A JERK.
GIMME THE LIST. I'LL WORK ON IT WHILE YER DOIN' YER PHONE CALL THING.
THANKS, DAVE.
NO PROBLEM.
HIS "FRIEND" SHE SAID. I THINK WE'VE GOT TO FIND OUT WHO THAT KID WAS, DAVE.
AGREED.
I'M JUST GOING TO GRAB A QUICK SHOWER.
'KAY.
OH HEY! I...UH...LOOKED INTO THE ASSISTANT MANAGER ALSO.
YEAH?...
YEAH...
psshhh!.....

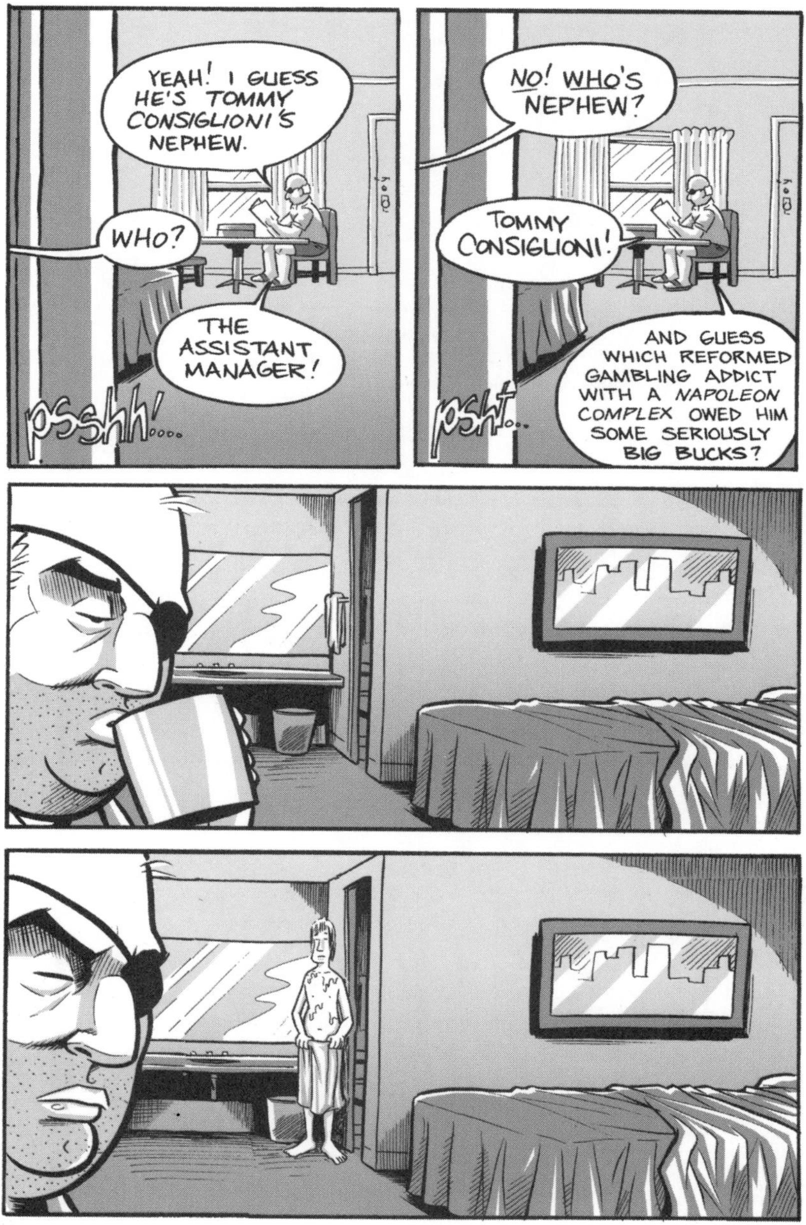

YEAH! I GUESS HE'S TOMMY CONSIGLIONI'S NEPHEW.
WHO?
THE ASSISTANT MANAGER!
psshh!....
NO! WHO'S NEPHEW?
TOMMY CONSIGLIONI!
AND GUESS WHICH REFORMED GAMBLING ADDICT WITH A *NAPOLEON COMPLEX* OWED HIM SOME SERIOUSLY BIG BUCKS?
psht...

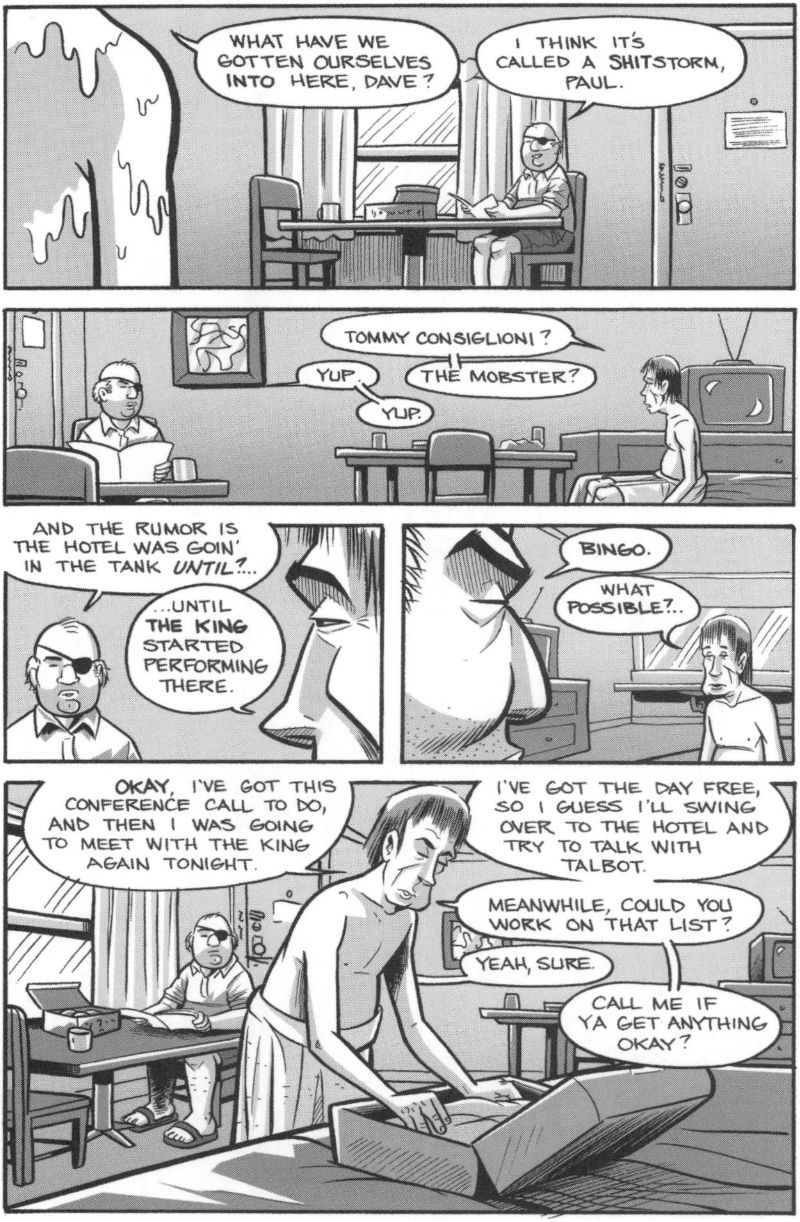
WHAT HAVE WE GOTTEN OURSELVES INTO HERE, DAVE?
I THINK IT'S CALLED A SHITSTORM, PAUL.
TOMMY CONSIGLIONI?
YUP.
THE MOBSTER?
YUP.
AND THE RUMOR IS THE HOTEL WAS GOIN' IN THE TANK UNTIL?...
...UNTIL THE KING STARTED PERFORMING THERE.
BINGO.
WHAT POSSIBLE?..
OKAY, I'VE GOT THIS CONFERENCE CALL TO DO, AND THEN I WAS GOING TO MEET WITH THE KING AGAIN TONIGHT.
I'VE GOT THE DAY FREE, SO I GUESS I'LL SWING OVER TO THE HOTEL AND TRY TO TALK WITH TALBOT.
MEANWHILE, COULD YOU WORK ON THAT LIST?
YEAH, SURE.
CALL ME IF YA GET ANYTHING OKAY?

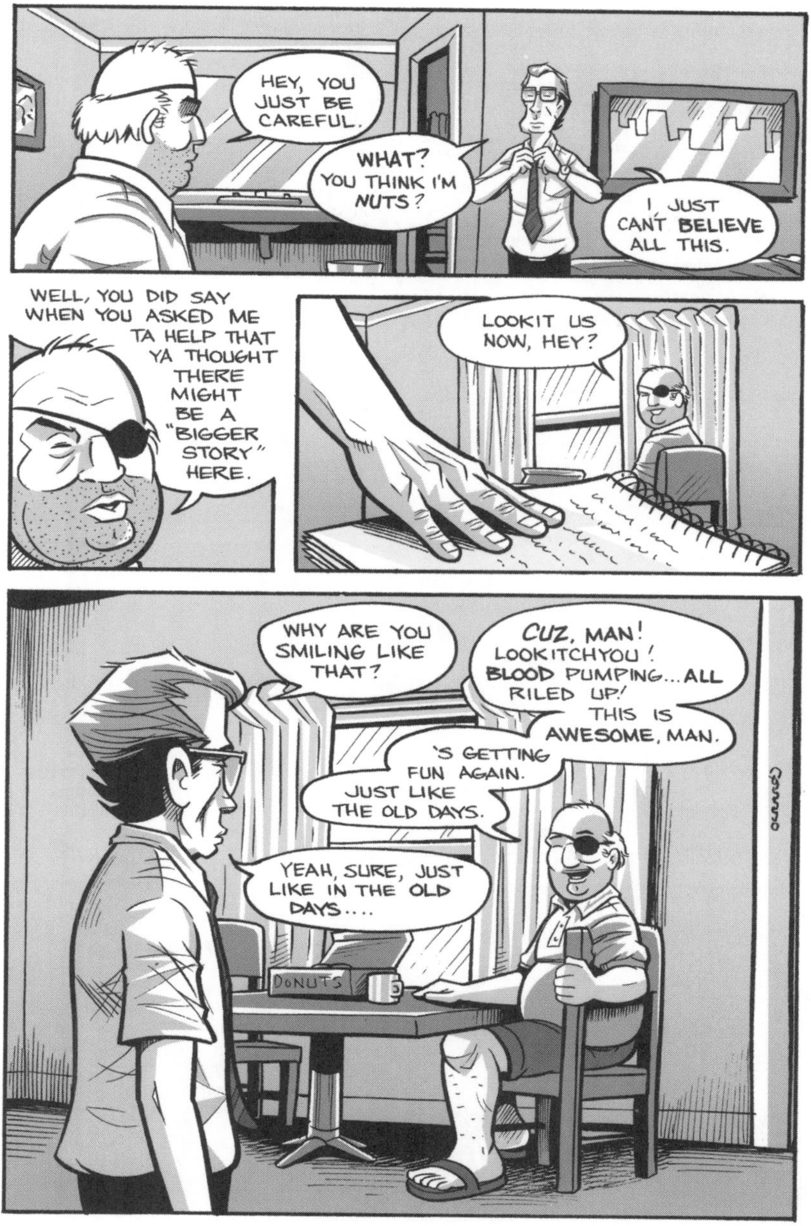
HEY, YOU JUST BE CAREFUL.
WHAT? YOU THINK I'M NUTS?
I JUST CAN'T BELIEVE ALL THIS.
WELL, YOU DID SAY WHEN YOU ASKED ME TA HELP THAT YA THOUGHT THERE MIGHT BE A "BIGGER STORY" HERE.
LOOKIT US NOW, HEY?
WHY ARE YOU SMILING LIKE THAT?
CUZ, MAN! LOOKITCHYOU! BLOOD PUMPING... ALL RILED UP!
THIS IS AWESOME, MAN.
'S GETTING FUN AGAIN. JUST LIKE THE OLD DAYS.
YEAH, SURE, JUST LIKE IN THE OLD DAYS....
DONUTS

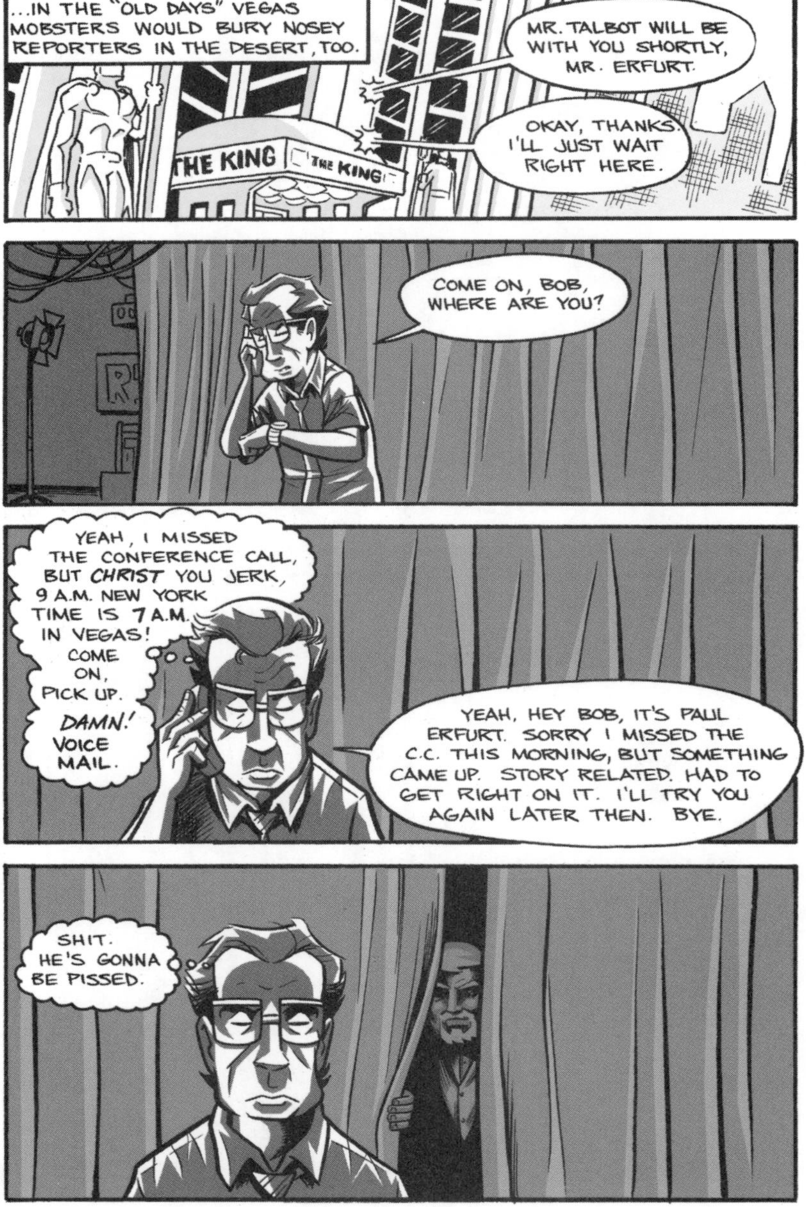
...IN THE "OLD DAYS" VEGAS MOBSTERS WOULD BURY NOSEY REPORTERS IN THE DESERT, TOO.
MR. TALBOT WILL BE WITH YOU SHORTLY, MR. ERFURT.
OKAY, THANKS. I'LL JUST WAIT RIGHT HERE.
THE KING
THE KING
COME ON, BOB, WHERE ARE YOU?
YEAH, I MISSED THE CONFERENCE CALL, BUT CHRIST YOU JERK, 9 A.M. NEW YORK TIME IS 7 A.M. IN VEGAS! COME ON, PICK UP. DAMN! VOICE MAIL.
YEAH, HEY BOB, IT'S PAUL ERFURT. SORRY I MISSED THE C.C. THIS MORNING, BUT SOMETHING CAME UP. STORY RELATED. HAD TO GET RIGHT ON IT. I'LL TRY YOU AGAIN LATER THEN. BYE.
SHIT. HE'S GONNA BE PISSED.

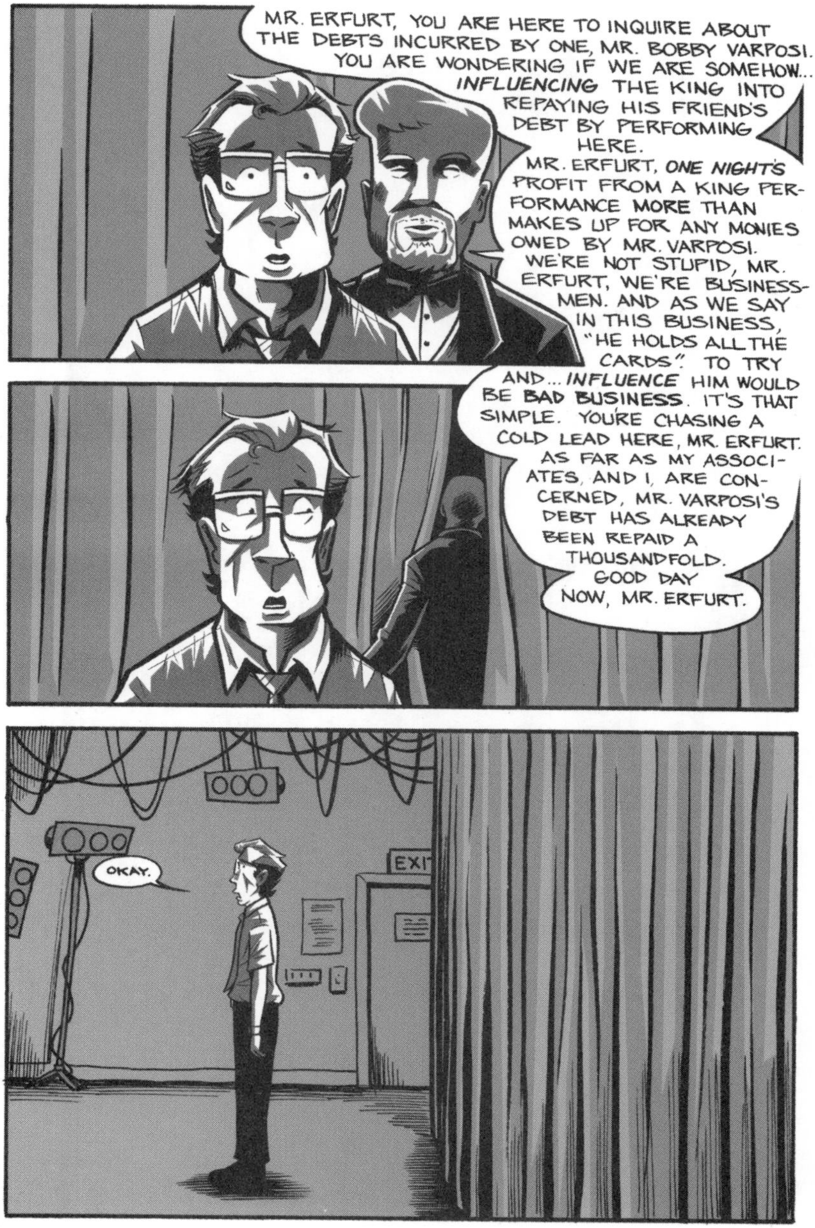
MR. ERFURT, YOU ARE HERE TO INQUIRE ABOUT THE DEBTS INCURRED BY ONE, MR. BOBBY VARPOSI. YOU ARE WONDERING IF WE ARE SOMEHOW... *INFLUENCING* THE KING INTO REPAYING HIS FRIEND'S DEBT BY PERFORMING HERE.
MR. ERFURT, *ONE NIGHT'S* PROFIT FROM A KING PERFORMANCE **MORE** THAN MAKES UP FOR ANY MONIES OWED BY MR. VARPOSI. WE'RE NOT STUPID, MR. ERFURT, WE'RE BUSINESSMEN. AND AS WE SAY IN THIS BUSINESS, "HE HOLDS ALL THE CARDS". TO TRY AND... *INFLUENCE* HIM WOULD BE **BAD BUSINESS**. IT'S THAT SIMPLE. YOU'RE CHASING A COLD LEAD HERE, MR. ERFURT. AS FAR AS MY ASSOCIATES, AND I, ARE CONCERNED, MR. VARPOSI'S DEBT HAS ALREADY BEEN REPAID A THOUSANDFOLD. GOOD DAY NOW, MR. ERFURT.
OKAY.
EXIT

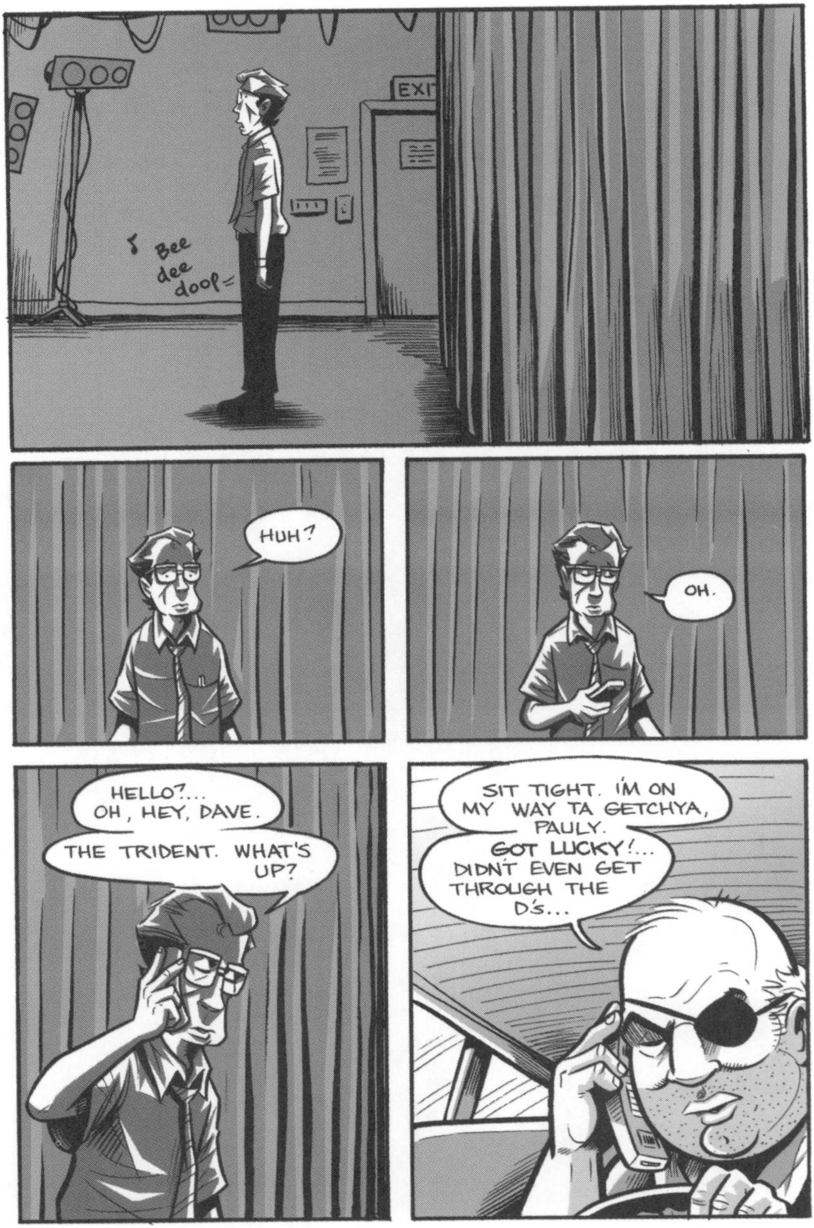
Bee dee doop
HUH?
OH.
HELLO?... OH, HEY, DAVE.
THE TRIDENT. WHAT'S UP?
SIT TIGHT. I'M ON MY WAY TA GETCHYA, PAULY.
GOT LUCKY!... DIDN'T EVEN GET THROUGH THE D's...

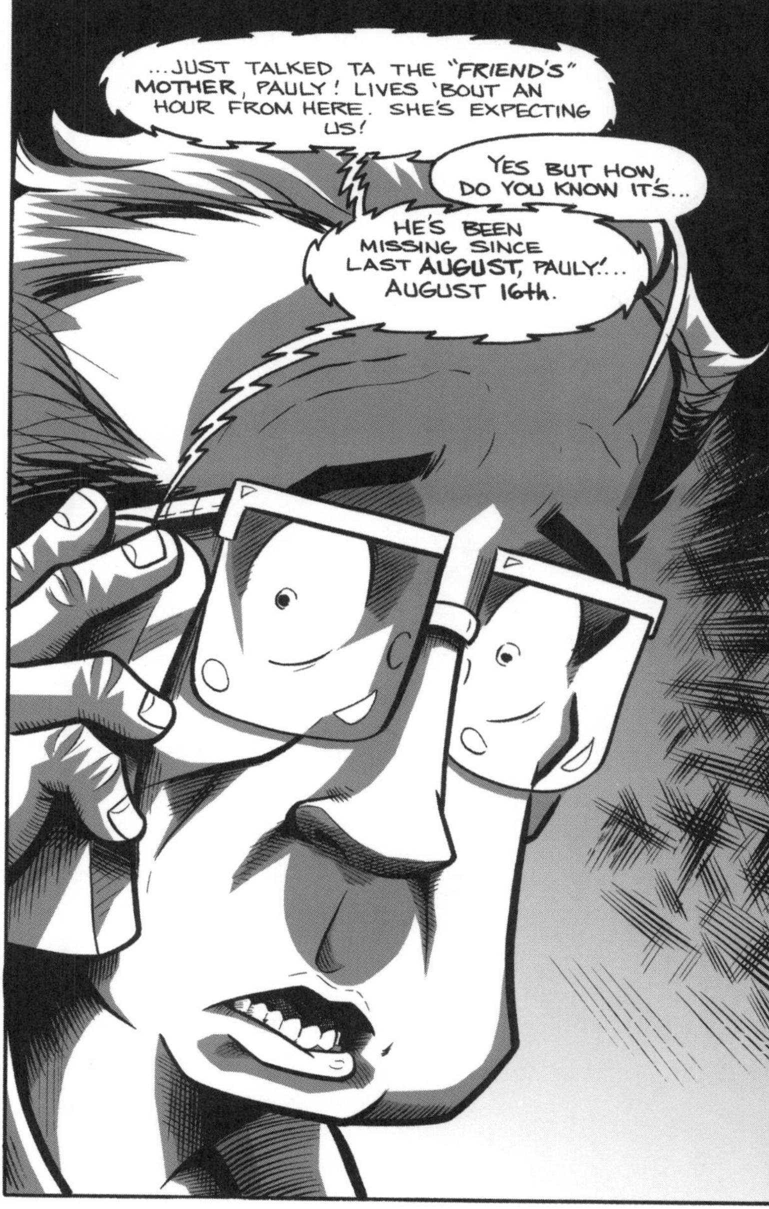
...JUST TALKED TA THE "FRIEND'S" MOTHER, PAULY! LIVES 'BOUT AN HOUR FROM HERE. SHE'S EXPECTING US!
YES BUT HOW, DO YOU KNOW IT'S...
HE'S BEEN MISSING SINCE LAST AUGUST, PAULY!... AUGUST 16th.

"THERE HAVE BEEN PRETENDERS,
THERE HAVE BEEN CONTENDERS.
BUT THERE IS ONLY ONE **KING**."

— BRUCE SPRINGSTEEN

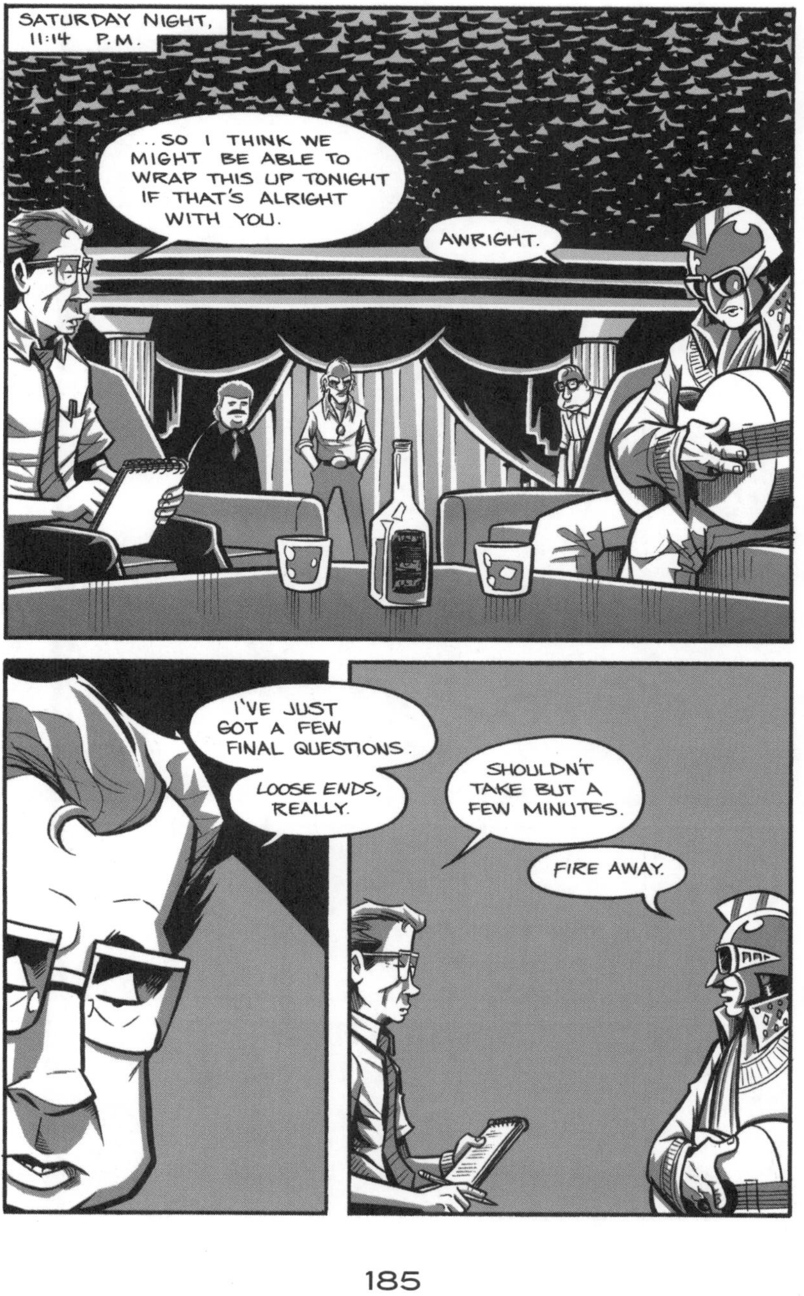
SATURDAY NIGHT, 11:14 P.M.
...SO I THINK WE MIGHT BE ABLE TO WRAP THIS UP TONIGHT IF THAT'S ALRIGHT WITH YOU.
AWRIGHT.
I'VE JUST GOT A FEW FINAL QUESTIONS.
LOOSE ENDS, REALLY.
SHOULDN'T TAKE BUT A FEW MINUTES.
FIRE AWAY.

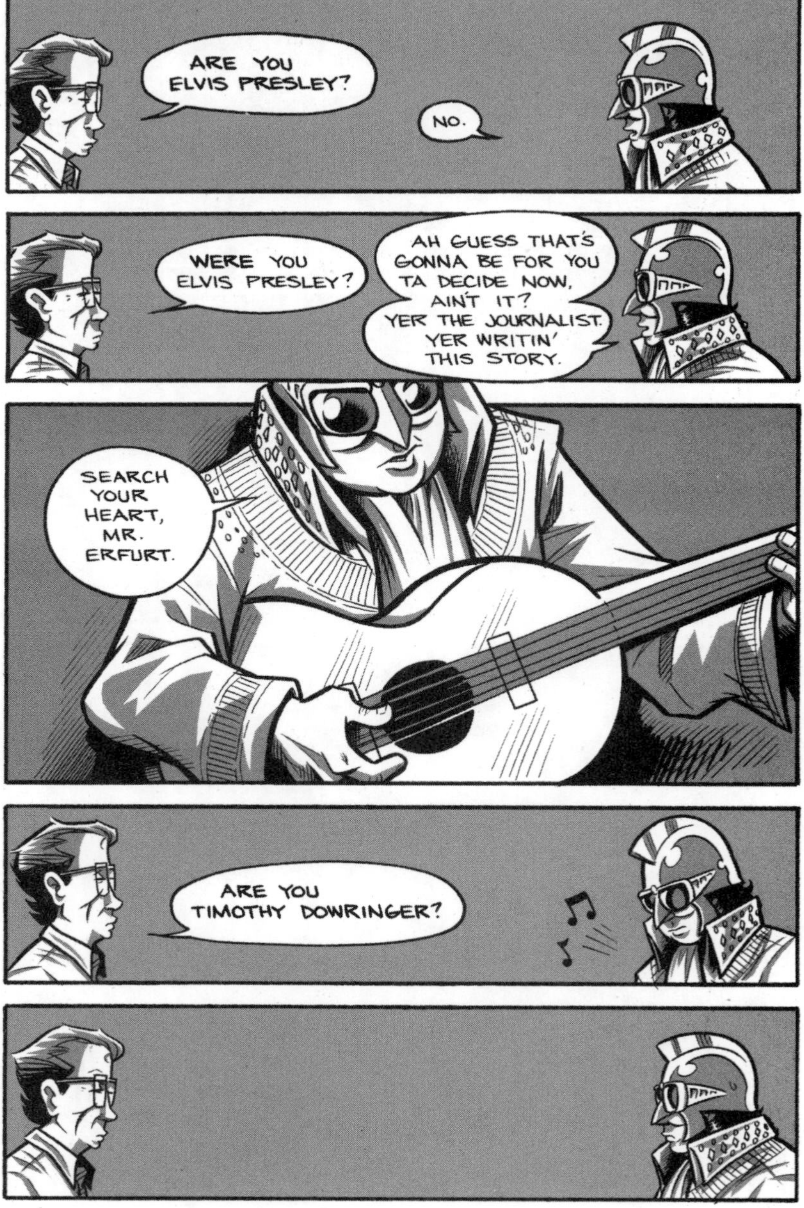
ARE YOU ELVIS PRESLEY?
NO.
WERE YOU ELVIS PRESLEY?
AH GUESS THAT'S GONNA BE FOR YOU TA DECIDE NOW, AIN'T IT? YER THE JOURNALIST. YER WRITIN' THIS STORY.
SEARCH YOUR HEART, MR. ERFURT.
ARE YOU TIMOTHY DOWRINGER?

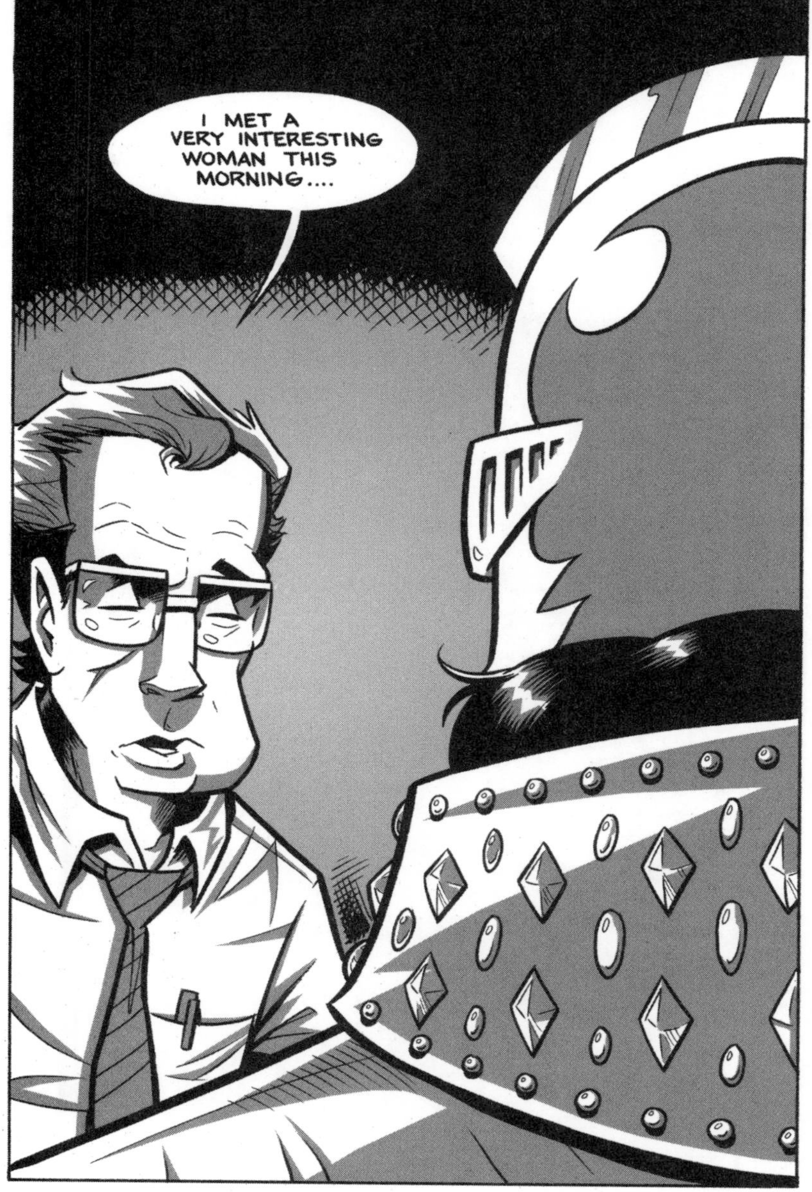
I MET A VERY INTERESTING WOMAN THIS MORNING....

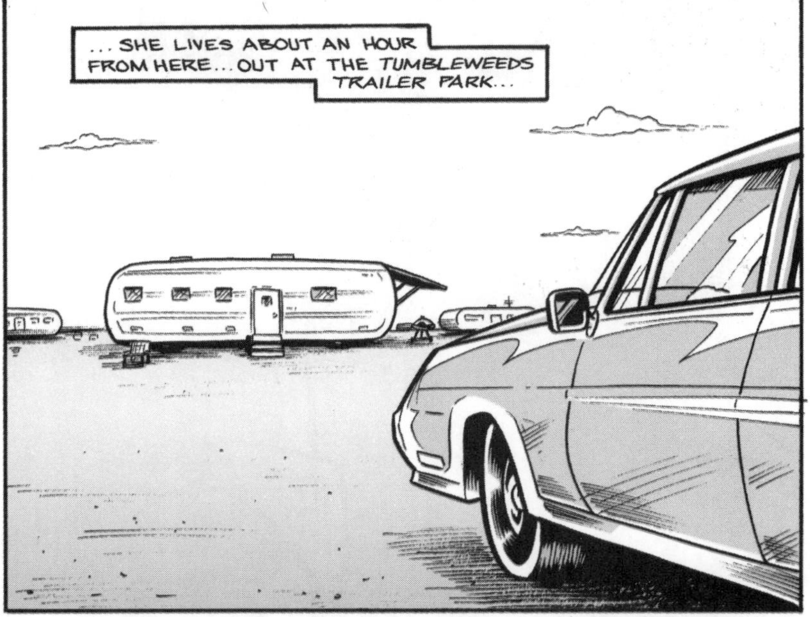
... SHE LIVES ABOUT AN HOUR FROM HERE... OUT AT THE TUMBLEWEEDS TRAILER PARK...

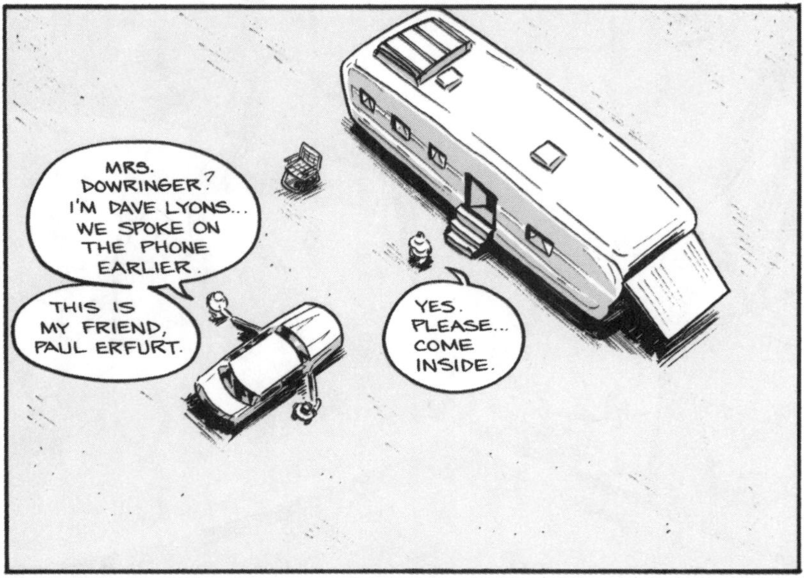
MRS. DOWRINGER? I'M DAVE LYONS... WE SPOKE ON THE PHONE EARLIER.
THIS IS MY FRIEND, PAUL ERFURT.
YES. PLEASE... COME INSIDE.

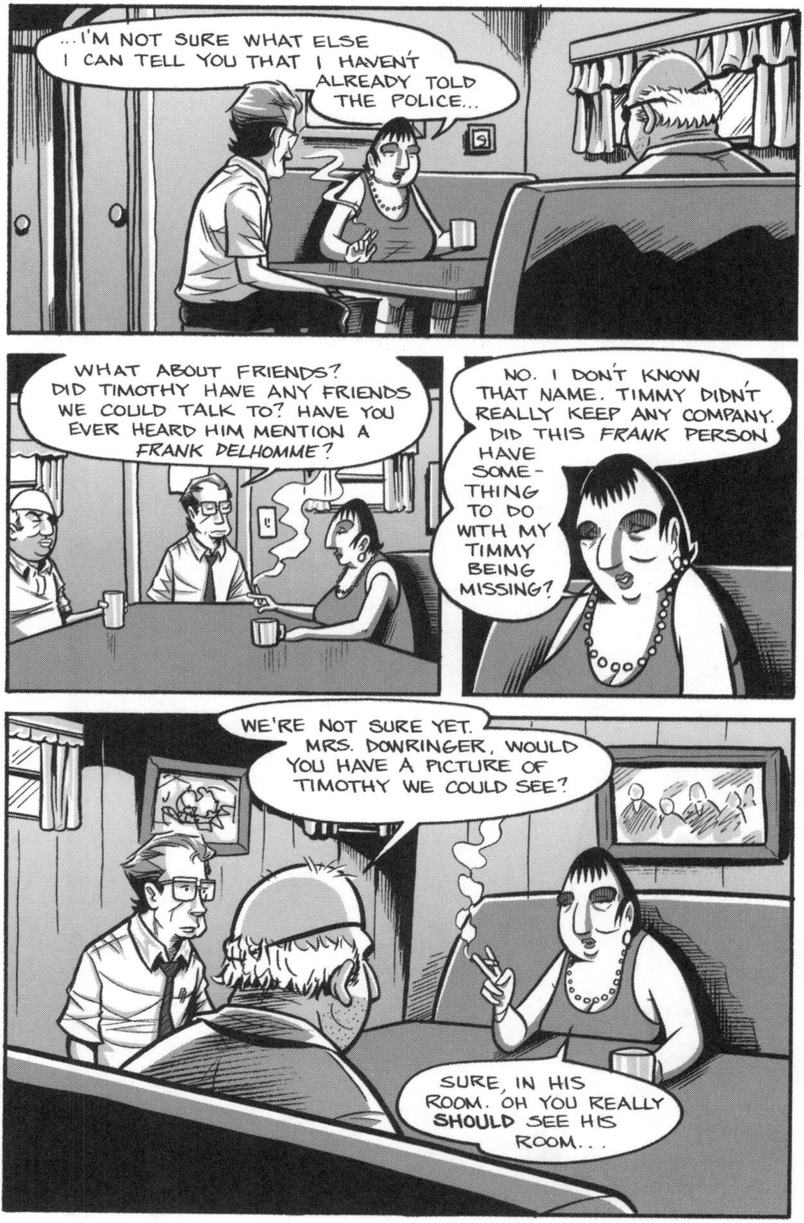
...I'M NOT SURE WHAT ELSE I CAN TELL YOU THAT I HAVEN'T ALREADY TOLD THE POLICE...
WHAT ABOUT FRIENDS? DID TIMOTHY HAVE ANY FRIENDS WE COULD TALK TO? HAVE YOU EVER HEARD HIM MENTION A *FRANK DELHOMME*?
NO. I DON'T KNOW THAT NAME. TIMMY DIDN'T REALLY KEEP ANY COMPANY. DID THIS *FRANK* PERSON HAVE SOME-THING TO DO WITH MY TIMMY BEING MISSING?
WE'RE NOT SURE YET. MRS. DOWRINGER, WOULD YOU HAVE A PICTURE OF TIMOTHY WE COULD SEE?
SURE, IN HIS ROOM. OH YOU REALLY **SHOULD** SEE HIS ROOM...

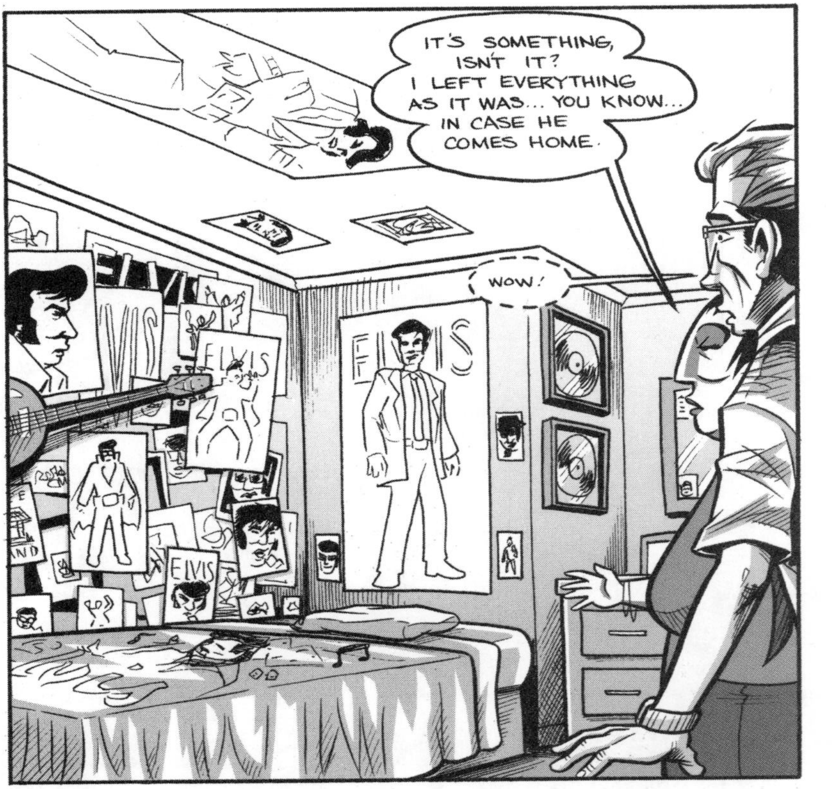
IT'S SOMETHING, ISN'T IT? I LEFT EVERYTHING AS IT WAS... YOU KNOW... IN CASE HE COMES HOME.
WOW!
ELVIS

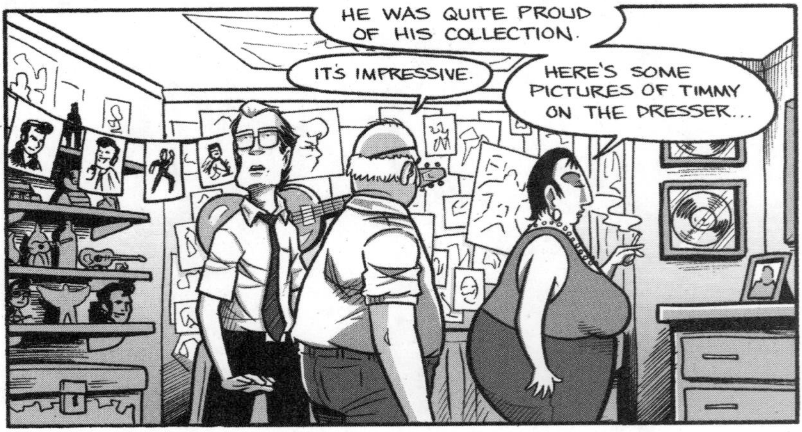
HE WAS QUITE PROUD OF HIS COLLECTION.
IT'S IMPRESSIVE.
HERE'S SOME PICTURES OF TIMMY ON THE DRESSER...

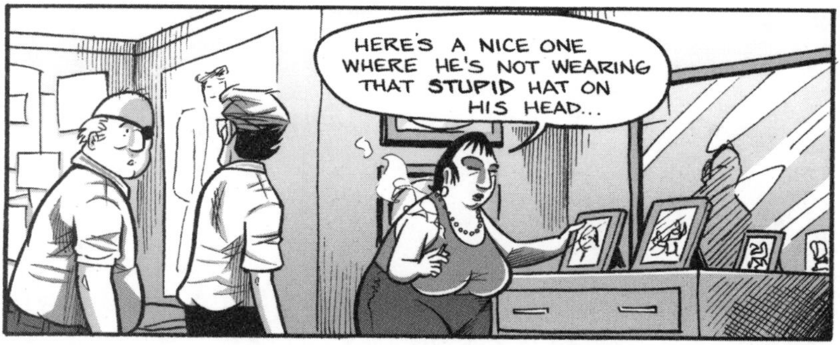
HERE'S A NICE ONE WHERE HE'S NOT WEARING THAT STUPID HAT ON HIS HEAD...

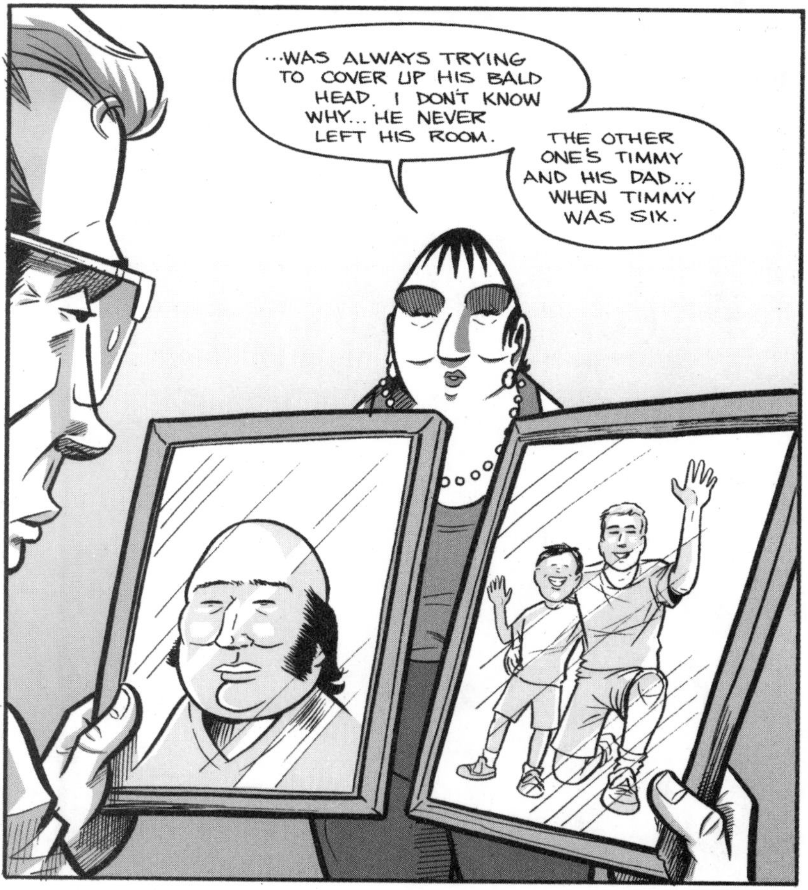
...WAS ALWAYS TRYING TO COVER UP HIS BALD HEAD. I DON'T KNOW WHY... HE NEVER LEFT HIS ROOM.
THE OTHER ONE'S TIMMY AND HIS DAD... WHEN TIMMY WAS SIX.

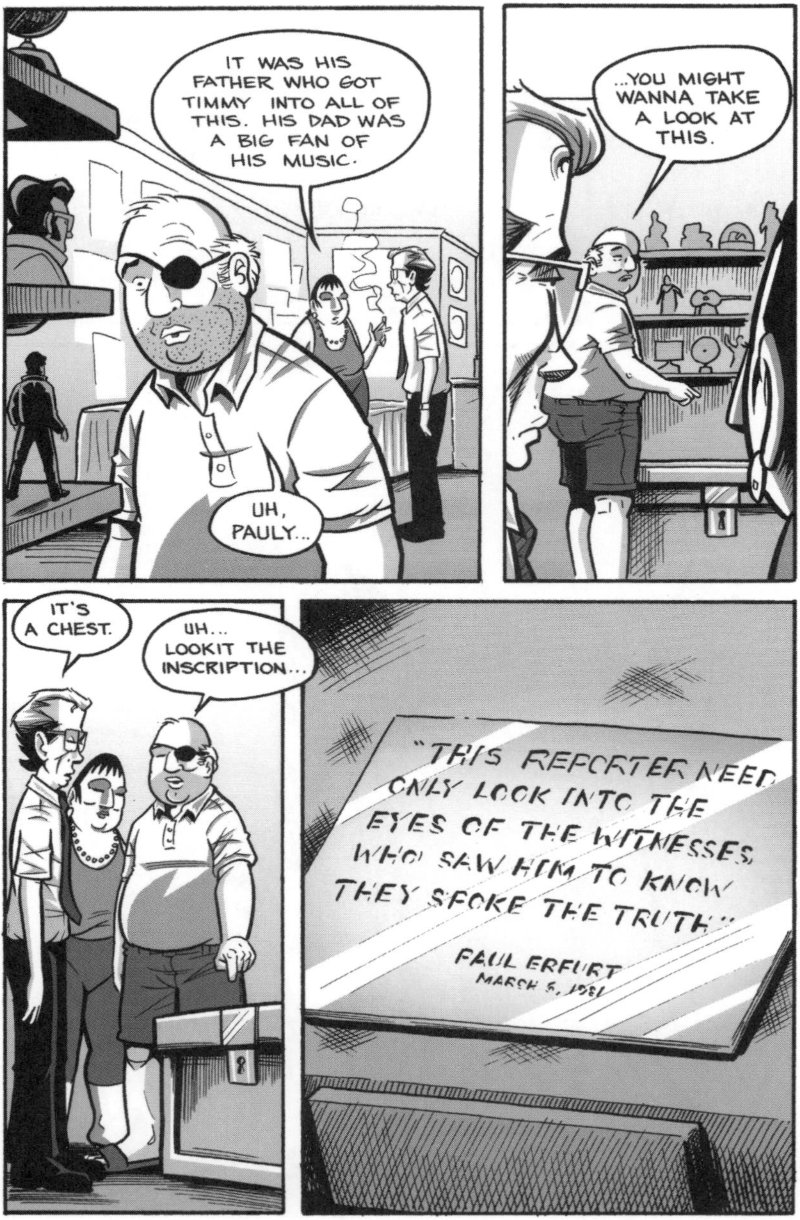

IT WAS HIS FATHER WHO GOT TIMMY INTO ALL OF THIS. HIS DAD WAS A BIG FAN OF HIS MUSIC.
UH, PAULY...
...YOU MIGHT WANNA TAKE A LOOK AT THIS.
IT'S A CHEST.
UH... LOOKIT THE INSCRIPTION...
"THIS REPORTER NEED ONLY LOOK INTO THE EYES OF THE WITNESSES WHO SAW HIM TO KNOW THEY SPOKE THE TRUTH."
PAUL ERFURT
MARCH 5, 1981

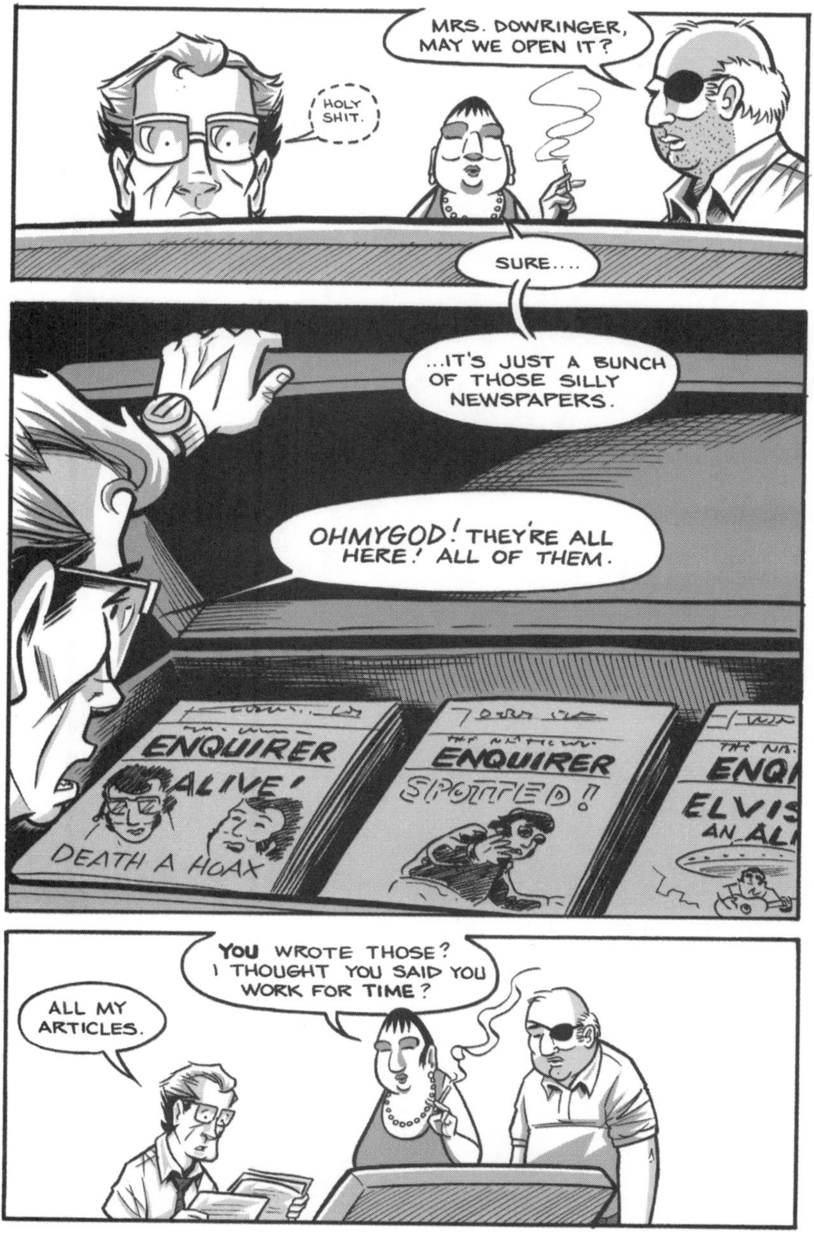
MRS. DOWRINGER, MAY WE OPEN IT?
HOLY SHIT.
SURE....
...IT'S JUST A BUNCH OF THOSE SILLY NEWSPAPERS.
OHMYGOD! THEY'RE ALL HERE! ALL OF THEM.
ENQUIRER
ALIVE!
DEATH A HOAX
ENQUIRER
SPOTTED!
ELVIS
ALL MY ARTICLES.
YOU WROTE THOSE? I THOUGHT YOU SAID YOU WORK FOR TIME?

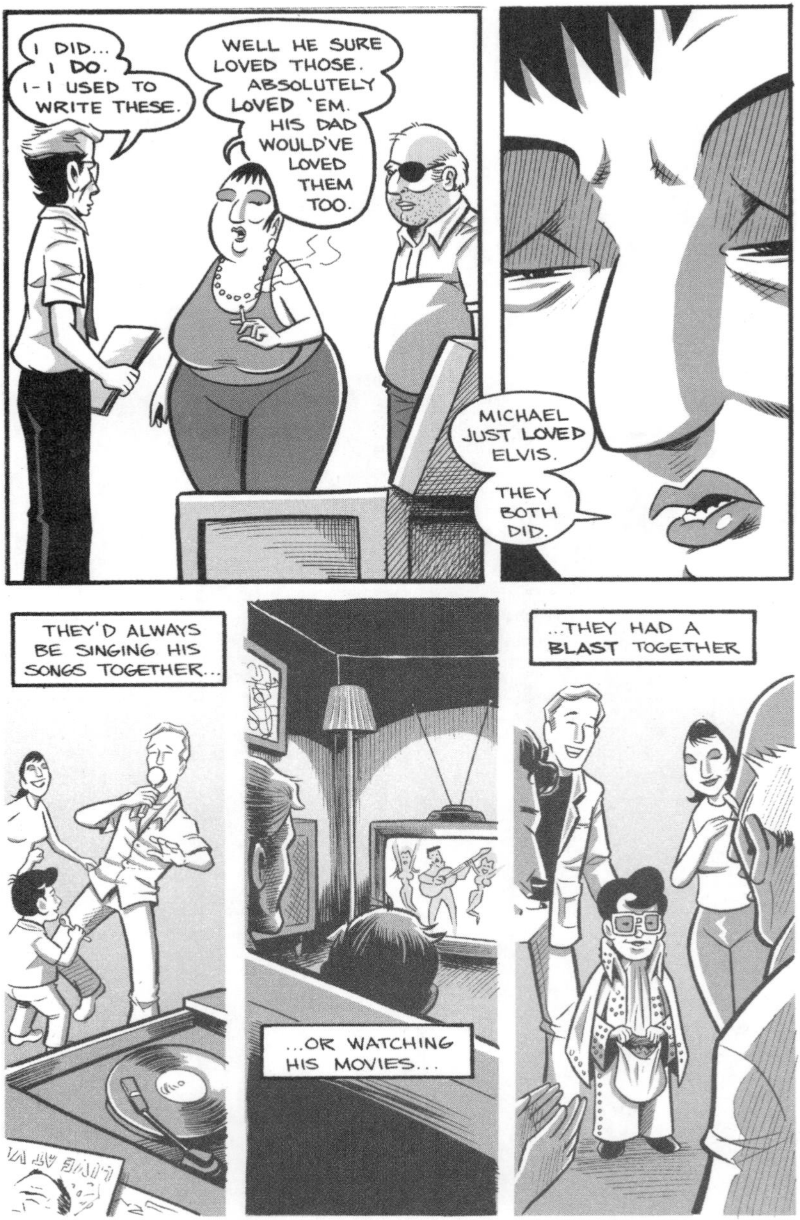
I DID...
I DO.
I-I USED TO WRITE THESE.
WELL HE SURE LOVED THOSE. ABSOLUTELY LOVED 'EM.
HIS DAD WOULD'VE LOVED THEM TOO.
MICHAEL JUST LOVED ELVIS.
THEY BOTH DID.
THEY'D ALWAYS BE SINGING HIS SONGS TOGETHER...
...OR WATCHING HIS MOVIES...
...THEY HAD A BLAST TOGETHER

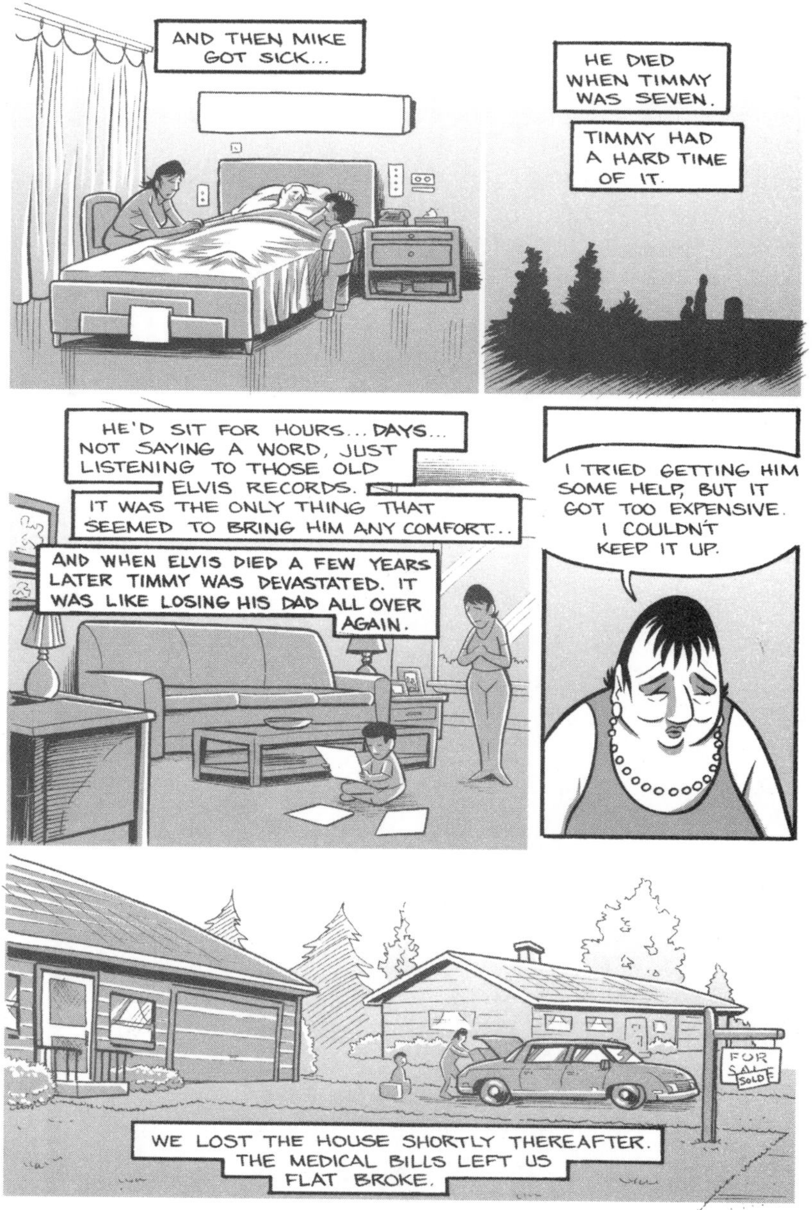
AND THEN MIKE GOT SICK...
HE DIED WHEN TIMMY WAS SEVEN.
TIMMY HAD A HARD TIME OF IT.
HE'D SIT FOR HOURS... DAYS... NOT SAYING A WORD, JUST LISTENING TO THOSE OLD ELVIS RECORDS.
IT WAS THE ONLY THING THAT SEEMED TO BRING HIM ANY COMFORT...
AND WHEN ELVIS DIED A FEW YEARS LATER TIMMY WAS DEVASTATED. IT WAS LIKE LOSING HIS DAD ALL OVER AGAIN.
I TRIED GETTING HIM SOME HELP, BUT IT GOT TOO EXPENSIVE. I COULDN'T KEEP IT UP.
FOR
SOLD
WE LOST THE HOUSE SHORTLY THEREAFTER. THE MEDICAL BILLS LEFT US FLAT BROKE.

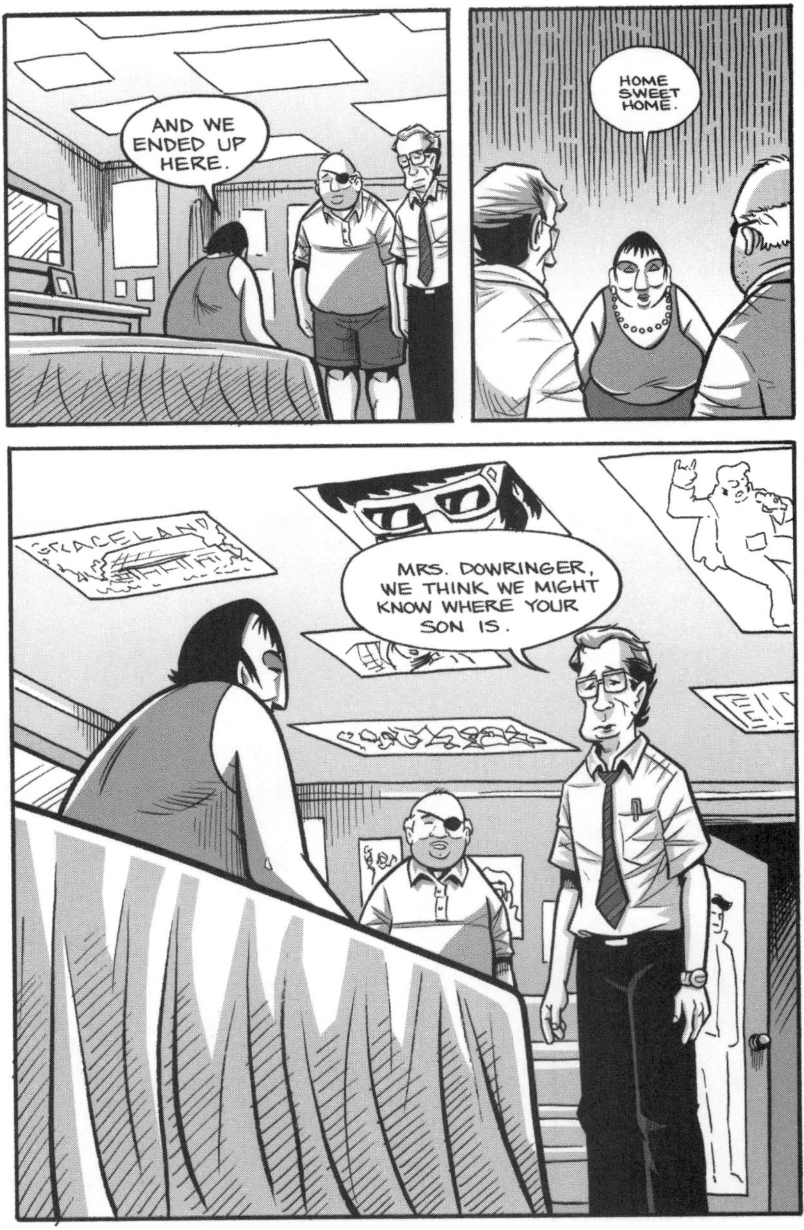
AND WE ENDED UP HERE.
HOME SWEET HOME.
GRACELAND
MRS. DOWRINGER, WE THINK WE MIGHT KNOW WHERE YOUR SON IS.

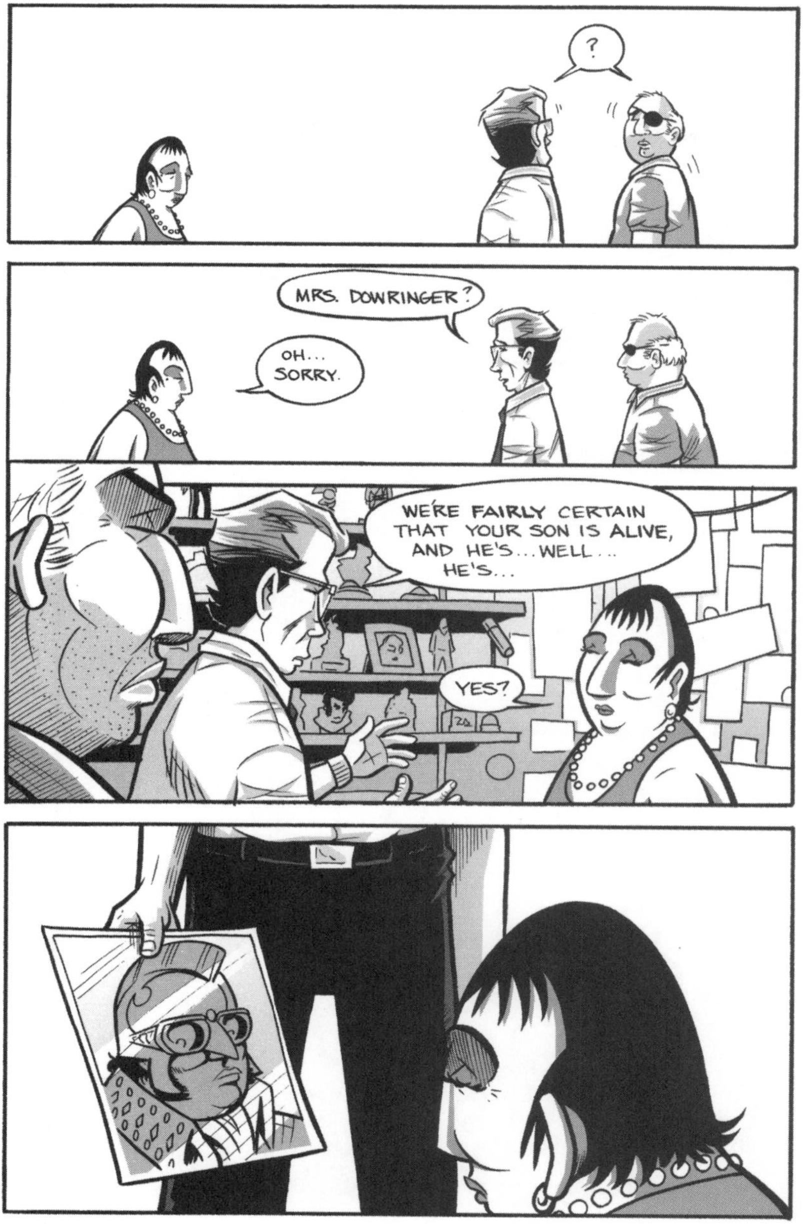
?
MRS. DOWRINGER?
OH... SORRY.
WE'RE FAIRLY CERTAIN THAT YOUR SON IS ALIVE, AND HE'S...WELL... HE'S...
YES?

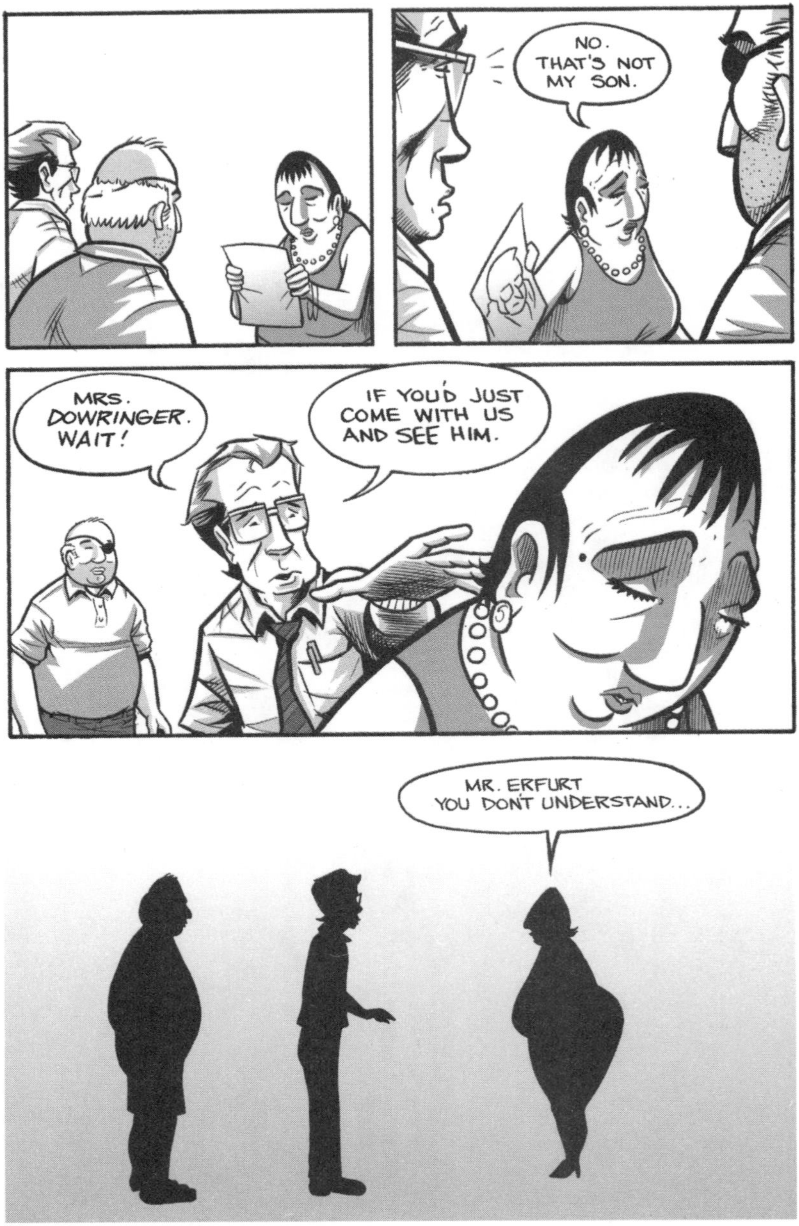

NO. THAT'S NOT MY SON.
MRS. DOWRINGER. WAIT!
IF YOU'D JUST COME WITH US AND SEE HIM.
MR. ERFURT YOU DON'T UNDERSTAND...

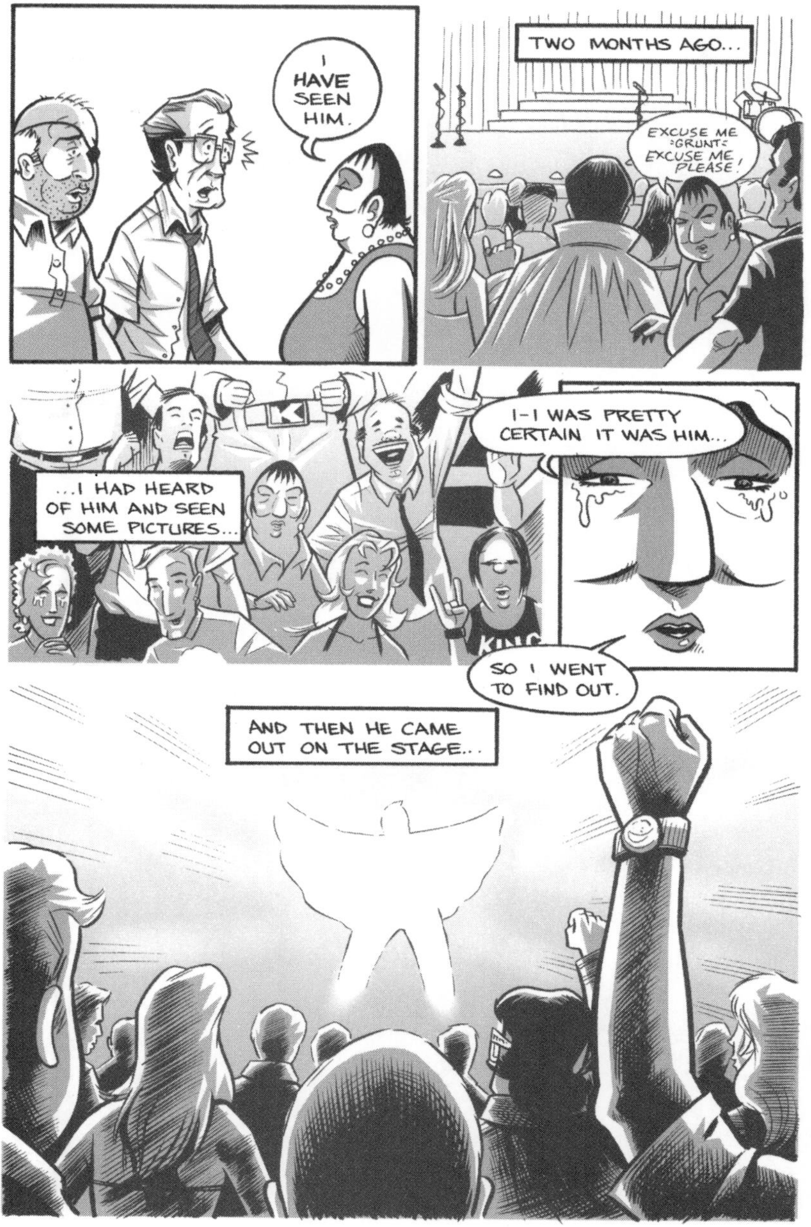
I HAVE SEEN HIM.
TWO MONTHS AGO...
EXCUSE ME :GRUNT: EXCUSE ME PLEASE!
I-I WAS PRETTY CERTAIN IT WAS HIM...
...I HAD HEARD OF HIM AND SEEN SOME PICTURES...
KING
SO I WENT TO FIND OUT.
AND THEN HE CAME OUT ON THE STAGE...

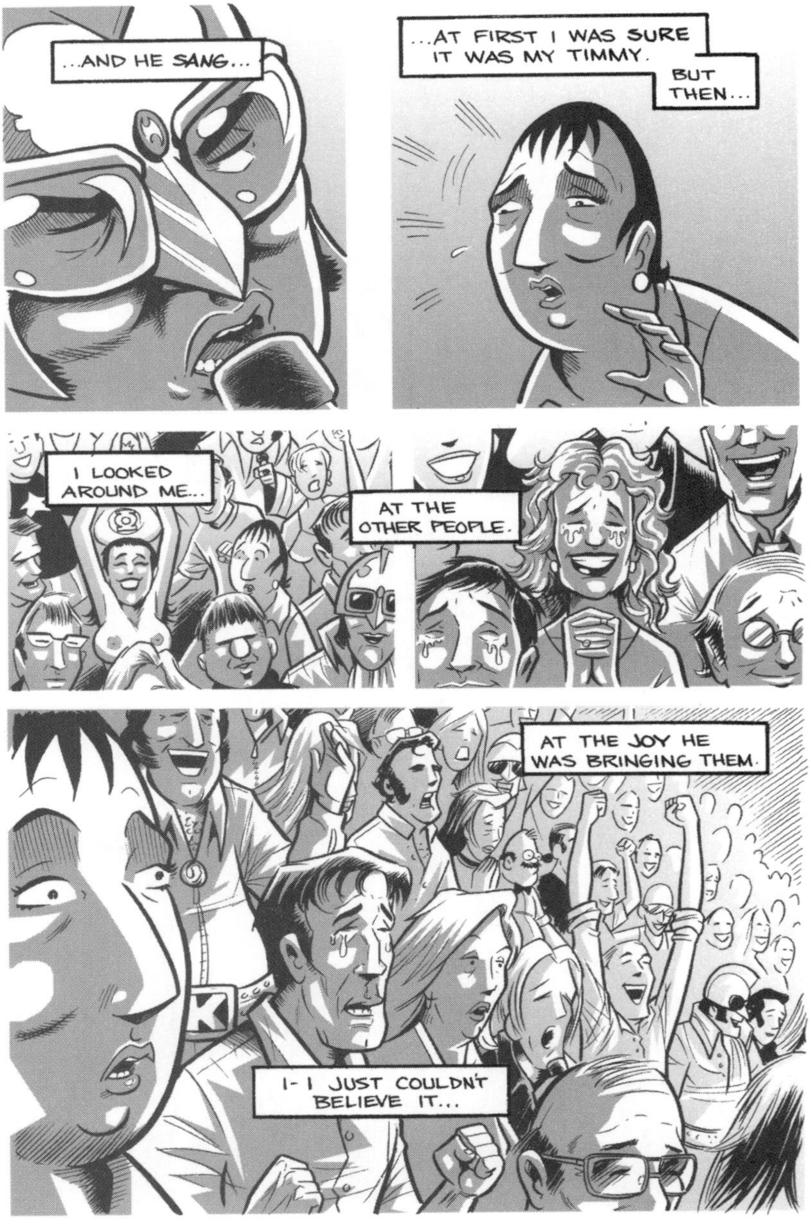
...AND HE SANG...
...AT FIRST I WAS SURE IT WAS MY TIMMY.
BUT THEN...
I LOOKED AROUND ME...
AT THE OTHER PEOPLE.
AT THE JOY HE WAS BRINGING THEM.
I- I JUST COULDN'T BELIEVE IT...

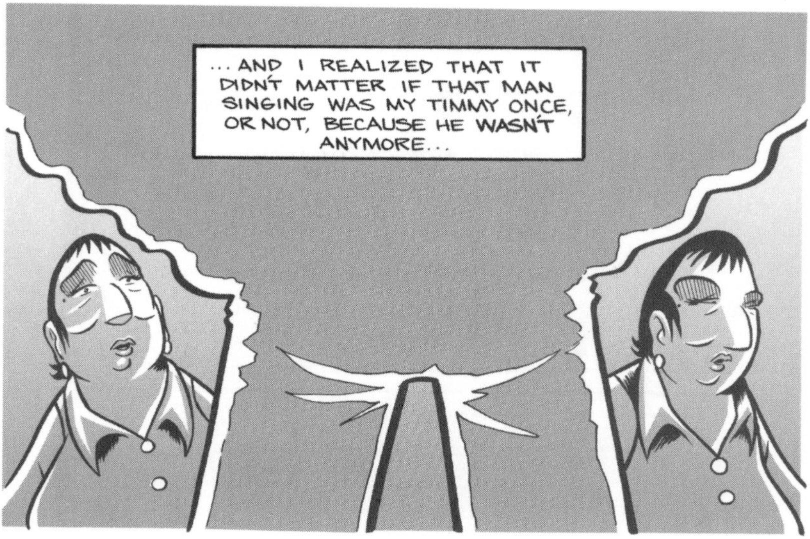
...AND I REALIZED THAT IT DIDN'T MATTER IF THAT MAN SINGING WAS MY TIMMY ONCE, OR NOT, BECAUSE HE WASN'T ANYMORE...

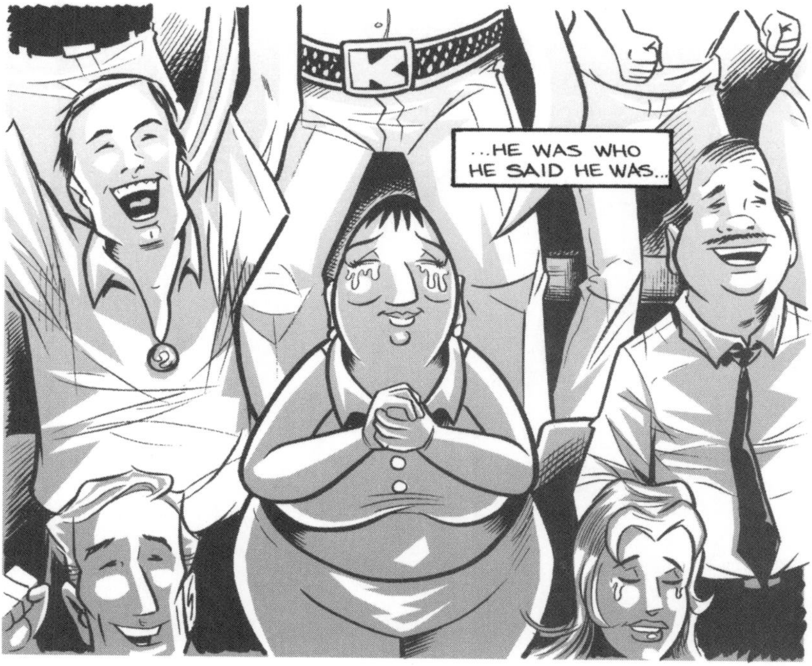
...HE WAS WHO HE SAID HE WAS...

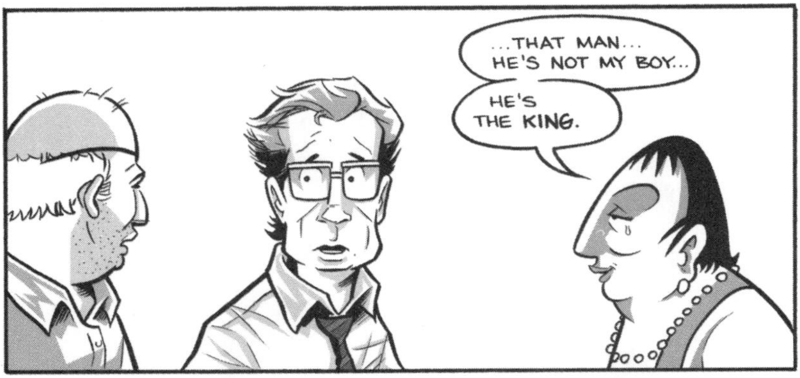
...THAT MAN...
HE'S NOT MY BOY...
HE'S
THE KING.

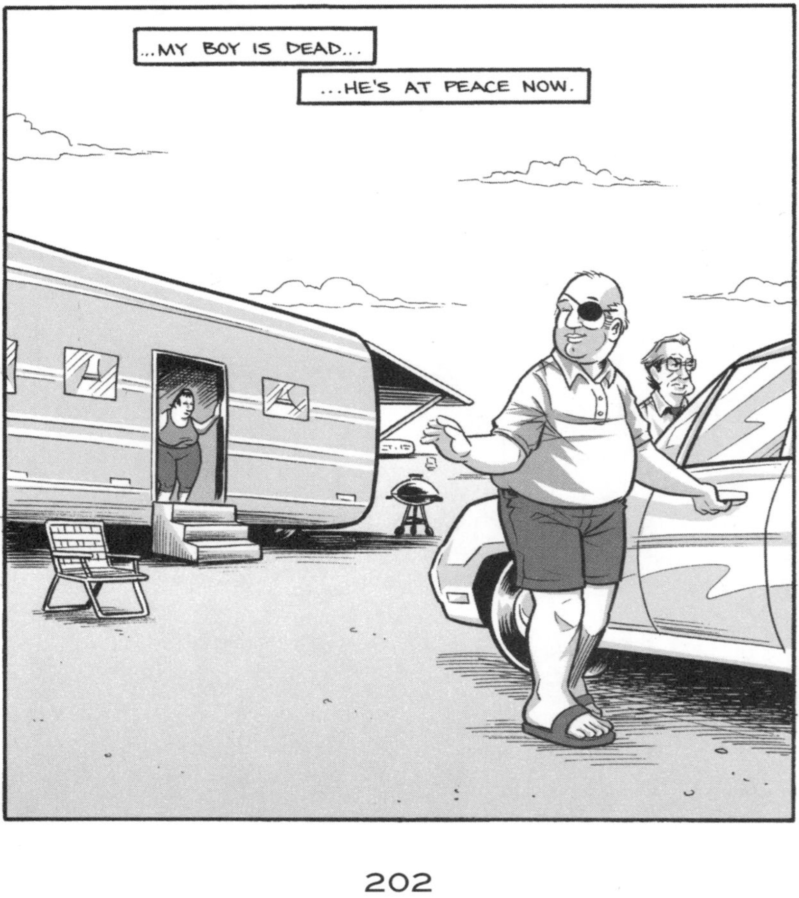
...MY BOY IS DEAD...
...HE'S AT PEACE NOW.

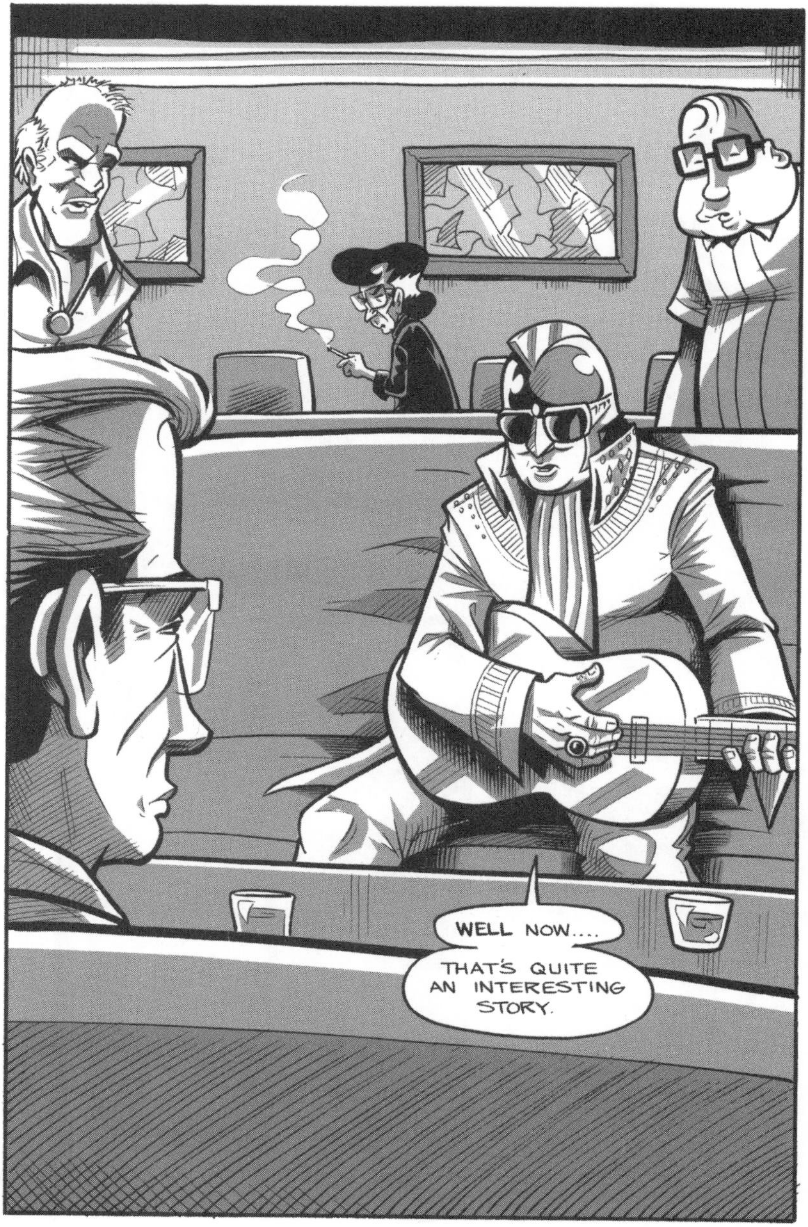
WELL NOW....
THAT'S QUITE AN INTERESTING STORY.

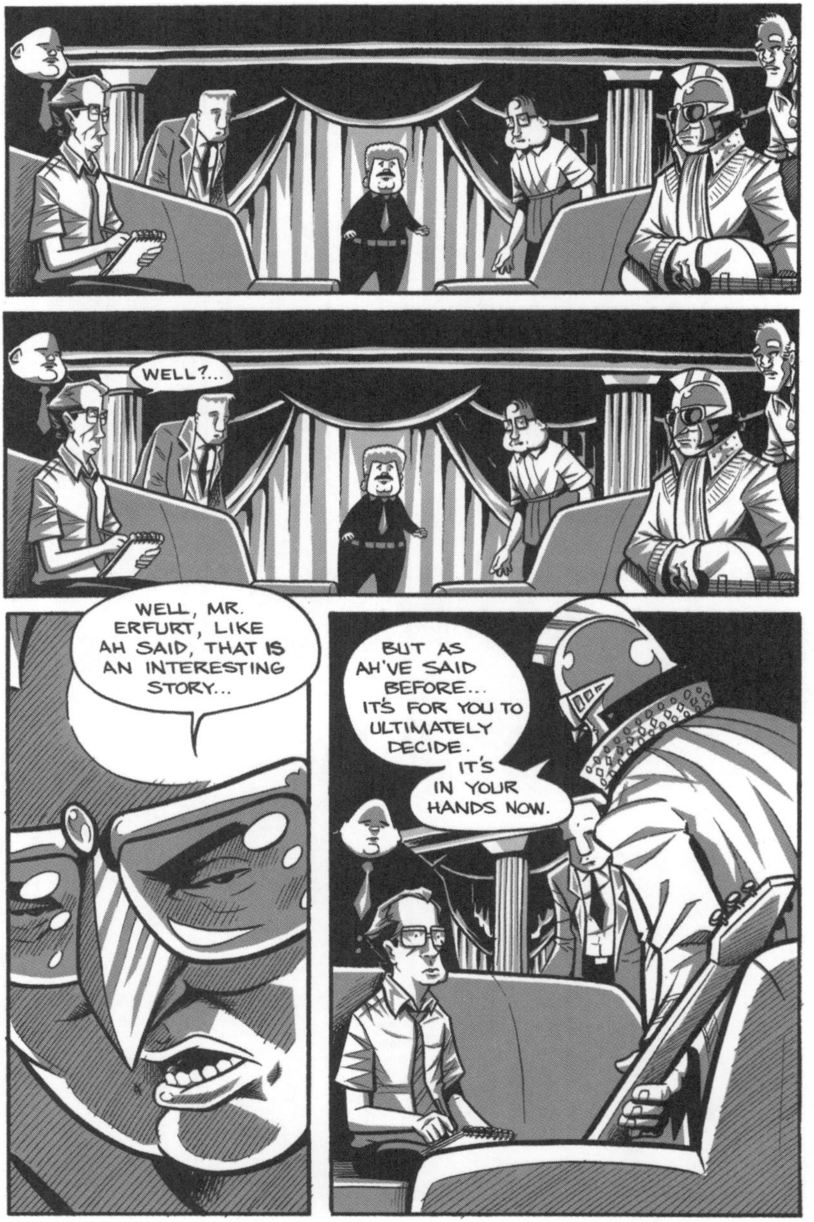
WELL?...
WELL, MR. ERFURT, LIKE AH SAID, THAT IS AN INTERESTING STORY...
BUT AS AH'VE SAID BEFORE... IT'S FOR YOU TO ULTIMATELY DECIDE.
IT'S IN YOUR HANDS NOW.

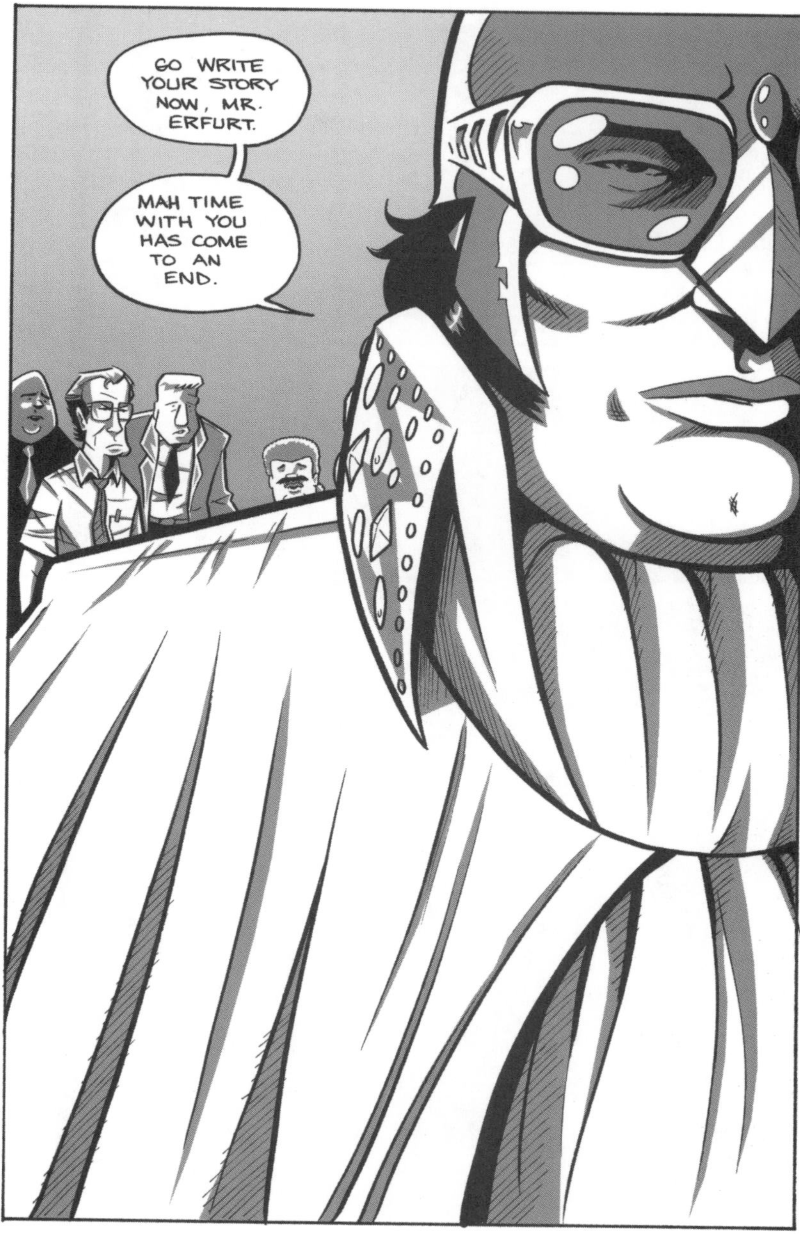
GO WRITE YOUR STORY NOW, MR. ERFURT.
MAH TIME WITH YOU HAS COME TO AN END.

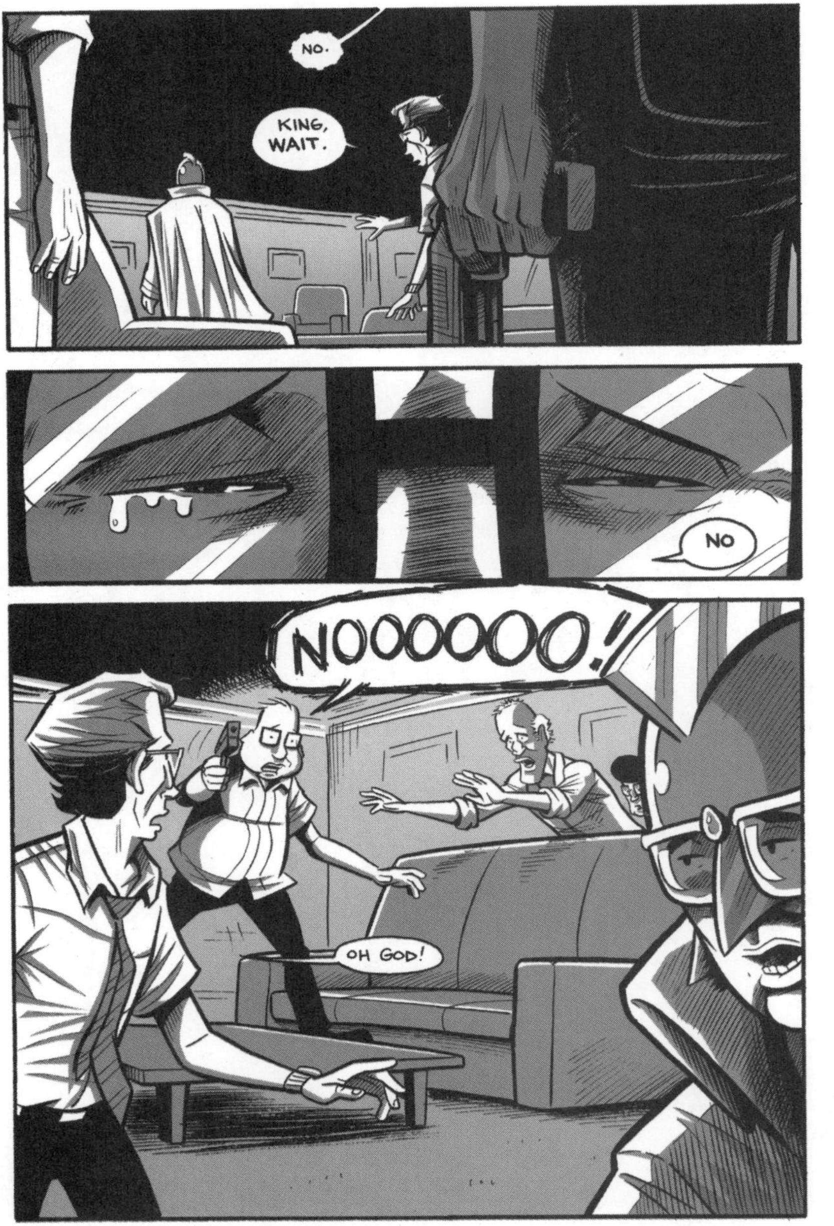
NO.
KING, WAIT.
NO
NOOOOOO!
OH GOD!

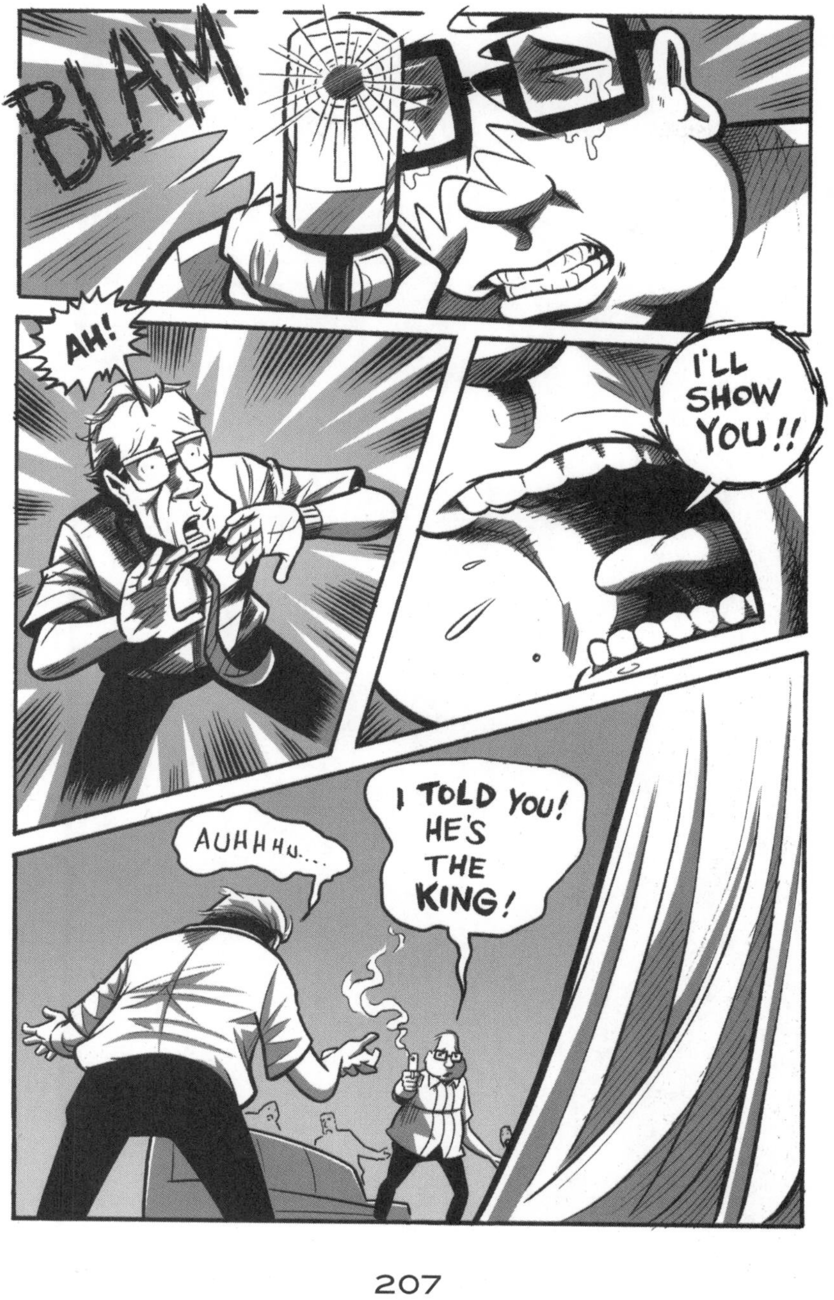
BLAM
AH!
I'LL SHOW YOU!!
AUHHHN...
I TOLD YOU! HE'S THE KING!

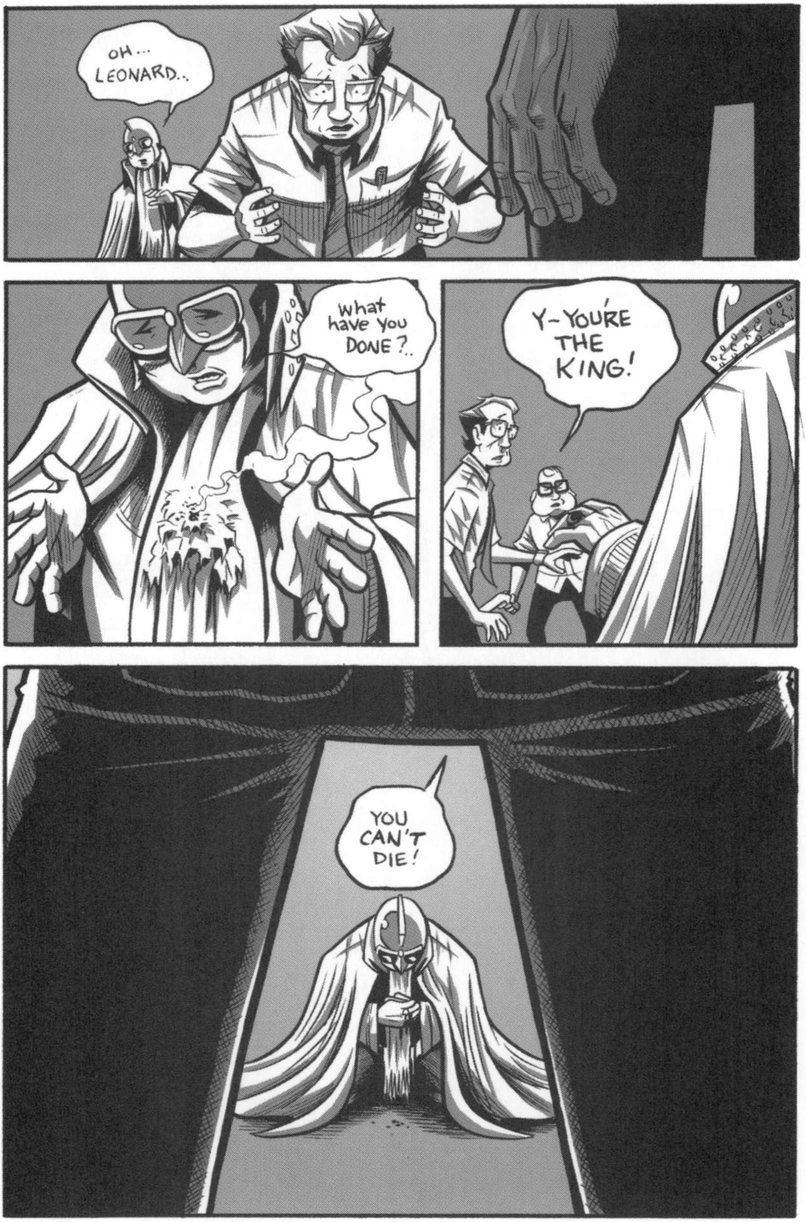
OH... LEONARD..
What have you DONE?..
Y-YOU'RE THE KING!
YOU CAN'T DIE!

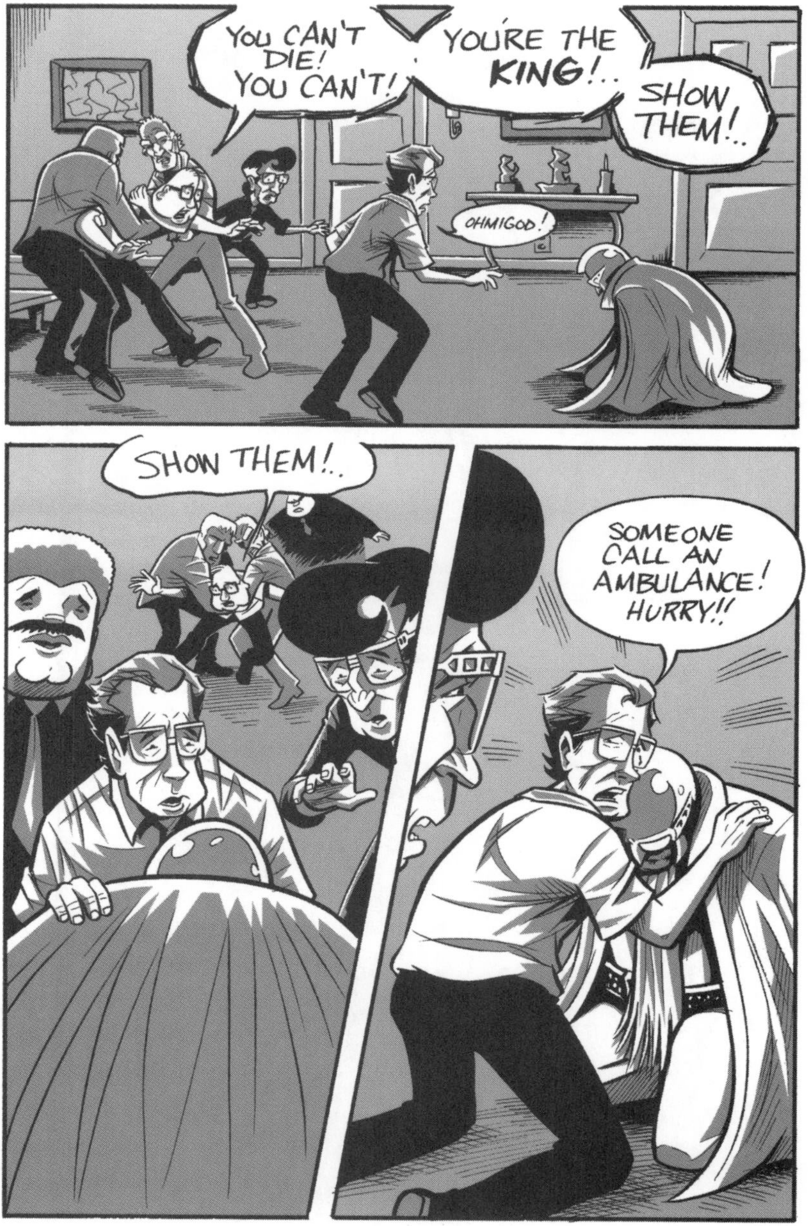
YOU CAN'T DIE! YOU CAN'T!
YOU'RE THE KING!..
SHOW THEM!..
OHMIGOD!
SHOW THEM!..
SOMEONE CALL AN AMBULANCE! HURRY!!

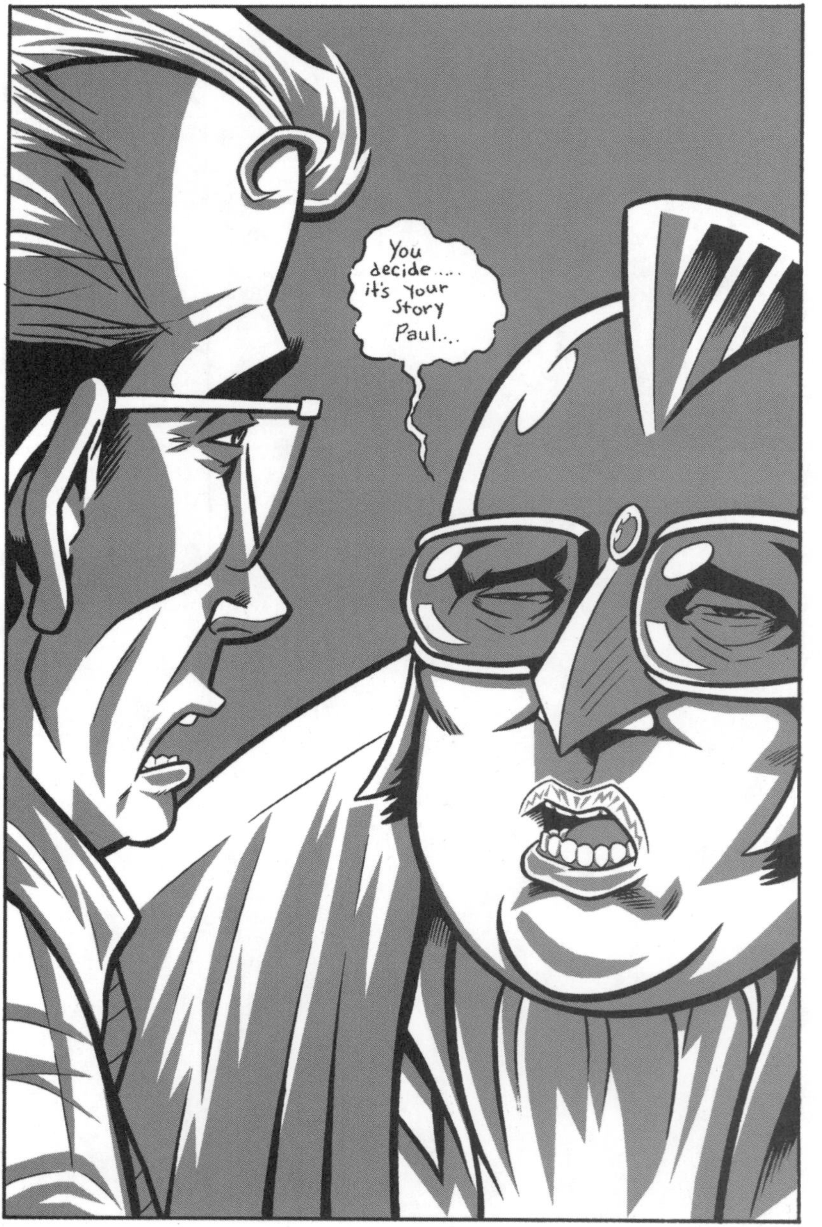
You decide..... it's your story Paul....

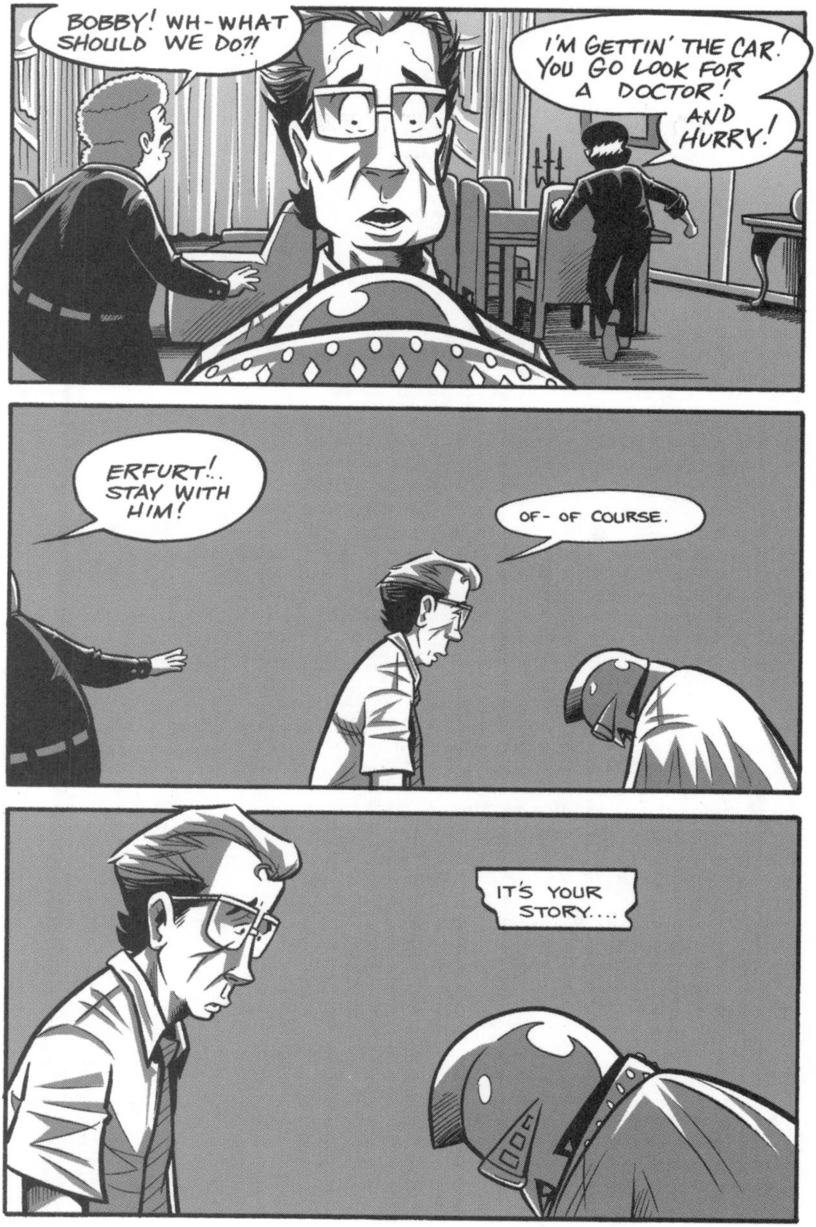
BOBBY! WH-WHAT SHOULD WE DO?!
I'M GETTIN' THE CAR! YOU GO LOOK FOR A DOCTOR!
AND HURRY!
ERFURT!.. STAY WITH HIM!
OF- OF COURSE.
IT'S YOUR STORY....

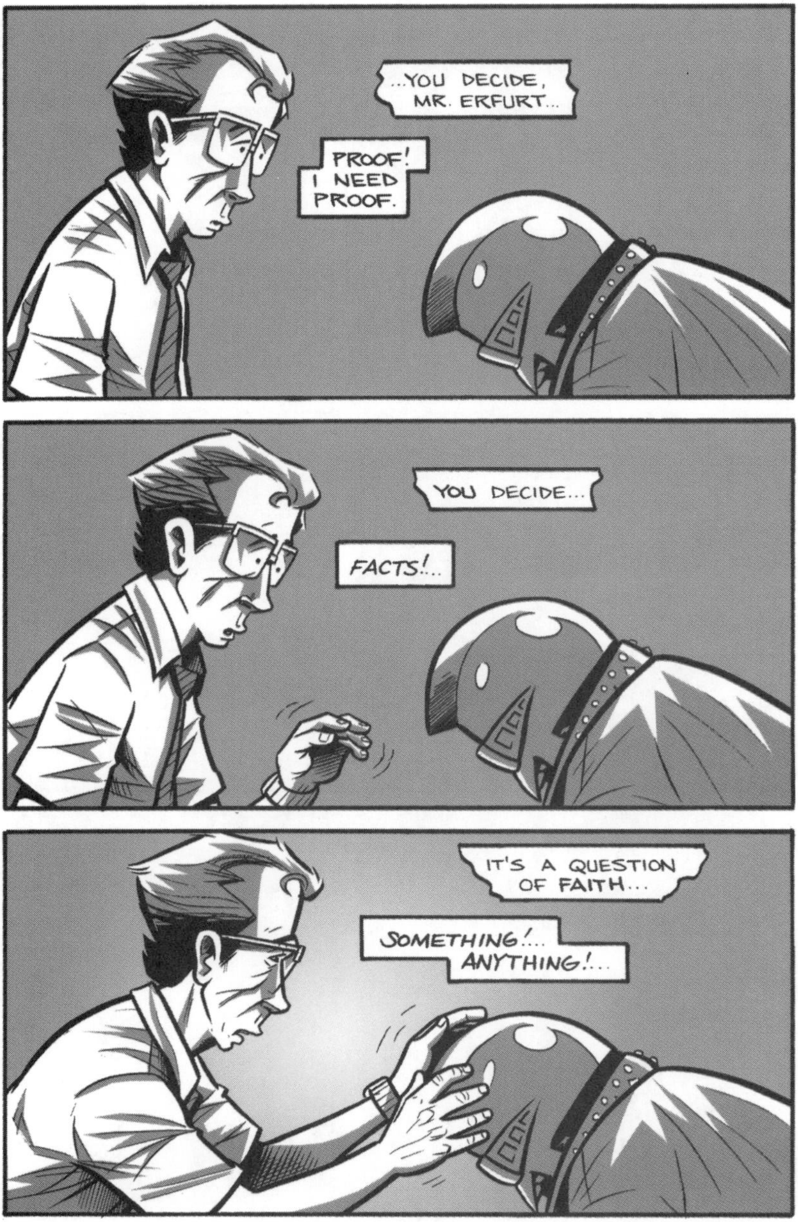
...YOU DECIDE, MR. ERFURT...
PROOF! I NEED PROOF.
YOU DECIDE...
FACTS!...
IT'S A QUESTION OF FAITH...
SOMETHING!... ANYTHING!...

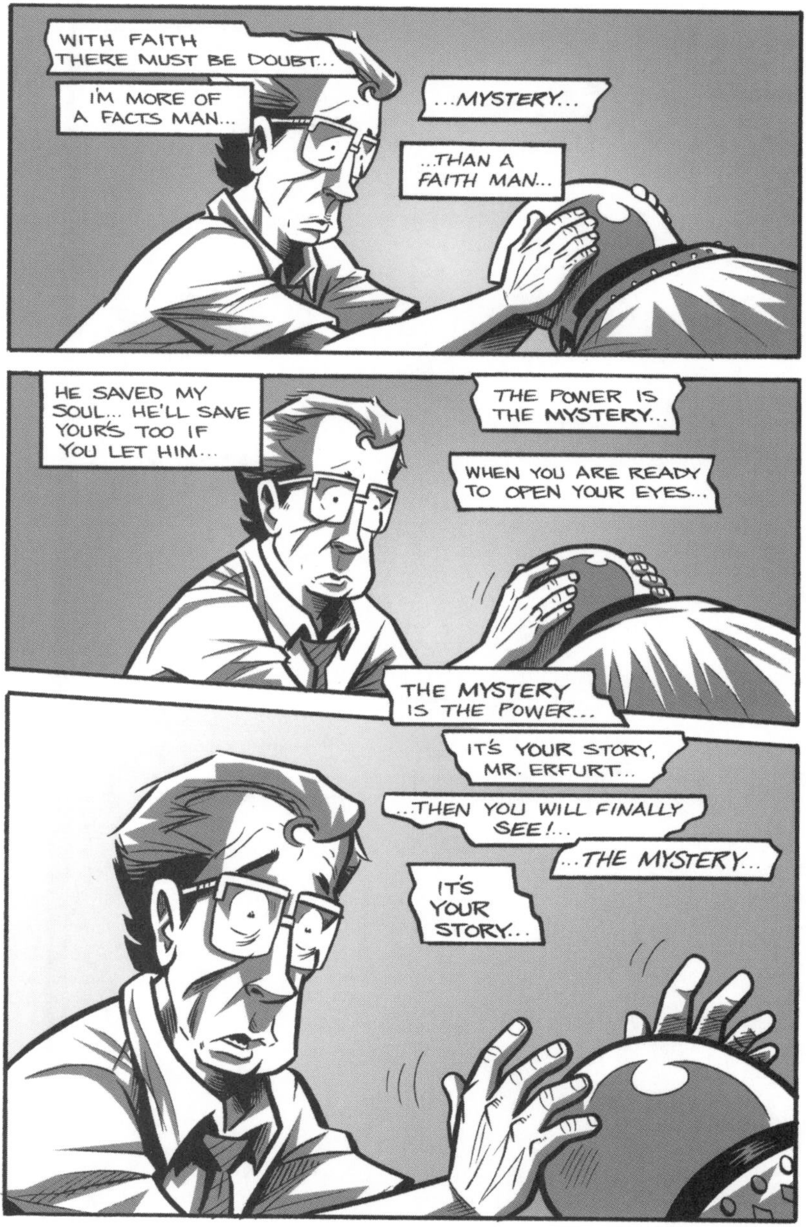
WITH FAITH THERE MUST BE DOUBT...
I'M MORE OF A FACTS MAN...
...MYSTERY...
...THAN A FAITH MAN...
HE SAVED MY SOUL... HE'LL SAVE YOUR'S TOO IF YOU LET HIM...
THE POWER IS THE MYSTERY...
WHEN YOU ARE READY TO OPEN YOUR EYES...
THE MYSTERY IS THE POWER...
IT'S YOUR STORY, MR. ERFURT...
...THEN YOU WILL FINALLY SEE!...
...THE MYSTERY...
IT'S YOUR STORY...

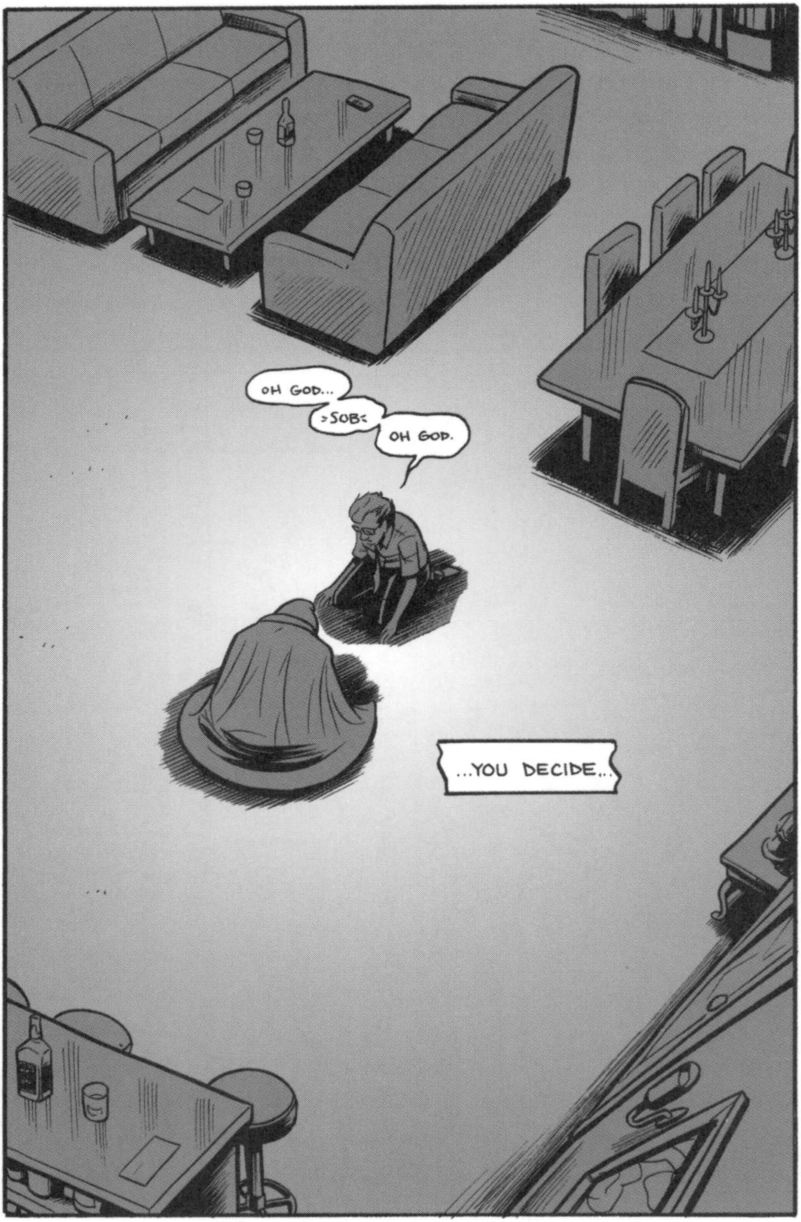
OH GOD...
>SOB<
OH GOD.
...YOU DECIDE...

"LIFE IS MORE THAN DRAWING BREATH."

— ELVIS

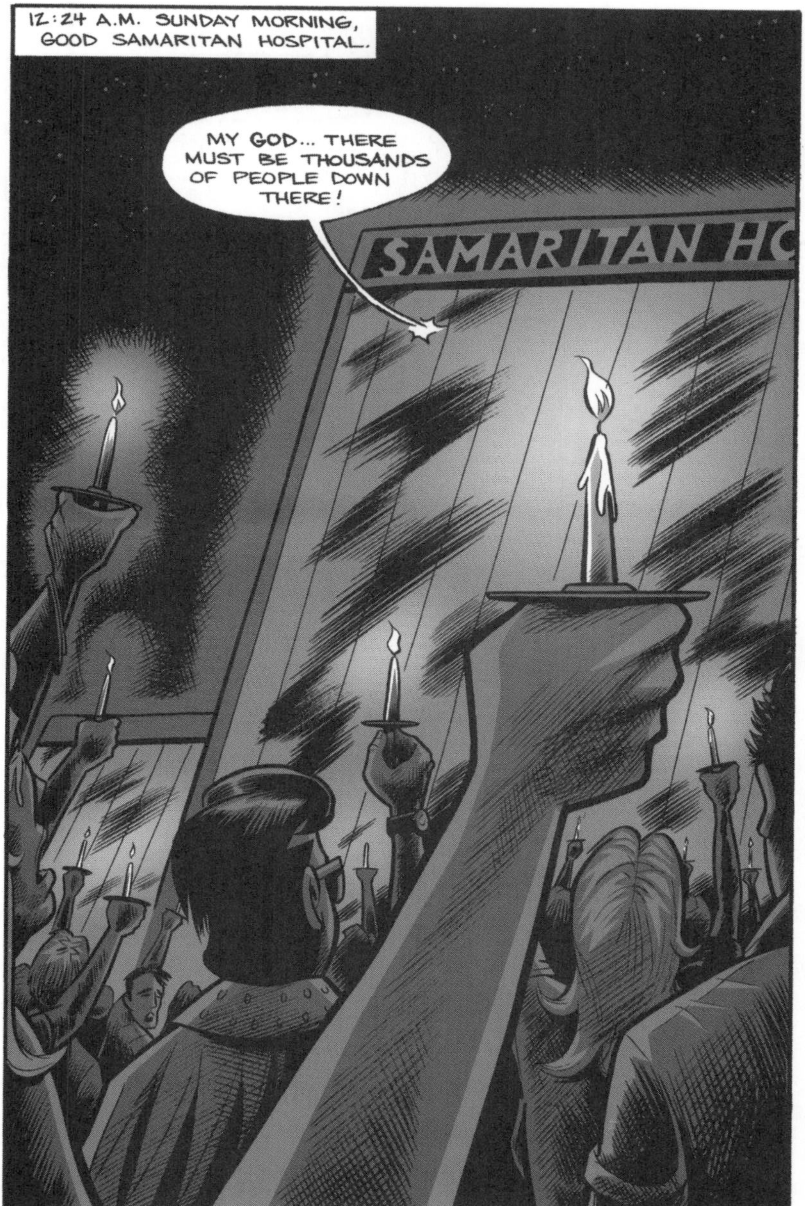
12:24 A.M. SUNDAY MORNING, GOOD SAMARITAN HOSPITAL.
MY GOD... THERE MUST BE THOUSANDS OF PEOPLE DOWN THERE!
SAMARITAN HO

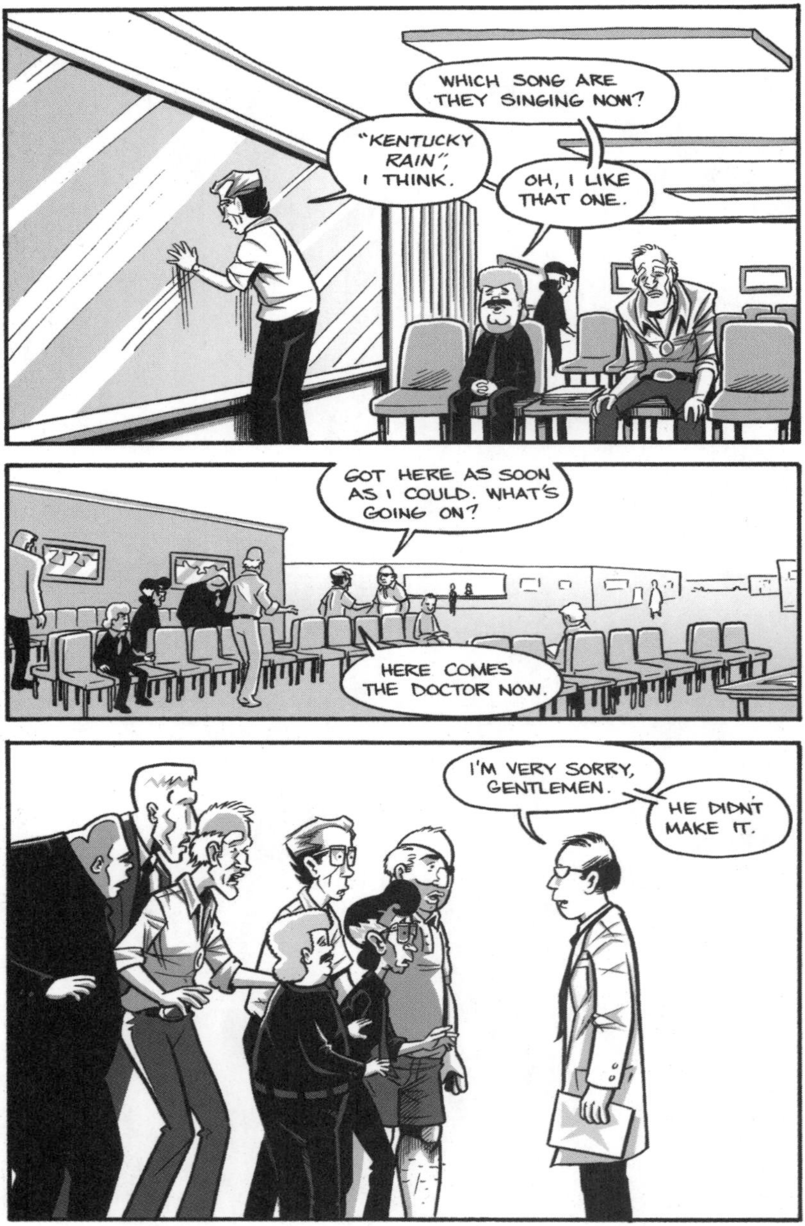
WHICH SONG ARE THEY SINGING NOW?
"KENTUCKY RAIN", I THINK.
OH, I LIKE THAT ONE.
GOT HERE AS SOON AS I COULD. WHAT'S GOING ON?
HERE COMES THE DOCTOR NOW.
I'M VERY SORRY, GENTLEMEN.
HE DIDN'T MAKE IT.

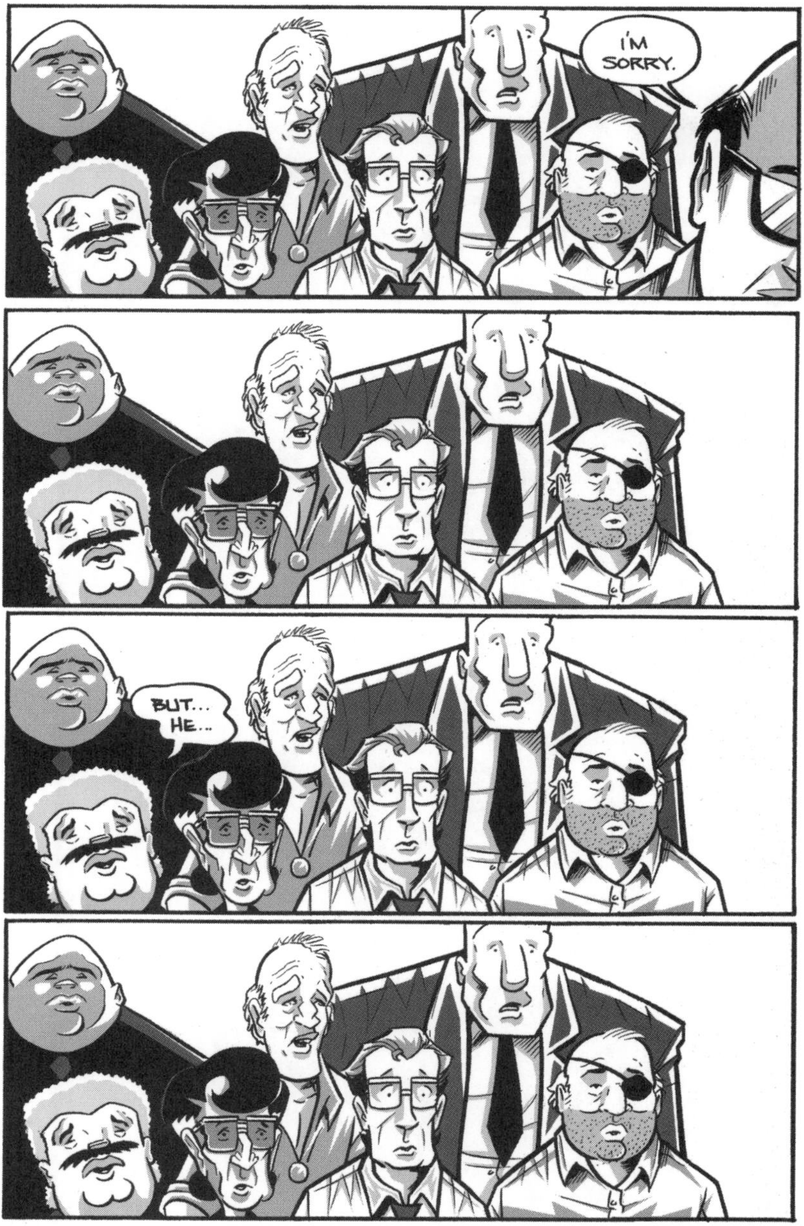
I'M SORRY.
BUT... HE...

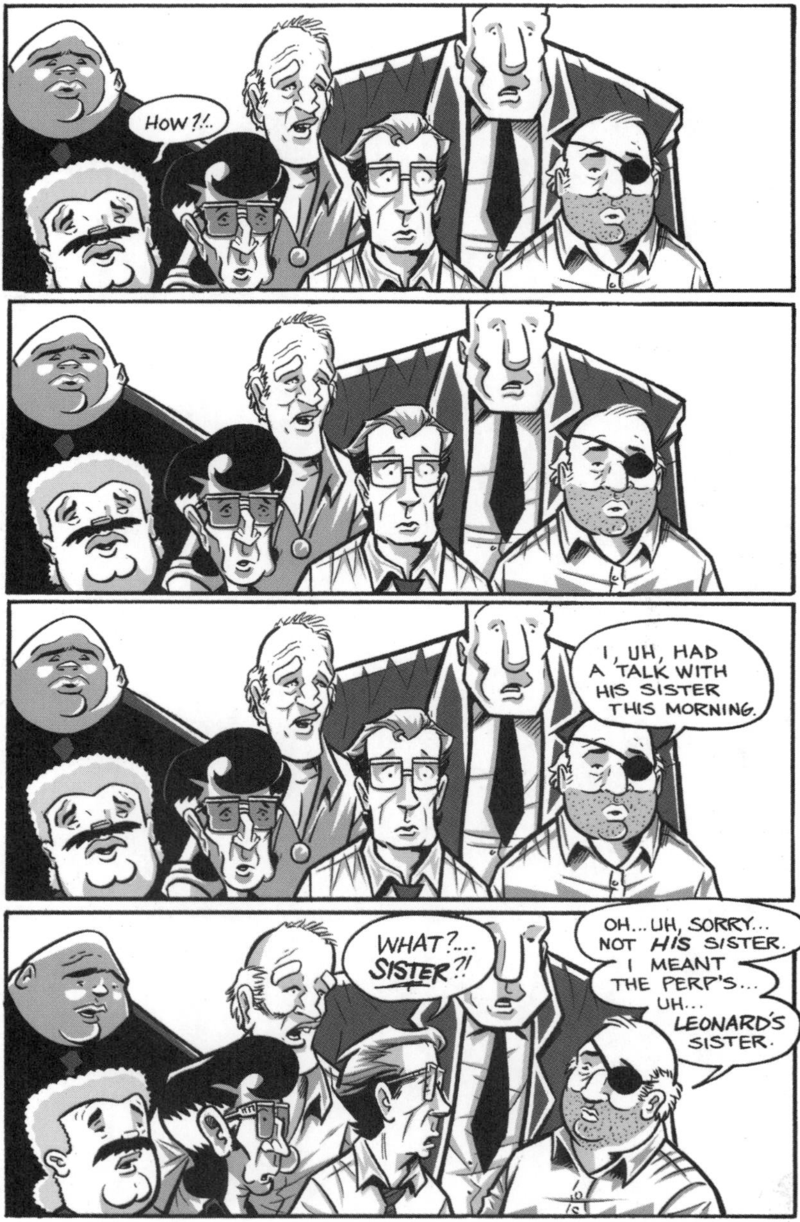
HOW?!..
I, UH, HAD A TALK WITH HIS SISTER THIS MORNING.
WHAT?... SISTER?!
OH... UH, SORRY... NOT HIS SISTER. I MEANT THE PERP'S... UH... LEONARD'S SISTER.

...DOWN AT THE P.D. WHERE THEY'RE HOLDIN' HIM. I SWUNG BY THERE QUICK BEFORE HEADIN' HERE.

...BUDDY THERE CALLED ME SOON AS THEY GOT THE CALL 'BOUT THE SHOOTING.

...SHE WAS GLAD TA TALK TA ME... TA ANYONE.

TOLD ME ABOUT WHEN THEY WERE KIDS...

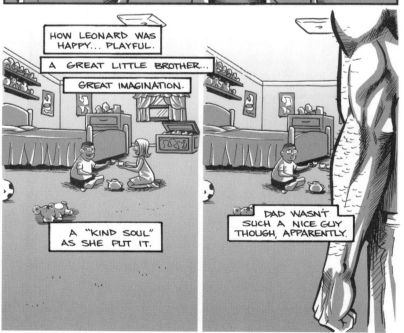

HOW LEONARD WAS HAPPY... PLAYFUL.

A GREAT LITTLE BROTHER...

GREAT IMAGINATION.

A "KIND SOUL" AS SHE PUT IT.

DAD WASN'T SUCH A NICE GUY THOUGH, APPARENTLY.

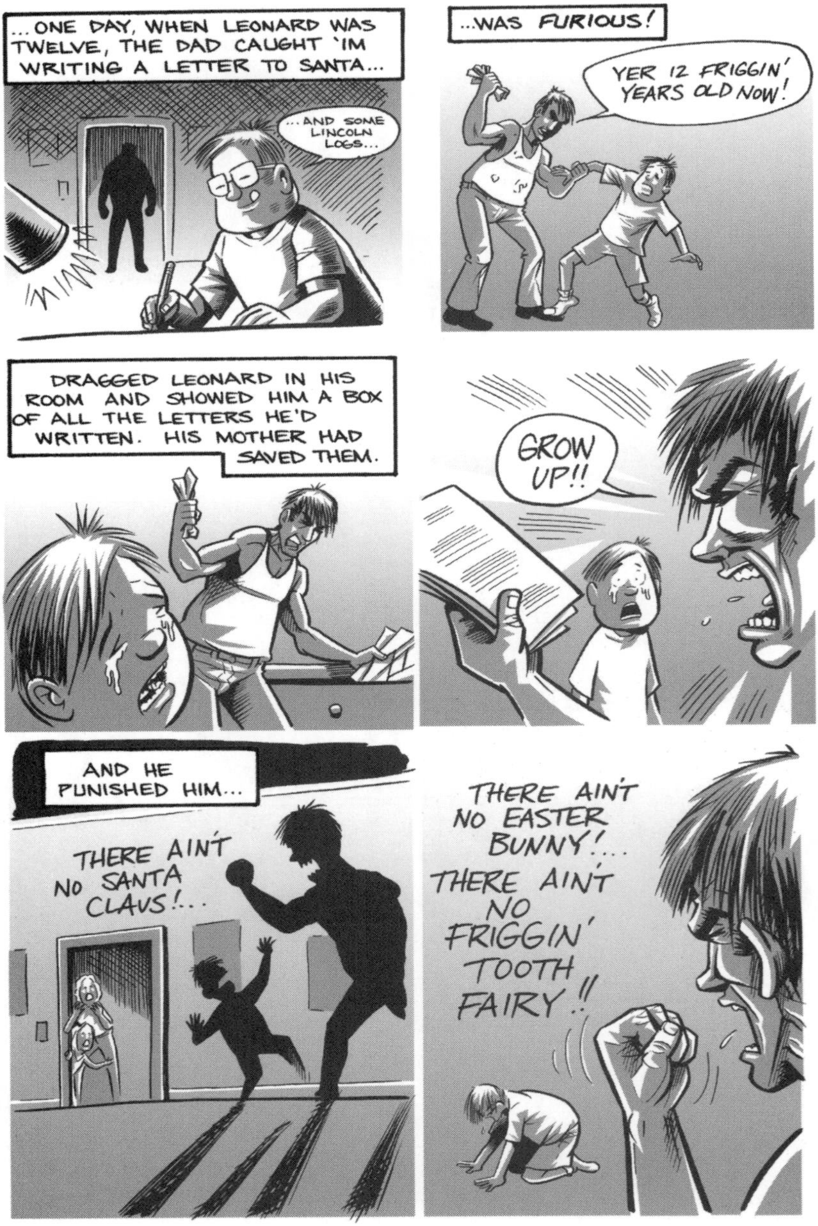
...ONE DAY, WHEN LEONARD WAS TWELVE, THE DAD CAUGHT 'IM WRITING A LETTER TO SANTA...
...AND SOME LINCOLN LOGS...
...WAS FURIOUS!
YER 12 FRIGGIN' YEARS OLD NOW!
DRAGGED LEONARD IN HIS ROOM AND SHOWED HIM A BOX OF ALL THE LETTERS HE'D WRITTEN. HIS MOTHER HAD SAVED THEM.
GROW UP!!
AND HE PUNISHED HIM...
THERE AIN'T NO SANTA CLAUS!...
THERE AIN'T NO EASTER BUNNY!... THERE AIN'T NO FRIGGIN' TOOTH FAIRY!!

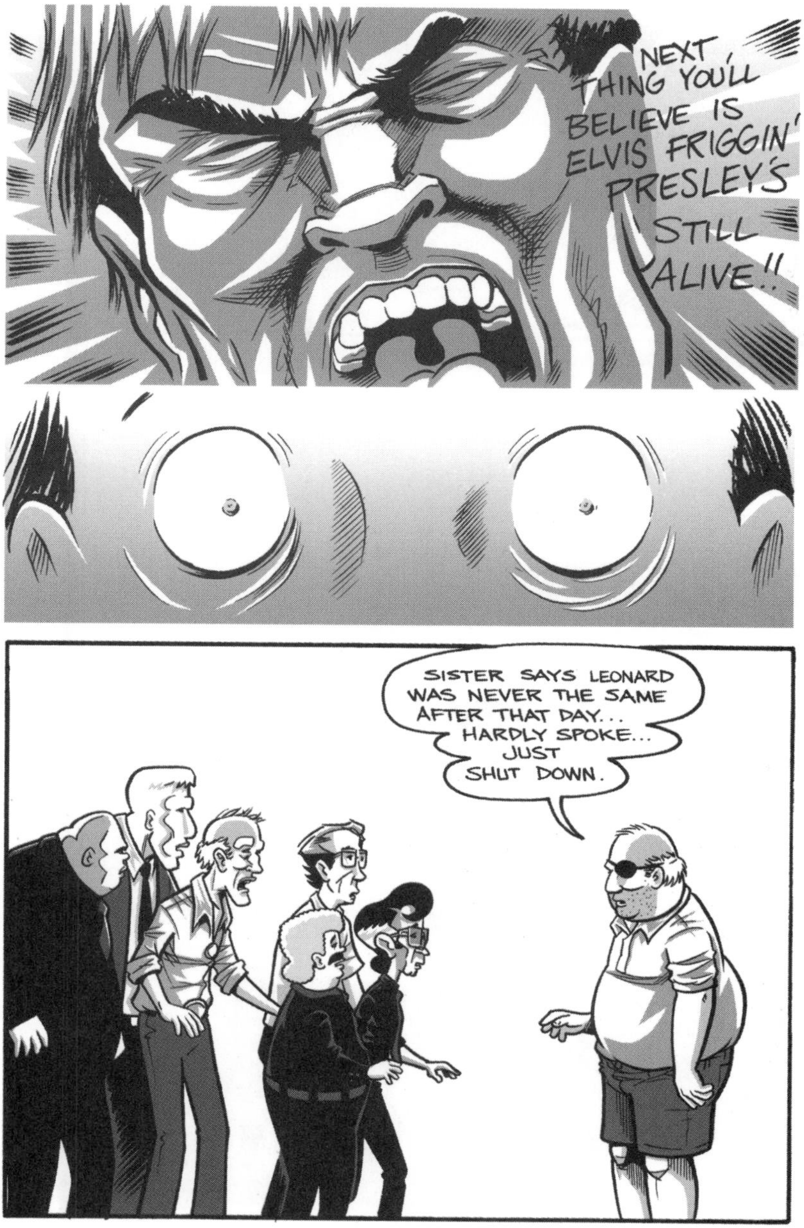
NEXT THING YOU'LL BELIEVE IS ELVIS FRIGGIN' PRESLEY'S STILL ALIVE!!
SISTER SAYS LEONARD WAS NEVER THE SAME AFTER THAT DAY... HARDLY SPOKE... JUST SHUT DOWN.

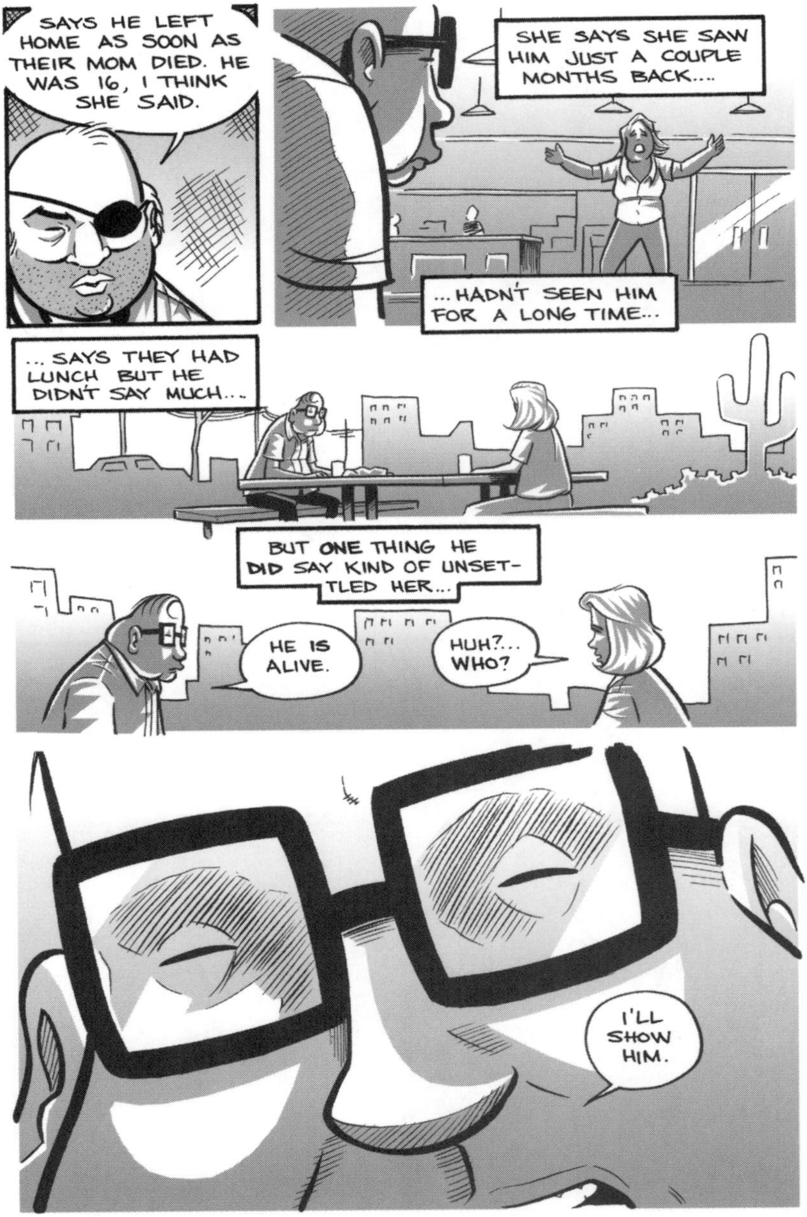
SAYS HE LEFT HOME AS SOON AS THEIR MOM DIED. HE WAS 16, I THINK SHE SAID.
SHE SAYS SHE SAW HIM JUST A COUPLE MONTHS BACK....
...HADN'T SEEN HIM FOR A LONG TIME...
...SAYS THEY HAD LUNCH BUT HE DIDN'T SAY MUCH...
BUT ONE THING HE DID SAY KIND OF UNSET-TLED HER...
HE IS ALIVE.
HUH?... WHO?
I'LL SHOW HIM.

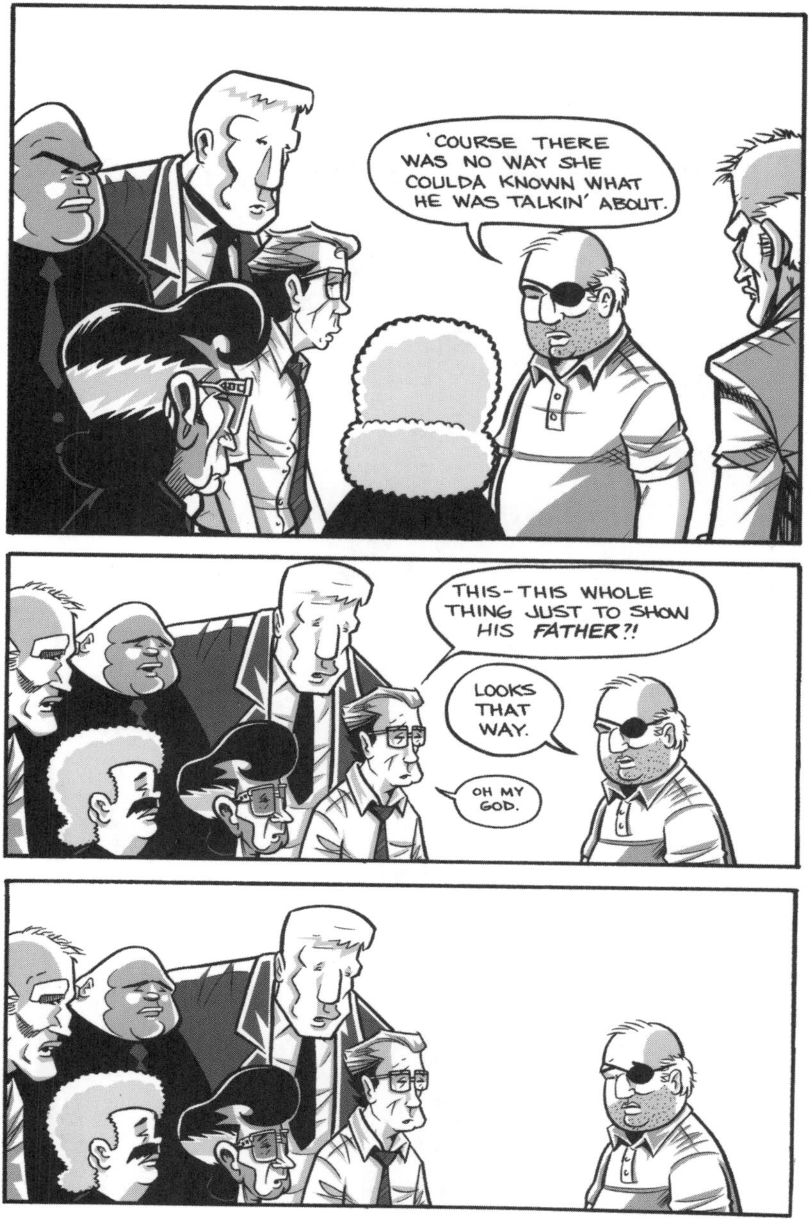
'COURSE THERE WAS NO WAY SHE COULDA KNOWN WHAT HE WAS TALKIN' ABOUT.
THIS-THIS WHOLE THING JUST TO SHOW HIS *FATHER*?!
LOOKS THAT WAY.
OH MY GOD.

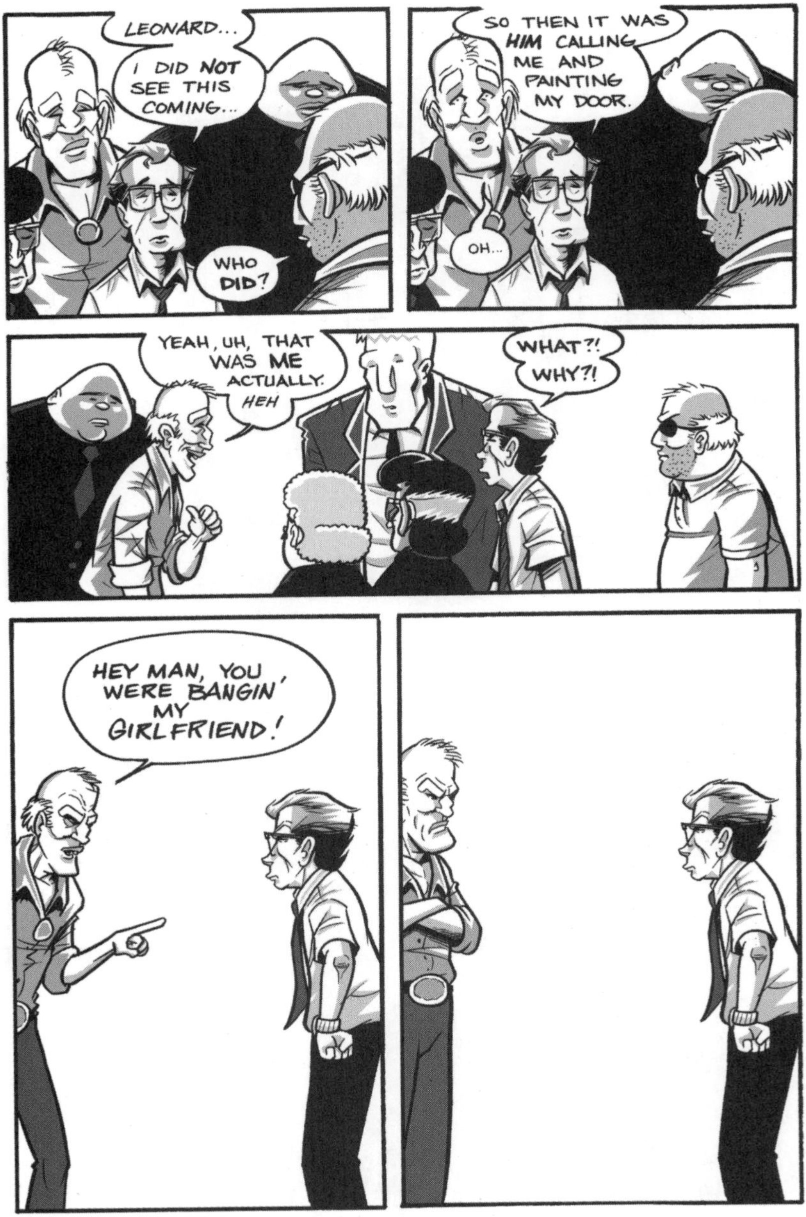
LEONARD...
I DID NOT SEE THIS COMING...
WHO DID?
SO THEN IT WAS HIM CALLING ME AND PAINTING MY DOOR.
OH...
YEAH, UH, THAT WAS ME ACTUALLY. HEH
WHAT?! WHY?!
HEY MAN, YOU WERE BANGIN' MY GIRLFRIEND!

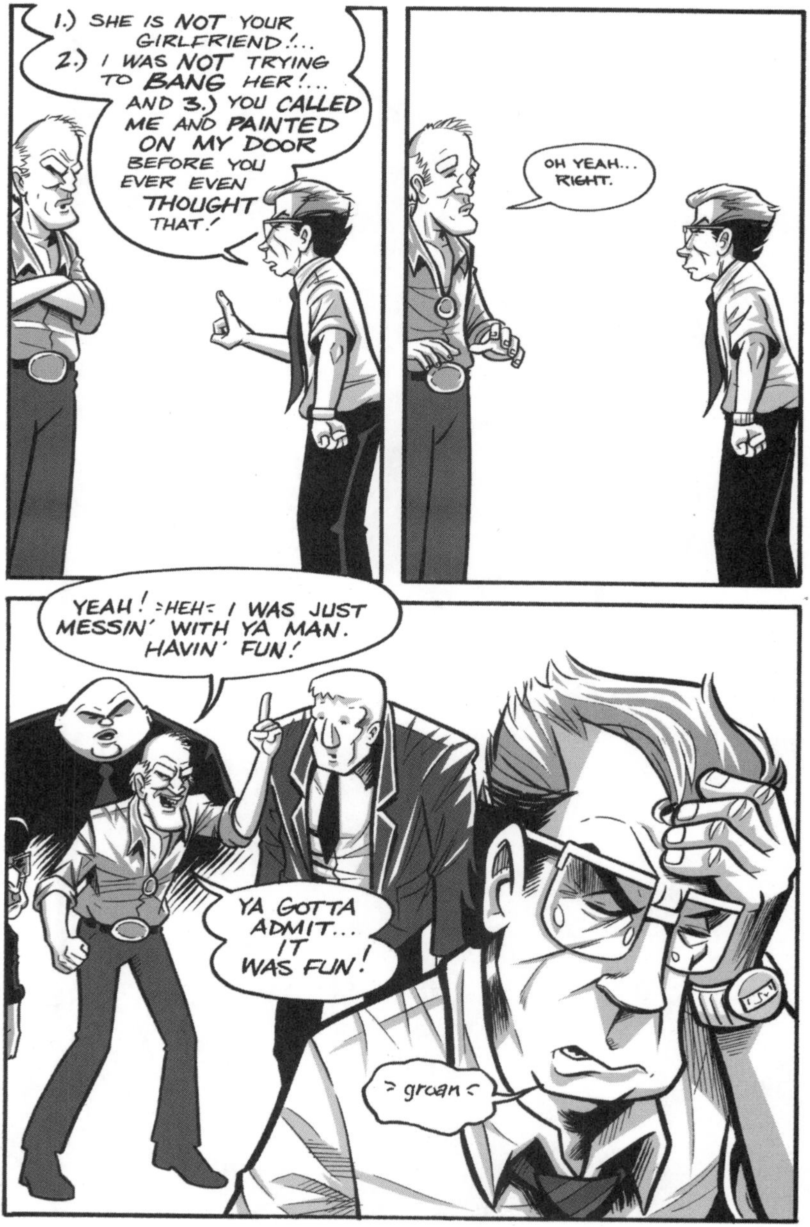
1.) SHE IS NOT YOUR GIRLFRIEND!... 2.) I WAS NOT TRYING TO BANG HER!... AND 3.) YOU CALLED ME AND PAINTED ON MY DOOR BEFORE YOU EVER EVEN THOUGHT THAT!
OH YEAH... RIGHT.
YEAH! =HEH= I WAS JUST MESSIN' WITH YA MAN. HAVIN' FUN!
YA GOTTA ADMIT... IT WAS FUN!
>groan<

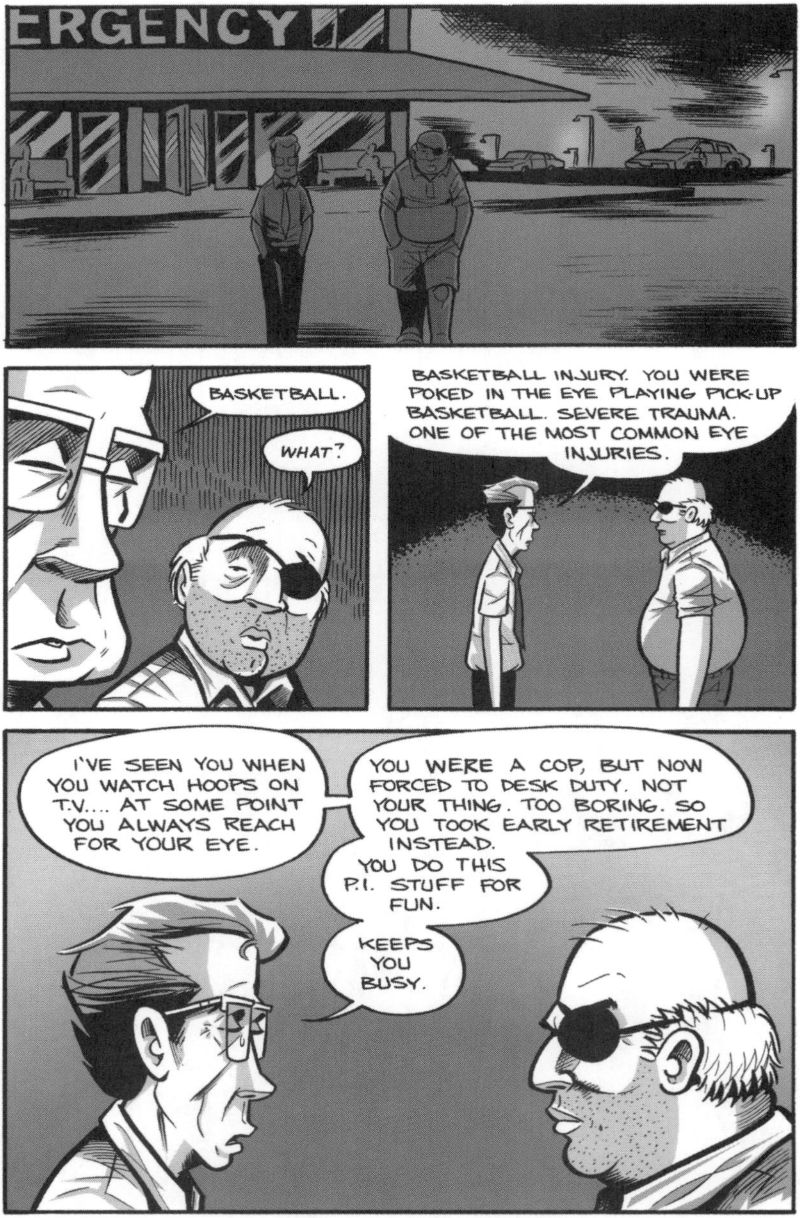
ERGENCY
BASKETBALL.
WHAT?
BASKETBALL INJURY. YOU WERE POKED IN THE EYE PLAYING PICK-UP BASKETBALL. SEVERE TRAUMA. ONE OF THE MOST COMMON EYE INJURIES.
I'VE SEEN YOU WHEN YOU WATCH HOOPS ON T.V.... AT SOME POINT YOU ALWAYS REACH FOR YOUR EYE.
YOU WERE A COP, BUT NOW FORCED TO DESK DUTY. NOT YOUR THING. TOO BORING. SO YOU TOOK EARLY RETIREMENT INSTEAD.
YOU DO THIS P.I. STUFF FOR FUN.
KEEPS YOU BUSY.

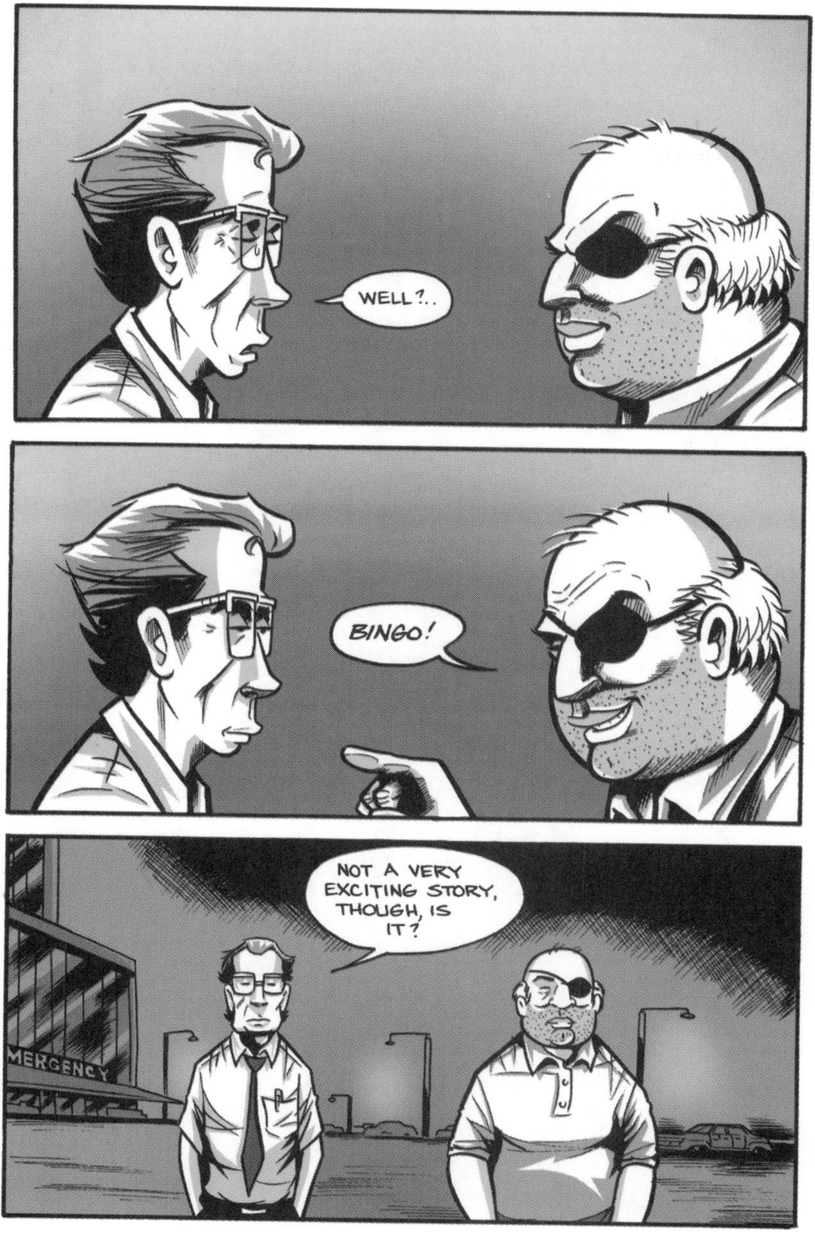
WELL?..
BINGO!
NOT A VERY EXCITING STORY, THOUGH, IS IT?
MERGENCY

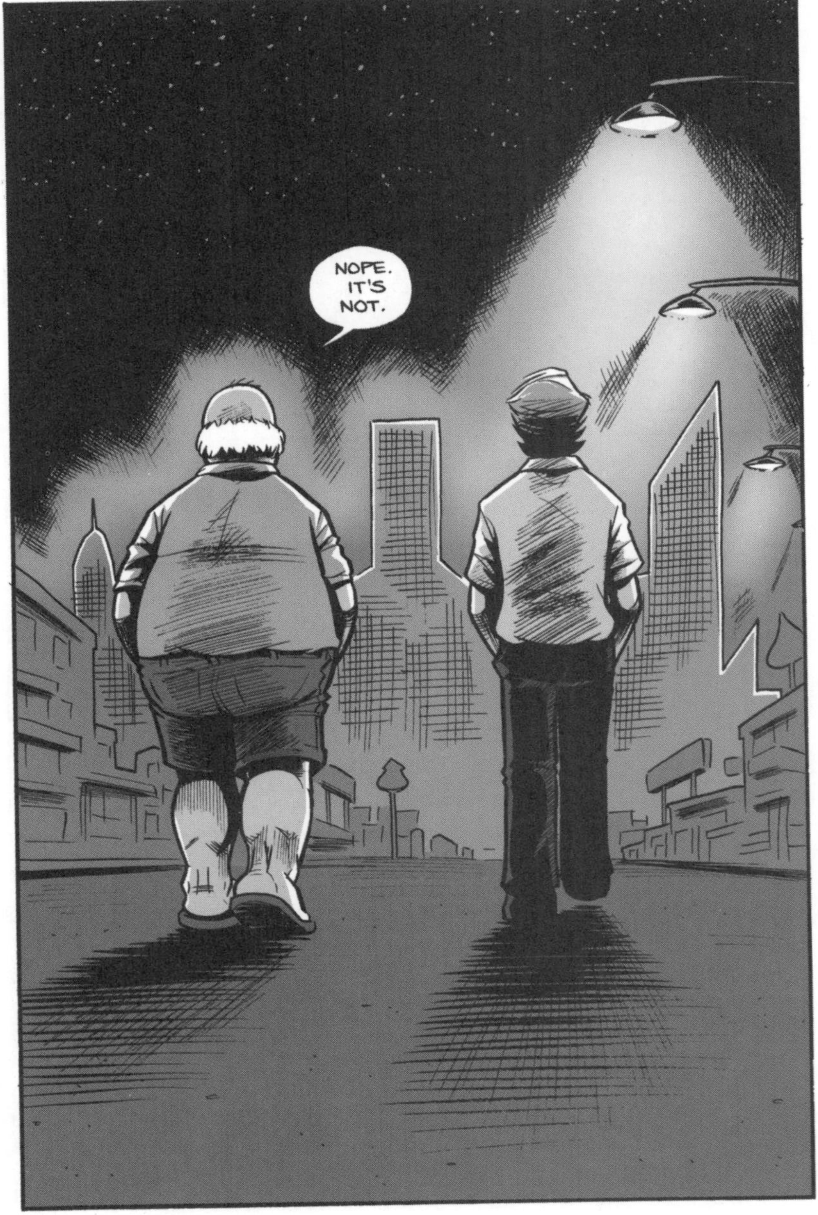
NOPE. IT'S NOT.

"IT WAS LIKE HE CAME ALONG AND
WHISPERED SOME DREAM IN EVERYBODY'S
EAR, AND SOMEHOW WE ALL DREAMED IT."

— BRUCE SPRINGSTEEN

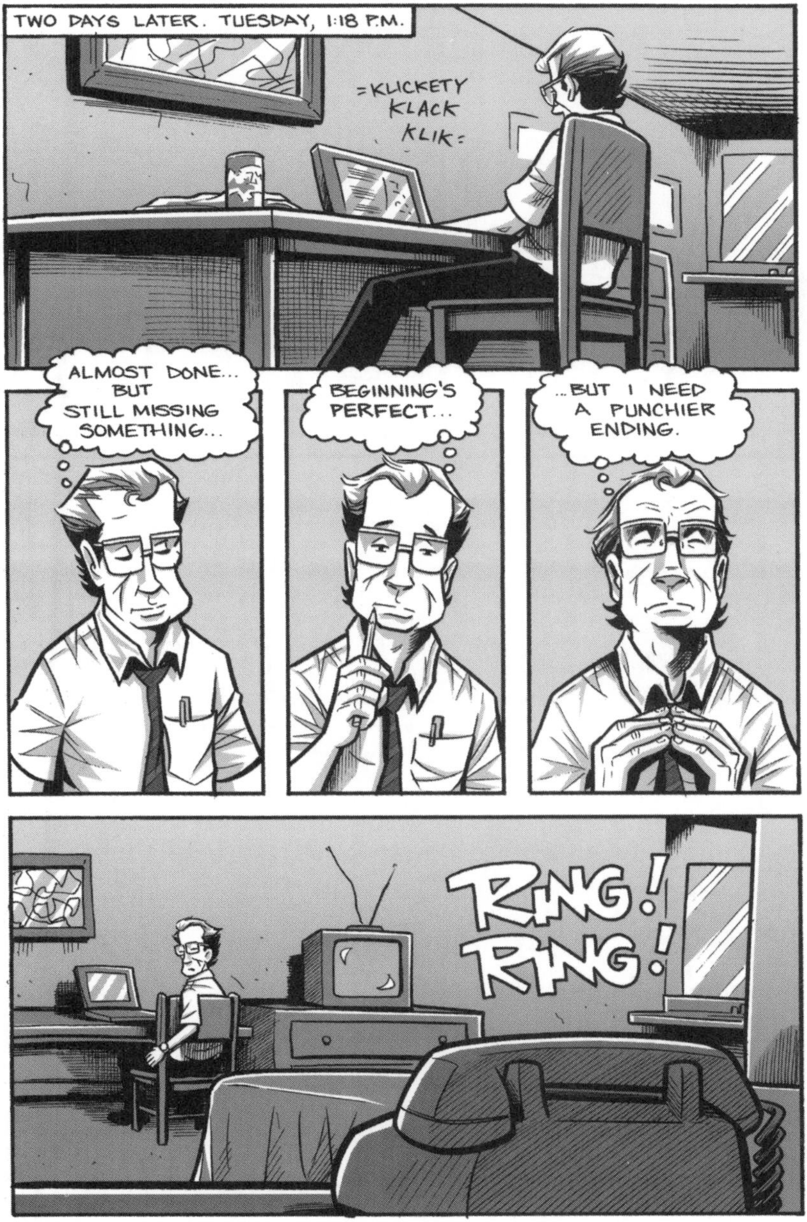
TWO DAYS LATER. TUESDAY, 1:18 P.M.
=KLICKETY KLACK KLIK=
ALMOST DONE... BUT STILL MISSING SOMETHING...
BEGINNING'S PERFECT...
...BUT I NEED A PUNCHIER ENDING.
RING! RING!

YES...HELLO...

YES, THIS IS PAUL ERFURT.

I'LL BE RIGHT THERE.

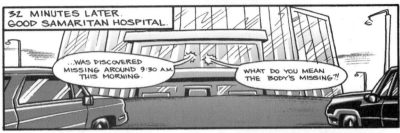

32 MINUTES LATER. GOOD SAMARITAN HOSPITAL.

...WAS DISCOVERED MISSING AROUND 9:30 A.M. THIS MORNING.

WHAT DO YOU MEAN THE BODY'S MISSING?!

I CANNOT EXPLAIN THIS UNFORTUNATE OCCURRENCE JUST YET. WE ARE LOOKING INTO IT, OF COURSE. AND HAVE NOTIFIED THE PROPER AUTHORITIES.

THIS IS ≈AHEM≈ SOMETHING OF AN EMBARRASSMENT. WE'RE HOPING THAT OUR BEING FORTHRIGHT WITH YOU MIGHT SPARE US UNDO CRITICISM IN YOUR ARTICLE.

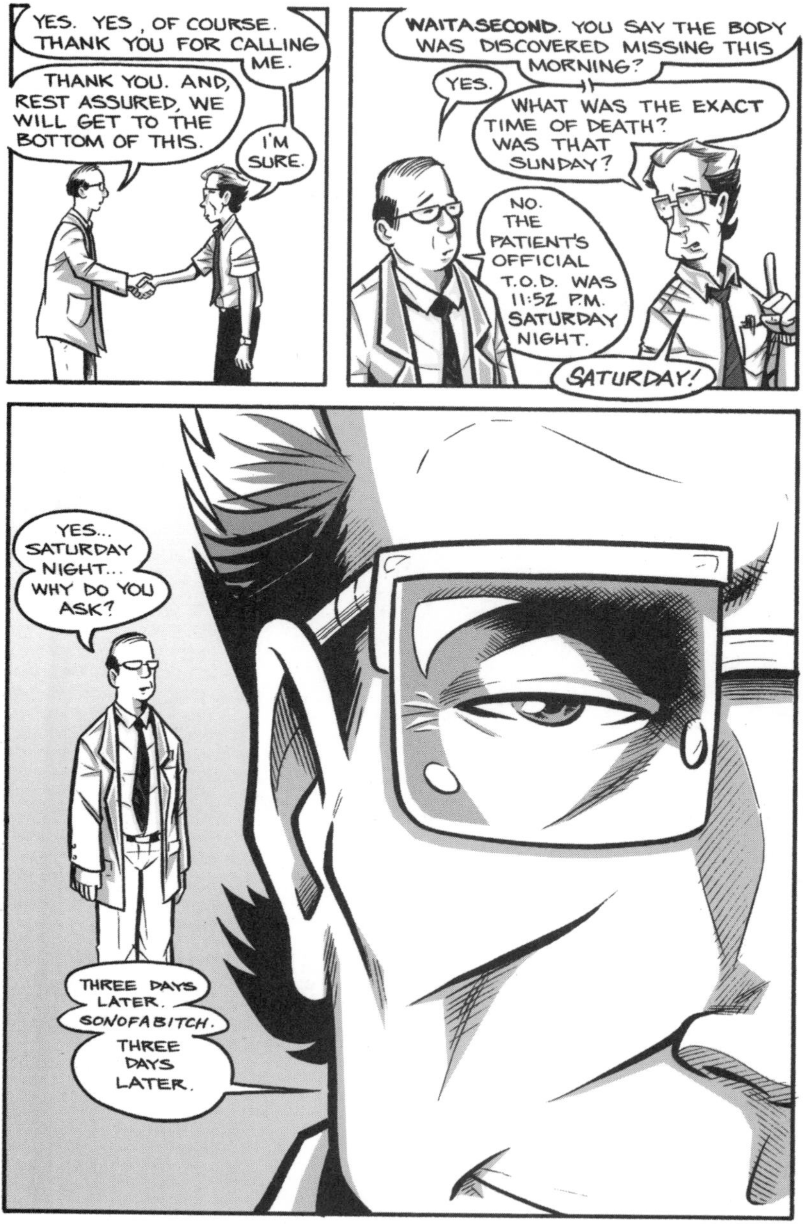
YES. YES, OF COURSE. THANK YOU FOR CALLING ME.
THANK YOU. AND, REST ASSURED, WE WILL GET TO THE BOTTOM OF THIS.
I'M SURE.
WAITASECOND. YOU SAY THE BODY WAS DISCOVERED MISSING THIS MORNING?
YES.
WHAT WAS THE EXACT TIME OF DEATH? WAS THAT SUNDAY?
NO. THE PATIENT'S OFFICIAL T.O.D. WAS 11:52 P.M. SATURDAY NIGHT.
SATURDAY!
YES... SATURDAY NIGHT... WHY DO YOU ASK?
THREE DAYS LATER.
SONOFABITCH.
THREE DAYS LATER.

"WHEN THERE'S NO CONTROVERSY, THERE'S NO NEWS. WHEN THEY QUIT TALKING ABOUT YOU, YOU'RE DEAD."

— ELVIS

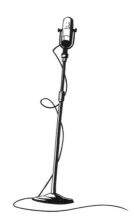

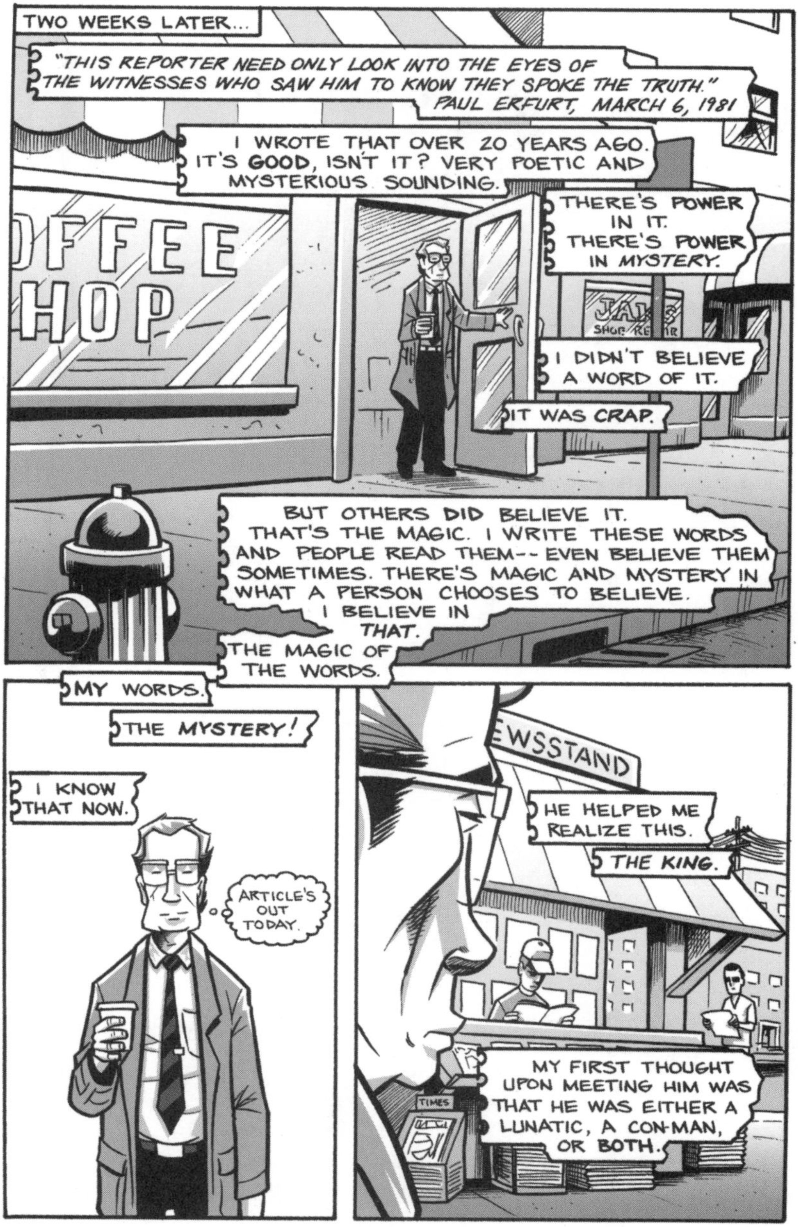
TWO WEEKS LATER...
"THIS REPORTER NEED ONLY LOOK INTO THE EYES OF THE WITNESSES WHO SAW HIM TO KNOW THEY SPOKE THE TRUTH." PAUL ERFURT, MARCH 6, 1981
I WROTE THAT OVER 20 YEARS AGO. IT'S GOOD, ISN'T IT? VERY POETIC AND MYSTERIOUS SOUNDING.
OFFEE HOP
THERE'S POWER IN IT. THERE'S POWER IN MYSTERY.
I DIDN'T BELIEVE A WORD OF IT.
IT WAS CRAP.
BUT OTHERS DID BELIEVE IT. THAT'S THE MAGIC. I WRITE THESE WORDS AND PEOPLE READ THEM-- EVEN BELIEVE THEM SOMETIMES. THERE'S MAGIC AND MYSTERY IN WHAT A PERSON CHOOSES TO BELIEVE. I BELIEVE IN THAT.
THE MAGIC OF THE WORDS.
MY WORDS.
THE MYSTERY!
I KNOW THAT NOW.
ARTICLE'S OUT TODAY.
EWSSTAND
HE HELPED ME REALIZE THIS.
THE KING.
MY FIRST THOUGHT UPON MEETING HIM WAS THAT HE WAS EITHER A LUNATIC, A CON-MAN, OR BOTH.
TIMES

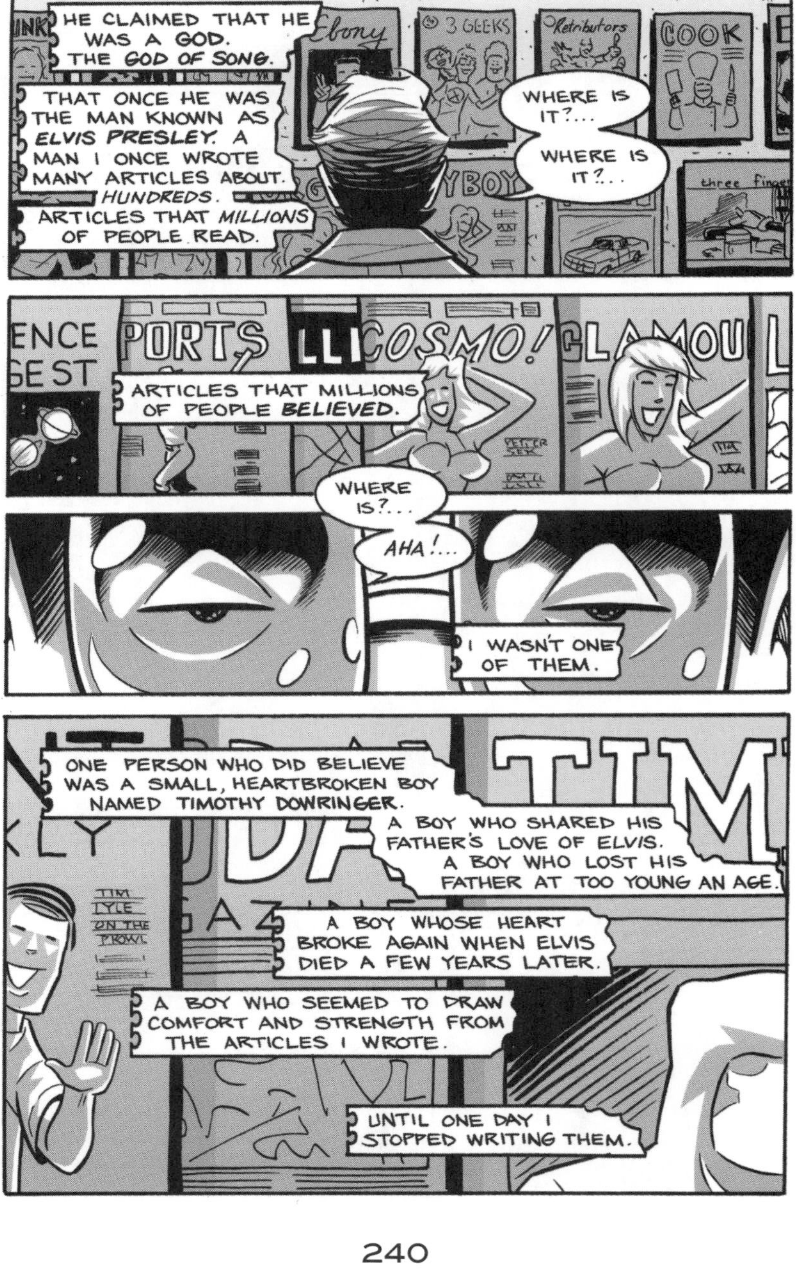
HE CLAIMED THAT HE WAS A GOD. THE GOD OF SONG.
THAT ONCE HE WAS THE MAN KNOWN AS ELVIS PRESLEY. A MAN I ONCE WROTE MANY ARTICLES ABOUT. HUNDREDS.
ARTICLES THAT MILLIONS OF PEOPLE READ.
WHERE IS IT?...
WHERE IS IT?...
Ebony
3 GEEKS
Retributors
COOK
ARTICLES THAT MILLIONS OF PEOPLE BELIEVED.
COSMO!
WHERE IS?...
AHA!...
I WASN'T ONE OF THEM.
ONE PERSON WHO DID BELIEVE WAS A SMALL, HEARTBROKEN BOY NAMED TIMOTHY DOWRINGER.
A BOY WHO SHARED HIS FATHER'S LOVE OF ELVIS. A BOY WHO LOST HIS FATHER AT TOO YOUNG AN AGE.
A BOY WHOSE HEART BROKE AGAIN WHEN ELVIS DIED A FEW YEARS LATER.
A BOY WHO SEEMED TO DRAW COMFORT AND STRENGTH FROM THE ARTICLES I WROTE.
UNTIL ONE DAY I STOPPED WRITING THEM.

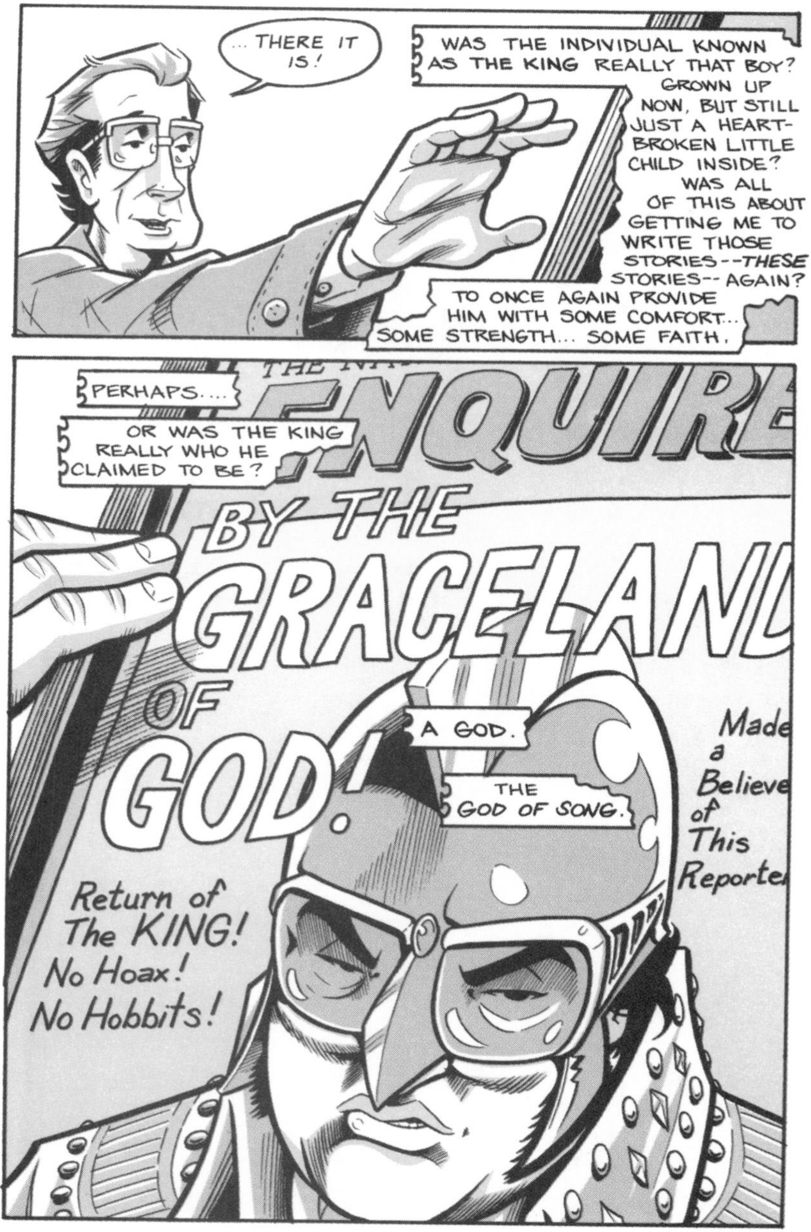
...THERE IT IS!
WAS THE INDIVIDUAL KNOWN AS THE KING REALLY THAT BOY? GROWN UP NOW, BUT STILL JUST A HEART-BROKEN LITTLE CHILD INSIDE? WAS ALL OF THIS ABOUT GETTING ME TO WRITE THOSE STORIES--THESE STORIES--AGAIN?
TO ONCE AGAIN PROVIDE HIM WITH SOME COMFORT... SOME STRENGTH... SOME FAITH.
PERHAPS....
OR WAS THE KING REALLY WHO HE CLAIMED TO BE?
ENQUIRE
BY THE GRACELAND OF GOD!
A GOD.
THE GOD OF SONG.
Made a Believe of This Reporte
Return of The KING! No Hoax! No Hobbits!

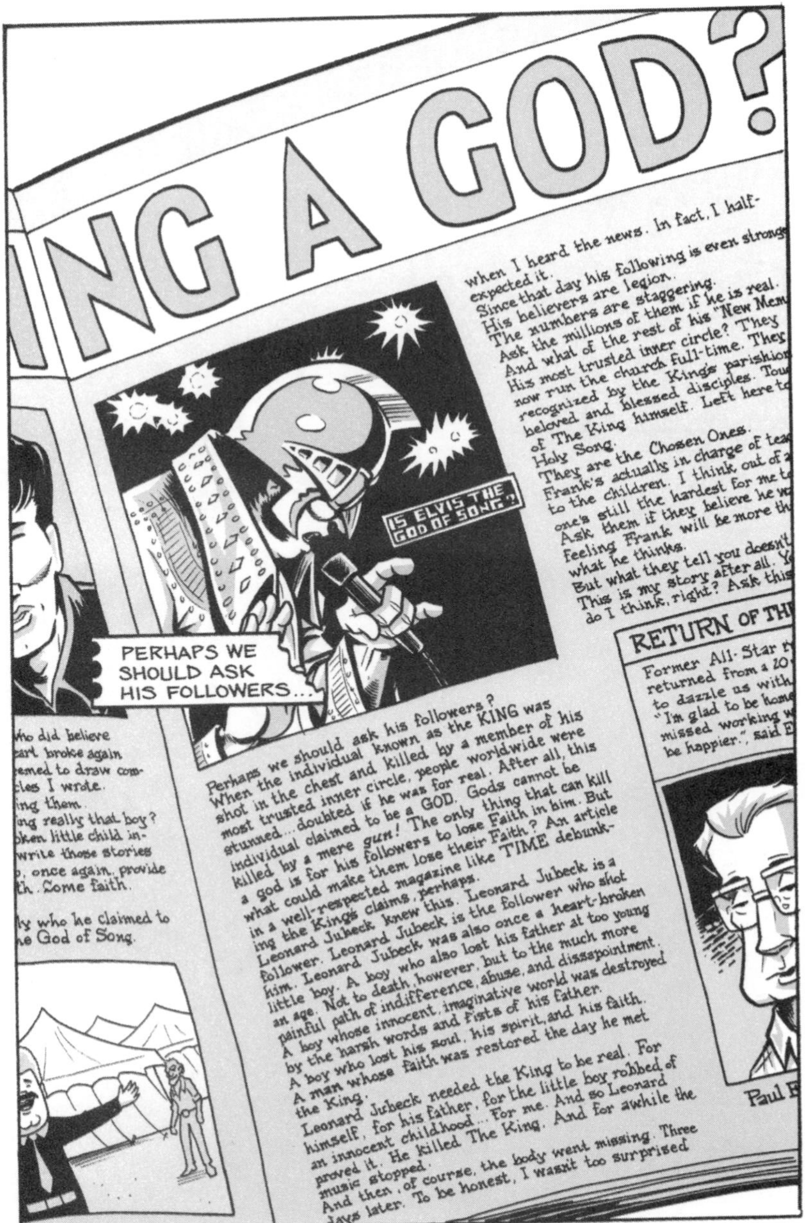
NG A GOD?
IS ELVIS THE GOD OF SONG?
PERHAPS WE SHOULD ASK HIS FOLLOWERS...
when I heard the news. In fact, I half-
expected it.
Since that day his following is even
His believers are legion.
The numbers are staggering.
Ask the millions of them if he is real.
And what of the rest of his "New
His most trusted inner circle? They
now run the church full-time. They
recognized by the King's
beloved and blessed disciples.
of The King himself. Left here
Holy Song.
They are the Chosen Ones.
Frank's actually in charge of
to the children. I think out of
one's still the hardest for me
Ask them if they believe he
Feeling Frank will be more
what he thinks.
But what they tell you
This is my story after all.
do I think, right? Ask this
Perhaps we should ask his followers?
When the individual known as the KING was
shot in the chest and killed by a member of his
most trusted inner circle, people worldwide were
stunned... doubted if he was for real. After all, this
individual claimed to be a GOD. Gods cannot be
killed by a mere gun! The only thing that can kill
a god is for his followers to lose Faith in him. But
what could make them lose their Faith? An article
in a well-respected magazine like TIME debunk-
ing the King's claims, perhaps.
Leonard Jubeck knew this. Leonard Jubeck is a
follower. Leonard Jubeck is the follower who shot
him. Leonard Jubeck was also once a heart-broken
little boy. A boy who also lost his father at too young
an age. Not to death, however, but to the much more
painful path of indifference, abuse, and dissapointment.
A boy whose innocent, imaginative world was destroyed
by the harsh words and fists of his father.
A boy who lost his soul, his spirit, and his faith.
A man whose faith was restored the day he met
the King.
Leonard Jubeck needed the King to be real. For
himself, for his father, for the little boy robbed of
an innocent childhood... For me. And so Leonard
proved it. He killed The King. And for awhile the
music stopped.
And then, of course, the body went missing. Three
days later. To be honest, I wasn't too surprised
RETURN OF TH
Former All-Star
returned from a
to dazzle us with
"I'm glad to be
missed working
be happier.", said
Paul

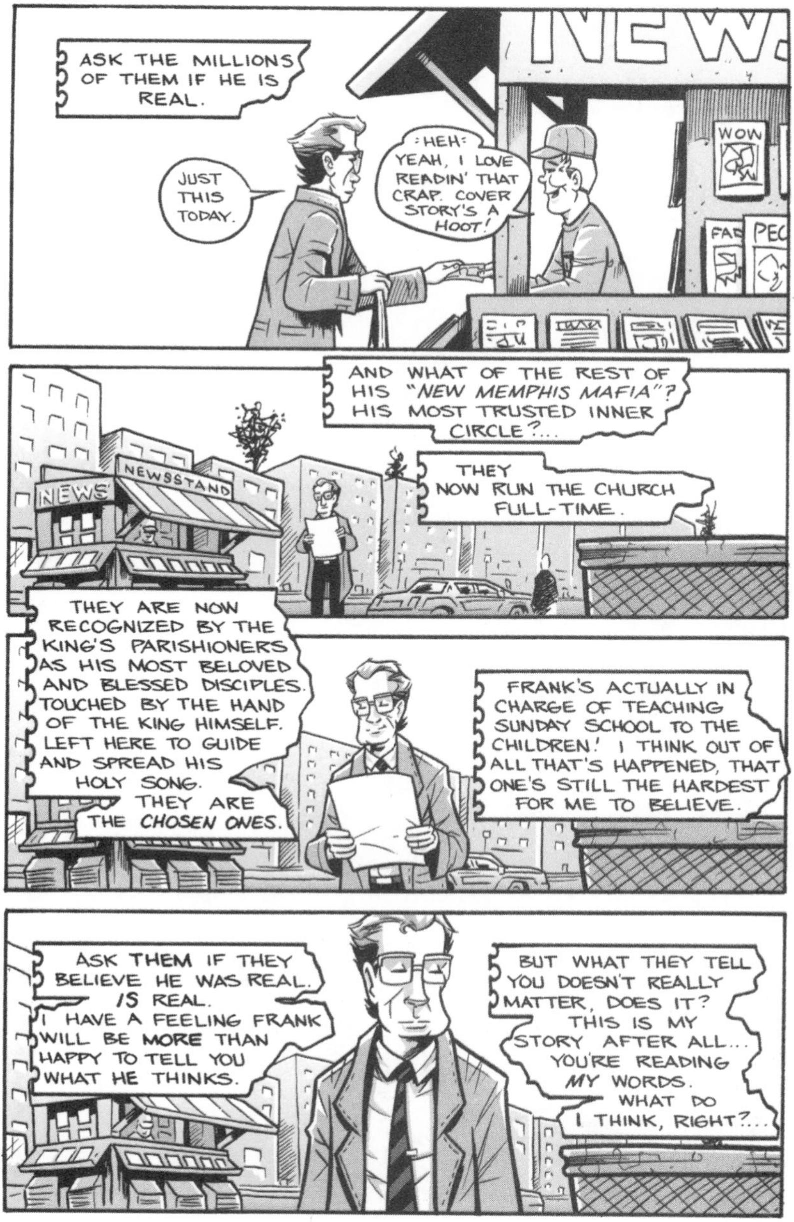
ASK THE MILLIONS OF THEM IF HE IS REAL.
JUST THIS TODAY.
:HEH: YEAH, I LOVE READIN' THAT CRAP. COVER STORY'S A HOOT!
NEWS
WOW
AND WHAT OF THE REST OF HIS "NEW MEMPHIS MAFIA"? HIS MOST TRUSTED INNER CIRCLE?...
NEWSSTAND
NEWS
THEY NOW RUN THE CHURCH FULL-TIME.
THEY ARE NOW RECOGNIZED BY THE KING'S PARISHIONERS AS HIS MOST BELOVED AND BLESSED DISCIPLES. TOUCHED BY THE HAND OF THE KING HIMSELF. LEFT HERE TO GUIDE AND SPREAD HIS HOLY SONG.
THEY ARE THE CHOSEN ONES.
FRANK'S ACTUALLY IN CHARGE OF TEACHING SUNDAY SCHOOL TO THE CHILDREN! I THINK OUT OF ALL THAT'S HAPPENED, THAT ONE'S STILL THE HARDEST FOR ME TO BELIEVE.
ASK THEM IF THEY BELIEVE HE WAS REAL. IS REAL.
I HAVE A FEELING FRANK WILL BE MORE THAN HAPPY TO TELL YOU WHAT HE THINKS.
BUT WHAT THEY TELL YOU DOESN'T REALLY MATTER, DOES IT?
THIS IS MY STORY AFTER ALL... YOU'RE READING MY WORDS.
WHAT DO I THINK, RIGHT?...

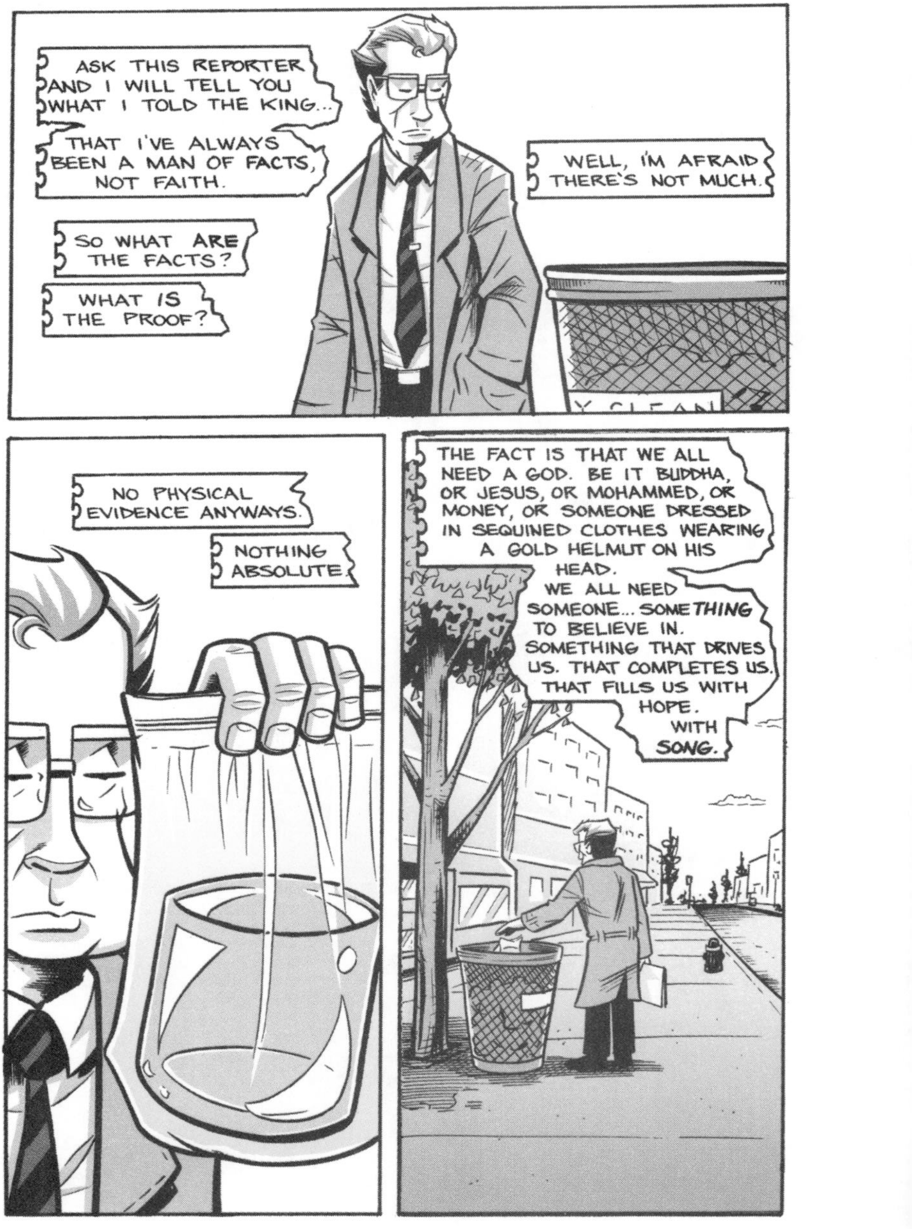

ASK THIS REPORTER AND I WILL TELL YOU WHAT I TOLD THE KING...
THAT I'VE ALWAYS BEEN A MAN OF FACTS, NOT FAITH.
SO WHAT ARE THE FACTS?
WHAT IS THE PROOF?
WELL, I'M AFRAID THERE'S NOT MUCH.
NO PHYSICAL EVIDENCE ANYWAYS.
NOTHING ABSOLUTE.
THE FACT IS THAT WE ALL NEED A GOD. BE IT BUDDHA, OR JESUS, OR MOHAMMED, OR MONEY, OR SOMEONE DRESSED IN SEQUINED CLOTHES WEARING A GOLD HELMUT ON HIS HEAD.
WE ALL NEED SOMEONE... SOMETHING TO BELIEVE IN. SOMETHING THAT DRIVES US. THAT COMPLETES US. THAT FILLS US WITH HOPE. WITH SONG.

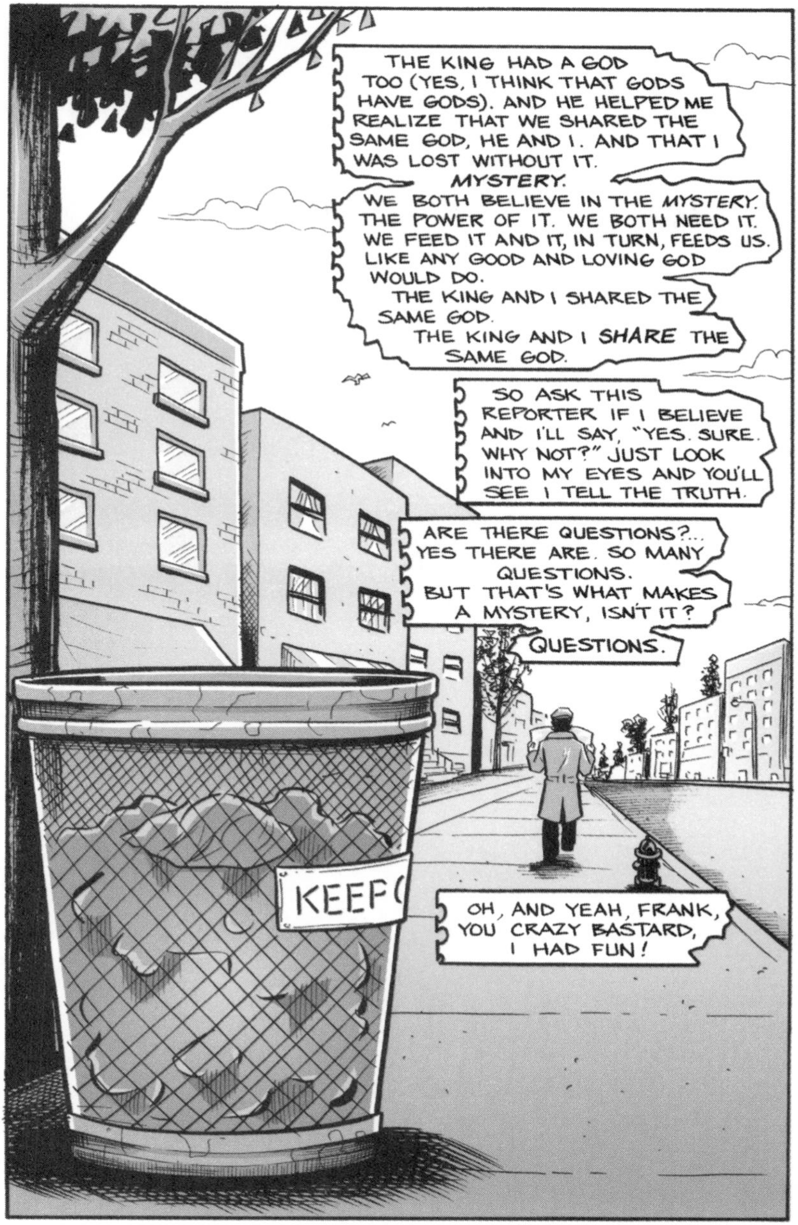
THE KING HAD A GOD TOO (YES, I THINK THAT GODS HAVE GODS). AND HE HELPED ME REALIZE THAT WE SHARED THE SAME GOD, HE AND I. AND THAT I WAS LOST WITHOUT IT.
MYSTERY.
WE BOTH BELIEVE IN THE MYSTERY. THE POWER OF IT. WE BOTH NEED IT. WE FEED IT AND IT, IN TURN, FEEDS US. LIKE ANY GOOD AND LOVING GOD WOULD DO.
THE KING AND I SHARED THE SAME GOD.
THE KING AND I SHARE THE SAME GOD.
SO ASK THIS REPORTER IF I BELIEVE AND I'LL SAY, "YES. SURE. WHY NOT?" JUST LOOK INTO MY EYES AND YOU'LL SEE I TELL THE TRUTH.
ARE THERE QUESTIONS?... YES THERE ARE. SO MANY QUESTIONS.
BUT THAT'S WHAT MAKES A MYSTERY, ISN'T IT?
QUESTIONS.
KEEP
OH, AND YEAH, FRANK, YOU CRAZY BASTARD, I HAD FUN!

"I'M TIRED OF BEING ME."

— ELVIS

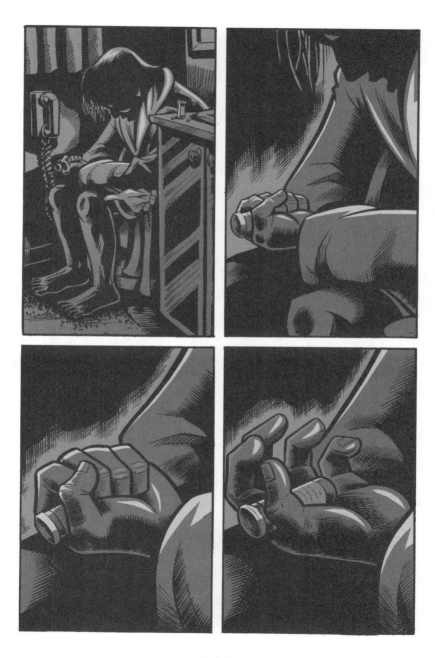

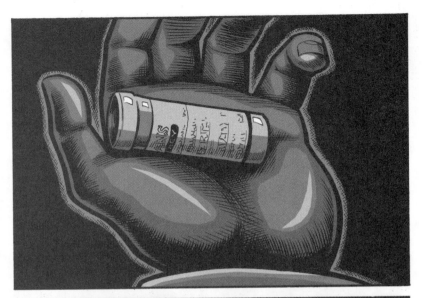

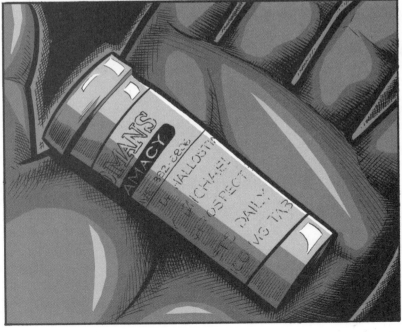

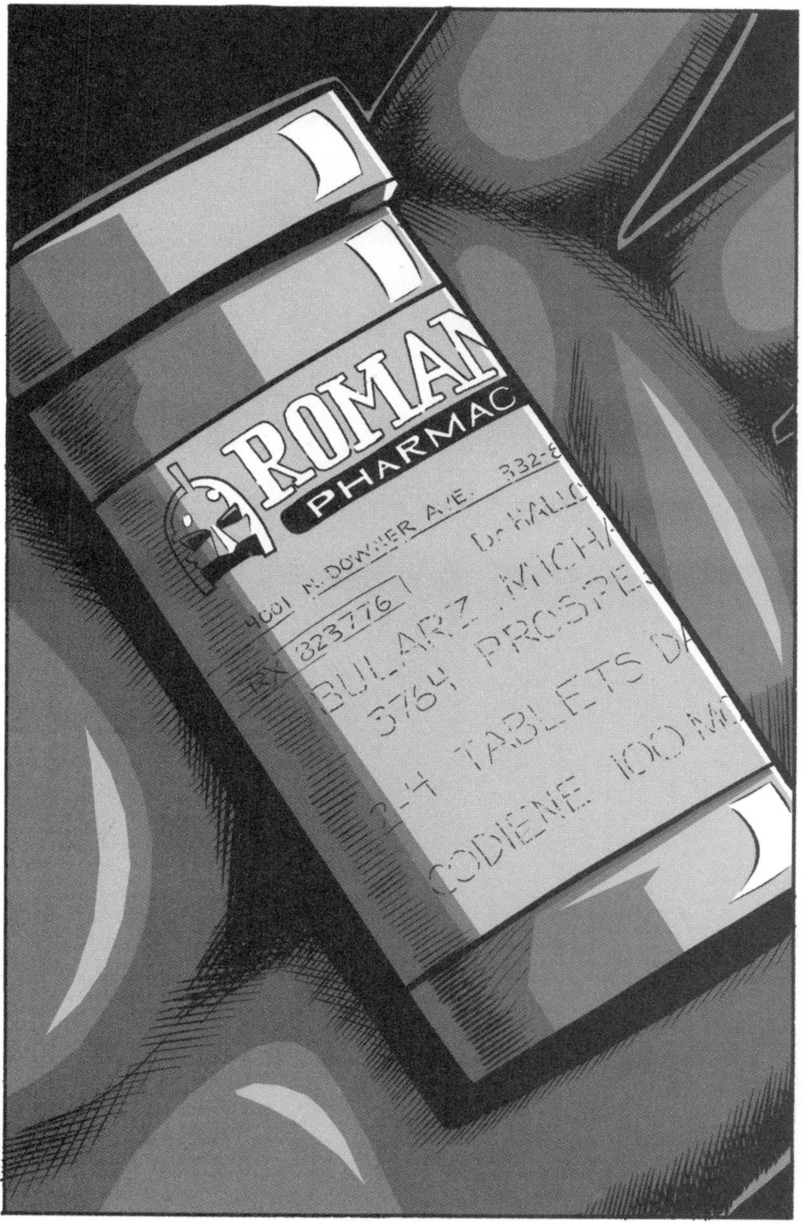
ROMAN
PHARMAC
4001 N. DOWNER AVE.
RX 823776
BULARZ MICH
3764 PROSPE
TABLETS DA
CODIENE 100 M

"ELVIS HAS LEFT THE BUILDING."

———AL DVORIN

Rich Koslowski has worked in the animation and comic book industry for the past fourteen years. He is best known for his groundbreaking, Ignatz award-winning graphic novel *Three Fingers*, and his Eisner award-nominated work on the self-published parody title *The 3 Geeks*.

He got his start in comics working as an inker at Archie on the popular *Sonic the Hedgehog* series, and has since worked on *Jughead*, *Veronica*, and *Archie's Weird Mysteries*.

Rich lives with his wife Sandra (who helps on all his books) and their lovely daughter Stella, in Shorewood, Wisconsin.

Adam Wallenta's career in comics began in the mid-nineties, coloring such books as *Namor*, *X-Men Adventures*, and *Cable* for Marvel. He later formed *American Mule Entertainment* and published the underground cult-hit *The True Adventures of Adam and Bryon*, and more recently *The Retributors*.

In addition to his coloring work, Wallenta has illustrated everything from children's books to clothing lines. His future projects include writing and drawing the official comic book release for the revolutionary hip-hop band Public Enemy, and several top-secret collaborations with Rich Koslowski.

Adam lives in Connecticut, and his work can be found at:
http://adam.americanmule.com/
www.illusarts.com

We went
the king a bit
less dowdy. A
bit more confident
looking. Still
overweight but
carries himself
with pride.

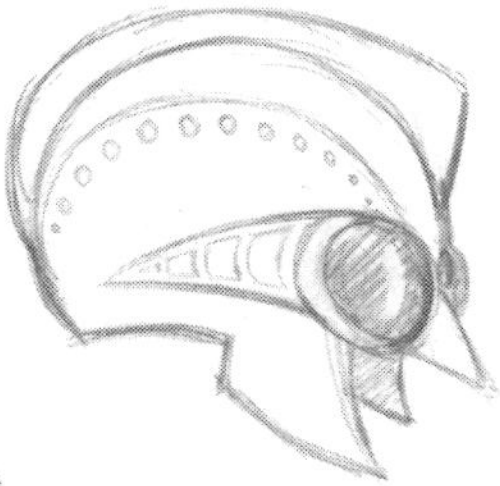

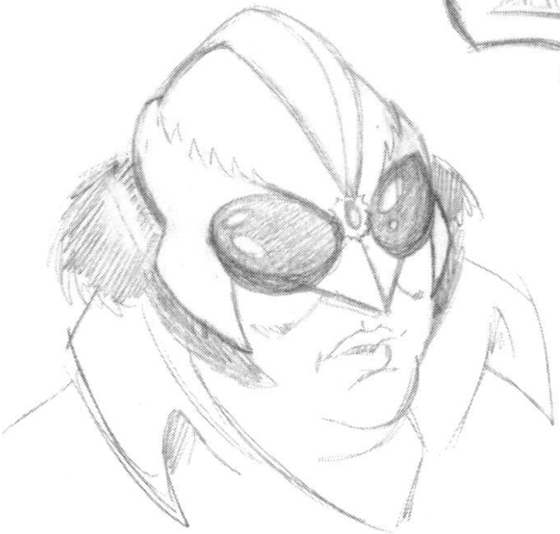

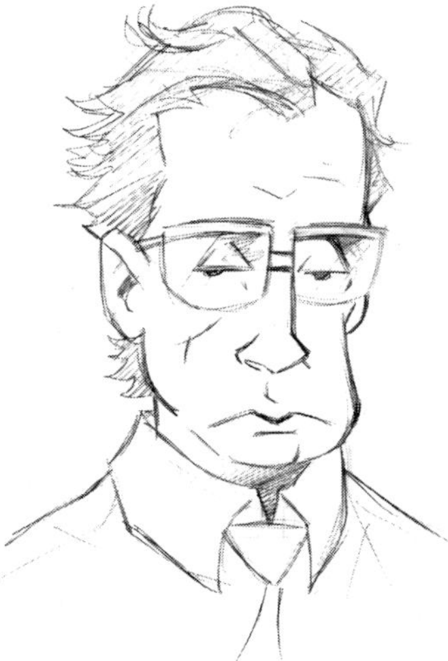

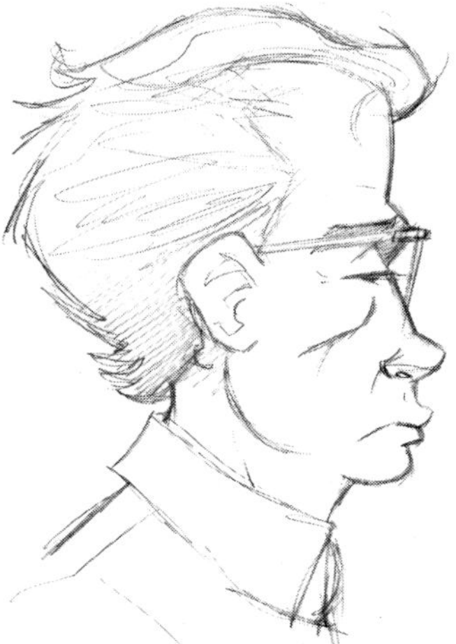

5'10" ish
thin with
a pot belly

My first thought on how Karl Erfurt should look. He's in his late forties, slight build, hair thinning, slightly unkempt but not a total slob. He could've been handsome once. He should look tired, worn down, you know, the typical down-and-out old sleazy reporter look.

Of course he won't be wearing a trench coat in Las Vegas. I'm thinking short sleaved dress shirts with ties.

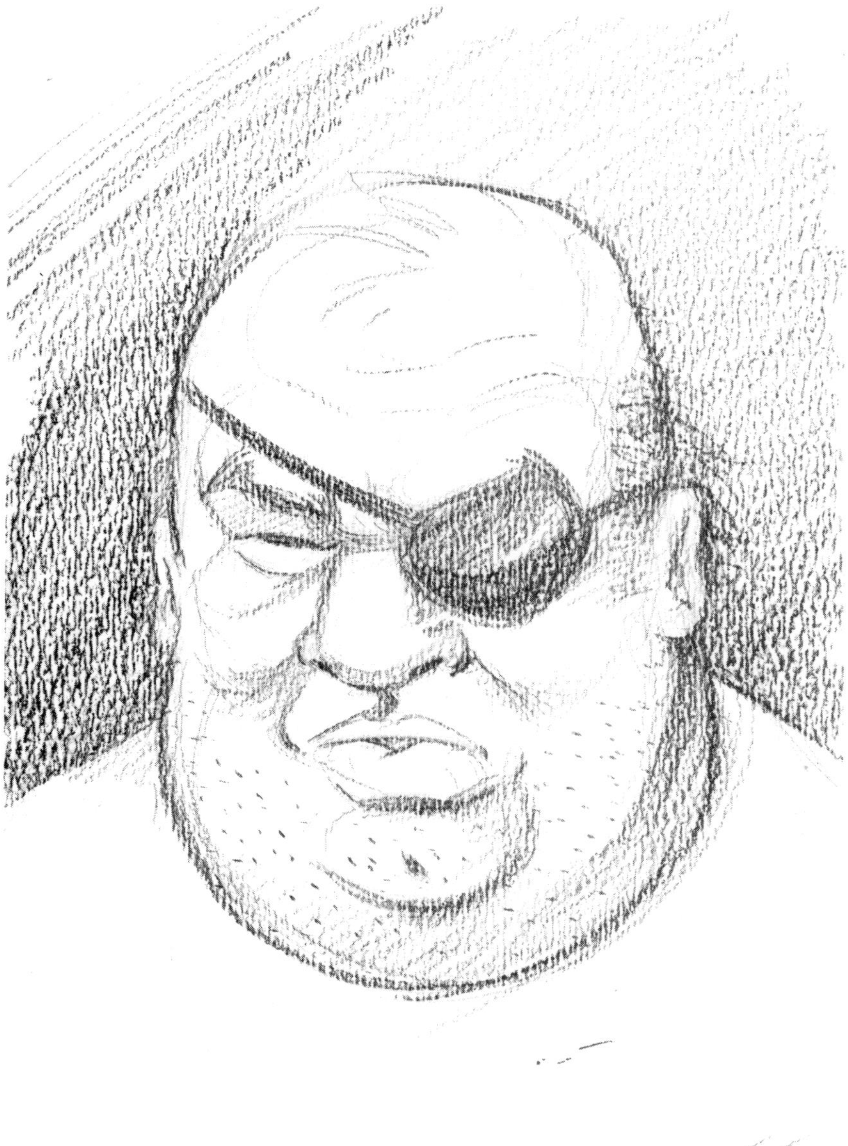

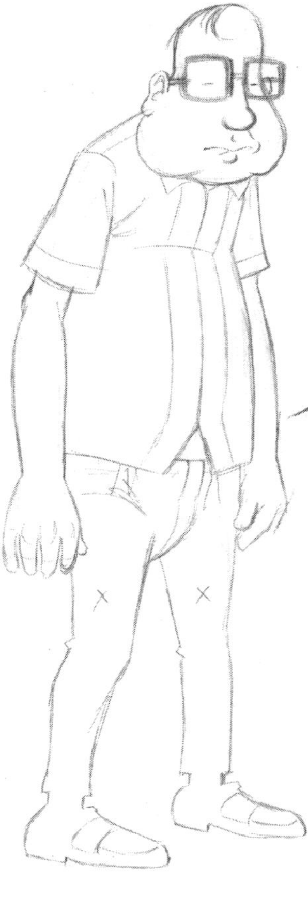

LEONARD JUBECK

~~PAULY [illegible]~~

<u>KILLER</u>

TORMENTED AS A SMALL BOY BY HIS FATHER. ONE DAY, AT AGE 12, FOUND BOX OF SANTA LETTERS IN DAD'S CLOSET. DAD FLEW INTO RAGE OVER HIS SNOOPING. BEAT HIM AND SCREAMED TO "GROW UP YOU LITTLE IDIOT! THERE AIN'T NO SANTA! THERE AIN'T NO EASTER BUNNY! NEXT THING Y'ALL BELIEVE IS ELVIS PRESLEY'S STILL ALIVE!"

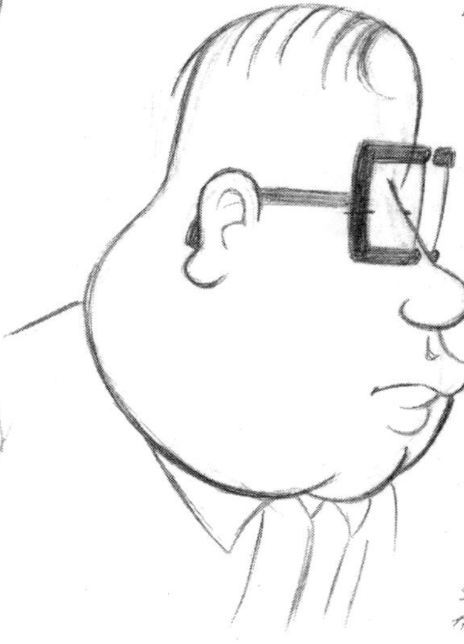

YEARS LATER HE GOT JOB AT POST OFFICE. SAW ALL THE LETTERS ADDRESSED TO "THE KING" JUST LIKE OLD SANTA LETTERS.

PAULY CLUNG TO THE HOPE THAT THE KING <u>WAS</u> ALIVE SO IN SOME TWISTED WAY HE COULD SHOW HIS <u>FATHER</u>!

THAT'S WHY HE SHOOTS HIM IN THE END.

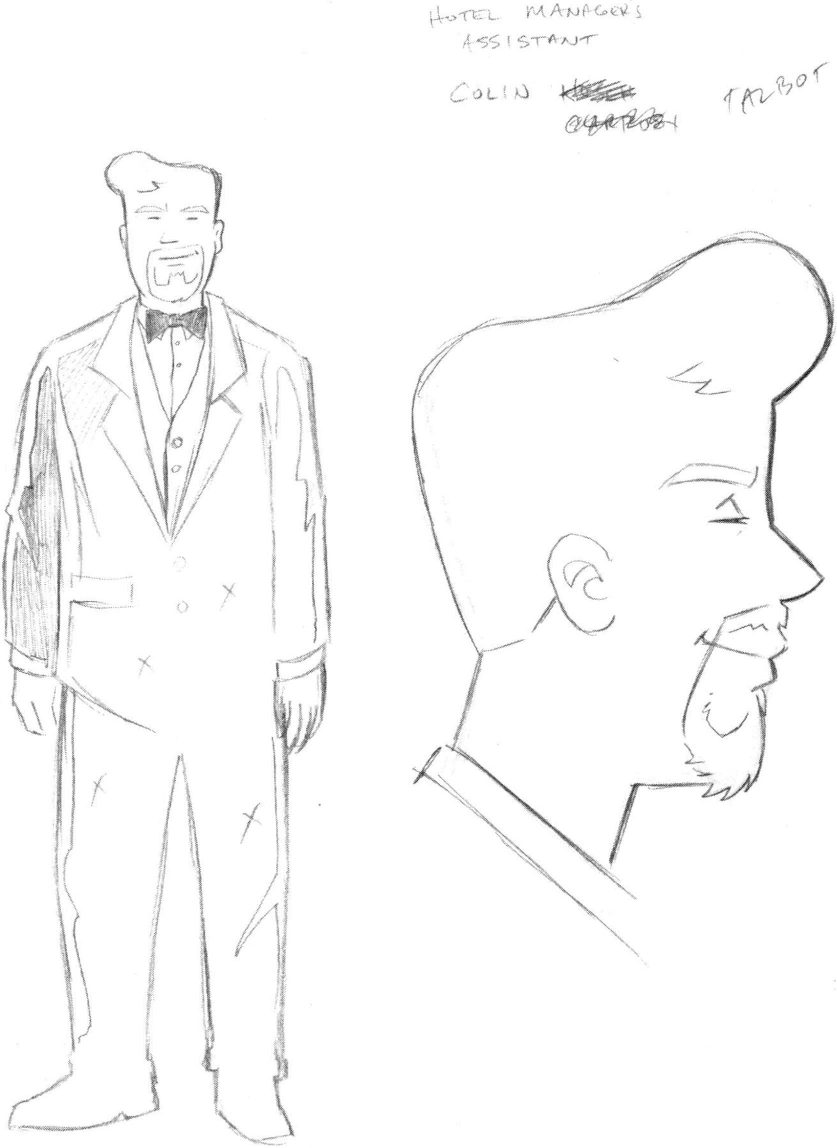
HOTEL MANAGER'S
ASSISTANT
COLIN
TALBOT

There were several books I referenced while making this book:

ELVIS SPEAKS by Elizabeth McKeon & Linda Everett

ELVIS, THE KING REMEMBERED by Susan M. Moyer

ELVIS, THE KING OF ROCK 'N' ROLL by Rupert Matthews

THE ELVIS ENCYCLOPEDIA by David E. Stanley with Frank Coffey

I'd like to thank the following people for their support and help on this book: First and foremost my wife, Sandy, whose support is always amazing to me. My daughter, Stella, for inspiring me every day. Dr. Mark Ruttum who saved my eyesight and my career. Dr. Russell Gonnering who directed me to Dr. Ruttum, and all the other doctors and nurses and staff at Froederdt Eye Institute of Milwaukee, WI. Also all of you who encouraged me after my eye injury with your advice and well-wishes! Chris Staros and Brett Warnock for their patience with me and this project. Adam Wallenta for his incredible color work! Rob Venditti for his insightful edits. Chris Staros and all the millions of Elvis fans for their inspiration and for helping me to fully understand the genius of Elvis Presley. Art Mawhinney and C.J. Bettin for their help early on with the technical computer stuff (I really need to learn all this computer stuff one day). Zach Howard for his helping define the look of the two main characters, The King and Paul Erfurt. My grandfather, Paul Erfurt (who my reporter is named after), for bringing all those Enquirers over for Sunday lunches back in the early eighties. And lastly, Elvis!

Rich

Special Note from the Author:
It's funny to me that this is a book about a musician and yet there is no music! Music is so critical to the very nature of this story and yet the reader has no soundtrack. So, I highly recommend that you read this book again and softly play some of the King's tunes in the background while you do so. I played them constantly while creating this book and it really helps...invoke the true spirit of the subject matter.